COLLECTED ESSAYS IN LAW

Democracy Through Law

The Collected Essays in Law Series
General Editor: Tom D. Campbell

Law's Premises, Law's Promise:
Jurisprudence after Wittgenstein

Thomas Morawetz

ISBN: 0 7546 2013 1

The Jurisprudence of
Law's Form and Substance

Robert S. Summers

ISBN: 0 7546 2024 7

Regulation, Crime, Freedom

John Braithwaite

ISBN: 0 7546 2005 0

Legal Rules and Legal Reasoning

Larry Alexander

ISBN: 0 7546 2004 2

The Great Juristic Bazaar:
Jurists' Texts and Lawyers' Stories

William Twining

ISBN: 0 7546 2211 8

Dispute Processing and Conflict Resolution

Carrie Menkel-Meadow

0 7546 2305 X

Objectivity in Ethics and Law

Michael Moore

0 7546 2329 7

Crime, Compliance and Control

Doreen McBarnet

0 7546 2349 1

Johan Steyn
A Lord of Appeal in Ordinary

Democracy Through Law

Selected Speeches
and Judgments

LONDON AND NEW YORK

First published 2004 by Dartmouth Publishing Company and Ashgate Publishing

2 Park Square, Milton Park, Abingdon, Oxfordshire OX14 4RN
711 Third Avenue, New York, NY 10017

Routledge is an imprint of the Taylor & Francis Group, an informa business

First issued in paperback 2018

Copyright © Johan Steyn 2004

Johan Steyn hereby asserts his moral right to be identified as the author of the Work in accordance with the Copyright, Designs and Patents Act 1988.

All rights reserved. No part of this book may be reprinted or reproduced or utilised in any form or by any electronic, mechanical, or other means, now known or hereafter invented, including photocopying and recording, or in any information storage or retrieval system, without permission in writing from the publishers.

Notice:
Product or corporate names may be trademarks or registered trademarks, and are used only for identification and explanation without intent to infringe.

British Library Cataloguing in Publication Data
Steyn, Lord, 1932–
    Democracy through law: selected speeches and judgments. –
    (Collected essays in Law)
    1. Law 2. Human rights 3. Constitutional law 4. Contracts
    5. Torts 6. Procedure (Law) 7. Justice, Administration of
    I. Title
    340

Library of Congress Cataloging-in-Publication Data
Steyn, Lord, 1932–
    Democracy through law: selected speeches and judgments /
    Johan Steyn.
      p. cm. – (Collected Essays in Law)
    1. Law–England. 2. Democracy–England.
    I. Title. II. Series.

    KD358.S74 2005
    349.42–dc22   2004054818

ISBN 13: 978-0-7546-2404-2 (hbk)
ISBN 13: 978-1-138-37506-2 (pbk)

Contents

Acknowledgements ix

Series Editor's Preface x

Introduction xiii

PART ONE: THEORY AND PRACTICE

1   A Common Bond
         American Bar Association Conference, London
         17 July 2000   3

2   Does Legal Formalism Hold Sway in England?
         The Bentham Club, University College, London
         1996   11

3   *Pepper v Hart*: A Re-Examination
         Herbert Hart Memorial Lecture 2000, Oxford
         17 May 2000   27

4   The Intractable Problem of the Interpretation of Legal Texts
         The John Lehane Memorial Lecture 2002
         The University of Sydney, Sydney, Australia
         25 September 2002   41

5   Dynamic Intepretation Amidst an Orgy of Statutes
         The Brian Dickson Memorial Lecture, University of Ottawa,
         Ottawa, Canada
         2 October 2003   57

6   The Role of the Bar, the Judge and the Jury: Winds of Change
         The 1998 Kalisher Memeorial Lecture, London
         13 October 1998   71

7   The Value of Dissenting Judgments: *Fisher v Minister of*
         Public Safety and Immigration [1998] AC 673, 686   85

PART TWO: CONSTITUTIONAL LAW AND PUBLIC LAW

8   The Weakest and Least Dangerous Department of Government
Administrative Law Bar Association, The Old Hall Lincoln's Inn, London
1997   97

9   The Case for a Supreme Court
The Neill Lecture, All Souls College, Oxford
1 March 2002   109

10   Creating a Supreme Court
Counsel Magazine
October 2003   125

11   Democracy Through Law
The 2002 Robin Cooke Lecture, University of Wellington, Wellington, New Zealand
18 September 2002   129

12   Constitutional Principle in Action: *R. (Anufrijeva) v Secretary of State for the Home Department* [2004] 1AC 604, 618   143

PART THREE: HUMAN RIGHTS LAW

13   Human Rights: The Legacy of Mrs Roosevelt
The Holdsworth Club, University of Birmingham, Birmingham
30 November 2001   151

14   The Case of Augusto Pinochet: A Breakthrough: *R. v Bow Street Metropolitan Stipendiary Magistrate Ex parte Pinochet Ugarte* [2002] 1 AC 61, 111   163

15   The New Legal Landscape
Justice/Sweet & Maxwell Conference Speech, London
19 October 2000   171

16   The Ethos of the European Convention on Human Rights: *Brown v Stott* [2003] 1 AC 681, 706   177

| 17 | The Centrality of the Right to Fair Trial as a Human Rights Norm
*Judicial Colloquium on the Domestic Application of International Human Rights Norms, Bangalore, India
December 1998* | 185 |

PART FOUR: HUMANITARIAN LAW

| 18 | Guantanamo Bay: The Legal Black Hole
*Twenty-seventh F A Mann Lecture
The Old Hall, Lincoln's Inn, London
25 November 2003* | 195 |

PART FIVE: CONTRACT AND TORT LAW

| 19 | The Role of Good Faith and Fair Dealing in Contract Law: A Hair-shirt Philosophy?
*The Royal Bank of Scotland Law Lecture 1991, Oxford
1991* | 213 |

| 20 | Contract Law: Fulfilling the Reasonable Expectations of Honest Men
*The Eleventh Sultan Azlan Shah Lecture 1996, Kuala Lumpur, Malaysia
1996* | 225 |

| 21 | Written Contracts: To What Extent may Evidence Control Language?
*University College, London
26 November 1987* | 235 |

| 22 | A Kind of Esperanto?
*Frontiers of Liability Seminar, All Souls College, Oxford University
1994* | 245 |

| 23 | Perspectives of Corrective and Distributive Justice in Tort Law
*The 2001 John Maurice Kelly Memorial Lecture, University College, Dublin
1 November 2001* | 253 |

| 24 | Immunity of Suit of Advocates: *Arthur J.S. Hall Co. v Simons* [2002] 1 AC 615, 675 | 275 |

PART SIX: ARBITRATION

25 England's Response to the UNCITRAL Model Law of
    Arbitration
    Freshfields Lecture, London
    1994   287

PART SEVEN: WESTMINSTER ABBEY

26 Address at Memorial Service for the Rt Hon The Lord
    Williams of Mostyn Q.C. 20 January 2004
    Westminster Abbey, London
    20 January 2004   305

Name Index   309

Acknowledgements

My debt to the Bar of England and Wales is enormous. The friendly and civilised ambiance of the Temple epitomises for me excellence of the English legal system. Since I am still a serving judge I feel a little inhibited about explaining how much I owe to my fellow judges. It has, however, been a privilege to be part of a wonderful collegiate community, dedicated only to the examination of issues in the public interest.

I am grateful to Professor Tom Campbell for suggesting that some of my papers ought to be published in book form. My publishers have been extraordinarily patient about the time I have taken in selecting the pieces and delivering the materials. I am also grateful in particular to John Irwin for his advice about editorial matters.

Through the years, Gail Munden, my secretary, has handled my habit of constantly redrafting judgments and lectures with great skill and charm. She also assembled the materials which make up the book. I have indeed been fortunate. Laura Johnson, my former judicial assistant, helped me in preparing the final text. She played a large part in the preparation of some of the lectures, notably my F.A. Mann lecture on Guantanamo Bay. Diane Procter, a law reporter par excellence, saved me from many errors.

I have had the advantage of discussing some of the lectures in this book, as well as the Introduction, with Professor Jeffrey Jowell Q.C. and profited from his advice.

I dedicate this book to my wife, Susan, in appreciation of her unfailing support. She played an invaluable role in suggesting changes of content, tone and style in many of the papers.

Grateful acknowledgement is made to the following persons, editors, publishers and institutions for their kind permission to reprint the essays included in this volume: Oxford University Press, Oxford; Sydney Law Review, Australia; European Human Rights Law Review, London; Sweet & Maxwell Limited, London; Incorporated Council of Law Reporting, London; Counsel Magazine, Croydon; Interights, London; Denning Law Journal, Buckingham; Paul O'Conner, University of College Dublin; London Court of International Arbitration, London.

Series Editor's Preface

Collected Essays in Law makes available some of the most important work of scholars who have made a major contribution to the study of law. Each volume brings together a selection of writings by a leading authority on a particular subject. The series gives authors an opportunity to present and comment on what they regard as their most important work in a specific area. Within their chosen subject area, the collections aim to give a comprehensive coverage of the authors' research. Care is taken to include essays and articles which are less readily accessible and to give the reader a picture of the development of the authors' work and an indication of research in progress.

Johan Steyn

Photo by Universal Pictorial Press Agency Ltd.

Introduction

This is a collection of lectures, speeches, addresses and essays, interspersed with a few judgments, all prepared since 1985 in a career of nearly 20 years as an English judge. If there is such a thing as a traditional route to appointment as a judge in England, my career has not followed it.

I studied law at the University of Stellenbosch, the town where my father had been a Professor of Law. The influence of the civilian legal tradition was great. Yet the Roman Dutch legacy was overlaid by the influence of English law. It was an education in a hybrid legal system. Thanks to a Rhodes Scholarship, I went to University College, Oxford, where I studied English law for two years. It was, of course, a truly wonderful experience. But Oxford University was then a far more complacent place than it is today. Sceptical questions about the English legal system were often met with the knock-down argument that 'it works'. Returning to South Africa during the apartheid era, I practised there as an advocate for some 15 years. It was a period of institutionalised tyranny and cruelty in the richest country in Africa, inflicting great suffering on millions of black people. As a lawyer I was aware that the Government by and large could and did achieve its oppressive purposes by a scrupulous observance of legality. It made an indelible impression on me.

In February 1973 I left South Africa and settled in England. After a brief pupillage I started to practise at 4 Essex Court, Temple, London, EC4, in a set of chambers which largely concentrated on international trade disputes. I took silk in 1979. For me this period (1973–1985) was immensely valuable: it was a window to the real world of international commerce.

Out of the blue in January 1985, I received a message to call on Lord Hailsham of St. Marylebone, the Lord Chancellor, at an appointed hour. In my chambers practical jokes on unsuspecting members were the order of the day. I suspected one. I made elaborate enquiries to verify the authenticity of the invitation. In the event, Lord Hailsham offered me a High Court judgeship, and I was assigned to the Commercial Court. I was astonished that such a position could be offered to a relatively recent émigré. I accepted with delight and I have never regretted this decision. But I have always been slightly puzzled by the fact that I was made a High Court judge at all. Some years later my doubt became intensified when I met Lord Hailsham in the House of Lords. He called me 'Charles' and afterwards when we occasionally met by chance in the corridors of the House of Lords, I obediently answered to that name. Was my appointment a case of error in persona?

I was a judge of the Commercial Court for about 7½ years. The international flavour of the work, and frequent experience of foreign legal systems, appealed to me. During this period I was also a Presiding Judge on the Northern Circuit. For three to four years I sat for about half the legal year in either Manchester, Liverpool, Preston or Carlisle. The experience was a primer in trying heavy criminal cases and it gave me a broader view of how at different levels the English legal system works. This period was followed by three fascinating years in the Court of Appeal sitting both in the civil and criminal divisions. The pace and diversity of the work appealed to me. My exposure to public law issues was initially limited but it gradually increased.

In January 1995 I was appointed as a Law Lord. The Appellate Committee of the House of Lords only hears cases on issues of law of general public importance. In my period in the House of Lords there has been a shift towards hearing more public law cases. The way in which cases are decided is very different from the usual pattern in the Court of Appeal. The rival arguments are subjected to searching enquiry. A discussion between the Law Lords after the close of the oral argument is only a step towards the disposal of the case. There is time for individual reflection and research. In the close collegiate community (called the Law Lords corridor) there is a constant exchange of ideas about a pending case, and frequent circulation and re-circulation of opinions in response to other views. Given that I am *parti pris* I would say that it is a system worthy of a supreme court of a modern democracy. Mistakes are, of course, made but decisions are reached as a result of reasoned debate. This is the system in the House of Lords.

A Law Lord spends a large part of his time sitting in the Privy Council which hears *inter alia* appeals from a group of former dependencies, colonies and dominions. The procedure in the Privy Council contemplates a single judgment to which all members assent. In my period dissenting judgments were accepted but regarded as exceptional. Strangely enough there is still some doubt whether a concurring judgment on a ground different from a majority view can be given.[1] Lord Reid stated that the jurisprudence of the House of Lords is of a significantly higher quality than that of the Privy Council, and he ascribed it to the fact that in the former individual judgments are regularly given.[2]

When deciding cases under constitutions incorporating bills of rights on the model of the European Convention on Human Rights, the Privy Council, has had the opportunity over more than 40 years to develop human rights law. In

---

[1] In Scottish appeals on devolution issues individual judgments are customary.

[2] Lord Reid, 'The Judge as Lawmaker' (1972) 12 JSPTL 22, at 29.

a detailed examination of decisions of the Privy Council Professor Ewing has concluded in 1991 that the Board has made no positive contribution to the jurisprudence of human rights.[3] His assessment is not easy to counter. Since 1991 there has been some progress. But the decisions of the Privy Council in death sentence cases from Caribbean countries over the last decade cast a sombre shadow. My dissenting judgment in *Fisher v Minister of Public Safety and Immigration* (1998) gives some insight into the role and case law of the Privy Council in capital cases. Progress towards a full acceptance of the higher legal order created by a bill of rights and the recognition of dynamic methods of interpretation appropriate to constitutional adjudication have not been rapid. Beyond that, as a serving Law Lord, I refrain from commenting on the role and jurisprudence of the Privy Council.

I must give what is nowadays called a health warning about the contents of this book. I have deliberately not altered any texts. There is inevitably some overlap between the essays. Some I would now prepare differently. I have also changed my mind about some important issues. For example, I originally supported the proposition that *ultra vires* was the foundation of statute based judicial review but in a lecture delivered in New Zealand in September 2002 I acknowledged that this position is no longer maintainable. It is sufficient to say that in a democracy the judiciary is the guardian of the rule of law. In other respects my points of view have become more refined and focused in recent years. The topics covered are certainly of interest. I would, however, not claim that my treatment of them always matched their intrinsic importance.

It may be helpful if I outline what I see as some of the great changes that have taken place during my period as a judge. It is the backcloth to many of the subjects which I discuss in this book. Inevitably, my summary is influenced by my own views and I accept that often there are other reasonable points of view. And what I say is incomplete. Yet it has the advantage of drawing some threads together.

In the western democratic world the United Kingdom may be alone in not having a written constitution. On the other hand, it has the priceless advantage of a tried and tested constitutional monarchy which enjoys the confidence of the British people. There is no need for a written constitution. But until 2 October 2000 when the incorporation of the European Convention on Human Rights into our domestic law came into force the United Kingdom had no bill of rights. That was a disadvantage for individuals who are subject to the laws of the United Kingdom. The filling of that gap has set the United Kingdom on course to becoming a true constitutional state. Traditionally, in

---

[3] K.D. Ewing. 'A Bill of Rights: Lessons from the Privy Council' in W. Finnie, C.M.G. Himsworth and N. Walker (eds.) *Edinburgh Essays in Public Law* (1991), 231, at 241.

English law the "state" has no legal identity and is not a legal concept. Why that was so is unclear. The explanation may lie in mystical concepts of anointed Kings with the Crown at the apex of the legal order. Since the incorporation of the ECHR, the state is now indubitably a concept of English law. Not surprisingly, but unannounced, English courts have started speaking of citizens rather than subjects.

The overarching principle of our constitutional law, classically explained by A.V. Dicey in 1875, was the supremacy of Parliament. Dicey wrote:[4]

> The principle of parliamentary sovereignty means neither more nor less than this, namely, that Parliament thus defined has, under the English constitution, the right to make or unmake any law whatever; and, further, that no person or body is recognised by the law of England as having a right to override or set aside the legislation of Parliament.

In 1973 the United Kingdom entered into the European Community. From that time the supremacy of Parliament was no longer absolute. Subject to Parliament's power to legislate expressly to withdraw from the European Union — an unthinkable hypothesis — there has been a divided concept of legal sovereignty. The European Communities Act 1972 is a truly fundamental law. Community law is a higher legal order than domestic law and within its sphere the Luxembourg court is the supreme judicial authority in our country. That was vividly illustrated in 1991 by the second *Factortame* case.[5] There was a clash between community law and a later act of the United Kingdom Parliament. The House of Lords granted an injunction to forbid a minister from obeying an act of Parliament. The act was disapplied. This decision sent seismic shock waves through our legal system.

Our law has been transformed by the European Community institutions. In 1974 in *Bulmer Limited v Bollinger*,[6] Lord Denning M.R., said '. . . the Treaty [of Rome] is like an incoming tide. It flows into the estuaries and up the rivers. It cannot be held back . . .'. So it has continued. The process has been carried forward by European directives, regulations and the jurisprudence of the Luxembourg court in many areas as diverse as contracts of employment and the quality of our beaches. Principles such as legal certainty and proportionality became part of our law. All this is too well known to require explanation.

In 1998 the narrow Diceyan view of sovereignty of Parliament was fundamentally qualified by devolution legislation and the Human Rights Act 1998. The enactment of the Scotland Act 1998, and the Government of Wales

---

[4] Introduction to the Law of the Constitution, Liberty Fund ed, based on the eighth ed., 3.
[5] [1991] 1 AC 603.
[6] [1974] Ch 401, at 418.

Act 1998, which devolved powers in different ways to Scotland and Wales, are best seen as political settlements recognising the value of diversity. In theory the Westminster Parliament can take back what it gave. In practice the political damage of doing so would emphatically rule it out. These two acts are in a real sense constitutional measures. Professor Vernon Bogdanor has pointed out that 'at the very least, the sovereignty of Parliament means something very different in Scotland and, to some extent, Wales from what it means in England'.[7] A real federal element has *de facto* been entrenched in our constitutional arrangements. The simplistic views of Dicey do not fit the contours of modern Britain.

But the greatest change must be the enactment of the Human Rights Act 1998. The United Kingdom signed and ratified the European Convention on Human Rights in 1951. The Convention exerted some influence on the development of our law. Since the creation in 1966 of the right of petition for its citizens to the European Court of Human Rights the impact of the ECHR on our law has increased. Established doctrine decreed that the ECHR was still not part of domestic law. Since 2 October 2000 the ECHR is now our Bill of Rights. Fundamental convention rights have been brought 'home' and we have at last joined the rights revolution. It is important to understand the nature of human rights treaties, such as the ECHR. Only too frequently in legal analysis they are assimilated with multilateral treaties of the traditional type which are concluded to accomplish the reciprocal exchange of benefits between contracting states. The Inter-American Court has observed about human rights treaties:[8]

> Their object and purpose is the protection of the basic rights of individual human beings irrespective of their nationality, both against the State of their nationality and all other contracting States. In concluding these human rights treaties, the States can be deemed to submit themselves to a legal order within which they, for the common good, assume various obligations, not in relation to other States, but towards all individuals within their jurisdiction.

The Human Rights Act 1998 is a constitutional measure protecting fundamental individual rights. It formally preserves Parliamentary supremacy. But the reality is again that the doctrine of Parliamentary supremacy has been fundamentally qualified. In practice the final word will usually rest with the Strasbourg court. This new legal order renders much of Dicey's account of our constitution irrelevant.

Due in a large measure to the European dimension on both fronts, there have been consequences which I have examined in detail in some of my

---

[7] Our New Constitution, (2004) 120 LQR 242, at 256.
[8] Advisory Opinion OC – 2/82, September 24, 1982, Inter-Am. Ct H.R., (Series A) (No. 2 (1982)), para 29.

essays. First the isolation of English law from European legal culture and tradition has come to an end. Multilateral treaties, representing a blend of common law and civil law principles, demonstrate this ever more important international process. Moreover, at our universities the *jus commune* of modern Western Europe is taught. The publication of the influential Principles of International Commercial Contracts by Unidroit[9] and the Principles of European Contract Law by the Commission on European Contract Law[10] are significant examples of this process. Secondly, in our highest court, the House of Lords, comparative law methods have in recent years come of age. The members of the court not only welcome citation of foreign materials but expect practitioners to research comparative law sources. I recently summarised the true purpose of comparative law methods as follows:[11]

> The aim is decidedly not to arrive at some sort of poll of the solutions adopted in a majority of jurisdictions. The real function of comparative law in practical jurisprudence is to throw light on the competing advantages and disadvantages of feasible solutions. It enables courts to re-examine the merits and demerits of our legal institutions in a rigorous manner. Such an enquiry must be approached from the vantage point of principled decision making. Where possible, it must also be tested against empirical evidence: see *Arthur J.S. Hall & Co v Simons* [2002] 1 AC 615 at pp 680G–681F, for the value of empirical evidence of foreign experience of the impact of the abolition of the immunity of suit of advocates.

The result of such a beneficial cross fertilisation of ideas between, for example, Britain and Canada are evident in a series of decisions of the highest courts of our two respective countries in the last few years.

Thirdly, in recent years the phenomenon of legal formalism has receded. At its core was the idea that the inner logic of the law, often made more attractive by an appeal to common sense, ought to be the lodestar of judges. They do now take into account the results to which rules lead and they decide difficult cases on the basis of weighing in the balance broader considerations of legal principle, justice, and policy.

Fourthly, in the last two decades there has been an intense debate about the problems of interpreting legal texts. There has been a general shift from literal interpretation to purposive interpretation. On the other hand, much depends on the particular text. Fiscal legal legislation may require a rather different approach from social welfare legislation. A letter of credit in an international sale involving third party interests may have to receive a relatively strict interpretation while, on the other hand, on a higher plane a

---

[9] Rome, 1994.
[10] Parts I and II, 2000, 342–344 (April 2004).
[11] (2004) 120 L.Q.R. 342–344.

constitution must 'be capable of growth and development over time to meet new social, political and historical realities often unimagined by its framers'.[12] Whatever the document under consideration the context is always relevant. The insight was provided by Lord Wilberforce in *Reardon Smith*[13] that one does not have to identify an ambiguity in order to take into account the setting in which the language of a commercial contract has to be construed. The same applies to all legal texts. Before forming views about the meaning of a text it is always necessary to take into account the contextual scene. On the other hand, the idea that one must identify an ambiguity before one can take into account the contextual scene of a text lives on in arguments of counsel and occasionally in decisions of courts. Old habits of thought die hard.

In parallel the process of the constitutionalisation of our public law has accelerated. Over the last 20 years public law has been transformed by judges to become, under the umbrella of Parliamentary supremacy, a meaningful and effective brake on the executive. The claim that the courts stand between the executive and the citizen is no longer an empty constitutional idea. It has been invigorated and become a foundation of our modern democracy. It is a vast subject. In this introduction I can do no more than outline the advances in legal analysis in four areas which I trace in some of my papers.

First, the distinction between two senses of the rule of law is now better understood. As a principle of institutional morality it contemplates a civil society under equal and just laws. In this sense it is expressly mentioned in the preamble to the ECHR and permeates the later more comprehensive International Covenant of Civil and Political Rights (1966). It is the greatest moulding force of customary international and domestic law. But the rule of law is also an overarching principle of our domestic law. It protects minimum standards of substantive and procedural fairness through public law. It has a major role to play in protecting the values of a liberal democracy in which the rights of minorities are effectively protected. It has been invoked in many diverse circumstances. There is no closed category of cases in which it may be applied.

Secondly, the principle of legality, which for too long was dormant in our law, became authoritatively restated by the House of Lords. In *Pierson*[14] a majority were not prepared to endorse it. But two years later in *Simms*[15] a majority did affirm it. Why is it significant? The premise is that Parliament does not write on a blank sheet. It legislates for a modern European liberal democracy. If Parliament wishes to annul or qualify fundamental rights of

---

[12] *Hunter v Southam Inc* [1984] 2 SCR 145, at 155.
[13] [1976] 2 Lloyd's Rep 621.
[14] [1998] AC 539.
[15] [2000] 2 AC 115.

individuals it must legislate in crystal clear terms and accept the political cost of doing so. General language cannot override fundamental rights. Since most legislation is framed in general language this principle is of supreme importance.

Thirdly, in recent years the courts have recognised certain fundamental rights as constitutional. Thus the courts protect as constitutional the right of participation in the democratic process, equality of treatment, freedom of expression, religious freedom, the right of unimpeded access to the courts, and the right to a fair trial. This classification of such rights strengthens their normative force. The duty of the court is to vindicate the breach of a constitutional right depending on its nature, by an appropriate remedy. The organic development of constitutional rights is a parallel and complementary process to the protection of fundamental rights under the ageing ECHR. For example, the antidiscrimination provision contained in article 14 of the ECHR is a weak and parasitic provision as it serves to protect only other convention rights. By contrast the constitutional principle of equality developed domestically by English courts is broader in scope.[16]

The fourth theme of judicial review is the separation of powers. A distinctive feature of a democracy is the separation of powers between a legislature, the executive, and the judiciary. The independent roles of the three branches of government is inherent in the very concept of a democracy. As Justice Brandeis observed separation of powers serves not to promote efficiency but to preclude the exercise of arbitrary power'.[17] But the separation of powers is never absolute. It may range from a relatively weak principle, as in Britain, to a strong principle, as in the United States. Gradually the insulation of the judicial function from the legislative and executive functions has come to be seen as a necessary corollary of true judicial independence and the rule of law. This perception has gathered pace since the incorporation of the ECHR, and in particular article 6, which requires fair trials before independent tribunals, in our domestic law.

Two historical anomalies lingered on. Until 2003, the Lord Chancellor, Lord Irvine of Lairg, insisted that, despite being a Cabinet Minister, he was entitled to sit as a member of the Appellate Committee of the House of Lords and preside over it. At the same time serving Law Lords from time to time exercised the right to act as legislators in the Upper House. The government resolved in 2003 that these curiosities should be brought to an end and that a Supreme Court for the United Kingdom should be created.

Unfortunately, the obvious and sensible decision to create a Supreme Court was handled in a singularly inept way and caused widespread resentment.

---

[16] *R (Anufreijeva) v Secretary of State for the Home Department* [2004] 1 AC 604 (HL) which is included in this book is an instructive example.

[17] *Myers v U.S.* 272 U.S. 52 (1926).

Many feel that to achieve the main aim, namely to create a Supreme Court fit for a modern liberal democracy, it was unnecessary to dismantle the historic office of Lord Chancellor. History and symbolism matter greatly. It would have been relatively easy to achieve the core objectives of the package of reforms by remoulding the office of the Lord Chancellor. Some of the Law Lords also resented the proposed termination of their privilege to speak and vote in the House of Lords. The truth is that it is wonderful to work in the magnificent splendour of the Palace of Westminster. It is difficult not to be seduced by it. But there is no redeeming public interest in maintaining these anomalies. There may be rough patches but I think the reform will in due course be put in place. We have come a long way since 1860 when lay peers regularly sat on appeals in the House of Lords. It is worth recalling that in 1860 when the Duke of Buccleuch, who was not a lawyer, doubted the wisdom of his sitting in an Indian appeal lasting nine days, he was assured that he might 'depend upon it, the natives of India would much rather have this case decided by a great Scotch Duke than by lawyers'.[18]

Since 1997 there has also been an ambitious programme of constitutional reform by statute. The Bank of England Act 1998 gave the Bank of England independence in the setting of interest rates. The post of a Mayor of London was created in 1999. A plan to create Regional Assemblies in regions of England is advancing. Following a number of public health scares, an independent Food Standards Agency has been set up under the Food Standards Act 1999. The Freedom of Information Act 2000 has been enacted. Unfortunately, it is a rather weak measure, notably because the information commissioner is given limited powers. Yet overall constitutionalism has in some areas been advanced in recent years.

The story is one of the gradual development of a European democracy towards becoming a constitutional state. It is an encouraging story. Unfortunately, it is an incomplete picture. I must describe the position as I see it warts and all. The ideological conflicts of our time have had an impact on democratic values.

Recent years have witnessed a wave of intolerance towards minorities sweeping across Europe and exorbitant and excessive responses of governments seeking short term popularity. It has not bypassed the United Kingdom. The horrific events of 11 September 2001, and the responses to it, have not only fractured the international legal order but have cast a shadow over the protection of human rights worldwide. It is documented that the outrageous lawlessness of the United States of America at Guantanamo Bay has encouraged and is encouraging many governments, including the United

---

[18] Robert Stevens, Law and Politics: The House of Lords as a Judicial Body, 1800–1976, 1978, 45 (note 37).

Kingdom government, to try to undermine human rights. The outlook for human rights is bleak.

Undoubtedly, governments need space to govern, and to protect the public against terrorism. But what governments may do must have limits. Here the legal profession and the judiciary have a role to play. Even in an emergency fundamental rights must not be curtailed further than is absolutely necessary. The courts must never abdicate their constitutional duty to examine abuses of power even in an emergency. They must never acquiesce in governments trampling over democratic values. They must persevere in protecting the rule of law. 'It is not necessary to hope in order to work, and it is not necessary to succeed in order to persevere'.[19]

---

[19] Attributed to William of Orange (1533–1584).

Part One

Theory and Practice

[1]
A Common Bond

The Democratic Ideal

The commitment of our nations to the democratic ideal is longstanding and unswerving. It is anchored in the enlightened public opinion and constitutional habits of our peoples. It embraces the idea of government under law and not under men and women. The first premise of the democratic ideal is that government exists for one purpose only: to protect and enhance the welfare of the people. In our fully representative systems the people therefore decide who should govern them. Regular and orderly transfer of power in accordance with the wishes of the majority is the hallmark of our systems. The people entrust power to the government in accordance with the principle of majority rule. The second premise of the democratic ideal is that the basic values of liberty and justice for all and respect for human rights and fundamental freedoms are guaranteed. Where a tension develops between these two premises a balance has to be struck. And the guarantor of that balance is an impartial and independent judiciary carrying out its task in accordance with principles of institutional integrity. Alone the judiciary would be unequal to this vital and delicate task. It is critically dependent on a free and courageous legal profession, all serving the course of justice.

Constitutionalism

The United States of America has the priceless advantage of a written constitution incorporating its paramount law. It ensures that public affairs are conducted in an orderly manner. It stands guard against the abuse of public power. It nurtures the democratic ideal by an entrenchment of rights. By confining the legislature, the executive and the judiciary to their own provinces, protected by a broad principle of separation of powers and guarantees of fundamental rights, it strives for the optimal conditions in which democracy can flourish. This equilibrium depends in a large measure on the settled view that it is the province and duty of the judiciary to say what the constitution requires and what the law is. By contrast the United Kingdom does not have a written constitution. But the second half of the twentieth century has witnessed a widespread renaissance of constitutionalism in many countries including Australia, Canada, India, New Zealand and South Africa. This movement has not bypassed the United Kingdom. It is now set on a programme of major constitutional reform. It involves the incorporation of the European Convention of Human Rights and Freedoms as a higher legal order as well as the devolution of powers to Scotland, Wales and Northern Ireland. And in parallel the courts have embarked on a process of constitutionalisation of public law. A culture of justification now prevails: it requires constitutional arrangements which diverge from constitutional principle to be justified in the public interest.

The Core Principles

Among the distinctive features of our democracies certain core principles stand out. First, there is the principle of freedom of expression. It serves several broad objectives. It promotes the self-fulfilment of individuals in society. It enables the truth to emerge from the free expression of conflicting views. More than 80 years ago, Mr Justice Holmes (echoing John Stuart Mill) saw truth emerging in a marketplace of ideas. He said:

> "When men have realised that time has upset many fighting faiths, they may come to believe even more than they believe the very foundations of their own conduct that the ultimate good desired is better reached by free trade in ideas – that the best test of truth is the power of the thought to get itself accepted in the competition of the market."

Freedom of speech encourages the free flow of information and ideas which informs political debate. It enables electors to make well-informed choices and the elected to make well-instructed decisions. It is the life-blood of democracy.

Second, deeply embedded in our systems is the principle of equality. It is a fundamental tenet of democracy that both law and government accord every individual equal concern and respect for their welfare and dignity. Everyone is entitled to equal protection of the law, which should be applied without fear or favour. Law's necessary distinctions must be justified but must never be made on the grounds of race, colour, belief, gender or any other irrational ground. Individuals in both our countries are protected by law from discrimination on those grounds.

Third, the imprint of the rule of law pervades our systems. It holds that no one purporting to exercise public power has any authority to do so unless given it by law. But it goes further. It requires an independent and impartial judiciary with the exclusive responsibility of declaring what law is and deciding whether other branches of government have the power which they claim. It also requires that the law itself should be both accessible and certain, so that the citizens may know how to conduct their affairs, and that the law should not confer discretionary powers on the executive which are so broad and uncertain that they may be exercised in an arbitrary or discriminatory manner.

Fourth, our systems uphold the principle of the due process. It requires that anyone exercising public power should act fairly. No one should be deprived of liberty or property except in accordance with a fair procedure. Everyone is entitled to a fair hearing of civil disputes by an independent and impartial court or tribunal. Everyone charged with a criminal offence is entitled to a fair trial including the right to be presumed innocent until proved guilty according to law.

The Human Rights Movement

The fundamental principles of our systems have been reinforced by the human rights movement which gained impetus after the Second World War. It was the result of mankind's revulsion at the barbarism of the Holocaust and other crimes against humanity. The landmark was the adoption of Universal Declaration of Human Rights in 1948. This text, which drew heavily on the language of the United States' Constitution, proclaimed in the first three lines of its preamble the essence of its theme

XVI OVERVIEW

by asserting that "recognition of the inherent dignity and of the equal and unalienable rights of all members of the human family is the foundation of freedom, justice and peace in the world." The Universal Declaration was drafted as an aspirational text, articulating the faith of members of the United Nations in the development of fundamental human rights. It provided the moral basis for the evolution of human rights law as a rights-based system. It played an important role in the development of customary international law. It also provided the framework for multi-lateral treaties which extended human rights law. Our countries have signed and ratified the International Covenant on Civil and Political Rights (1966) which is the most important of those treaties. The Covenant has been signed and ratified by 95 nations. Despite the flowering of the human rights movement, the period since the Second World War has seen great ideological storms, generated by nationalism, racism and religious bigotry. Perhaps conflict is endemic in the human condition. Nevertheless, it is the resolve of our nations to continue to work for the advancement of human rights because it is morally right and is our best hope for peace.

The Role of the Courts

The court system plays an indispensable part in the functioning of a democracy. It exists in order to serve the needs of a civil society. To carry out that task in a manner which will inspire public confidence various conditions must be met. The judiciary must fulfil and observe requirements of independence and impartiality. The court system must be backed by proper constitutional arrangements to ensure that the administration of justice is not affected by the involvement or pressure from the executive or public officials. It must also be adequately funded in order to ensure that justice is properly done and not unduly delayed. To this end, and consistent with the overriding requirement of justice, the court system must aim to simplify proceedings and make them intelligible to the public. It must aim to shorten proceedings so as to ensure that justice is not done at too high a price. At the same time our legal systems are fully committed to continuing the development of alternative methods of dispute resolution, thereby further improving access to justice. These are our goals in the year 2000. It is our resolve to work ceaselessly to improve our court systems.

Substantive Law

A distinctive feature of the common law is the case-by-case development of legal rules. It is the source of its enduring strength. Judges concentrate on the attainment of pragmatic justice, anchoring their decisions in custom and experience. This methodology is to be contrasted with the civilian tradition, influenced by systematic codes and cultural traditions favouring doctrine rather than experience.

The spirit of liberty is the dominant theme of the common law. Whatever is not specifically forbidden, individuals and their enterprises are free to do. By contrast the government and its agencies may only do what the law permits: what is done in the name of people requires constant examination and justification.

The differences between our systems are marked but those differences do not obscure unifying features. The right of everyone to own property, and enjoy the fruits of his or her labours, is the very foundation of our societies. The objective of the law of contract in both countries is fair dealing and giving effect to the reasonable expectations of honest men and women. The law of tort in our countries, although materially different in significant respects, is based on the interplay of two themes. First, the principle of corrective justice requires compensation to be paid for the infliction of unjustified harm on another. Second, the principle of distributive justice which requires tort law sometimes to take into account the position of citizens as members of a community among whom the burdens and risk of loss must be distributed on a basis of equality and fairness. The law of restitution is based on the fundamental precept that nobody should be unjustly enriched at the expense of another. Through the web of the law of obligations in our countries there runs a golden thread: the pursuit of a just settlement of civil disputes between citizens.

The family is the natural and fundamental group unit of society. It is therefore fit and proper that in the development of the law priority is given to family law in all its aspects, paying due regard at all times to the paramount welfare of children.

The purpose of the criminal law is not punishment for its own sake. Its aim is to permit everyone to go about their daily lives without fear of harm to person or property. It promotes values of stability and order in which democracy can flourish for the benefit of all. It is the premise of our criminal justice systems that in the words of John Stuart Mill the only purpose for which power can be rightfully exercised over any member of a civilised community is to prevent harm to others.

Law Reform

The law is about the world of ideas. It is not and cannot be static. It must from time to time be re-examined and adapted to take account of the changing needs of society. So far as that task is consistent with principles of institutional integrity, which bind all judges, the primary role in such development must belong to the judiciary. In performing this task the judges rely heavily on practising lawyers. The calling of a lawyer is an honourable one. It involves more than the pursuit of personal interest. It involves an allegiance to the rule of law and a responsibility to improve the law and the legal system. In their separate roles judges and lawyers depend heavily on the universities and academic lawyers for the best explanation of the law and answers to the questions whether in particular areas the existing law serves the ends for which it exists. In the pursuit of the rationality of the law judges, practitioners and academic lawyers act as partners in a common endeavour.

It has, however, also been necessary in both our countries to have in place institutional arrangements for promoting systematic law reform. This is necessary in order to deal with the persistent problems of the uncertainty and complexity of the law. In the United States of America the American Law Institute and the National Conference of Commissioners on Uniform State Laws have made a major contribution in developing and modernising law. In the United Kingdom the key institutions have been the Law Commission for England and Wales and the Scottish Law Commission. The debt of our countries to these agencies is enormous. And we commit ourselves to assist in their endeavours whenever called upon and in whatever manner we can assist.

The Challenge of 2000

The great success story of the twentieth century was the rapidly accelerating development of the natural sciences and technology. But sombrely we must acknowledge that this progress has sometimes been at the expense of the environment which we hold in trust for future generations.

It must be our resolve for the twenty-first century to develop principles of environment law which respect the planet on which we live.

The potential of scientific progress to contribute to the administration of justice in our countries is great. It is a challenge for the lawyers in both countries to ensure that the advance is harnessed to the attainment, so far as is possible, of practical justice for all.

Ultimately, we must go back to the roots of the common law which is our shared heritage. In his Commentaries on the Laws of England, first published in the 1760s, Blackstone wrote that law is the principal and most perfect branch of ethics. He was right. Ethics and law are inextricably intertwined. The sense of what is morally right is the greatest of all the moulding forces of the law. It underpins practical decisions made, day after day, by lawyers and judges. The ethical and moral foundations of the law enjoin us as lawyers to join in a common endeavour to conduct ourselves in a spirit of civility, generosity and humanity conducive to the welfare of the public whom we serve.[*]

---

[*] I acknowledge assistance given to me in the drafting of this introductory piece by members of the British team.

[2]
Does Legal Formalism Hold Sway in England?

Bentham railed against the mystique of the law, or what he called the theatre of the judiciary. He said that the inhabitants of the world of the law, and particularly its higher regions 'form a sort of celestial conclave, of the secrets of which, whatsoever observation is endeavoured to be made from subjacent low grounds, is made through a medium impregnated with awe, admiration, and conjecture'.[1] With profound respect to our patron there was nothing celestial about the accommodation provided for Lord Hoffmann and myself upon our appointment as Law Lords. Lord Hoffmann was told that he could not have the broom cupboard in the Law Lords corridor since I was already in it. Instead Lord Hoffmann got the ladies' lavatory.

Bentham promised a peep into the mysteries of the world of the law. Invoking the image of the famous robber of classical mythology he added loftily: 'A more particular object is the throwing of light into the den of the long-robed Cacus. Cacus felt the light and trembled.'[2] Mundanely, in Eurospeak the buzz words are now the imperative of transparency. Bentham would generally speaking have applauded the European move towards greater openness in legal institutions. The only qualification is that Bentham, like many great men who want to change the world, would not necessarily on *a priori* grounds have welcomed the propagation of ideas running counter to his own fixed views.

One of the mysteries of the law which attracted the attention of Bentham was the nature of legal reasoning, and the permissible bounds of legal reasoning. Bentham discussed this subject at some length.[3] He also examined the kindred subject of 'strict' and

---

[1] *The Works of Bentham* (1843), i, 242.   [2] *Ibid.*
[3] *The Theory of Legislation* (trs. from the French by Dumont, 1911), 66 ff.

'liberal' interpretation of statutes.[4] He described liberal interpretation as 'that delicate and important branch of judiciary power, the concession of which is dangerous, the denial ruinous'. Since the time of Bentham much has been written on the subject of the nature of legal reasoning, particularly by legal philosophers. Tonight, as a judge and not a legal philosopher, I would like to explore in a speculative way a feature of legal reasoning. The topic to which I would like to turn is the question whether legal formalism holds sway in England. The description of the role of a modern English judge upon which I am about to embark would not have pleased Bentham. He accorded only a limited role to judges. Indeed he called them judicial functionaries. Dogmatically, he argued that progress was only possible along the legislative route. Fellow Benthamites, my speculations will not satisfy our patron's principle of utility. Nevertheless, by command of the Honorary Secretary I must press on.

Legal formalism is really shorthand for a number of different ideas.[5] While it smacks a little of the licence in the use of language, which Humpty-Dumpty claimed for himself, I will use the word formalism as covering two phenomena. The first is a tendency for judges in searching for applicable rules to decide cases on narrow grounds of the inner logic of the law. But as Professor MacCormick pointed out—and I am greatly indebted to that distinguished legal philosopher—lawyers tend to use the word 'logic' not only in the strict sense to cover the case where a conclusion necessarily follows from given premises but also in the wider sense that a conclusion 'does not make sense'.[6] The opposite tendency to legal formalism is for judges also to take into account the results to which rules lead and to decide cases on the basis of weighing in the balance broader considerations of legal principle, justice, and policy. It may be convenient to describe the narrower tendency as substantive formalism. In this sense Bentham was a formalist. The second phenomenon is of a different character. It relates to the extent to which judges expose the real grounds for their decisions in their judgments. I do not, of course, have in mind the deliberate

---

[4] *Of Laws in General* (ed. H. L. A. Hart, London, 1970), 162.
[5] See, for example, 'Statutes and Contracts as Founts of Legal Reasoning', in P. Cane and J. Stapleton (eds.), *Essays for Patrick Atiyah* (Oxford, 1991).
[6] *Legal Reasoning and Legal Theory* (1994), 38.

concealment of a judge's real reasons. That could occur but it must be rare. Rather I have in mind the unconscious tendency to express judgments in purely formal language although consequentialist arguments and policy factors also play a role in the decision.

Substantive Formalism

What I have so far said about formalism has been rather abstract. It may now be useful if I give an example of formalism at work. It comes from the field of contract law, which traditionally has been fertile ground for formalism. In 1915 in *Dunlop Pneumatic Tyre Co. Ltd* v. *Selfridge and Co. Ltd*[7] the House of Lords enunciated the rule of privity of contract, namely that our law does not recognize a contract for the benefit of a third party. The Lord Chancellor, Viscount Haldane, said:[8] 'In the law of England certain principles are fundamental. One is that only a person who is a party to a contract can sue on it. Our law knows nothing of a *jus quaesitum tertio* arising by way of contract.' Lord Haldane regarded the conclusion as a self-evident result of legal logic. An echo of that conceptual reasoning is to be found in *Midland Silicones Ltd* v. *Scruttons Ltd*.[9] The Lord Chancellor ignored the countervailing considerations that the rule of privity of contract frustrates the autonomy of the will of the parties and disregards their reasonable expectations. He also ignored the element of reliance by parties on a contract for the benefit of a third party. Moreover, the rule enunciated by the Lord Chancellor ignored the needs of commerce, e.g. if an insurance policy confers a benefit on a third party, the latter has no claim at common law.[10] In truth there are at stake competing principles and policy factors. That was obscured by the formalist approach adopted by the House of Lords. It is not my purpose tonight to argue that the House of Lords should necessarily review the decision in *Dunlop Pneumatic*.[11] But I cite the case to illustrate the limitations of single bright line logic.

Dunlop Pneumatic is representative of a way of formal legal reasoning which was until recent times common in England.

---

[7] [1915] AC 847.   [8] At 853.   [9] [1962] AC 446.
[10] Cheshire, Fifoot, and Furmston, *Law of Contract*, (12th edn.) 454.
[11] In *Darlington Borough Council* v. *Wiltshier Northern Limited* [1995] 1 WLR 68, at 76E–78B, I examined the privity rule in greater detail.

Certain consequences flow from an exclusive reliance on formalist reasoning. It tends to emphasize form rather than substance in judicial decisions. It tends to ignore new and changing needs of society. There is good sense in the maxim that the rule ought to follow where reason leads, and where reason stops there ought to stop the rule. But the formalist judge is likely to say that it is not the duty of the court to rationalize the law of England. Moreover, formalism inculcates an intense respect for *stare decisis* whatever the lessons of experience and the force of better reasoning. I will argue that formalism tends to impose a stranglehold on the capacity of a legal system to develop in a disciplined, orderly, and just way. Above all, it fails to do *justice* in accordance with law in keeping with the traditional judicial oath. I will argue that in a modern liberal democracy the shift should generally be away from formalism.

But I must put matters in context. Logic in a broad sense plays an essential role in legal reasoning. In cases involving open questions of law it is inevitable that a judge will in the first place reason from established rules or use the methodology of analogies to be found in authoritative decisions or even occasionally in statute law.[12] Together these methods of legal reasoning constitute the inner logic of the law. Reasoning in this way tends to encourage coherence in a legal system in the sense that the rules of the system as a whole will knit together; it tends to promote consistency and uniformity in the resolution of disputes; and it tends to ensure that like cases are decided alike. It therefore improves the structure of the law and that matters. It can be called the argument of consistency: it will usually prevail. Indeed in most cases broader considerations will support the promptings of legal logic. But in some cases, particularly at appellate level, doing justice in accordance with law requires a court additionally to take into account general principles of law, countervailing policy factors, and the balance of arguments about practical justice. The concept of general principles of law, as opposed to rules, is far from straightforward. What I have in mind are principles such as that a court must seek to uphold the contractual bargains of persons of competent understanding; that a court ought to strive to satisfy the reasonable expectations of parties to a contract; that a court ought to recoil from a result

---

[12] P. S. Atiyah, 'Common Law and Statute Law' (1985) 48 *MLR* 1.

which would permit somebody to benefit from his own deliberate wrongdoing; and so forth. In the same way as there may be competing arguments on policy and justice, general principles may struggle for supremacy in a particular case. For example, the principle of freedom of expression is a fundamental right in a liberal democracy but it may, in exceptional circumstances, arguably have to yield to the principle that it is justifiable to take measures to protect the security of the state.

Often the subtle interaction of legal logic and broader considerations will form the basis of a judicial decision. Logical symmetry is not the ultimate aim of the law. Sometimes consistency must be sacrificed in favour of wider considerations. But if a judge comes to such a decision, it must be on the basis that like cases will be decided in a like way. It assuredly does not mean some kind of individualized or palm-tree justice. And the discipline of the law imposes an undefinable limit on the extent to which a judge may develop the law. His decision must be one of integrity: it must be permissible, if not necessarily commanded, by general principles of law. If the judge strays beyond that limit he enters forbidden territory and puts at risk the delicate balance of power in a democracy: he will imperil the rule of law itself.

That brings me to my main task, namely to attempt an assessment of the extent to which formalism is still a significant force in modern English jurisprudence. I believe that in the last twenty-five years there has been a gradual shift away from using exclusively formalist techniques. No single appellate judge or academic lawyer could possibly be responsible for such a change in direction. Yet to my mind two names stand out, in very different ways, as great contributors to this movement. In this period, Lord Denning, despite occasional remonstration by the House of Lords, left an indelible imprint on English law. Generally his judgments became famous for his insistence on intuitive, robust, and practical justice. Moreover, in the last twenty-five years the broad-minded philosophy of Lord Reid rather than that of the literalist Viscount Simonds has, by and large, become dominant. At first the process was tentative but it accelerated. Formalism in the sense of an exclusive reliance on formalist methods has not been exorcised. It never will be. But it is on the wane.

I am uncomfortably aware that I cannot in this article prove these assertions. A *magnum opus* by an academic lawyer would be necessary to do justice to the topic. All I can do is to place before you my impressions. I think Lord Reid's paper, 'The Judge as Law Maker', published in 1972 in the *Journal of the Society of Public Teachers of Law* was a critical breakthrough.[13] Every lawyer already knew that judges sometimes make law. But until 1972 it was considered impolitic for judges to acknowledge their creative role openly. Lord Reid dispelled the mystery. And he made clear that in a situation of choice a judge may be guided by common sense, legal principles, his sense of justice, and by public policy by which, in the context, he meant relevant policy factors. That position was perfectly consistent with Lord Reid's unswerving loyalty to the supremacy of Parliament. Given the recent debate about the relationship between Parliament and the courts I make clear that on the constitutional position I take the same view as Lord Reid.

The last quarter of a century has also witnessed the ending of the virtual isolation of the English legal system from the broad sweep of the Western European legal tradition. That came about not only by virtue of the participation of this country in the legal institutions of Europe. Multilateral treaties, representing a blend of civil law and common law principles, have played a role. So did the growing awareness of the emerging *jus commune* of continental Europe. On a broader basis comparative law caused English lawyers to re-examine the merits of the solutions offered by their own system.

It is necessary to look at the development of our law more concretely. It is a vast subject. But I must be economical. I will start with legislation, since its impact on the lives of citizens is even greater than that of the common law. So great is the veneration of English lawyers for the common law that legislation is regrettably largely neglected as an independent and coherent subject at our universities. There is, however, not time to explore this theme tonight. I propose to concentrate on the approach of judges to the interpretation of statutes. Towards the end of the last century Pollock characterized the approach of judges as follows: 'Parliament generally changes the law for the worse, and that the business of judges is to keep the mischief of its interference within the narrowest possible bounds'.[14] That was no doubt true until fairly

---

[13] (1972) 12 *JSPTL (NS)* 22.
[14] *Essays on Jurisprudence and Ethics* (1882), 85.

recent times: a literalist interpretation often prevailed and presumptions were often used to defeat the purpose of a statute. But Pollock's statement is no longer true. The modern approach is illustrated by the decision of the House of Lords in the *The Boucraa*.[15] By statute a new procedural power was created enabling an arbitrator to dismiss a claim for inordinate and inexcusable delay in pursuing it. The statute did not contain a provision making clear whether it was to be retrospective or not. In a case which arose before the statute came into force the respondents in an arbitration sought an order dismissing the claim. The claimants in the arbitration contended that the presumption against retrospectivity required a restrictive interpretation of the statute. Lord Mustill spoke for all members of the House when he said:

> I must own up to reservations about the reliability of generalised presumptions and maxims when engaged in the task of finding out what Parliament intended by a particular form of words, for they too readily confine the court to a perspective which treats all statutes, and all situations to which they apply, as if they were the same. This is misleading, for the basis of the rule is no more than simple fairness, which ought to be the basis of every legal rule.[16]

The House of Lords held that the statute was retrospective. The noteworthy feature of this case is the emphasis on a contextual approach and the need to go back to the reason for the presumption, i.e. fairness. This is a very far cry from the picture sketched by Pollock.

In a 1969 Report the Law Commission still commented on a tendency for judges to over-emphasize the literal meaning of a statutory provision at the expense of the meaning to be derived from contextual aids.[17] In the last twenty-five years purposive construction, giving due effect to the whole contextual scene of a statute, has come of age. This change was not started by the teleological approach of European Community jurisprudence but it has probably been accelerated by European ideas. By and large

---

[15] *L'Office Cherifien des Phosphates* v. *Yamashita-Shinnion Steamship Co. Ltd* [1994] 1 All ER 20.
[16] At 29.
[17] *The Interpretation of Statutes* (Law Com. No. 21), para. 80(c).

judges have proved themselves willing to use broader, non-formalist methods. No doubt judges sometimes go astray, particularly in interpreting unfamiliar and complex legislation the purpose and scheme of which they have not mastered. That is ultimately the fault of judges but it has to be said that the Bar also has a responsibility. It should be axiomatic that a barrister should be able to explain preferably in written form the relevant contextual scene of such a statute. The important point is, however, that judges no longer feel constrained to use the restrictive methodology of formalism in the interpretation of statutes. Indeed, the myth of a statute as being a self-sufficient fixed verbal formula, always yielding an obvious or ordinary meaning, has been exposed. The bold decision of the House of Lords in *Pepper* v. *Hart*[18] is simply a culmination of a more realistic approach to the interpretation of statutes. Pollock would have been astounded.

In the compass of this article it is impossible to explore the different facets of the trend away from formalism in the field of statutory interpretation. Perhaps I may be permitted a few generalizations. The meaning of language has been called a labyrinth of paths. Often there is no obvious or ordinary meaning. But there is always a contextual meaning. And the context is relevant at two levels: first, it is relevant to the question what meanings the language is capable of letting in. Secondly, it is relevant to the question which of the several interpretations best matches the purpose of the provision. All these matters are part of the very alphabet of a modern English judge. And since fairness ought to be the basis of every statutory provision it is inevitable that the more demonstrably unfair a suggested interpretation is the clearer must be the statutory wording necessary to support it.

That brings me to the development of the common law. Largely as a result of the ever-increasing influence of academic writers the approach of Lord Reid has become the new orthodoxy. Again, I can only touch on a few major developments. I start with criminal law and procedure, a corner of the law inclined to formalism. On the one hand, the view of a criminal trial as a sporting contest is now eschewed: convictions are not often set aside for purely technical reasons. On the other hand, the idea that a defendant is entitled to irreducible minimum standards of fairness has firmly

---

[18] [1992] 3 WLR 1032.

taken root. Absent fair and effective procedures the rights of an accused cannot be effectively vindicated. Formalism coped badly with this notion. Before the 1990s discovery in criminal cases was often woefully deficient. Trust the prosecutor's sense of fairness was the policy. A series of well-documented miscarriages of justice led to a re-examination of this approach. *Ward*,[19] and subsequent cases,[20] placed the problem in the framework of our evolving constitution. A defendant has a constitutional right to a fair trial. And a trial involving material non-disclosure by the prosecution is not a fair trial. The court protects the right to a fair trial by vindicating the defendant's constitutional rights, the court being the final arbiter. Of course, we ought to trust our prosecutors but such trust was never a sufficient condition to vindicate fundamental rights. The new common law development of fair disclosure principles is a triumph of substance over form.

But academic lawyers and judges performed their most creative work in the administrative law field. They have freed this branch of the law from its formalist shackles. Consequentialist arguments and policy factors are the very stuff of decisions in the public law field. Once English judges fully accepted their constitutional role of protecting citizens against abuse of official power there was not much room for formalist techniques. One only has to recall the decision by the House of Lords refuting a ministerial assertion of immunity from contempt of court proceedings,[21] the decision of the Divisional Court in the *Pergau Dam* case,[22] and the decision of the House of Lords in the case of the Criminal Injuries Compensation Schemes[23] to appreciate that judges cannot avoid considering policy issues in the process of reviewing allegations of abuse of ministerial powers. Equally important was the decision of the House of Lords in *Derbyshire*,[24] based squarely on policy grounds, that the institutions of local government, like central government, have no right to sue in defamation. The great question remains

---

[19] 96 Cr.App.R 1.
[20] *R. v. Keane*, 99 Cr.App.R and *R. v. Brown* [1994] 1 WLR 1599.
[21] *M v. Home Office* [1994] 1 AC 377.
[22] *R. v. Secretary of State for Foreign and Commonwealth Affairs, ex parte World Development Movement Ltd* [1995] 1 WLR 386.
[23] *R. v. Secretary of State for the Home Department, ex parte Fire Brigades Union* [1955] 2 464.
[24] *Derbyshire County Council v. Times Newspapers Ltd* [1993] AC 534.

whether proportionality, already part of our law through Community law, ought to become part of our domestic law, in aid of constitutional and human rights. It is an open question. In the meantime, the standards applied by the courts in judicial review must ultimately be justified by constitutional principles, which govern the proper exercise of public power in a democracy.[25] Gradually, through the combined work of academic lawyers and judges, our unwritten constitution is assuming more coherent form.

The developments in other branches of the common law provide less heady stuff. And the picture is not monolithic. I do not suggest that formalism is dead and buried in the recesses of the Chancery Division! But the trend has generally been anti-formalist. On the other hand, despite the rise and growth of consumerism, pockets of the law of contract have proved remarkably resistant to the idea of giving effect to the standards and requirements of business people. That is a matter to which I have already alluded. But I would also mention *Walford* v. *Miles*[26] where in 1992 the House of Lords held that an express agreement to negotiate in good faith is invalid. The remedy for a breach of such an agreement can on any view only be compensation for wasted costs. While I do not argue for the introduction of a general duty of good faith in contract law, it is difficult to see why an express agreement to negotiate in good faith should be invalid. A best endeavours undertaking is apparently valid. That is a most technical distinction. What the difficulty is I do not know. After all, there is no reason to think that English judges are not capable of trying the issue whether a party has acted in bad faith by pretending to negotiate, thereby causing the other party wasted expenditure.

In the field of tort there will be many cases in which there is a tension between legal logic and practical justice. And it would be naïve to assume that practical justice will always triumph. One example of a close-run contest will suffice. The decision of the House of Lords in *White* v. *Jones*[27] is a legal philosopher's dream. By a majority of three to two the House of Lords held that a solicitor who negligently fails to carry out a testator's instructions to execute a will may in principle incur liability in tort to an

---

[25] S. De Smith, Woolf, and Jowell, *Judicial Review of Administrative Action* (5th edn., London, 1995) 14.   [26] [1992] 2 AC 128.
[27] [1995] 2 WLR 187.

intended beneficiary who suffers loss as a result of such carelessness. Lord Keith of Kinkel and Lord Mustill demonstrated convincingly that logic, deductive reasoning, and the absence of any supporting analogy militated against admitting the claim. In the speeches of the minority the plaintiff was found wanting in the seventh heaven of legal concepts. Lord Goff of Chieveley approached the matter differently. He recognized that consistency militated against admitting a remedy. But for Lord Goff (with whom Lords Browne-Wilkinson and Nolan in separate speeches agreed) the dictates of practical justice were decisive. For the majority the consequence that the aggrieved beneficiary should have to bear the loss whilst allowing the professional man to pocket his fee and go scot-free was simply unacceptable. Some say that the consequences of this decision will long reverberate through the law of tort. I would argue that the decision was made in a one-off situation and that it tells us little about other problems in the law of tort. But for a student of jurisprudence, and of the phenomenon of formalism, it is a fascinating case.

Less than twenty years ago it was still asserted that England had no law of unjust enrichment and reasoning in individual cases proceeded on that assumption.[28] It was as misleading a statement as the assertion that England has no law of privacy. Both assertions are classic examples of Begriffsjurisprudenz or jurisprudence by concepts. England already had a law of unjust enrichment: the terrain of debate was about the frontiers of the law and its capability of developing. Today, thanks to the pioneering work of Lord Goff of Chieveley and academic lawyers, our law of restitution, while still capable of substantial improvement, is a mature system. It is no longer in doubt that the unifying concept is the principle of unjust enrichment. Similarly, our law already protects in piecemeal fashion various interests of privacy: the only questions are the extent of the already recognized protection and the capability of the law to develop.[29] Here much work remains to be done. Given the compelling need to protect freedom of

---

[28] *Orakpo v. Manson Investments* [1978] AC 95, at 104D, *per* Lord Diplock.
[29] Sir Richard Scott, 'Developments in the Law of Confidentiality' [1990] *Denning LJ* 77; R. Beddard, 'Photographs and the Rights of the Individual' (1995), 58 *MLR* 771.

expression, the subject is complex and requires further systematic analysis by academic lawyers.

Looking to the future, the environment in which English judges work is important. Let me assure you at once that this is not a prelude to another plea for the provision of legal clerks! Once I became aware of the fact that about 95 per cent of appellate judgments in the United States are drafted by law clerks and that all judgments of the European Court of Justice are apparently drafted by legal assistants, my enthusiasm for law clerks waned. Every English judge at every level of the judicial hierarchy personally prepares all his own judgments. Long may that continue. But it is often essential for judges, particularly at appellate level, to do some independent research. The treadmill of the list of pending cases makes that difficult, particularly in the House of Lords with its meagre means of access to modern legal literature. It would be an enormous advantage for appellate judges to have access to a pool of energetic researchers.

But there is another dimension. In our adversarial system the court is usually asked to choose between rival cases. The quality of the arguments presented to the court is of crucial importance. Usually, in civil cases, counsel argue cases thoroughly from the vantage point of precedent. Candour compels me to say (and mine is not a lone view) that this cannot be said of the arguments of counsel in some criminal appeals. Unfortunately, among some criminal specialists research means no more than looking up the point in *Archbold* or *Blackstone*. But I sometimes wonder whether in some civil cases in the House of Lords counsel do not concentrate too much on precedent and narrow conceptual arguments at the expense of the wider implications of the case. Often the balance of substantive arguments, and the evaluation of what would be the best legal solution, will be decisive. Counsel do not always engage in argument on this higher ground. There also seems to be scope for some experimentation at the Bar with the technique of using something like a written Brandeis brief which explores in depth the consequences of the adoption of rival arguments. That technique was first used in 1908 by Louis Brandeis, who later became a member of the United States Supreme Court.[30] Since then this technique has been refined and is today widely used not only in

---

[30] *Muller v. Oregon*, 208 US 412 (1908).

constitutional cases but in a wide spectrum of cases involving countervailing policy considerations. Some ninety years later, I wonder whether the United States experience might help us in concentrating the minds of barristers and judges on policy factors and consequentialist arguments which sometimes go virtually unexplored or are mentioned only in a rather amateurish way. No doubt the technique of a Brandeis brief would have to be substantially modified and adapted to our conditions. But that should not be beyond the wit of experienced counsel.

There is another problem. The House of Lords generally adopts the practice that cases must be decided on the arguments and authorities produced by counsel. I regard this policy as unnecessarily restrictive. Given the fact that the House of Lords may not have occasion to reconsider the point for many years, I consider that there is much to be said for relaxing the present practice. But I would go further. Subject to the requirement of fairness, which governs all proceedings, I do not see that there is any good reason why the House of Lords should not overtly adopt the policy that the House, rather than counsel, is the master of the shape of the arguments. I ask rhetorically why should the House not in appropriate cases direct on what points it wants to be addressed orally. Such a development could contribute to the better exploration of the substantive issues in the case. It would not eliminate formalism. Nothing will: formalism will always play a role. But it would tend to promote the better development of arguments beyond the inner logic of the law. I would argue that such a reform would strengthen our system.

The Tendency to Give Formal Reasons Only

It is now an opportune moment to turn briefly to the subject of judicial candour, that is the question whether judges fully expose the real reasons for their decisions in their judgments. This subject has often attracted the interest of academic lawyers. For example, in 1981 two lecturers at the London School of Economics conducted what I would call a quality control test on the reasons given by Law Lords for decisions in the House of Lords in the period 1979–80.[31] Mercifully, they have, so far as I know, not as

---

[31] W. T. Murphy and R. W. Rawlings, 'After the *Ancien Regime*' (1981) 44 MLR 617 and (1982) 45 MLR 34.

yet embarked on a performance assessment for the period since I was appointed as a Law Lord in January last year! While defending in principle the importance and value of such work, I must say the results of this particular study seem to me somewhat controversial. I can understand criticism of what the authors describe as 'discursive techniques' found in House of Lords speeches, such as repetition, assertion, the use of common sense, the invocation of the ordinary man, and so forth. I can also understand the charge of superficiality. Moreover, before I gained a new perspective early last year I used to think that there was a phenomenon to be observed of Law Lords more and more substituting emphasis for analysis as the years rolled by. But I am a little puzzled about the way the authors marked Lord Wilberforce's papers. The authors said Lord Wilberforce's speeches played a central role in their discussion.[32] They stated that '[h]is speeches tend to be some of the least straightforward and most dense in our sample.'[33] Given that Lord Wilberforce was one of our great judges since the Second World War I wondered what the explanation is. Possibly it lies in the fact that Lord Wilberforce never pretended that there were easy solutions to complex problems. His mind was not stocked with certainties or absolutes. His judgments do not induce repose but they certainly are not dense.

Let me place the issue in context. In civil law countries there is usually only one judgment. That is also the invariable practice in the European Court of Justice. Dissent is suppressed in aid of certainty. Subject to the convention that there is only one judgment in appeals in the Criminal Division of the Court of Appeal, English judges are free to express their disagreement with one another, and they do so freely and robustly. Given that the judiciary is a branch of government in a broad sense, this seems to me a particularly healthy feature of our democratic system. And it must also enliven academic life to read about those disagreements.

After comparing the independence inculcated by a career at the English Bar with the career structure of continental judges, J. Gillis Wetter contrasted the style of English and continental judges as follows: 'The [English] style is that of masterful advocates defending their own conclusions—and, accordingly, the very opposite of that employed by members of a judiciary which is

---

[32] 44 MLR, n. 31 above, at 633.   [33] Ibid.

ingrained with notions of *Government*, officialdom, and concepts like *Staatsakt*.'[34]

Undoubtedly English judgments tend to be discursive. They differ markedly in style from the sibylline judgments of the European Court of Justice.[35] It is true that the Opinion of the Advocate General is usually more informative. But the Court does not always adopt the views of the Advocate General or make clear that it does so. Often judgments of the European Court of Justice are squarely based on policy grounds which are not spelt out. I prefer the English style. Ultimately, our liberties and the quality of our society depend on an informed public opinion. From a democratic point of view it is necessary that the judgments of our judges should be subject to constant public scrutiny. The style of English judgments facilitates that process.

I would accept that in the past judges have sometimes felt uncomfortable about including broader considerations, and in particular policy factors, in their judgments. It is even possible that a few still do. But I do not think that there is any substantial force in a suggestion that English judges do not openly express all their grounds of decision.

Conclusion

Lawyers sorely try the patience of the public. Hazlitt complained about what he called the quibbles and quillets of lawyers and, I would add, he expressly included 'the professors' in this charge.[36] He said:

A perfect lawyer is one whose understanding always keeps pace with the inability of words to keep pace with ideas: who by natural conformation of mind cannot get beyond the letter to the spirit of any thing; who, by a happy infirmity of soul, is sure never to lose the form in grasping at the substance. Such a one is sure to arrive at the head of his profession![37]

Since 1816 we have made some progress. Nevertheless, I do not think that we could even today conscientiously enter a demurrer to

---

[34] *The Styles of Appellate Judicial Decisions* (1960), 35.
[35] Brown and Kennedy, *The Court of Justice of the European Communities* (4th edn.) 52–4.
[36] Hazlitt, *Selected Writings* (ed. Jon Cook, 1991), 43.   [37] Ibid. 44.

the general charge. But of one thing I am absolutely sure: if confronted with the charge, the Bar Council, the Law Society, and the Judges' Council would in unison deny the charge in comprehensive terms and ask for further and better particulars of the slur on the profession, the request being drafted by a very experienced Chancery junior counsel in a form which would have pleased Lord Eldon.

Returning to the question which I posed at the beginning, I do not believe that there is a simple answer to it. Some cases are not capable of being analysed except in rather formal terms, e.g. some commercial cases. On the other hand, in some cases, particularly at appellate level, the court is confronted with situations of choice in which deductive reasoning competes for supremacy with considerations of general principle, policy, and justice. The modern trend is for English courts not to confine their reasoning to the narrow inner logic of the law. Judicial choice is, however, a rational, disciplined, and constrained process. On the other hand, it makes sense to accept openly that a judge does not work in a vacuum: he will inevitably consider the results of rival arguments on the basis of his perceptions of the parallel but separate systems of moral and political philosophy. The principles enshrined in the European Convention on Human Rights will probably be his irreducible minimum standards. He will be intensely aware that while the rationality of the law is an important goal, justice is even more important. After all, the law is simply a means of ordering a civilized society. And judges ought to approach controversial questions of law in an open-minded and sceptical way which acknowledges that rational men sometimes have radically different perspectives. It is often idle to pretend that there is only one right answer to a question of law. Simplistically, I end by saying that the imperative of judicial decision-making is that it must always be justified by reason, sharpened by meaningful and effective debate.

[3]
Pepper v Hart;
A Re-Examination

The great master of English legal philosophy, Herbert Hart, did not write about the theory of the interpretation of integrated legal texts such as wills, contracts, and statutes. Until fairly recently lawyers tended to think of the common law as the main part of our legal system. The reality today is quite different. When one considers disputes before tribunals, lower courts, the High Court, the Court of Appeal, and the House of Lords, the interpretation and application of legal texts is the dominant source of law of our time. Owing particularly to the flood of legislation to give effect to the requirements of the social welfare state, and the European dimension, the preponderance of enacted law over common law is increasing year by year. It is not surprising therefore that the subject of interpretation has moved to the centre of the legal stage. This process has been given added impetus by the fact that the devolution legislation and the Human Rights Act 1998 will require courts to adopt methods of interpretation suitable to constitutional adjudication. It is therefore an opportune time to take another look at the landmark decision of the House of Lords in *Pepper* v *Hart*[1] which relaxed the rule prohibiting courts from using ministerial explanations of Bills in Parliament in the construction of statutes. Some say that it was a great liberalizing decision, a blow against literalism in the construction of statutes, and entirely benign in its consequences. I propose to question all the constituent parts of this view.

---

[1] [1993] AC 593.

The interpretation of different types of legal text have much in common. Typically a text contains a register of words, sentences, and paragraphs. Admittedly, a dictionary gives a limited range of conventional meanings for a word. It cannot, however, yield the contextual meaning of words and sentences. In a legal text a word forms part of a sentence and subject to syntax sentences are unlimited in their variety of arrangement of words. Moreover, the sentence is embedded in a text which by virtue of its character and the general effect of its provisions adds colour to words and sentences. Even an agreed definition is of limited use: it takes no account of contextual requirements. Language is a labyrinth. As in ordinary life, words in a legal text cannot be understood except in relation to the circumstances in which they were used. It is sometimes assumed by judges that the existence of an ambiguity is a precondition to admitting evidence of the context of legal text. That is wrong. Language can never be understood divorced from its context. The full impact of the classic judgment of Lord Wilberforce in *Reardon Smith*[2] is not always appreciated. Speaking of contracts Lord Wilberforce said that there is always a setting in which they have to be placed.[3] He made clear that the court is always entitled to be informed of the contextual scene of a contract.[4] The same must apply to the interpretation of all legal texts. The aim of interpretation of a legal text, whether it be a private instrument or a public statute, must be to derive a meaning from its nature and contents. The mandated point of departure must be the text itself. The primacy of the text is the first rule of interpretation for the judge considering a point of interpretation. Extrinsic materials are therefore subordinate to the text itself. Justice Frankfurter's warning is still a salutary one:

> Spurious use of legislative history must not swallow the legislation so as to give point to the quip that only when the legislative history is doubtful do you go to the statute.[5]

This does not mean that contextual materials must be downgraded. On the contrary, it is a universal truth that any statement is only intelligible if one knows under what conditions it was made. The judge must consider all relevant contextual material in order to decide what different meanings the text is capable of letting in. But his task is interpretation not interpolation. What falls beyond that range of possible meanings of the text will not be a result attainable by interpretation. There is a Rubicon which judges may not cross: principles of institutional integrity forbid it.

These general propositions apply to the interpretation of statutes. But the process by which statutes come into existence must influence the approach to their interpretation. In our democracy the primary law-making function is entrusted to citizens assembled in two separate chambers of Parliament. The legislature enacts statutes in accordance with the law of Parliament for a European

---

[2] *Reardon Smith Line* v. *Yrgrar Hansen-Tangen (trading as Hansen-Tangen)* [1976] W.L.R. 989
[3] Ibid at 995H.
[4] Ibid at 997A–C.
[5] The Reading of Statutes (1947), published in *Of Law and Men: Papers and Addresses of Felix Frankfurter* 44 at 67.

liberal democracy. Subject to general presumptions of constitutional importance, such as the rule of law and the principle of constitutionality, the critical thing is what the text of the law so enacted by Parliament provides. When controversy arises the contextual meaning of the enacted text is controlling. The intention of the majority of members of the legislature on the subject under discussion, assuming such a fact to be discoverable, does not have legal significance. Similarly, the views of the government, ministers, and whips—decisive as their decisions may be on the outcome of debates—do not have any relevance to the meaning of the legislation. Under our constitution Parliament enacts legislation, the courts interpret and apply the enacted laws and the executive acts in conformity with the law as interpreted by the courts. The executive is enormously powerful in getting its proposals enacted. But it has no law-making function and it has no authority to declare what the law is or will be if a Bill is enacted.

This is the background against which the Appellate Committee repeatedly held before 1993 that the official reports of proceedings in either House of Parliament, *Hansard* for short, may not be used as an aid to the interpretation of statutes. In *Pepper v Hart* the rule was relaxed.[6] The case concerned the interpretation of a taxation statute. Mr Hart was a schoolmaster at a fee-paying school. It operated a concessionary fee scheme which enabled members of staff to have their sons educated at the school at reduced fees if surplus places were available. Mr Hart was obliged to pay tax on 'the cash equivalent of the benefit'. The House regarded the statutory definition of that expression as ambiguous. The Financial Secretary to the Treasury had explained in a debate that the taxation of certain benefits in kind would be the extra cost caused by the provision of the benefit.[7] The additional cost to the school was negligible since the places would otherwise have been empty. Relying on the statute the Revenue had taxed a proportion of the total cost of providing the services. By a majority of six to one the House held that the Revenue's interpretation was in conflict with what the Financial Secretary had told Parliament. The House made the assumption that the explanation given by the Financial Secretary reflected the intention of Parliament when it passed the legislation. The House ruled against the Revenue. The leading judgment was given by Lord Browne-Wilkinson. Characteristically, it was a powerfully reasoned judgment. At the core of his reasoning was the following consideration:

> In many, I suspect most, cases references to Parliamentary materials will not throw any light on the matter. But in a few cases it may emerge that the very question was considered by Parliament in passing the legislation. Why in such a case should the courts blind themselves to a clear indication of what Parliament intended in using those words? The court cannot attach a meaning to words which they cannot bear, but if the words are capable of bearing more than one meaning why should not Parliament's true intention be enforced rather than thwarted?[8]

---

[6] *Davis v Johnson* [1979] AC 264; *Hadmor Production Ltd v Hamilton* [1983] AC 191, 232–3 *per* Lord Diplock.
[7] 11 HL Paper 43–1; HC 214–1.
[8] Above n 1 at 634H–635B.

Lord Denning had made the same point by saying 'Why should judges grope about in the dark searching for the meaning of an Act, when they can so easily switch on the light?' This is the argument which carried the day. Lord Browne-Wilkinson discussed the practical arguments against a relaxation of the rule in great detail, viz. the difficulty of obtaining access to such materials, the expense of searches, the increase in court time, and so forth. He concluded that those arguments could not prevail against the need to give effect to the true intention of Parliament. He said little about the constitutional implications of the relaxation. He did record that an argument was put forward that the exclusionary rule 'preserves the constitutional proprieties leaving Parliament to legislate in words and the courts (not Parliamentary speakers) to construe the words finally enacted'. And later he added:

> The Attorney-General raised a further constitutional point, namely, that for the court to use Parliamentary material in construing legislation would be to confuse the respective roles of Parliament as the maker of law and the courts as the interpreter. I am not impressed by this argument. The law, as I have said, is to be found in the words in which Parliament has enacted. It is for the courts to interpret those words so as to give effect to that purpose. The question is whether, in addition to other aids to the construction of statutory words, the courts should have regard to a further source. Recourse is already had to white papers and official reports not because they determine the meaning of the statutory words but because they assist the court to make its own determination. I can see no constitutional impropriety in this.[9]

Leaving aside the detailed consideration of an argument by the Attorney-General based on Article 9 of the Bill of Rights, this is the only discussion of the constitutional issues. In a passage which reflects the *ratio* of the case Lord Browne-Wilkinson observed:

> ... the exclusionary rule should be relaxed so as to permit reference to parliamentary materials where: (a) legislation is ambiguous or obscure, or leads to an absurdity; (b) the material relied on consists of one or more statements by a minister or other promoter of the Bill together if necessary with such other parliamentary material as is necessary to understand such statements and their effect; (c) the statements relied on are clear. Further than this, I would not at present go.[10]

Except for Lord MacKay of Clashfern, the Lord Chancellor, who dissented on pragmatic grounds, all the other members of the House expressly agreed with the reasons given by Lord Browne-Wilkinson.

By way of clearing the decks I must now identify two questions affecting *Pepper v Hart* which I will not discuss. The Attorney-General argued that the relaxation of the exclusionary rule would result in an infringement of Article 9 of the Bill of Rights 1689 which prohibits the questioning or impeaching proceedings in Parliament. It was a transparently weak argument. It was roundly rejected by all the law lords. As Lord Browne-Wilkinson observed: 'The purpose

---

[9] Ibid at 639H–640A.
[10] Ibid at 640C.

is to give effect to, not thwart, the intentions of Parliament'.[11] This view has been endorsed in the Report of 30 March 1999 by the Joint Committee on Parliamentary Privilege, which met under the Chairmanship of Lord Nicholls of Birkenhead.[12] Except to note that this issue may have deflected attention from more realistic constitutional arguments, it is unnecessary to exhume the arguments on Article 9. Secondly, experienced commentators with encyclopaedic knowledge of the circumstances of *Pepper v Hart* in all its ramifications have questioned the ruling of the House that the Financial Secretary's explanation was admissible under the requirements laid down by the House.[13] It is truly fascinating stuff. But I must treat these two topics as legal archaeology.

My concern is with the effect and consequences of the central ruling in *Pepper v Hart*. Initially, my untutored view was that it must be right to let in *Hansard* material which can cast light on an ambiguous provision. And in 1996 I expressed that opinion in a public lecture.[14] Recently, without expressing a view on the rival arguments of principle, I argued in a published essay that in the light of practical experience of the operation of *Pepper v Hart* it may have become an expensive luxury in our legal system.[15] This was a view based on the meagre results yielded by the resort to *Hansard* set against the cost of producing such material. It has become the duty of lawyers to conduct such searches at pain of being judged to have been professionally negligent. What is involved is well described by Bates:

> ... a legal adviser must be satisfied that, at each stage of the Bill in both Houses, no admissible statement of legislative intention has been made. This would entail, in most cases, at least an examination of, in the House of Commons, the opening and winding-up speeches at Second Reading, the consideration of the provision, and amendments moved to it, at the Committee Stage, and the opening and winding-up speeches at the Report Stage; and, in the House of Lords, the opening and winding-up speeches at Second Reading and the consideration of the provision, and amendments moved to it, at the Committee and Report Stages. If an admissible statement is identified, the legal adviser may then be required to conduct a more rigorous examination of the subsequent parliamentary proceedings to establish whether the statement has been repeated, varied or withdrawn and ... whether there has been a relevant subsequent amendment to the provision ... [it] also requires establishing a negative, namely that the subsequent parliamentary proceedings do not reveal that the statement was withdrawn or varied or that a relevant inconsistent amendment was successfully moved.[16]

Almost invariably such searches are fruitless. It remains my view that *Pepper v*

---

[11] Ibid at 646C.
[12] HL Paper 43-1; HC 214-1.
[13] Sir Nicholas Lyell QC, MP, '*Pepper v Hart:* The Government Perspective' (1995) 15 *Stat LR* 1–9; F. Bennion, 'How They All Got it Wrong in *Pepper v Hart*' [1995] British TR 325.
[14] 'Does Legal Formalism Hold Sway in England?' (1996) *CLP* 43 at 50.
[15] 'Interpretation: Legal Texts and their Landscapes: The Coming Together of the Common Law and Civil Law' in B. S. Markesinis (ed.) *The Clifford Chance Millennium Lectures* (2000) 87–8.
[16] 'Parliamentary Material and Statutory Construction: Aspects of the Practical Application of *Pepper v Hart*' (1993) 14 *Stat LR* 46 at 54.

Hart has substantially increased the cost of litigation to very little advantage. Many appellate judges share this view. But this occasion demanded that I should examine the subject more deeply and comprehensively. I have tried to do so.

A good place to start the enquiry is with the assumption of the House that the Financial Secretary's explanation reflected 'the intention of Parliament'. The question whether it is appropriate to speak about the intention of a multi-member legislature, which enacts legislation in accordance with set procedures, has been discussed by legal philosophers. In *Law's Empire* Ronald Dworkin wrote:

> So long as we think legislative intention is a matter of what someone has in mind and means to communicate by a vote, we must take as primary the mental states of particular people because institutions do not have minds, and then we must worry about how to consolidate individual intentions into a collective, fictitious group intention.[17]

Jeremy Waldron has argued that 'there is no justification for privileging the mental states of any faction in the legislature as canonical with regard to the decision that he has made by the whole'.[18] There are also protagonists of intentionalism. I am not qualified to join in this philosophical debate. I am afraid I am going to elide the questions with respect to monkeys on typewriters, and the marks made by waves on a beach. Mundanely, I am going to approach the subject from the point of view of reasoned practicality.

It is sometimes meaningful and appropriate for a judge to refer to the intention of Parliament in recognition of its supreme law-making power. It is also perfectly sensible to say that legislation as duly promulgated reflects the will of Parliament. But it is quite a different matter to ascribe to a composite and artificial body such as a legislature a state of mind deduced from exchanges in debates. I am not saying that the law cannot ascribe to legal persons, such as companies and state agencies, an intention to commit particular acts. It can and often does. How and when it arises depends on the application of rules of attribution developed to suit the demands of particular contexts, e.g. on the one hand, a shipping company seeking to limit liability under the Merchant Shipping Acts and, on the other hand, statutes in the health and safety field.[19] Sometimes such questions may be controversial, as is shown by the current debate whether a company can commit the offence of manslaughter which requires proof of fault.[20] But the argument that a legislature, operating through two chambers, each consisting of hundreds of members, may have an intention revealed by statements in debates raises distinctive problems. And until *Pepper v Hart* the common law, the law of Parliament, and our constitution knew no rule of attribution, or rule of recognition, treating statements of ministers as Acts of Parliament.

---

[17] (1986) at 335–6.
[18] *Law and Interpretation* (1995) 329 at 355.
[19] *Meridian Global Funds Management Asia Ltd* [1995] 2 AC 500 at 506A–507F.
[20] T. Kaye, 'Corporate Manslaughter: Who Pays? The Ferryman?' in D. Feldman and F. Meisel (ed.), *Corporate and Commercial Law: Modern Developments* (1996) 349.

It is important to bear in mind precisely what is involved. The intention under consideration is one targeted on the meaning of language contained in a clause in a Bill and employed in a ministerial statement. A Bill is unique as a written document. First Parliamentary Counsel recently explained.

> [a] Bill is not there to inform, to explain, to entertain or to perform any of the other usual functions of literature. A Bill's sole reason for existence is to change the law. The resulting Act *is* the law. A consequence of this unique function is that a Bill cannot set about communicating with the reader in the same way that other forms of writing do. It cannot use the same range of tools. In particular, it cannot repeat important points simply to emphasize their importance or safely explain itself by restating a proposition in different words. To do so would risk creating doubts and ambiguities that would fuel litigation. As a result, legislation speaks in a monotone and its language is compressed.[21]

Parliament can legislate only through the combined action of both Houses acting in accordance with the elaborate stages prescribed by the rules of Parliament. Although the legislative powers of Parliament are exercised by human beings, Parliament as an abstraction cannot have a state of mind like an individual. Parliament legislates by the use of general words. It would be strange use of language to say even of an individual legislator that he intended something in regard to the meaning of a Bill which was never present in his mind. To ascribe to all, or a plurality of legislators, an intention in respect of the meaning of a clause in a complex Bill and how it interacts with a ministerial explanation is difficult.[22] The ministerial explanation in *Pepper* v *Hart* was made in the House of Commons only. What is said in one House in debates is not formally or in reality known to the members of the other House. How can it then be said that the minister's statement represents the intention of Parliament, i.e. both Houses. The Appellate Committee took the view that opposing views expressed by a person other than the promoter can safely be disregarded whenever a statement by a promoter is admitted. The statement of the promoter is treated as canonical. This is also an assumption which seems inherently implausible in respect of the ebb and flow of parliamentary debates. The relevant exchanges sometimes take place late at night in nearly empty chambers. Sometimes it is a party political debate with whips on. The questions are often difficult but political warfare sometimes leaves little time for reflection. These are not ideal conditions for the making of authoritative statements about the meaning of a clause in a Bill. In truth a minister speaks for the government and not for Parliament. The statements of a minister are no more than indications of what the government would like the law to be. In any event, it is not discoverable from the printed record whether individual members of the legislature, let alone a plurality in each chamber, understood and accepted a ministerial explanation of the suggested meaning of the words. For many the spectre of the ever watchful whips will be enough.

---

[21] Extract from Note from First Parliamentary Counsel to the Select Committee on the Modernization of the House of Commons: Second Report, HC 389 (3 December 1997) Appendix 2 at 2.

[22] Compare R. Dworkin, *Law's Empire* (1986) ch 9.

They may agree on only one thing, namely, to vote yes. And they have no means of voting yes and registering at the same time disagreement with the explanation of the minister. Their silence is therefore equivocal. When one ponders such realities of parliamentary life the idea of determining from *Hansard* the true intention of Parliament on the meaning of a clause in a Bill, and an associated ministerial statement, looks more and more farfetched. In *Black-Clawson* Lord Reid, speaking with enormous parliamentary experience, said: 'We often say that we are looking for the intention of Parliament but that is not quite accurate. We are seeking the meaning of the words which Parliament use.'[23] It would have been a fiction for the House to say in *Pepper* v *Hart* that as a matter of historical fact the explanation of the Financial Secretary reflected the intention of Parliament. Such a fact cannot in the nature of things be deduced from *Hansard*. Arguably the House may have had in mind in *Pepper* v *Hart* that an intention derivable from the Financial Secretary's statement ought to be imputed to Parliament. If that were the case, the reasoning would rest on a complete fiction. My view is that the only relevant intention of Parliament can be the intention of the composite and artificial body to enact the statute as printed. If there is substance in this part of my analysis, it tends to undermine the very core of the reasoning in *Pepper* v *Hart*.

It is now necessary to examine *Pepper* v *Hart* against a broader canvass. This requires consideration of the legal and practical consequences of the decision. I would argue that four propositions are sustainable. First, if the foundation requirements for the admission of a statement in *Hansard* are established it must be admitted. The court has no discretion. Secondly, the occasion to admit such a statement arises where, after exhausting normal methods of interpretation, there is an ambiguity, obscurity or absurdity in respect of the particular point of statutory interpretation and a promoting minister's statement is clear on the very question. In these circumstances it seems likely that a properly admitted statement will be a trump card or at the very least of considerable weight. Thirdly, in the real world of litigation it is impossible for a court to decline *in limine* to receive such a statement on the ground that the requirements of ambiguity, obscurity or absurdity are not satisfied. Such a refusal before all arguments have been deployed would be seen as a prejudgment of the case. This factor creates the opportunity for the full deployment of *Hansard* in a wide category of cases. Fourthly, it is in practice inevitable that the courts will from time to time allow such statements to determine whether there is an ambiguity. Lord Browne-Wilkinson said: 'Having once looked at what was said in Parliament, it is difficult to put it out of mind'. This is underlined by the fact that, but for *Hansard*, the majority in *Pepper* v *Hart* would have decided in favour of the Revenue. In the real world it will be difficult to hold to a line that ambiguity, and so forth, must be determined only by reference to normal methods of interpretation. The third

---

[23] *Black-Cawson International Ltd* v *Papierwerke Waldhoff Anschaffenberg AG* [1975] AC 591 at 613–15.

and fourth points are not critical to the rest of my argument but they underline the potential scope of *Pepper* v *Hart*.

There is a case for allowing a statute to be interpreted in favour of the taxpayer in accordance with a considered explanation given by a minister promoting the Bill. It is the argument that the executive ought not to get away with saying in a parliamentary debate that the proposed legislation means one thing in order to ensure the passing of the legislation and then to argue in court that the legislation bears the opposite meaning. That is what happened in *Pepper* v *Hart*.[24] Lord Bridge of Harwich said that the Financial Secretary 'assured' the House that it was not intended to impose the relevant tax. He must have taken the view, as did other members of the majority, that the Revenue in imposing the tax were going back on an assurance to the House of Commons. That would have been an unfair result in a mature democracy. If such a consequence prevailed it might tend to undermine confidence in the legal system. Presented in this way the reasoning begins to look like an estoppel argument. An analogy springs to mind. English law adopts an objective approach to the construction of written contracts. The question is not what the parties subjectively intended. The task of the judge is to ascertain what in the context of the contract the language must reasonably be taken to mean. Evidence of what the parties intended is generally excluded. On the other hand, if one party has led the other to act in the belief that in their dealings the contract will have a certain meaning the first party will be estopped from raising a contrary contention. In this way English law tempers the rigidity of the objective theory and the relevant exclusionary rules. Whether one calls it an estoppel or not *Pepper* v *Hart* as decided on its facts can similarly be viewed as a tempering of the exclusionary rule in the interests of fairness. On this basis the impact of the decision could be confined to the admission against the executive of categorical assurances given by ministers to Parliament. This may be a defensible and principled justification of *Pepper* v *Hart*. And it does not involve a search for the phantom of a parliamentary intention.

But that is not how the reasoning of the House in *Pepper* v *Hart* was formulated. The House had before it a ministerial statement which it regarded as favouring the taxpayer. This framework dictated the shape of the arguments and the judgments. The converse case was not considered. What would the position have been if the statutory position had been truly ambiguous and the ministerial statement favoured the Revenue? *Ex hypothesi* the statement would have come from a minister promoting the Bill and would have been clear on the very question in issue. It would therefore have been a trump card. A judge who declined to give effect to it would, on the reasoning in *Pepper* v *Hart*, be thwarting the intention of Parliament. What then happens to the principle that if a taxation provision is reasonably capable of two alternative meanings, the courts will prefer the meaning more favourable to the subject? *Pepper* v *Hart* does not address this question. It also does not address the position where, in the face of an ambiguity,

---

[24] Above n 1 at 643C.

presumptions of general application with constitutional import, e.g. restrictively construing general words in a statute which appear wide enough to trench on the rule of law, would otherwise have been regarded as decisive. The criteria laid down for the admissibility of statements made by a minister are wide enough to cover any case where the statement supports the government view. Nevertheless, as I have explained, there may be a new but respectable argument that in the field of taxation and elsewhere *Pepper* v *Hart* may only be used against the executive.

The basis on which the exclusionary rule was relaxed ignores constitutional arguments of substance. Lord Bridge described the rule as 'a technical rule of construction'.[25] And implicitly that is how the majority approached the matter. Surely, it was much more. It was a rule of a constitutional importance which guaranteed that only Parliament, and not the executive, ultimately legislates; and that the courts are obliged to interpret and apply what Parliament has enacted, and nothing more or less. To give the executive, which promotes a Bill, the right to put its own gloss on the Bill is a substantial inroad on a constitutional principle, shifting legislative power from Parliament to the executive. Given that the ministerial explanation is *ex hypothesi* clear on the very point of construction, *Pepper* v *Hart* treats qualifying ministerial policy statements as canonical. It treats them as a source of law. It is in constitutional terms a retrograde step: it enables the executive to make law. It is to be noted that the objection is not to the idea of a judge looking at *Hansard*. For example, it may be unobjectionable for a judge to identify the mischief of a statute from *Hansard*. What is constitutionally unacceptable is to treat the intentions of the government as revealed in debates as reflecting the will of Parliament.

Let me look at some of the wider consequences of *Pepper* v *Hart*. Prima facie the statutes of our Parliament are regarded as 'always speaking' and not tied to the circumstances in which they were passed. A statute 'has a legal existence independently of the historical contingencies of its promulgation, and accordingly should be interpreted in the light of its place within the system of legal norms currently in force'.[26] This is a benign principle which allows for statutes to apply despite the inevitable changes in social conditions of society. It seems to me, however, that where there has been a qualifying statement under *Pepper* v *Hart* it may be said that the position is crystallized as explained by the minister at that time. In the result the reference to *Hansard* settles an interpretation within the contemporary understanding of government and this introduces a new form of literalism.[27] If that is so, a valuable capacity of our legal system to cope with changing conditions is lost. Another feature of our system which must be considered is the principle of legality. It does not permit general wording in statutes to erode basic rights and freedoms. There is too great a risk that the

---

[25] Ibid at 616H.
[26] Sir Rupert Cross, *Statutory Interpretation* (3rd edn, 1995) 52; *Reg.* v *Ireland* [1998] AC 147 at 158C–D; see also S. A. De Smith, Lord Woolf, and J. Jowell, *Judicial Review of Administrative Action* (5th edn) para 6-07.
[27] *Reg.* v *Secretary of State for the Home Department, ex parte Simms* [1993] 3 WLR 328.

implications of general words may go unnoticed in the democratic process. If Parliament wishes to make inroads on basic rights it must squarely confront what it is doing. But what happens if the minister made a *Pepper* v *Hart* statement indicating an intention by general words to modify such a basic right? Lord Lester of Herne Hill, the barrister who so ably and successfully argued *Pepper* v *Hart* in the House of Lords, has subsequently written that the courts will not 'permit ministers to interfere with basic rights and freedoms on the basis of what ministers say in Parliament'.[28] But how can that be guaranteed if the legislation is ambiguous and there is a clear ministerial statement indicating that such an inroad on fundamental rights is intended? After all, under *Pepper* v *Hart* the court has no element of discretion. Another consequence of *Pepper* v *Hart* is on the drafting of statutes. That draftsmen will continue to draft with care and precision I do not doubt. But when political issues arise and ministers become involved *Pepper* v *Hart* offers an opportunity to call off a search for precision by making a statement. A likely effect of *Pepper* v *Hart* is to encourage imprecision in drafting in controversial measures.

A matter not considered in *Pepper* v *Hart* is the likely impact of the relaxation of the exclusionary rule on executive practice. It was always predictable that the behaviour of ministers would alter in response to the change announced in *Pepper* v *Hart*. After all, why should ministers not take advantage of the opportunity under *Pepper* v *Hart* to explain the effect of the legislation in the way in which the government would like it to be understood? If this happens it must mark a constitutional shift in power from Parliament to ministers. Recently Dr Geoffrey Marshall wrote that 'there is likely to be a multiplication of Parliamentary attempts to place on the record statements of intention that will serve particular view points and to obtain favourable ministerial answers that can later be cited in litigation'.[29] My impression is that this prediction is already in the process of being fulfilled. I have been unable to trawl through *Hansard* to make good this point. A huge research programme would be needed to accomplish such a task. But with the aid of published commentaries on the course of the Parliamentary debates leading to the enactment of the Human Rights Act 1998 I have been able to study the use made of *Pepper* v *Hart* in this context.[30] *Hansard* reveals numerous questions designed to elicit *Pepper* v *Hart* material and responses by ministers having this decision in mind. When questioned about the effect of the omission to incorporate Article 13 of the European Convention on Human Rights the Lord Chancellor said: 'One always has in mind *Pepper* v *Hart* when one is asked questions of that kind. I shall reply as candidly as I may.'[31] This makes my point: executive practice is bound to be influenced by *Pepper* v *Hart*.

---

[28] '*Pepper* v *Hart* Revisited' (1994) 15 *Stat LR* 10.
[29] G. Marshall, '*Hansard* and the Interpretation of Statutes' in D. Oliver and G. Drewry (eds), *The Law in Parliament* (1998) 139 at 153.
[30] J. Wadham and H. Mountfield, *Blackstone's Guide to the Human Rights Act 1998* (1999) Appendix 4; Extracts from *Hansard* at 203 *et seq.*; F. Klug, 'The Human Rights Act 1998, *Pepper* v *Hart* and All That' [1999] PL 246 *et seq.*
[31] *Hansard* HL (18 November 1997) col. 475.

Planted questions are a well-known device employed by the government on the Westminster scene. There is every incentive for government to use this strategy to get on the record *Pepper* v *Hart* statements where it is reluctant to spell out its precise intentions on the face of the legislation. And the opportunities afforded to lobbyists are manifest.

All in all it may not be unfair to say that *Pepper* v *Hart* failed to address important constitutional matters. There are, however, those who believe that the relaxation of the exclusionary rule was the ultimate vindication of purposive construction. And purposive construction is like mother's milk and apple pie: who can argue against it? Lord Browne-Wilkinson relied on the fact that official reports and white papers were admissible for the purpose of identifying the mischief to be corrected. Lord Browne-Wilkinson said:

> Take the normal Law Commission Report which analyses the problem and then annexes a draft Bill to remedy it. It is now permissible to look at the report to find the mischief and at the draft Bill to see that a provision in the draft was *not* included in the legislation enacted: see the *Factortame* case [1990] 2 AC 85. There can be no logical distinction between that case and looking at the draft Bill to see that the statute as enacted reproduced, often in the same words, the provision in the Law Commission's draft. Given the purposive approach to construction now adopted by the courts in order to give effect to the true intentions of the legislature, the fine distinctions between looking for the mischief and looking for the intention in using words to provide the remedy are technical and inappropriate.[32]

I respectfully agree with Lord Browne-Wilkinson on this point. I would allow such reports to be admitted for what logical value they have. But the constitutional objections which I have discussed do not apply to such pre-existing material. They are part of the contextual scene against which Parliament legislates. In any event, to present the *Pepper* v *Hart* issue as depending on whether one adopts a literal or purposive approach to construction is wide off the mark. By the time *Pepper* v *Hart* was decided nobody supported literal methods of construction. The suggested antithesis misses the point of the fundamental and constitutional nature of the objections. The objections are not simply that a minister's view of a clause is irrelevant but that it is in principle profoundly objectionable to treat it as a trump card or even relevant in the interpretative process.

If the principal footholds of my reasoning are secure, it follows that *Pepper* v *Hart* is not good law. What are the chances of *Pepper* v *Hart* being reversed? Being a decision that marks a shift of power from Parliament to the executive, the prospect of any government initiating legislation to reverse it must be slight. It is, however, possible that *Pepper* v *Hart* may be confined by judicial decision to be used only *against* the executive when it seems to go back on an assurance given to Parliament. This would not require the overruling of *Pepper* v *Hart*. It would simply confine its legal force to the material circumstances of that case.

---

[32] Above n 1 at 635D-E.

Fortunately, there has been a development which may make it easier for the Court of Appeal or the Appellate Committee to revisit this corner of the law. Brief explanatory memoranda used to be printed at the front of a Bill. Such a document was a précis and did not provide background. In addition ministers were provided with notes on clauses. These were essentially briefing notes for use by ministers in debate. The notes on clauses did explain what each clause in a Bill was meant to do. Later such notes on clauses were made available to backbenchers. Since 1998 this system has been imaginatively refined by Explanatory Notes published in a single document alongside each Bill. The Explanatory Notes are not intended to make law and cannot be amended by Parliament. The notes are neutral in political tone: they aim to explain the effect of the text and not to justify it. The purpose is 'to help the reader to get his bearings and to ease the task of assimilating the law'.[33] This new procedure has the imprimatur of the House of Commons Select Committee on Modernization and the House of Lords Procedure Committee.[34] The Explanatory Notes accompany the Bill on introduction and are updated in the light of changes to a Bill made in the parliamentary process.[35] My information is that the Explanatory Notes are usually published before legislation comes in force. No costly researches will be required to identify them. The First Parliamentary Counsel has provided me with a sample of such Explanatory Notes.[36] On what I have so far seen there is much concrete and valuable contextual information in the Explanatory Notes. Such documents may prove to be a more immediate and informative aid than earlier official reports. The question of their use in court has not arisen. In a formal question the indefatigable Lord Lester of Herne Hill has, however, asked the Government in the House of Lords:

> Whether they consider that, in the light of the new procedure for the publication of updated notes on clauses (which provide an extrinsic source of statutory interpretation), the disadvantages of judicial recourse to parliamentary debates for the purpose of construing ambiguous legislation outweigh the benefits of the rule in *Pepper v Hart* [1993] AC 593.[37]

Not surprisingly, Lord Falconer of Thornton, replying on behalf of the Government, elided the question. He simply said that it is for the courts to decide whether they should take into account the Explanatory Notes. In my view the case for permitting reference to such documents is strong. I would expect such documents to be of great assistance to the courts in mastering the scheme and structure of sometimes impenetrable legislation. It is true that the Explanatory Notes may occasionally indicate the Government's intentions on the very question before the court. For my part I would not rule out otherwise useful information

---

[33] Above n 21.
[34] Ibid.
[35] Second Report, HL 98, 1997–1998 (19 November 1997).
[36] Mr Edward Caldwell CB has also given me much useful information. He is, however, not responsible for anything said in this lecture.
[37] HL 1031 (28 February 2000).

on this ground. How is this to be reconciled with my main thesis about *Pepper v Hart?* Consistently with confining that decision to the admission of ministerial assurances against the executive, I envisage that there may be clear statements on behalf of the Government in Explanatory Notes which ought to be treated in the same way. What is impermissible is to attribute such statements to Parliament as expressing the will of the legislature. If it is decided that in principle Explanatory Notes may be admitted, it is likely that the disinclination of judges to delve into Hansard will increase. Moreover, when the occasion presents itself to decide whether in principle such materials may be admitted, the question of the future status of *Pepper* v *Hart* is likely to arise. That may be an opportunity to confine *Pepper* v *Hart* as I have suggested.

I have challenged a judgment of Lord Browne-Wilkinson. His contribution to the development of English law as a judge, Vice-Chancellor, Law Lord and eventually Senior Law Lord has been immense. He is a great judge. But our allegiance must always be to the law. As lawyers our duty is to follow the evidence and arguments where they lead. I hope I have demonstrated that in *Pepper* v *Hart* issues of high principle were not examined and that a re-examination of that case is necessary. It is for you to judge whether I have succeeded in this task.

[4]
The Intractable Problem of the Interpretation of Legal Texts*

SOME MIGHT SAY that to speak of the intractable problem of interpretation of legal texts is an exaggeration. After all, unlike other professionals, a judge usually starts with the comfort that he has a 50 per cent chance of getting the answer to the question right. Moreover, he has the reassurance of Lord Reid's advice to judges that if your average drops significantly below 50 per cent you have a moral duty to spin a coin.

The centrality of the interpretation of legal texts is not always fully appreciated. Day by day, in Britain up and down the country, tribunals, lower courts, the High Court, the Court of Appeal, and the House of Lords, are concerned with the interpretation of a variety of legal texts ranging from wills, contracts, statutes, regulations, bye-laws, various types of 'soft laws' and so forth. It amounts to the preponderant part of the legal work of English judges, perhaps as high as 90 per cent. I would be surprised to hear that the position is significantly different in Australia. But the academic profession and universities have not entirely caught up with the reality that statute law is the dominant source of law of our time. The interpretation of legal texts is of supreme importance for a modern lawyer.

There are, of course, rules applicable to interpretation, some which are known by Latin expressions, such as *ejusdem generis, expressio unius est exclusio alterius,* and *noscitur a sociis*. These underlying rules of interpretation have a role to play. But, subject to what I will say about constitutional adjudication, ultimately interpretation does not generally depend on the application of rules. It is an art. And I would therefore like to start by taking a look at the subject in a more general way. But I am not putting forward a theory of interpretation. The subject is too elusive to be encapsulated in a theory. But as a

---

* This essay was first delivered as the John Lehane Memorial Lecture 2002 at the University of Sydney, 25 September 2002, and then published in *Sydney Law Review* [vol 25:5 2003]. It was reproduced for discussion at the Commercial Law & Commercial Practice Seminar, LSE, and again here with the kind permission of The Editors of the *Sydney Law Review.*

result of the work of legal philosophers, academic and practising lawyers, and judges it is possible to take stock of some modest insights.

I propose to discuss the interpretation of contracts, statutes and constitutional measures. But before I turn to these particular legal texts, I would put forward four general propositions which (if correct) go to the heart of interpretation.

First, it is a universal truth that words can only be understood in relation to the circumstances in which they are used. Adapting one of Wittgenstein's memorable examples, one can imagine parents telling a baby-sitter, who agreed to look after their five year old twins for some hours, that if the children become troublesome 'teach them a game'.[1] The parents return to find the baby-sitter playing poker with the children. Poker is a game. Did the context give a more restrictive colour to the word 'game'? Wittgenstein thought the answer was Yes. Judging by my own grandchildren I am not so sure.

The purpose of interpretation is sometimes mistakenly thought to be a search for the meaning of words. This in turn leads to the assumption that one must identify an ambiguity as a pre-condition to taking into account evidence of the setting of a legal text. Enormous energy and ingenuity is expended in finding ambiguities. This is the wrong starting point. Language can never be understood divorced from its context. In the words of Oliver Wendell Holmes a word is not a transparent crystal. The true purpose is to find the contextual meaning of the language of the text, ie what the words would convey to the reasonable person circumstanced as the parties were. In *Codelfa* Brennan J succinctly stated that 'the symbols of language convey meaning according to the circumstances in which they were used'.[2] Earlier this year in the *Royal Botanic Gardens* case your High Court reaffirmed this observation.[3] In his classic judgment in *Reardon Smith*[4] Lord Wilberforce illuminated this point. Speaking of contracts, Lord Wilberforce said that there is *invariably* a setting in which the language has to be placed. He made clear that the court is *always* entitled to be informed of the contextual scene of a contract. The same must apply to the interpretation of all legal texts. The failure to understand this fundamental principle of linguistic jurisprudence and legal logic has caused great injustices. An example in the field of wills is instructive. Consider the decision in *Re Fish: Ingram v Rayner*.[5] The testator gave his estate to 'his niece Eliza Waterhouse' during her life. The testator had no niece named Eliza Waterhouse. But his wife had a legitimate grand niece named Eliza Waterhouse and also an illegitimate grand niece of the same name. The illegitimate grand niece was living

---

[1] *Philosophical Investigations*, 1958, note to para 70.
[2] *Codelfa Construction Pty Ltd v State Rail Authority (NSW)* (1982) 149 CLR 337 at 401.
[3] *Royal Botanic Gardens and Domain Trust v Sydney City Council* (2002) 186 ALR 290, para 10.
[4] [1976] 2 Lloyd's Rep 621.
[5] [1894] 2 Ch 83.

with the testator and he was in the habit of calling her his niece. This was powerful objective evidence that the words in the will referred to her. With wringing protestations about the painful nature of their task, the Court of Appeal refused to admit the evidence. They held that there was no ambiguity. The illegitimate grand niece lost what had been left to her. What a grotesque result. The will could not be understood without knowing the context.

In the interpretation of legal texts the most frequent source of judicial error is the failure to understand the contextual scene of a legal text. Often judges are not provided with all the contextually relevant raw materials. The essential setting of a text may include in a contract case how a market works, in a breach of statutory duty case competing policy arguments, the structure of a complex statute, the historical development of legislation, and so forth. There is scope for the development of something like a *Brandeis* brief but carefully and concisely targeted to the relevant context.

The second proposition is that the aim of interpretation of a legal text, whether it be a private instrument or a public statute, must be to derive a meaning from its nature and contents. The mandated point of departure must be the text itself. The primacy of the text is the first rule of interpretation for the judge considering a point of interpretation. Extrinsic materials are therefore subordinate to the text itself. Often lawyers argue cases on the reverse hypothesis. Justice Frankfurter recalled the lawyer who said to the United States Supreme Court 'the legislative history is doubtful so I invite you to go to the statute'. Contextual materials must of course not be downgraded. On the contrary, the judge must consider all relevant contextual material in order to decide (a) what different meanings the text is capable of letting in and (b) what is the best interpretation among competing solutions. But the judge's task is interpretation not interpolation. What falls beyond that range of possible contextual meanings of the text will not be a result attainable by interpretation. There is a Rubicon which judges may not cross: principles of institutional integrity forbid it.

The third proposition relates to the generalisation that there has been a shift from literal interpretation to purposive interpretation. What is literalism? This is straightforward. The tyrant Temures promised the garrison of Sebastia that no blood would be shed if they surrendered to him. They surrendered to him. He shed no blood. He buried them all alive.[6] That is literalism. It has generally no place in modern law. On the other hand, it would be an over-simplification to say that there has been a homogenous shift towards a purposive interpretation of all legal texts. Much depends upon the particular text. A comparatively strict interpretation of a documentary credit issued in an international sale may be necessary because a third party (the bank) must be able to rely on a meaning gathered largely within the four corners of the text. In a network of contracts governing a construction project, parties ought

---

[6] This example is given in *The Works of William Paley* (1838 ed), v III, 60.

generally to be able to rely on the obvious meaning of the interlocking texts. Similarly, fiscal legislation may sometimes require a stricter approach than social welfare legislation. By contrast in a consumer transaction the purchaser of a fridge in a consumer sale may be entitled to a more generous interpretation of a right to reject a fridge which cannot make ice.

The fourth proposition I have already foreshadowed. Interpretation is not a science. It is an art. It is an exercise involving the making of choices between feasible interpretations. Structural arguments must be considered. Competing consequentialist arguments must be taken into account. Broader policy considerations may be relevant. Educated intuition may play a larger role than an examination of niceties of textual analysis. The judge's general philosophy may play a role. Ultimately, however, a judge must be guided by external standards in making his choice of the best contextual interpretation. He must put aside his subjective views and consider the matter from the point of view of the reasonable person.

I. COMMERCIAL CONTRACTS

Clarity is the aim in drafting commercial contracts but absolute clarity is unattainable. And it is impossible for contracting parties to foresee all the vicissitudes of commercial fortune to which their contract will be exposed. Moreover, and quite understandably, business bargains have to be struck under great pressure of time and events. Often the phenomenon of studied ambiguity obtrudes: the parties cannot resolve a particular difference but leave it to the court to settle the issue. It is therefore tiresome for judges to expatiate on the quality of draftsmanship of commercial contracts. Judges must simply do the best they can with the raw materials produced in the real world.

The common law does not in principle differentiate between the interpretation of a rudimentary cobbled-together contract and a sophisticated standard form contract; between the interpretation of a consumer contract and a commercial contract; or between the interpretation of a domestic and transnational contract. That is not, however, to say that in working out what is the best interpretation of a contract a court may not have to take into account, for example, a consumer as opposed to a commercial context, or the need for uniformity in international transactions.

In sharp contrast with civil law legal systems the common law adopts a largely objective theory to the interpretation of contracts. The purpose of the interpretation of a contract is not to discover how the parties understood the language of the text which they adopted. The aim is to determine the meaning of the contract against its objective contextual scene. By and large the objective approach to question of construction serves the needs of commerce. It is, however, less well suited to delivering practical justice in consumer transactions. There is much to be said for approaching commercial transactions and consumer agreements somewhat differently. This is already happening. One of the biggest modern developments in contract law has been the development of greater rights for consumers, notably in controls on exemption clauses and requirements of 'fairness' in consumer contracts. In England the principal impetus has been European directives for the protection of consumers. This has given rise to arguments that there should be two contract laws, one for consumer transactions, the other for commercial dealings.[7]

Two recent decisions in the House of Lords explored the extent to which the context may impress a meaning other than the obvious meaning on contractual language. In *Mannai Limited v Eagle Star Assurance Company Limited*[8] the issue was whether a contractual notice by a tenant to determine a lease was valid. The notice wrongly named the day upon which the tenant would do so as 12 January rather than 13 January. The majority held that the notice was valid. Essentially, they regarded it as wholly implausible that the tenant only wanted to terminate if he could do so on 12 rather than 13 January. Given this position the majority concluded that a reasonable recipient would have understood that the option was being exercised. In the context 12 meant 13. The minority held that the notice failed to conform to the requirements of the option reserved in the lease. As a member of the majority in *Mannai* I acknowledge that when judgments were delivered in the House of Lords Chancery practitioners hoisted a black flag over Lincoln's Inn.

The case of *Investors Compensation Scheme Limited v West Bromwich Building Society*[9] is important. The particular dispute can be put to one side. It is sufficient to say that by a majority of 4 to 1 the House of Lords upheld the conclusion of the judge that something had probably gone wrong in the drafting and reversed a ruling of the Court of Appeal. Lord Hoffmann, speaking for the majority, rejected the contention that judges cannot, short of rectification, decide on an issue of interpretation that parties had made mistakes of meaning or syntax. Lord Hoffmann observed that 'if one would nevertheless conclude from the background that something must have gone wrong with the language, the law does not require judges to attribute to the parties an intention which they plainly could not have had.' This was the ratio of the decision. However, in the course of his speech Lord Hoffmann also observed that the admissible background 'includes absolutely anything which would have affected the way in which the language would have been understood by a reasonable man'. This proposition upset the horses in the commercial paddock. Commercial judges vented their angst. Subsequently, in *BCCI v Ali* Lord Hoffmann explained that his observation only referred to anything which the reasonable man

---

[7] Appleby, *Contract Law*, (2001), chs 15 and 17.
[8] [1997] AC 749.
[9] [1998] 1 WLR 896.

would regard as relevant.[10] Relevance of the extrinsic evidence to the objective setting of the contract is the expressed criterion. It is, however, rare for a judge to decide that a text means something that it could not mean in ordinary or technical language. On the rare occasions when a judge does this, he does it because he thinks there is an obvious mistake which has been made by the author of the text and that he has a duty to correct it.

The decision in the *Investors Compensation Scheme* case raised questions about two sacred cows of English law, namely that the court is not permitted to use evidence of (1) pre-contractual negotiations of the parties or (2) of their subsequent conduct in aid of the construction of written contracts even if the material throws light on the subjective intentions of the parties.[11] One view is that these rules follow from the principle that the task of the court is simply to establish the objectively ascertained contextual meaning of the language of the contract. The other view is that the restrictive rules are imposed as a matter of legal policy to achieve certainty. It is, however, important to note that the Vienna Convention on the Sale of Goods (1980),[12] the Unidroit Principles of International Commercial Contracts,[13] and the Principles of European Contract Law (1998)[14] in principle permit such evidence to be taken into account. No doubt this liberality is due to the subjective approach of civil law system. Possibly we are swimming against the tide. In England the rule about prior negotiations may for the moment be relatively safe. I am less confident about the life expectancy of the rule excluding subsequent conduct. Business people and, for that matter, ordinary people, simply do not understand a rule which excludes from consideration how the parties have in the course of performance interpreted their contract. The law must not be allowed to drift too far from intuitive reactions of justice of men and women of good sense: the rule about subsequent conduct may have to be re-examined. In any event, the strict application of these rules had to be qualified in practice. Pragmatically, it has been decided that if pre-contractual exchanges show that the parties attached an agreed meaning to ambiguous expressions, that may be admitted in aid of interpretation.[15] That is a substantial inroad on the restrictive rules. The courts have resorted to estoppel to temper the rigidity of the orthodox rule regarding the inadmissibility of subsequent conduct. Thus in *Vistafjord* the Court of Appeal held that a party may be precluded by an estoppel by convention from raising a contention contrary to a common assumption of fact or law (including the interpretation of a contract)

---

[10] [2002] 1 AC 251, at 269 (para 39).
[11] *Prenn v Simmons* [1971] 1 WLR 1381; *James Millar and Partners v Whitworth Street Estates (Manchester) Ltd* [1970] AC 583.
[12] Art 8(3).
[13] Art 4(3).
[14] Art 5.102.
[15] *The Karen Oltmann* [1976] 2 Lloyd's Rep 708. See McLauchlan (1997) 113 LQR 237.

on which the parties have acted.[16] In this way the reasonable expectations of parties are given some protection. A more radical approach to the two restrictive rules may become necessary. It may be that the differences between commercial and consumer transactions should be more clearly recognised: a hard-nosed attitude to admitting such evidence in commercial transactions may be right but in consumer transactions a more relaxed approach may be necessary.

That brings me to the implication of terms.[17] It is part of the interpretative process. In systems of law where there is a general duty of good faith in the performance of contracts the need to supplement the written contract by implied terms is less than in the common law system. The implication of terms fulfils an important function in promoting the reasonable expectations of parties. Two types of implication are relevant. First, there are terms implied in fact, ie from the contextual scene of the particular contract. Such implied terms fulfil the role of ad hoc gap fillers. Often the expectations of the parties would be defeated if a term were not implied, eg sometimes a contract simply will not work unless a particular duty to cooperate is implied. The law has evolved practical tests for such an implication, such as the test whether the term is necessary to give business efficacy to the contract or whether the conventional bystander, when faced with the problem, would immediately say 'yes, it is obvious that there must be such a term'. The legal test for the implication of a term is the standard of strict necessity. And it is right that it should be so since courts ought not to supplement a contract by an implication unless it is perfectly obvious that it is necessary to give effect to the reasonable expectations of parties. It is, however, a myth to regard such an implied term as based on an inference of the actual intention of the parties. The reasonable expectations of the parties in an objective sense are controlling: they sometimes demand that such terms be imputed to the parties. The second category is terms implied by law. This occurs when incidents are impliedly annexed to particular forms of contracts, eg contracts for building work, contracts of sale, hire etc. Such implied terms operate as default rules. By and large such implied terms have crystallised in statute or case law. But there is scope for further development in a rapidly changing world. This function of the court is essential in providing a reasonable and fair framework for contracting. After all, there are many incidents of contracts which the parties cannot always be expected to reproduce in writing.

Ending my discussion of contracts, the black letter approach to interpretation of contracts has given way to a more commercial approach. It eschews niceties of language and concentrates on a contextual approach and the structure and purpose of the transaction. It is to be welcomed.

---

[16] [1988] 2 Lloyd's Rep 343.
[17] Andrew Phang, 'Implied Terms, Business Efficacy and the Officious Bystander' [1988] JBL 1.

130   *Lord Steyn*

On the other hand, the problem of the consumer perspective has not been completely solved.

II.   STATUTE LAW

In 1882 Pollock described the approach of English judges to statutes as follows: 'Parliament generally changes law for the worse, and... the business of the judges is to keep the mischief of its interference within the narrowest bounds.'[18] This was an accurate description of the judicial mindset in Victorian times. This approach led to restrictive interpretation by literalist methods which sometimes blocked social progress. It remained the approach of English judges until some time after the Second World War. But the legal world has changed. Like Australian judges, English judges now apply purposive methods of construction of statutes.

Except in the rare case where a statute reveals a contrary intention, it is now settled that every statute must be interpreted as an 'always speaking statute'. There are at least two strands to this principle. The first is that courts must interpret and apply a statute of any vintage to the world as it exists today. That is the basis of the decision of the House of Lords in *R v Ireland,* a case where 'bodily harm' in a Victorian statute governing assaults was held to cover psychiatric injury.[19] Equally important is the second strand, namely that a statute must be interpreted in the light of the legal system as it exists today.[20] Thus the importance the law nowadays attach to free speech is relevant background to the interpretation of earlier statutes. The rationale of this principle is that a statute is usually intended to endure for a long time in a changing world. This principle does not apply to contracts. Arguably, however, there could be a similar development in respect of international standard form contracts with an intended long life.

It will be rare for a statute to have one obvious meaning which can be determined without taking into account the context of the legislation. One might say that a statutory provision that a notice must be lodged within 30 days requires no resort to contextual material. But even this proposition is not necessarily correct. The context may throw light on the relative plausibility of interpretations holding that days include every day of the week or only week days. While the text of the statute is of pre-eminent importance, it cannot be understood in a vacuum.

---

[18] *Essays on Jurisprudence and Ethics* (1882) 85.
[19] [1988] AC 147, 158D-G.
[20] Cross, *Statutory Interpretation,* 3rd edn (1995), 51–52; *McCartan Turkington Breen v Times Newspapers Ltd* [2001] 2 AC 277, 296A-F.

This was lucidly explained by Lord Blackburn in *River Wear Commissioners v Adamson* as follows:[21]

> ... I shall ... state, as precisely as I can, what I understand from the decided cases to be the principles on which the Courts of Law act in construing instruments in writing; and a statute is an instrument in writing. In all cases the object is to see what is the intention expressed by the words used. But, from the imperfection of language, it is impossible to know what that intention is without inquiring farther, and seeing what the circumstances were with reference to which the words were used, and what was the object, appearing from those circumstances, which the person using them had in view; for the meaning of words varies according to the circumstances with respect to which they were used.

Legislative language can only be understood against the backcloth of the world to which it relates. Sometimes judgments do not fully take into account the different levels of reasoning at which the context is relevant. As in the case of commercial contracts, and other legal texts, the context is relevant to what possible different meanings the language of the text may let in. But the context is again relevant when the judge comes to select among the possible interpretations the best one. It is therefore a fundamental misconception to say that the background to the statute may only be admitted in the event of an ambiguity. The interpretative process requires judges to make informed choices.

That brings me to the use of Hansard in aid of interpretation of statutes. As in Australia, English courts regularly use reports, which led to or preceded legislation, in aid of interpretation. It is part of the setting of a statute. Australian and English lawyers would agree that there is no reason why Hansard materials should not be used to identify the mischief against which the statute is aimed. It helps to explain the background of the statute. Far more troublesome is the use in aid of interpretation of statements of a government minister in the promotion of a bill as reflecting the desired intent of the government. Section 15A-B of the Acts Interpretation Act 1901, as inserted in 1984, permits the use of such material where the legislation is ambiguous or obscure or its literal meaning leads to an absurdity. In England *Pepper v Hart*[22] heralded a parallel development. Doubts about the reach of that decision have arisen in England. It may be of interest if I explained the reservations which are now emerging in England.

Pepper v Hart broke new ground by holding that in cases of ambiguity it is permissible to refer in aid of construction of statutes to statements of a promoter of the bill. The rationale of this principle was memorably stated by Lord Denning:

> Why should judges grope about in the dark searching for the meaning of an Act, when they can so easily switch on the light?

[21] (1877) 2 App Cas 743, 763.
[22] [1993] AC 593.

132 Lord Steyn

I have, however, come to the conclusion that while the actual decision in *Pepper v Hart* was correct, the broadly based observations in that case are contrary to constitutional principle.[23]

In the Westminster Parliament exchanges sometimes take place late at night in nearly empty chambers whilst places of liquid refreshment are open. Sometimes there is a party political debate with whips on. The questions are often difficult but political warfare sometimes leaves little time for reflection. These are not ideal conditions for the making of authoritative statements about the meaning of a clause in a Bill. Let me give you the flavour from an explanation by Lord Hayhoe, reported in Hansard of 27 March 1996. He said:

> I remember only too well my first intervention as a new Minister at the Treasury on the Finance Bill in the very early hours of the morning on a subject about which I knew absolutely nothing but on which I had a marvellously thick book of briefing from the Inland Revenue. I appropriately read out the response to some detailed points that had been made by one of the Opposition spokesmen who stood up afterwards to say how well I had dealt with the point he had raised and welcomed my first intervention in Finance Bill Committees. However, I discovered from my private office afterwards that I had read out the wrong reply to the amendment. Clearly, it made not the slightest bit of difference.

It is sometimes meaningful and appropriate for a judge to refer to the intention of Parliament in recognition of its supreme law-making power. It is also perfectly sensible to say that legislation as duly promulgated reflects the will of Parliament. But it is quite a different matter to ascribe to a composite and artificial body such as a legislature a state of mind deduced from exchanges in debates. The law can ascribe to legal persons, such as companies and state agencies, an intention to commit particular acts. Rules of attribution have been developed to suit the demands of particular contexts. But the argument that a legislature, operating through two chambers, may have an intention revealed by statements in debates is altogether more ambitious. Until *Pepper v Hart*, under the common law, there was in England no rule of attribution, or rule of recognition, which treated statements of ministers as acts of Parliament.

The intention under consideration is one targeted on the meaning of language contained in a clause in a Bill and employed in a ministerial statement. A Bill is a unique document. It speaks in compressed language. Parliament legislates by the use of general words. It is difficult to ascribe to members of Parliament an intention in respect of the meaning of a clause in

---

[23] I have drawn on my paper '*Pepper v Hart:* A Re-examination' (2001) 21 *Oxford Journal of Legal Studies* 59.

a complex Bill and how it interacts with a ministerial explanation. The ministerial explanation in *Pepper v Hart* was made in the House of Commons only. What is said in one House in debates is not formally or in reality known to the members of the other House. How can it then be said that the minister's statement represents the intention of Parliament, ie both Houses. The Appellate Committee took the view that opposing views expressed by a person other than the promoter can safely be disregarded whenever a statement by a promoter is admitted. This is also an assumption which seems inherently implausible in respect of the ebb and flow of Parliamentary debates. In truth a minister speaks for the government and not for Parliament. The statements of a minister are no more than indications of what the government would like the law to be. In any event, it is not discoverable from the printed record whether individual members of the legislature, let alone a plurality in each chamber, understood and accepted a ministerial explanation of the suggested meaning of the words. For many the spectre of the ever watchful whips will be enough. They may agree on only one thing, namely to vote yes. And they have no means of voting yes and registering at the same time disagreement with the explanation of the minister. Their silence is therefore equivocal. When one considers such realities of Parliamentary life the idea of determining from Hansard the true intention of Parliament on the meaning of a clause in a Bill, and an associated ministerial statement, looks more and more farfetched. In *Black-Clawson*,[24] Lord Reid, speaking with enormous Parliamentary experience, said, 'We often say that we are looking for the intention of Parliament but that is not quite accurate. We are seeking the meaning of the words which Parliament use.' It would have been a fiction for the House to say in *Pepper v Hart* that as a matter of historical fact the explanation of the Financial Secretary reflected the intention of Parliament. Arguably the House may have had in mind in *Pepper v Hart* that an intention derivable from the Financial Secretary's statement ought to be *imputed* to Parliament. If that were the case, the reasoning would rest on a complete fiction. The only relevant intention of Parliament can be the intention of the composite and artificial body to enact the statute as printed.

There is a strong case for allowing a statute to be interpreted in favour of the citizen in accordance with a considered explanation given by a minister promoting the Bill. It is the argument that the executive ought not to get away with saying in a Parliamentary debate that the proposed legislation means one thing in order to ensure the passing of the legislation and then to argue in court that the legislation bears the opposite meaning. That is what happened in *Pepper v Hart*. Lord Bridge of Harwich said that the Financial Secretary 'assured' the House that it was not intended to impose the

---

[24] *Black-Clawson International Ltd v Papierwerke Waldhof-Aschaffenburg AG* [1975] AC 591.

134 Lord Steyn

relevant tax. He must have taken the view, as did other members of the majority, that the Revenue in imposing the tax were going back on an assurance to the House of Commons. That would have been an unfair and unacceptable result. If such a consequence prevailed it would tend to undermine confidence in the legal system.

Whether one calls it an estoppel, a legitimate expectation, a principle of fairness, or whatever, *Pepper v Hart* as decided on its facts can simply be viewed as a tempering of the traditional exclusionary rule in the interests of justice. On this basis the impact of the decision can be confined to the admission *against* the executive of categorical assurances given by ministers to Parliament. This may be a principled justification of *Pepper v Hart*. And it does not involve a search for the phantom of a Parliamentary intention.

Unfortunately, that is not how the reasoning of the House in *Pepper v Hart* was expressed. The House had before it a ministerial statement which it regarded as favouring the taxpayer. This framework dictated the shape of the arguments and the judgments. The converse case was not considered. What would the position have been if the statutory position had been truly ambiguous and the ministerial statement favoured the Revenue? *Ex hypothesi* the statement would have come from a minister promoting the Bill and would have been clear on the very question in issue. It would therefore have been a trump card. A judge who declined to give effect to it would, on the reasoning in *Pepper v Hart*, be thwarting the intention of Parliament. What then happens to the principle that if a taxation provision is reasonably capable of two alternative meanings, the courts will prefer the meaning more favourable to the subject? *Pepper v Hart* does not address this question.

The basis on which the exclusionary rule was relaxed ignores constitutional arguments of substance. Lord Bridge described the rule as 'a technical rule of construction'. And implicitly that is how the majority approached the matter. Surely, it was much more. It was a rule of constitutional importance which guaranteed that only Parliament, and not the executive ultimately legislates; and that the courts are obliged to interpret and apply what Parliament has enacted, and nothing more or less. To give the executive, which promotes a Bill, the right to put its own gloss on the Bill is a substantial inroad on a constitutional principle, shifting legislative power from Parliament to the executive. Given that the ministerial explanation is *ex hypothesi* clear on the very point of construction, *Pepper v Hart* treats qualifying ministerial policy statements as canonical. It treats them as a source of law. It is in constitutional terms a retrograde step: it enables the executive to make law. It is of fundamental importance to understand that the objection is not to the idea of a judge looking at Hansard. It is entirely acceptable for a judge to identify the mischief of a statute from Hansard. What is constitutionally wrong in the English system is to treat the intentions of the government as revealed in debates as reflecting the will of Parliament.

A matter not considered in *Pepper v Hart* is the likely impact of the relaxation of the exclusionary rule on executive practice. It was always predictable that the behaviour of ministers would alter in response to the change announced in *Pepper v Hart*. After all, why should ministers not take advantage of *Pepper v Hart* to explain the effect of the legislation in the way in which the government would like it to be understood? If this happens it must mark a constitutional shift of power from Parliament to ministers. The Parliamentary debates leading to the enactment of the Human Rights Act 1998 are revealing. When questioned about the effect of the omission to incorporate Article 13 of the European Convention on Human Rights the Lord Chancellor said: 'One always has in mind *Pepper v Hart* when one is asked questions of that kind. I shall reply as candidly as I may.'[25] This makes my point: executive practice is bound to be influenced by *Pepper v Hart*. There is a real incentive for government to use this strategy to get on the record *Pepper v Hart* statements when it is reluctant to spell out its precise intentions on the face of the bill.

In *Pepper v Hart* the House of Lords failed to consider important constitutional questions. There are, however, those who believe that the relaxation of the exclusionary rule was the ultimate vindication of purposive construction. And purposive construction is like mother's milk and apple pie: who can argue against it? The reasoning in *Pepper v Hart* sought to build on the fact that official reports and white papers are admissible for the purpose of identifying the mischief to be corrected. Such reports are always admissible for what logical value they have. But the constitutional objections do not apply to such reports. They are part of the contextual scene against which Parliament legislates. In any event, to present the *Pepper v Hart* issue as depending on whether one adopts a literal or purposive approach to construction is wide off the mark. By the time *Pepper v Hart* was decided nobody supported literal methods of construction. The suggested antithesis misses the point of the fundamental and constitutional nature of the objections. The objections are not simply that a minister's view of a clause is irrelevant but that it is in principle wrong to treat it as a trump card or even relevant in the interpretative process.

What are the chances of *Pepper v Hart* being reversed? Being a decision that marks a shift of power from Parliament to the executive, the prospect of any government initiating legislation to reverse it must be slight. It is, however, possible that *Pepper v Hart* may be confined by judicial decision to the use of Hansard *against* the executive when it goes back on an assurance given to Parliament. This would not require the overruling of *Pepper v Hart*. It would simply confine its legal force to the material circumstances of that case. In England this question will not go away. In two recent

---

[25] Hansard, HL (18 November 1997) Col 475.

136   *Lord Steyn*

decisions in the House of Lords there have been dicta raising these questions.[26] The debate continues.

III.   CONSTITUTIONAL MEASURES: FUNDAMENTAL RIGHTS

Constitutional adjudication affecting fundamental rights contained in a bill of rights requires a broader approach than is applicable to commercial contracts and statutes. It requires what Lord Wilberforce in *Foster* described as 'a generous interpretation avoiding what has been called 'the austerity of tabulated legalism', suitable to give to individuals the full measure of fundamental rights and freedoms'.[27]

Bills of rights have proved themselves in the common law world, influencing the common law and being influenced by it. The interpretative techniques adopted in common law countries vary. The Canadian Charter of Rights and Freedoms requires judges to interpret an impugned law in a way that conforms to the Charter. If it cannot be reconciled the court declares the inconsistency and the law is pro tanto void. The New Zealand Bill of Rights 1990 is a weaker model. While the court must strive to reach an interpretation compatible with the Bill of Rights, there is no express power for the court to go further. On the other hand, the New Zealand Court of Appeal has strengthened the regime by holding that there is an implied power make a declaration of inconsistency.[28] With the advantage of these earlier models the South African Constitution, and its Bills of Rights, was carefully crafted to entrench human rights strongly. Unlike Canada and New Zealand there is a Constitutional Court to adjudicate on constitutional issues. It has the power to declare legislation unconstitutional. The United Kingdom Bill of Rights is a relative newcomer in the field. The Human Rights Act 1998, which incorporates the European Convention on Human Rights into our law, came into force in October 2000. There is a strong interpretative obligation on the court to interpret legislation so as to be compatible with the Convention. If it is impossible to do so, the court must make a declaration of incompatibility. Parliamentary supremacy is respected. The expectation is, however, that Parliament will consider the law on an early occasion and amend it.

In advance of the Human Rights Act 1998 coming into operation there was much hysteria. Newspapers described the Act as a recipe for chaos. They feared that traffic would be brought to a halt; that serious crime

---

[26] *Regina v Secretary of State for the Environment, Transport and Regions, ex parte Spath Holme* [2001] 2 AC 349, at 407 (*per* Lord Hope of Craighead); *Robinson v Secretary of State for Northern Ireland and Others* [2002] UKHL 32, *per* Lord Hoffmann and Lord Millett.
[27] *Ministry of Home Affairs v Fisher* [1980] AC 319, at 328.
[28] *Moohen v Film & Literature Board of Review* [2000] 2 NZLR 9; *Poumaka* [2000] 2 NZLR 37.

would go unpunished; and that the prison gates would be left permanently open. The forecast was that it would rain sulphur and brimstone. The premise of this hysteria was that the courts would accede to every impractical and implausible claim, ignoring the balance inherent in the Convention between individual rights and conditions of stability and order required in a liberal democracy. This ignored the fact that the direct application of the Convention has caused no such chaos in other European democracies. Nevertheless, Lord McCluskey, a Scottish judge, joined in by saying that the Human Rights Act 'would provide a field-day for crackpots, a pain in the neck for judges and legislators, and a goldmine for lawyers'. Unsurprisingly, the judge was held to be disqualified from sitting in a human rights case.[29] The predicted legal revolution has not taken place. Instead there has been a subtle process of weaving human rights law into United Kingdom law. The Act has bedded down in a sensible and satisfactory way. Only a small percentage of challenges have succeeded. But it has afforded an opportunity for the courts to examine critically but constructively a few murkier areas of English law. It has strengthened our democracy.

It is undoubtedly the case that human rights are protected at many levels in the Australian system.[30] But unlike Western European countries and major Commonwealth countries, Australia has no express bill of rights. For Australian courts, fulfilling their constitutional duties of standing between the people and the executive, and protecting fundamental rights, this is a disadvantage.

Much can, however, be done through the common law. In England, the courts have recognised certain fundamental rights as constitutional. The courts protect as constitutional the right of participation in the democratic process, equality of treatment, freedom of expression, religious freedom and the right of unimpeded access to the courts. Even before the incorporation of the European Convention on Human Rights into English law the courts held that everybody has an absolute constitutional right to a fair trial which if breached must lead to the setting aside of the conviction.[31] What is the significance of classifying a right as constitutional? It is meaningful. It is a powerful indication that added value is attached to the protection of the right. It strengthens the normative force of such rights.[32] It virtually rules out arguments that such rights can be impliedly repealed by subsequent legislation.[33] Generally only an express repeal will suffice. The constitutionality of a right is also important in regard to remedies. The duty of the court is to

---

[29] *Hoekstra and Others v HM Advocate* [2001] 1 AC 216.
[30] George Williams, *Human Rights Under the Australian Constitution*, (1999), *passim*.
[31] *R v Brown (Winston)* [1998] AC 367; *R v Bentley* [2001] 1 Cr App Rep 307. Now the absolute guarantee of a fair trial is governed by Art 6.1 of the European Convention: the relevant case law is reviewed in *Mills v HM Advocate and Another* [2002] 3 WLR 1597.
[32] *Mohammed v The State* [1999] 2 AC 111.
[33] *Thoburn and Others v Sunderford City Council and Others* [2003] QB 151.

138 *Lord Steyn*

vindicate the breach of a constitutional right, depending on its nature, by an appropriate remedy.

There is another important common law development. Parliament does not legislate on a blank sheet. In the case of Britain it legislates for a European liberal democracy. This gives rise to what Sir Rupert Cross described as a presumption of general application which operates as a constitutional principle.[34] General words in a statute should not be allowed to abrogate fundamental rights. This principle has a considerable common law pedigree but in practice judges often failed to observe it. In 1998 in *Pierson*[35] in separate judgments Lord Browne-Wilkinson and I tried to bring together the rich strands of authority in support of this principle. At that time our views did not attract the support of a majority. Two years later in *Simms*[36] the House of Lords unambiguously reaffirmed the principle. Lord Hoffmann explained the rationale of the principle:

> Parliamentary sovereignty means that Parliament can, if it chooses, legislate contrary to fundamental principles of human rights.... The constraints upon its exercise by Parliament are ultimately political, not legal. But the principle of legality means that Parliament must squarely confront what it is doing and accept the political cost. Fundamental rights cannot be overridden by general or ambiguous words. This is because there is too great a risk that the full implications of their unqualified meaning may have passed unnoticed in the democratic process. In the absence of express language or necessary implication to the contrary, the courts therefore presume that even the most general words were intended to be subject to the basic rights of the individual.

This principle is now firmly entrenched in English law.[37] If it is applied by your courts, it will strongly reinforce the protection of fundamental rights in Australia.

IV. CONCLUSION

I end by saying that in the interpretative process the judiciary owes allegiance to nothing except the constitutional duty of reaching through reasoned debate the best attainable judgments in accordance with justice and law. This is their role in the democratic governance of our countries.[38]

---

[34] *Statutory Interpretation*, 3rd edn, at 166.
[35] [1998] AC 539, 575D.
[36] *R v Secretary for the Home Department ex parte Simms* [2000] 2 AC 131.
[37] *R v Special Commissioner and Another, ex parte Morgan Grenfell & Co Ltd* [2003] 1 AC 563.
[38] I am indebted to Lydia Clapinska, a Judicial Assistant in the House of Lords, now based in Sydney, and to Karen Steyn, for suggestions about my lecture.

[5]
Dynamic Interpretation Amidst an Orgy of Statutes[1]

Brian Dickson was an outstanding jurist. Stendhal said that there is only one rule: style cannot be too clear, too simple. Brian Dickson followed this rule. His meticulous, carefully crafted and thoughtful judgments were and are admired throughout the common law world. With the advent of the Charter of Rights and Freedoms in 1992 the Supreme Court became seised of some of the most difficult and delicate issues in Canadian society, upon which reasonable people held strong and divergent views. Brian Dickson rose to the challenge. He set the Charter on track during its early years. He said that Canada had moved from a system of parliamentary supremacy to constitutional supremacy where each Canadian was given individual rights which the Government or legislature could not take away. He placed Charter jurisprudence on solid jurisprudential and principled foundations that will continue to be of enduring benefit to Canadians. He had in full measure all the qualities of a great judge and great Chief Justice. It is a privilege for me to deliver the first Brian Dickson Memorial Lecture.

My subject is the interpretation of legal texts, and particularly the interpretation of statutes, seen inevitably from an English perspective. You may think that some of my reflections exaggerate the complexities of the subject. It is true that, unlike other

[1] Delivered as the first Brian Dickson Memorial Lecture. Ottawa, October 2, 2003.

professionals, judges are usually able to start with a comforting feeling that they have a 50 per cent chance of getting the answer to the question right. Moreover, judges can be reassured by the fact that Lord Reid advised judges that if their average success rate drops significantly below 50 per cent they have a moral duty to spin a coin.

To set the subject in context I would mention two preliminary matters. In his influential book *A Common Law for the Age of Statutes* Guido Calabresi described what he called the "statutorification" of the law. He referred to the modern phenomenon of an orgy of statute making.[2] That description is particularly apt in the case of my country. In the last 20 years there has been an orgy of legislation in Britain, particularly in the criminal justice field. Almost every year there is a huge Criminal Justice Act. One feature of this frenzied statute making in the criminal justice field is a legislative see-saw: measures based on half-baked ideas are adopted in haste, published with minimal consultation, and puffed up to be the ideal solution for solving problems of crime but then abandoned very soon after and replaced by yet another solution said to be the perfect one. The complexity of each new statute defies belief. And so, to the bewilderment of the public and judges, the process continues. Year after year the editors of our major criminal treatise have commented adversely on this phenomenon. They have said[3]:

> "Major criminal legislation is now an annual event; the quality of it borders on the scandalous. If testimony to this were needed, it is only necessary to look at the way in which each year's Act is extensively amended or repealed by the next. If any government really wanted to improve the quality of the criminal justice it would announce a moratorium on criminal legislation for five or seven or, even, 10 years."

The blame does not rest with parliamentary draftsmen: they do excellent work. The packages of ill thought out expedients are the result of governments seeking short-term political popularity. Often the legislation is an instant response to particularly outrageous crimes, which grabbed the headlines during the parliamentary session. In this way the Dangerous Dogs Act 1991 was enacted. In a strong field it won the accolade as the worst piece of legislation ever to go on the English statute book. In a forum where reasoned and balanced debate prevails judges try to make sense of a system choked with legislation.

The second preliminary matter is that in my country day-by-day tribunals, lower courts, the High Court, the Court of Appeal and the House of Lords are concerned with the interpretation of a variety of legal texts ranging from statutes, regulations, byelaws, rules, various types of "soft laws," contracts, and so forth. Interpreting and applying various types of legislation amounts to the major part of the legal work of English judges, perhaps as high as 90 per cent. I would be surprised to hear that the position is significantly different in Canada. But universities in England have not entirely adjusted to the reality that statute law is the dominant source of law of our time. They arrange courses very much as if statute law fills the gaps left by the beloved common law rather than the other way around. The truth is that the common law has an important but nevertheless residual role to play. That this is the case should cause no

---

[2] Guido Calabresi, *A Common Law for the Age of Statutes* (1982), p.1.
[3] Archbold, *Criminal Pleading, Evidence and Practice* (1995 ed.), Preface.

surprise. The common law, entirely judge-made, is not in all respects ideally equipped to serve the needs of a modern social democracy. The mordant description of Anatole France springs to mind: "La majestueuse égalité des lois qui interdit au riche comme au pauvre de coucher sous les ponts, de mendier dans les rues et de voler du pain".[4]

The question may legitimately be posed: What is the justification for unelected judges deciding the meaning and effect of laws enacted by Parliament? How does this fit into so-called majoritarian and counter-majoritarian arguments? There is a defensible explanation. The democratic ideal has two strands. The first premise is that the people entrust power to the government to carry on its business in accordance with the principle of majority rule. The second premise of the democratic ideal is that the basic values of liberty and justice for all and respect for human rights and fundamental freedoms must be guaranteed. Where a tension develops between these two premises a balance has to be struck. And in a democracy the guarantor of that balance can generally only be an impartial and independent judiciary carrying out its task in accordance with principles of institutional integrity. The language used by Parliament does not interpret itself. Somebody must interpret and apply it. A democracy may, and almost invariably does, entrust the task of interpretation to the neutral decision-making of the judiciary. Alone the judiciary would be unequal to this task. It is critically dependent on a free and courageous legal profession, academic and practising, all serving the course of justice.

It may be useful to look at interpretation in a general way. The subject is too elusive to be encapsulated in a single theory. But as a result of the work of legal philosophers, academic and practising lawyers, and judges, it is possible to take stock of some modest insights.[5]

The first general proposition is that the aim of interpretation of a legal text, whether it be a private instrument or a public statute, must be to derive a meaning from its nature and contents. The starting point must be the text itself. The primacy of the text is the first principle of interpretation for the judge considering a point of interpretation. External materials ought therefore to be subordinate to the text itself. Often lawyers argue cases on the reverse hypothesis. Justice Frankfurter recalled the lawyer who said to the US Supreme Court, "the legislative history is doubtful so I invite you to go to the statute". The apparent meaning of statutory language is the starting point but not the end of interpretation. A judge must consider all relevant contextual material in order to decide what different meanings the text is capable of letting in and what is the best interpretation among competing solutions. But the judge's task is interpretation not interpolation. Interpretation is not infinitely expandable. What falls beyond that range of possible contextual meanings of the text will not be a result attainable by interpretation. There is a Rubicon that judges may not cross: principles of institutional integrity forbid it.

Secondly, words can only be understood in relation to the circumstances in which they are used. Adapting one of Wittgenstein's memorable examples, one can imagine parents telling a baby-sitter, who agreed to look after their five-year-old twins for some

---

[4] "The majestic egalitarianism of the law, which forbids rich and poor alike to sleep under bridges, to beg in the streets, and to steal bread." *Le Lys Rouge* (1894), Ch.7 (translation taken from the *Oxford Dictionary of Quotations*).

[5] See *e.g.* Eskridge, *Dynamic Statutory Interpretation* (1994); A.P. Martinich, ed., *The Philosophy of Language* (1996); A. Marmor, ed., *Law and Interpretation: Essays in Legal Philosophy* (1995).

248 Dynamic Interpretation Amidst an Orgy of Statutes

hours, that if the children become troublesome, "teach them a game".[6] The parents return to find the baby-sitter playing poker with the children. Poker is a game. Did the context give a more restrictive colour to the word "game"? Wittgenstein thought the answer was Yes. Judging by my own grandchildren I am not so sure.

Let me now attempt to extirpate what I regard as two jurisprudential heresies. In English law the interpretation of the meaning of a legal text is always a question of law, with attendant consequences for the possible reversibility of decisions judged to be wrong. In other words English law does not subscribe to the US Chevron doctrine, which holds that an interpretation by a federal agency is protected from review if it is a permissible or reasonable interpretation.[7] So much is clear. But sometimes loosely worded dicta create the impression that the task of an interpreter is to find the meaning of a word or words. Such an inquiry is of no legal interest. The aim of interpretation is emphatically not a search for the meaning of words. Instead the purpose of interpretation is to ascertain the meaning of the language employed in a text, taking into account syntax, background, and social context.

The next heresy is the assumption that one must identify a relevant ambiguity as a precondition to taking into account evidence of the setting of a legal text. Enormous energy and ingenuity is employed by lawyers in trying to find relevant ambiguities. This is the wrong starting point. Language can never be understood divorced from its context. The symbols of language convey meaning according to the circumstances in which they were used. The true purpose of interpretation is to find the contextual meaning of the language of the text, *i.e.* what the words would convey to the reasonable person circumstanced as the parties were. Speaking of contracts, Lord Wilberforce said that there is invariably a setting in which the language has to be placed.[8] The court is always entitled to be informed of the contextual scene of a contract. The same principle applies to the interpretation of all legal texts. The failure to understand this fundamental principle of linguistic jurisprudence and legal logic has caused great injustices. An example in the field of wills is instructive. Consider the decision in *Re Fish; Ingram v Rayner*.[9] The testator gave his estate to "his niece Eliza Waterhouse" during her life. The testator had no niece named Eliza Waterhouse. But his wife had a legitimate grandniece named Eliza Waterhouse and also an illegitimate grandniece of the same name. The illegitimate grandniece was living with the testator and he was in the habit of calling her his niece. This was powerful objective evidence that the words in the will referred to her. With wringing protestations about the painful nature of their task, the Court of Appeal refused to admit the evidence. They held that there was no ambiguity. The illegitimate grandniece lost what had been left to her. What a grotesque result. The will could not be understood without knowing the context.

In the interpretation of legal texts the most frequent source of error is the failure to understand the matrix of a legal text. Often judges in my country are not provided with all the contextually relevant raw materials. Doing so requires imaginative preparation of cases. The essential setting of a text may include in a contract case how a market works, in a breach of statutory duty case interacting social policies, the structure of a

---

[6] *Philosophical Investigations* (2nd ed., 1958), note to para.70.
[7] Tribe, *American Constitutional Law* (3rd ed., 2000), Vol.1, pp.993–997.
[8] *Reardon Smith Ltd v Hansen-Tangen* [1976] 2 Lloyd's Rep. 621.
[9] [1894] 2 Ch. 83.

complex statute, the historical development of legislation, and so forth. There is scope for the development of something like a Brandeis brief but concisely targeted to the relevant context.

But at this point a question arises: if one accepts the premise about context giving colour to the meaning of language, does it not follow that the case for interpretation in accordance with the original intent of the framers of the text is made out? It will be necessary to return to this question.

In the meantime I turn to my third general proposition. In 1882 Sir Frederic Pollock described the approach of English judges to statutes as follows[10]:

> "Parliament generally changes law for the worse, and ... the business of the judges is to keep the mischief of its interference within the narrowest bounds."

This was an accurate description of the judicial mindset in Victorian times. This approach led to restrictive interpretation by literalist methods which often blocked social progress. It remained the approach of English judges until some time after the Second World War. But the legal world has changed. Like Canadian judges, English judges now apply purposive methods of construction of statutes. Almost 60 years ago Learned Hand J. explained the merits of purposive interpretation[11]:

> "Of course it is true that the words used, even in their literal sense, are the primary, and ordinarily the most reliable, source of interpreting the meaning of any writing: be it a statute, a contract, or anything else. But it is one of the surest indexes of a mature developed jurisprudence not to make a fortress out of the dictionary; but to remember that statutes always have some purpose or objective to accomplish, whose sympathetic and imaginative discovery is the surest guide to their meaning."

Having identified the legislative purpose, the question then usually becomes one of determining which of the competing interpretations is most consistent with the goal. That will often depend on policy choices. The pendulum has swung towards purposive methods of construction. This change was accelerated by European ideas. Nowadays the shift towards purposive interpretation is not in doubt. On the other hand, the degree of liberality allowed in interpretation is crucially dependent on the context. A comparatively strict interpretation of a documentary credit issued in an international sale may be necessary because a third party (the bank) must be able to rely on a meaning gathered largely within the four corners of the text. In a network of contracts governing a construction project, parties ought generally to be able to rely on the obvious meaning of the interlocking texts. Similarly, fiscal legislation may sometimes require a stricter approach than social welfare legislation. In law context is everything.

I now move on to consider directly the position in regard to statutes. A statute is a unique document. It has a public character. It speaks in monotone and its language is compressed. It is the law. Lord Reid observed that: "We often say that we are looking for the intention of Parliament but that is not quite right. We are seeking the meaning

---

[10] *Essays on Jurisprudence and Ethics* (1882), p.85.
[11] *Cabell v Markham* (1945) 148 F 2nd 737, at 735.

250 Dynamic Interpretation Amidst an Orgy of Statutes

of the words which Parliament uses."[12] This is not a recipe for excluding consideration of the setting of a statute. Legislative language can only be understood against the backcloth of the world to which it relates. Sometimes judgments do not fully take into account the different levels of reasoning at which the context is relevant. As in the case of other legal texts, the setting is relevant to what different meanings the language of the text may let in. But it is also relevant when the judge comes to select among the possible interpretations the best one. It is a fundamental misconception to think that the background to the statute may only be admitted in the event of an ambiguity. Interpretation requires judges to make informed choices.

That brings me to the subject of intentionalism, originalism and textualism. In England the interpretation of private instruments, such as contracts and wills, focuses on the colour given to the language of the text by the circumstances existing at time of the making of it. That is so even if, for example, the contract is a long-term one. The position is different in regard to the interpretation of statutes. There is no statutory provision equivalent to s.10 of the Federal Interpretation Act which provides that statutes shall be considered as always speaking. But our courts developed a similar principle: it is now accepted that interpretation is not an archaeological dig. The controlling decision is *R v Ireland*.[13] The question arose whether the phrase "bodily harm" in the Offences Against the Person Act 1861 covers psychiatric harm done to a victim by a stalker. In 1861 the idea of psychiatric harm was not known. It was certainly not in the mind of the Victorian legislators. The question was whether the House had to treat the meaning as having been fixed at the time of enactment. The House held that the words of the statute must be interpreted in the light of contemporary scientific knowledge. The statute was interpreted as covering psychiatric harm. The House decided that it is a question of interpretation whether a statute is to be treated as always speaking or is to be given an historic interpretation. Since indication of an intent to tie the meaning to circumstances existing at the time of the enactment of the legislation is rarely to be found in a statute, statutes will generally be found to be of the always speaking variety. The logic of dynamic interpretation is inexorably that the meaning of a statute may change over time. It is a fairy tale to think otherwise.

This principle is not restricted to giving an updating interpretation in the light of new scientific developments. Sir Rupert Cross stated[14].

> "[A statute] has a legal existence independently of the historical contingencies of its promulgation, and accordingly should be interpreted in the light of its place within the system of legal norms currently in force. Such an approach takes account of the viewpoint of the ordinary legal interpreter of today, who expects to apply ordinary current meanings to legal texts, rather than to embark on research into linguistic, cultural and political history, unless he is specifically put on notice that the latter approach is required."

In *McCarten Turkington Breen (A Firm) v Times Newspapers Ltd*[15] the question arose whether under a statute dating from 1888 a qualified privilege that attaches to things

---

[12] *Black Clawson International Litd v Papierwerke Waldhof-Aschaffenberg AG* [1975] A.C. 591.
[13] [1998] A.C. 147.
[14] *Statutory Interpretation* (3rd ed., 1995), pp.51–52.
[15] [2001] 2 A.C. 277.

said at "a public meeting" covered a press conference. If it did, there was a defence to a claim in defamation. But in 1888 press conferences did not exist. The argument was that under the statute public meetings did not include press conferences. The House rejected this argument. The House construed the legislation in the light of the utility of press conferences in the modern world, taking into account the law of freedom of expression as it exists today. Again, the appeal to the original intent was rejected. In our system these are beneficial developments which enhance the utility of statutes. Parliament must be deemed to contemplate that generally its statutes will endure for a considerable time, and that unless statutes evince a contrary intention, they will be judged to be constantly speaking.

On a broader basis judges are inevitably influenced by changes in public attitudes. For example, in 1996 the Court of Appeal was dismayed by the fact that it was unable to hold that a ministerial decision excluding homosexuals from service in the army was not reviewable.[16] Three years later the European Court of Human Rights declared that restriction was unlawful.[17] In the Second World War such individuals had fought and died for their country in large numbers. Two years ago the House ruled that under the Rent Act a same sex partner of a tenant qualified for purposes of succession as "a member of the original tenant's family".[18] The House reached this conclusion on the basis of changing social habits and opinions. On the other hand, earlier this year the reassignment of gender, after surgery, for the purposes of marriage was a step too far for the House.[19] Interpretation is an evolutive process.

Our courts have over the last few years developed constitutional principles which protect the rule of law. Parliament legislates for a European liberal democracy. Even outside the field covered by the Human Rights Act (HRA) 1998 Parliament is presumed not to legislate contrary to the rule of law and fundamental rights. If Parliament wishes to do so it must squarely confront what it is doing and accept the political cost. General words cannot achieve such a result: only an unmistakeable parliamentary intent will be sufficient. This is called the principle of legality. It is a strong presumption. In 1999 it was reaffirmed and explained in *R. v Secretary of State for the Home Department Ex p. Simms*.[20] The Home Office interpreted prison rules as authorising a ban on visits by journalists to prisoners who wanted to use the interviews to mount media campaigns to demonstrate their innocence. The House declined to follow a decision of the US Supreme Court denying to prisoners such a right, read down the prison rules in accordance with the principle of legality, and declared the ban unlawful. Another example is *R. (on the application of Anufrijeva) v Secretary of State for the Home Department*.[21] In that case there were legislative indications that an uncommunicated decision denying asylum status to an individual was immediately binding. Invoking the constitutional principle requiring the rule of law to be observed, the House by a 4:1 majority held as one of the grounds of decision:

---

[16] *R. v Ministry of Defence Ex p. Smith* [1996] Q.B. 517.
[17] *Smith and Grady v United Kingdom* (1999) 29 E.H.R.R. 493.
[18] *Fitzpatrick v Sterling Housing Association* [2001] 1 A.C. 27.
[19] *Bellinger v Bellinger* [2003] UKHL 21; [2003] 2 A.C. 467.
[20] [2000] 2 A.C. 115 at 131E–G, *per* Lord Hoffmann.
[21] [2003] UKHL 36; [2003] 3 W.L.R. 252.

252 Dynamic Interpretation Amidst an Orgy of Statutes

"That principle too requires that a constitutional state must accord to individuals the right to know of a decision before their rights can be adversely affected. The antithesis of such a state was described by Kafka: a state where the rights of individuals are overridden by hole in the corner decisions or knocks on doors in the early hours. That is not our system... there must be exceptions to this approach, notably in the criminal field, e.g. arrests and search warrants, where notification is not possible. But it is difficult to visualise a rational argument which could even arguably justify putting the present case in the exceptional category."

The House held that a decision can take effect only upon notification to the individual concerned.

There is yet another constitutional development in England that touches on interpretation. Although the United Kingdom has no written constitution, the courts have recognised certain fundamental rights as constitutional. This development predates the HRA 1998 and is the common law at work in protection of fundamental rights. Thus the courts protect as constitutional the right of participation in the democratic process, equality of treatment, freedom of expression, religious freedom, and the right of unimpeded access to the courts. Even before the incorporation of the European Convention on Human Rights into English law the courts held that everybody has an absolute constitutional right to a fair trial which, if breached, must lead to the setting aside of the conviction.[22] What is the significance of classifying a right as constitutional? It is meaningful. It is a powerful indication that added value is attached to the protection of the right. It strengthens the normative force of such rights.[23] It virtually rules out arguments that such rights can be impliedly repealed by subsequent legislation.[24] Generally, only an express repeal will suffice. The constitutionality of a right is also important in regard to remedies. The duty of the court is to vindicate the breach of a constitutional right, depending on its nature, by an appropriate remedy.

Finally, in regard to the interpretation of statutes, the relaxation of the old rule prohibiting the courts from using *Hansard* has caused difficulties. In the landmark case of *Pepper v Hart* the House sanctioned resort to *Hansard*[25] where an explanation given by a Minister promoting the Bill was directly in point on an ambiguous provision in an Act. For my part such use of *Hansard* was fully justified. Whether one calls it an estoppel, legitimate expectation, a principle of fairness, that was a sensible tempering of the traditional exclusionary rule in favour of the citizen in the interests of justice. It is also sensible to allow *Hansard* to be used to identify the mischief that Parliament tried to correct. What I regard as constitutionally wrong in the English system is to treat the intentions of the government as revealed in debates as the will of Parliament. That is

---

[22] *R. v Brown* [1994] 1 W.L.R. 1599; *R. v Bentley* (2001) 1 Cr.App.R. 307. Now the absolute guarantee of a fair trial is governed by Art.6(1) ECHR: the relevant case law is reviewed in *Mills v Lord Advocate (Scotland Act)* [2002] UKPC D2; [2002] 3 W.L.R. 1597.
[23] *Mohammed v Trinidad and Tobago* [1999] 2 A.C. 111.
[24] *Thoburn v Sunderland City Council* [2002] EWHC (Admin) 195; [2003] Q.B. 151.
[25] [1993] A.C. 593.

how the dicta in *Pepper v Hart* had until recently been interpreted. Slowly these distinctions and clarification of *Pepper v Hart* are gaining ground in England.[26]

Now I turn to constitutional interpretation. An eloquent explanation was given in *Hunter v Southam Inc*[27] by Dickson C.J. He said:

> "The task of expounding a constitution is crucially different from that of construing a statute. A statute defines present rights and obligations. It is easily enacted and as easily repealed. A constitution, by contrast, is drafted with an eye to the future. Its function is to provide a continuing framework for the legitimate exercise of governmental power and, when joined by a Bill or Charter of Rights, for the unremitting protection of individual rights and liberties. Once enacted, its provisions cannot easily be repealed or amended. It must, therefore, be capable of growth and development over time to meet new social, political and historical realities often unimagined by its framers. The judiciary is the guardian of the constitution and must, in interpreting its provisions, bear these considerations in mind."

As Cardozo said, "[a] constitution states or ought to state not rules for the passing hour, but principles for an expanding future".[28]

The United Kingdom is a newcomer among countries that have adopted bills of rights. Today is the third anniversary of the HRA, which incorporated the European Convention on Human Rights into our law. The essential shape of the European Convention is very different from, for example, the bill of rights under the United States Constitution and much closer to your bill of rights. The framers proceeded on the basis that from time to time the fundamental right of one individual may conflict with the human rights of another.[29] Thus the principles of free speech and privacy may collide. They also thought that a single-minded concentration on the pursuit of fundamental rights of individuals to the exclusion of the interests of the wider public might be subversive of the ideal of tolerant European liberal democracies. The fundamental rights of individuals are of supreme importance but those rights are not unlimited: we live in communities of individuals who also have rights. Thus, notwithstanding the danger of intolerance towards ideas, the Convention system draws a line which does not accord the protection of free speech to those who propagate racial hatred against minorities.[30] This is to be contrasted with the categorical provision of the First Amendment to the US Constitution that "Congress shall make no law ... abridging the freedom of speech". The European Convention requires that where difficult questions arise a balance must be struck. Subject to a limited number of absolute guarantees such as the one against torture, the scheme and structure of the Convention reflects this balanced approach. The Convention is today an ageing instrument in urgent need of updating. For example, there is no freestanding

---

[26] *Wilson v First County Trust Ltd (No.2)* [2003] UKHL 40; [2003] 3 W.L.R. 568 at [58]–[59], per Lord Nicholls of Birkenhead.
[27] [1984] 2 S.C.R. 145.
[28] *The Nature of the Judicial Process*, p.20.
[29] I have used part of my description in *Brown v Stott* [2003] 1 A.C. 681 at 707E–708D.
[30] Art.10; *Jersild v Denmark* (1994) 19 E.H.R.R. 1, 26 at [31].

254 Dynamic Interpretation Amidst an Orgy of Statutes

guarantee against discrimination.[31] The UK Government is opposed to the incorporation into our law of a free-standing non-discrimination guarantee modelled on such a guarantee in the International Covenant of Civil and Political Rights (1966).[32] The constitutional principle of equality developed by the courts has therefore an important role to play.

The very purpose of a bill of rights is to give rights to individual citizens against an all powerful state. It creates a culture of justification. But techniques used in bills of rights vary. The Canadian Charter of Rights and Freedoms requires judges to interpret an impugned law in a way that conforms to the Charter. If it cannot be reconciled the court declares the inconsistency and to the extent of the incompatibility the law is void. The New Zealand Bill of Rights 1990 is a weaker model. While the court must strive to reach an interpretation compatible with the bill of rights, there is no express power for the court to go further. But the New Zealand Court of Appeal has strengthened the regime by holding that there is an implied power to make a declaration of inconsistency. With the advantage of these earlier models the South African Constitution, and its bills of rights, has entrenched human rights strongly. There is a Constitutional Court to adjudicate on constitutional issues. It has the power to declare legislation unconstitutional. In the UK HRA 1998 there is a strong interpretative obligation on the court to interpret legislation, in so far as it is possible to do so, as compatible with the Convention. The court is not entitled to interpret black as white but the obligation is much more than a mere obligation to adopt a purposive approach. It is clearly based on the obligation in EC law for national courts to reach an interpretation compatible with European law unless the language makes such an interpretation impossible. As a last resort the court must make a declaration of incompatibility. Parliamentary supremacy is respected. On the other hand, the HRA is no ordinary statute: it has a constitutional status.[33] The expectation is that Parliament will consider the law on an early occasion and amend it. The Canadian bill of rights is stronger than the UK one. In practice, however, the results produced by our two systems are not very different.

Bills of rights apply vertically, in other words they protect fundamental rights of individuals against the state and its agencies. The question may be raised whether a bill of rights also has direct horizontal application between private parties. Generalisations on this subject are unwise. It depends crucially on the terms of each instrument. There has been a vigorous debate on the point in England. The importance of the point can be illustrated by the potential scope of the guarantee of privacy in the Convention. English law knows no tort of privacy. Does the guarantee of privacy under the Convention empower the English courts to create a free-standing tort of privacy? The matter is not settled and any view must be provisional. I am inclined to think that the structure of our Act rules out direct horizontal application. If this is right, it may be beyond the power of the English courts to develop a general tort of privacy. On the other hand, as your Chief Justice has pointed out, bills of rights influence the common law and are in turn influenced by the common law.[34] Like your bill of rights ours has

[31] Art.14; see Professor Bob Hepple, "Race and Law in Fortress Europe", Chorley Lecture, London School of Economics, June 11, 2003.
[32] Art.26.
[33] *Brown v Stott* [2003] 1 A.C. 681, *per* Lord Bingham of Cornhill at 703G.
[34] The Chief Justice of Canada, "Bills of Rights in Common Law Countries" (2002) 50 I.C.L.Q. 197–204.

or should have a radiating effect on the general law. After all, ultimately common law, statute law and constitutional law coalesce in one legal system. In my country this may indirectly lead to the incremental development of remedies that protect rights of privacy, such as the duty of confidentiality in a relatively broad sense. Some may be disappointed by this unheroic stance. For my part, freedom of expression in a democracy is the most fundamental of all rights and without it an effective rule of law is impossible. Restraints on freedom of expression must therefore be admitted only when compelling considerations of public interest and justice demand it.

There are many areas of bills of right jurisprudence where we in England have much to learn from your jurisprudence. I would in particular single out one field. A key question is when and to what extent should the courts defer to the decisions of other branches of government. In England the spatial metaphor of a "discretionary area of judgment" on the part of Parliament or the executive with which the courts should not interfere is frequently employed.[35] It has overtones of a decision beyond the reach of judicial review. It has in effect been said that on constitutional grounds the court may not adjudicate on matters of national security.[36] It has further in effect been said that a decision on policy or allocation of resources is on constitutional grounds not for the courts.[37] While I respect these views I cannot accept them.

A core characteristic of a constitutional democracy is the protection it offers to the rights of individuals against the majority view as reflected by an elected government. In our new constitutional order Parliament itself has placed this duty on the courts. It permits judicial review of Acts of Parliament. The scope of the duties of the courts under our bill of rights are not limited in respect of subject-matter. There are no zones of immunity. The doors of the court must always be open to anyone with a complaint. The courts may not abdicate their responsibilities by developing self-denying constitutional limitations on their powers. McLachlin J. put the principled position as follows[38]:

"Care must be taken not to extend the notion of deference too far... Parliament has its role: to choose the appropriate response to social problems within the limiting framework of the Constitution. But the courts also have a role: to determine, objectively and impartially, whether Parliament's choice falls within the limiting framework of the Constitution. The courts are no more permitted to abdicate their responsibility than is Parliament. To carry judicial deference to the point of accepting Parliament's view simply on the basis that the problem is so serious and the solution difficult, would be to diminish the role of the courts in the constitutional process and to weaken the structure of rights upon which our constitution and nation is founded."

---

[35] A powerful critique of this spatial label with its overtones of a decision beyond the reach of judicial interference is to be found in Murray Hunt, "Sovereignty's Blight: Why Contemporary Public Law Needs The Concept of 'Due Deference' " in N. Bamforth and P. Leyland, eds, *Public Law in a Multi-Layered Constitution* (Hart, Oxford, 2003).

[36] *Secretary of State for the Home Department v Rehman* [2001] UKHL 47; [2003] 1 A.C. 153, per Lord Hoffmann at [50]–[54].

[37] *R. (on the application of ProLife Alliance) v BBC* [2003] UKHL 23; [2003] 2 All E.R. 977, per Lord Hoffmann at [74]–[77].

[38] *RJR McDonald v Att-Gen (Canada)* (1993) 3 S.C.R. 199 at [133]–[137].

256 Dynamic Interpretation Amidst an Orgy of Statutes

Making due allowance for the fact that, unlike the Canadian Charter, the HRA preserves parliamentary supremacy, this is also an accurate description of the function of the English courts under the HRA. The courts are charged with the adjudicative function of deciding whether Convention rights have been breached: in point of principle there are not any no-go areas.

On the other hand the courts may recognise that in respect of a particular dispute Parliament or the executive may be better placed to decide certain questions. The courts should not take such decisions on *a priori* grounds without scrutiny of the decision since one cannot know in advance whether it has not been infected by manifest illegality. So far as the courts desist from making decisions in a particular case it should not be on grounds of non-justiciability, separation of powers, or constitutional principle. The true justification for courts exceptionally declining to decide an issue is the relative institutional competence or capacity of the branches of government.[39]

The ideological storms of our age, and the rise of international terrorism, threaten allegiance to the rule of law in many countries. The tragic events of September 11, 2001, and the response to them, have fractured the international legal order, interrupted the development of international law and placed in jeopardy the protection of human rights far and wide. Recognising the dangers of terrorism, Aharon Barak, the President of the Israeli Supreme Court, said that it is a defining feature of a liberal democracy that "not all means are acceptable to it, and not all practices employed by its enemies are open before it".[40] Such restraint is the very core of democratic values. Yet at Guantanamo Bay hundreds of foot soldiers of the Taliban, denied prisoner of war status because they did not wear uniforms, have already been detained for some 18 months in what is a legal black hole. Despite its long tradition of allegiance to the rule of law the United States is, for the moment, engaged on a process which has not a vestige of legitimacy in municipal or international law. Our Court of Appeal has expressed its deep concern that such prisoners may be subject to indefinite detention in territory over which the United States has exclusive control with no opportunity to challenge the legitimacy of their detention before any court or tribunal.[41] There is no rule of law at Guantanamo Bay: that is the whole idea. The US courts have so far firmly declined jurisdiction in respect of the prisoners. Military tribunals with power of imposing death sentences will try the prisoners with an ultimate review by a President who has described the prisoners as "killers". Professor Ronald Dworkin has rightly said that the procedures contemplated are the kind of trials one associates with the most lawless totalitarian regimes.[42] What must authoritarian regimes, or countries with dubious human rights records, make of the example set by the most powerful of all democracies? It is also a perilous course: far from discouraging terrorism the outcome may further inflame passions in the Muslim world. Guantanamo Bay must be one of the lowest points in the distinguished story of US jurisprudence.

---

[39] J. Jowell, "Judicial Deference and Human Rights: A Question of Competence", in P. Craig and R. Rawlings, eds, *Law and Administration in Europe* (Oxford University Press, 2003).
[40] The citation relies on the magisterial essay of President Aharon Barak, "A Judge on Judging: The Role of a Supreme Court in a Democracy" (2002) 116 *Harvard Law Review* 148.
[41] *R. (on the application of Abbasi) v Secretary of State for Foreign and Commonwealth Affairs* [2002] EWCA Civ 1598; [2003] U.K.H.R.R. 76.
[42] "The Threat to Patriotism", *New York Review of Books*, February 28, 2002, p.44.

There has so far been no Al Qaeda attack on British soil. Nevertheless, the UK Parliament agreed to a derogation from the terms of the European Convention under Art.15 in order to permit detention without trial of foreign nationals suspected of links with terrorism. Article 15 permits such a derogation in time of war or other public emergency threatening the life of the nation. The Court of Appeal has upheld this action.[43] Later this year the issue comes before the House sitting with seven rather than the usual five members. It would be wrong for me to say anything about the merits of the case. It may turn out to be one of the most important cases ever to come before the House of Lords.

These days there exists a dialogue between the final courts of appeal in various democracies. There is already much contact between Canada and the United Kingdom. The values we share are more significant than those that divide us. We have much to learn from each other. This is perhaps the time to create regular judicial exchanges between our countries.

---

[43] *A v Secretary of State for the Home Department* [2002] EWCA Civ 1502; [2002] 2 W.L.R. 564.

[6]
The Role of the Bar, The Judge and the Jury: Winds of Change*

The Lord Chancellor's Consultation Paper on Rights of Audience and Rights to Conduct Litigation

This country has above all the priceless advantage of a long history of constitutional habits. It has, and has given a large part of the world, a parliamentary form of government. Next to the language of Shakespeare and Milton, and the common law, the system of parliamentary government is one of the great legacies of England to many nations. But like all democratic systems of government, it has a weakness. When the government has a massive majority in the House of Commons the executive becomes all powerful and parliamentary scrutiny of the acts and intentions of the executive is not always as careful as it ought to be. That is when the constitutional principle of the separation of powers becomes important.[1] In its judicial capacity the House of Lords has emphasized that the British Constitution is firmly based on the separation of powers.[2] For present purposes the separation of powers between the executive and the judiciary is at stake. It is to the judiciary that the citizen must look for protection from abuses by the executive and for a vindication of his rights against the state. But without an independent bar, and the jury system, the judiciary would be unequal to its task. Together the bar, the judiciary and the jury is a guarantor of the quality of our democracy. No government inclined to authoritarianism could long tolerate such institutions. It would quickly in populist language proclaim them to be contrary to the public interest. It is interesting to consider the South African experience. In the apartheid era the Nationalist government succeeded in restraining the press by repressive legislation. But it never did succeed in establishing control over the Bar. At least one lamp flickered on. Fortunately, we live in a European liberal democracy. But even in England we must be ever watchful and guard against executive encroachments on the separation of powers.

---

* This article is based on the 1998 Kalisher memorial lecture, delivered on October 13, 1998.

[1] I discussed separation of powers in some detail in "The Weakest and Least Dangerous Department of Government", [1997] P.L. 84.

[2] *Hinds v. The Queen* [1977] A.C. 195, at 212, *per* Lord Diplock; *Dupont v. Steel Ltd v. Sirs* [1980] 1 W.L.R. 142 at 157, *per* Lord Diplock.

For my part I regard a highly qualified, independent and courageous Bar as of central importance in our system. It was, therefore, with great concern that I read the Lord Chancellor's Consultation Paper published in June 1998. One does not have to pull away any veil to expose the major purpose of the Lord Chancellor. The Consultation Paper makes clear that the Lord Chancellor wishes to confer full rights of audience on State employees. He proposes to do so, not directly by promoting primary legislation to that end, but by asking Parliament to entrust that decision to his discretion. But the Lord Chancellor has left nobody in any doubt that he is determined that State employees should have such rights. I can fully understand that the Lord Chancellor now wants to abolish the Lord Chancellor's Advisory Committee on Legal Education and Conduct (ACLEC). It was my misfortune to chair that ill-starred committee for two years. So far as rights of audience are concerned it is certainly dispensable in its present form.[3] Moreover I support the conferment of rights of audience in the higher courts on all properly qualified solicitors in private practice. And I accept that there is a legitimate public interest in the availability and affordability of high class legal services. But in my view the proposed granting of full rights of audience to lawyers working for the Crown Prosecution Service (CPS) would be a mistake. I make no criticism of the CPS or of the dedicated lawyers who work for the CPS. The point is an institutional one. On grounds of constitutionalism it would be a mistake to grant such rights to State employees: prosecution in the Crown Court by members of an independent bar places a brake on the executive. It is no answer to say that CPS lawyers already prosecute in the magistrates courts. The important cases where tensions between the liberty of the citizen and the interests of the executive arise are heard in the Crown Court. It is an illusion to believe that CPS lawyers work in the same culture of independence as barristers in private practice. Inevitably, CPS lawyers have to display a loyalty to the organization which employs them and that imposes direct and indirect pressures on them. Failure to fit into the corporate culture of the CPS may result in dismissal or denial of promotion. That is one of the reasons why after careful investigation ACLEC by a majority advised against the conferment of full rights of audience on lawyers working for the State.

The advice given by ACLEC in June 1995 was not based on protecting any interests of the Bar. The majority was, amongst other things, concerned about "the reality of the likely pressures on CPS employers" and about "the extent to which, without the requirement of an independent advocate, those pressures might make it more difficult for the individual advocate to adopt a position contrary to the possible wishes and assumptions of the CPS as his or her employer". While there has been much criticism in the press directed at the advice of ACLEC not a single journalist has ever even in passing reported the true ground of our advice. On constitutional grounds I regard it as undesirable for State employees to be given rights of audience in the higher courts. If such

---

[3] ACLEC also has functions to advise on legal education, continuing professional development in advocacy and litigation. It has played a valuable role in this respect and an *independent* standing body will be needed for these tasks. Anything less would be a retrograde step.

rights are given there would be no justification for not in due course appointing such State employees as High Court judges. And that would be a development with undesirable implications for the quality of the administration of justice in the High Court which is constantly concerned with disputes between citizens and the State. Here too the earlier South African experience is instructive. Magistrates and regional magistrates with extended criminal jurisdiction were appointed from the State prosecution service. That ensured a largely complaisant magistrates bench under the Nationalist government.

But there is an even more important point. The proposals of the Lord Chancellor seek to concentrate in his hands the power over rights of audience. He will be able "to call in" any professional rule of either branch of the profession and eventually pass judgment on it. It is cold comfort that such powers would only be exercisable after consultation. A similar proposal made by the previous Lord Chancellor had to be withdrawn after the judges' written response described it as unconstitutional. In May 1989 the judges pointed out that the independence of the judiciary and the independence of the Bar are inextricably interwoven. The judges then stated:

> It is of fundamental importance that the existing degree of separation of the powers and functions of the Judiciary from those of Parliament and the Government, evolved gradually over the centuries, should be maintained. The independence of the Judiciary and of advocates is perhaps more important now than ever, because one of the great constitutional tasks of the Courts today is to control misuse of powers by Government ministers and departments.
>
> The Government is proposing that in the future the Lord Chancellor should make the final decision on standards of education and training for advocates, prescribe the principles to be embodied in codes of conduct for advocates, and be empowered to make decisions on rights of audience in the High Court and Court of Appeal by means of subordinate legislation. These proposals represent a grave breach of the doctrine of separation of powers.
>
> Until now no Government minister has had, and no Government has sought power to exercise ultimate control over the profession of advocacy in the courts. Once a power is given, the risk that it may be misused by some future Government cannot be disregarded.
>
> The Government should recognise that it has gone too far in making these proposals and should accept that such powers as the Lord Chancellor may require should only be exercised by him with the concurrence of the judiciary.
>
> In this way the necessary separation of the proper powers of the Judiciary from those of the Executive would be preserved.

The Government backed down. That is how ACLEC came to be set up by the Courts and Legal Services Act 1990. There is at present a system of statutory checks and balances. Extensions of rights of audience involves a process of decision making involving ACLEC, the Director General of Fair Trading, the four designated Judges and the Lord Chancellor. All have to agree to changes.

Unfortunately, the Consultation Paper misdescribes the purpose of the 1990 Act. The Lord Chancellor is wrong on a fundamental point in stating, amongst other things, that the 1990 Act was "intended to enable Crown Prosecutors to appear in the higher courts". On the contrary, as the terms of the Act of 1990 and the parliamentary debates make clear beyond any doubt, this controversial issue was left to be considered in accordance with the decision making processes of the Act. For my part I agree that ACLEC was too large a committee, with unwieldy procedures and too wide terms of reference. And the system was no doubt flawed inasmuch as it gave a power of veto to a single designated judge. But ACLEC was independent and the role of the designated Judges was at least a recognition of the doctrine of separation of powers. And constitutionalism requires the dispersal rather than the centralization of power notably where that power affects the impartial administration of justice.

Under the new proposals the judiciary will lose its powers over rights of audience and the Lord Chancellor would take over those powers. In the Consultation Paper the Lord Chancellor states that he would be acting as the head of the judiciary. But he is hardly a neutral and impartial figure. The Lord Chancellor is a member of the cabinet and he chairs a number of cabinet committees. He is a member of the executive carrying out the party political agenda of the Labour administration. He is a politician. The argument of the Lord Chancellor is seductive: he says in effect trust me to use these powers only in the public interest. In the Federalist (No. 10) James Madison answered such an argument by saying that "Enlightened statesmen will not always be at the helm". More than 200 years on we can go further than James Madison did. In their own estimation governments of all political complexions are always engaged on plans for the execution of policies that cannot but serve the public good. We know better. The world we live in is complex: more often than not there are countervailing arguments to be weighed and choices to be made. And history shows that even the most enlightened statesmen are prone to error. That is why constitutionalism enjoins us as a democratic society to disperse power. To entrust to a cabinet minister the power to control the legal profession would be an exorbitant inroad on the constitutional principle of the separation of powers. And the threat to the independence of the Bar is a threat to the independence of the judiciary. The Lord Chancellor is a constitutionalist. The Lord Chancellor stated in his speech at the Judges Dinner in July 1997 that the government of which he is a member would uphold the doctrine of separation of powers. He is engaged on a far reaching programme of constitutional reform. There is ample scope for constructive reform consistent with constitutional principle. But as a matter of high principle the proposals in the Lord Chancellor's consultation paper are wholly unacceptable.

The right to a fair trial and European Convention on Human Rights

The written constitutions of many democracies contain guarantees of a right to a fair trial. What is the position in England? Lord Taylor of Gosforth, C.J., had no doubt that in England a defendant has a right to a fair trial.[4] In *Bentley* Lord Bingham of Cornhill, C.J., recently described a defendant's right to a fair trial as the birth right of every English citizen.[5] The existence of the right seems beyond question. Moreover it is clearly a special and fundamental right. But I raise two questions: is it a constitutional right under our unwritten constitution? And, if it is, what flows from it? For my part, the second question can be answered quite simply. If a defendant has in breach of a constitutional right not in substance received a fair trial his conviction ought not to stand. And the court's view that the defendant was undoubtedly guilty ought to be no answer. In my view that is how it should be. But is it a recognised constitutional right? In 1994 in *Brown* in giving the judgment of the Court of Appeal, I described the right of an accused to a fair trial as a right protected by our unwritten constitution.[6] The House of Lords dismissed an appeal against the actual decision in *Brown*. In the leading judgment Lord Hope of Craighead did not expressly call a defendant's right to a fair trial a constitutional one. He called it "the elementary right of every defendant to a fair trial".[7] There is no inconsistency. Under the law of England a defendant has a constitutional right to a fair trial. That is coherent with the constitutional principle that a citizen has a right of unimpeded access to the courts.[8] But, in any event, a new legal order will come into existence when the Human Rights Act comes into effect.

The incorporation of the European Convention on Human Rights will be an enormous advance. From the point of view of the criminal law Article 6 is the core provision. It contains a guarantee of a fair trial within a reasonable time by an independent and impartial tribunal. It is described as a basic element of the rule of law in a democratic society. Article 6 will no doubt be the battleground upon which many issues will be contested in the criminal courts. How those issues will be resolved only the future can tell. But I make two general observations. First, the Convention is a living instrument which requires a broad and dynamic interpretation in the light of modern conditions. That does not mean that the degree of protection under the Convention is dependent on the unfettered intuitions of judges. But a decision about human rights is not a technical exercise in textual analysis: the jurisprudence of the European Court of Human Rights shows that ultimately judgments about political morality are involved. Secondly, subject always to the primacy of freedom of expression, there is often a need to balance competing values.[9] The interests of the individual and the interests of society in the stability needed even in a democracy will sometimes conflict. How such tensions are to be

---

[4] *R. v. Gibbons & Winterburn*, CA, 22 June 1993, cited at length in Robertshaw, *Summary Justice: Judges Address Juries* (1997), pp. 26–28.
[5] CA, July 30, 1998.
[6] [1994] 1 W.L.R. 1599 at 1606E.
[7] *R. v. Brown* [1998] A.C. 367 at 374G.
[8] *Raymond v. Honey* [1983] 1 A.C. 1 at 13, per Lord Wilberforce; *R. v. Home Secretary for Home Department, ex p. Leech* [1994] Q.B. 198 at 210A; and compare *Attorney-General v. Times Newspapers Ltd* [1974] A.C. 273 at 307F, per Lord Diplock; *Bremer Vulkan Schiffbau und Maschinenfabrik v. South India Shipping Corporation* [1981] A.C. 909 at 977E, per Lord Diplock.
[9] See Jacobs and White, *The European Convention on Human Rights* (2nd ed., 1996), Chap. 5.

resolved will depend on the balance of arguments. But the constitutionality of a defendant's right to a fair trial will be reinforced by the new legal order. On the other hand, while Article 6 covers pre-trial issues, it is debatable whether the enactment of the convention will necessarily have much effect on the vital issue of pre-trial disclosure. After all, the scope of the duty of disclosure in most convention countries is far narrower than in England. Realistically, that may well influence the jurisprudence of the European Court of Human Rights. On the other hand, there is an important contextual difference: in most convention countries judicial involvement in the criminal process begins earlier than in England.[10] In a sense the role of the *Juge d'instruction* or examining magistrate compensates for the more restricted duty of disclosure. These procedural differences may give rise to difficult points under the convention about the duty of disclosure in England. The existence of a constitutional right to a fair trial under our unwritten constitution may still be relevant on the issue of disclosure. One thing is certain. We all have much to learn. The vocabulary and discipline of the Convention, as well as the jurisprudence of the European Court of Human Rights, will become minimum basic knowledge for barristers and judges alike.

Formalism and justice

Next I turn to some reflections on the criminal law in action. In Victorian times the criminal law was harsh and the penalties severe. In the middle of the nineteenth century a witness who for reasons of conscience could not take the Christian oath was not allowed to testify. The testimony of a witness with previous convictions was excluded. An accused person could not go in the witness box. The peril of being a defendant was great. In those circumstances judges sometimes moderated the application of the law by formalistic distinctions which enabled the guilty to escape severe penalties. Substantive formalism played a role. The outlines of our modern criminal law were set in Victorian times. Since then there have been great improvements and the criminal law has become less technical. But the historical baggage of substantive formalism has in some areas of substantive criminal law not been left behind. In the House of Lords we recently had a good example of it in *Jackson*.[11] It was yet another appeal involving the procedures to be adopted when the police request a driver to provide a sample of urine or blood. It became clear that the Divisional Court had on a number of occasions upheld appeals on the grounds of trivial divergences from procedure which had nothing whatever to do with the guilt or innocence of the defendant or with any prejudice to him. As in the Roman formulary system the view often prevailed that the *ipsissima verba* of the warnings set out in *Warren*[12] by Lord Bridge of Harwich had to be used or the conviction could not stand. Lord Hutton's judgment in *Jackson* has possibly put an end to formalism in this

---

[10] Van den Wijngaert, *Criminal Procedure in the European Community* (Butterworths, 1993), *passim*.
[11] [1998] 3 W.L.R. 514.
[12] [1992] 4 All E.R. 865.

corner of the criminal law. Another example is the rule in *R. v. Morais* that an indictment which has not been properly signed by the clerk of the court the trial is a nullity.[13] That is apparently thought to be so even if the trial was in all other respects conducted flawlessly and the conviction was inevitable. Given that the signature of the clerk is a mere ministerial act this is an absurdly formalistic decision. A criminal trial is not a sporting contest. Justice does not require the acquittal of the guilty on the grounds of mere technicalities. Substantive formalism has no place in the modern criminal law. The other side of the coin is that it is imperative that our criminal law and procedure must always be morally defensible. Moreover, a defendant is entitled to irreducible standards of fairness encapsulated by the idea of a constitutional right to a fair trial.

Skilled advocates

The administration of justice is crucially dependent on competent and well prepared advocates. Sir Owen Dixon memorably summarized the duty of counsel. He said[14]:

> To be a good lawyer is difficult. To master the law is impossible. But I should have thought that the first rule of conduct for counsel, the first and paramount ethical rule, was to do his best to acquire such a knowledge of the law that he really knows what he is doing when he stands between his client and the court. . . .

That duty counsel owes to his client and to the court. In a criminal case a trial judge is entitled to well prepared submissions from both counsel for the prosecution and defence. In some quarters of the Bar it is apparently still thought acceptable for defence counsel to adopt the strategy of saying "let us leave it to the judge, if he errs we have a ground of appeal". In my view that is unacceptable conduct. For my part there is a general duty not only on counsel for the prosecution but also on defence counsel to raise any pertinent issues of substantive law or procedure with the trial judge in the absence of the jury so that, if possible, justice in accordance with law can be done at the trial.[15] The only exception I would make is the rare case where counsel for the defence reasonably feels that the judge has by his unfair conduct of the trial and summing up made such an intervention unrealistic. In any event, the general moral is: do not expect sympathy at appellate level about clear errors in a summing up which could have been corrected at a trial.

Appeals

The Court of Appeal (Criminal Division) is by far the most important appellate tribunal and, despite a daunting workload, produces work of very high quality. But my recent experience is of criminal appeals in the House of Lords. The

---

[13] 87 Cr.App.R.
[14] *Jesting Pilate* (1965), p. 131.
[15] *Code of Conduct of The Bar*, para. 610.

Law Lords expect a high standard of research and presentation from barristers. Looking up the point in Archbold is not research. Consulting secondary materials is not research. For example, if the appeal involves a statutory offence we would expect counsel to be familiar with the genesis of the statutory provision, the mischief to which it is directed, Law Commission Reports, White Papers, academic comment, comparative material from, say, Australia and New Zealand and so forth. Let me take another very specific example: let us assume that the correctness of an old decision is an issue. It should be routine research to check whether in contemporary journals, and contemporary editions of text books, there was comment on the decision which might show how the decision was received before it became encrusted with the label of orthodoxy. And the House of Lords would expect counsel to have explored all available sources as to the shape of the arguments in the case being reviewed. Such a demanding approach should cause no surprise. After all, the only reason for having criminal appeals to the House of Lords as the final court of appeal is that it is our duty to take cases apart. That task we can only properly perform if we are given assistance of a high quality by the Bar.

The jury system and fraud trials

Now I turn to the jury system. Like Lord Devlin I believe "that trial by jury is more than an instrument of justice and more than one wheel of the constitution: it is the lamp that shows that freedom lives".[16] The jury system is an integral and indispensable part of our constitutional arrangements. Only the most compelling grounds of public interest could ever justify the abandonment of trial by jury in any area. The Home Office consultation paper, published in July 1998, would in effect abolish the right to a jury trial in respect of a range of offences, including grievous bodily harm and theft. The purpose is to cut costs. It has nothing to do with justice. It is a bad proposal. It should be abandoned. But in my view there is such a justification in one narrow area: I would abolish juries in complex fraud trials. The jury system is inherently ill-suited to cope with serious fraud cases. I do not say that jurors cannot understand complex fraud cases. No doubt they can. The case for a change is more subtle. It is the dynamics of a complex fraud trial which militates against trial by jury. I have asked the Director of the Serious Fraud Office for some detailed information about the course of serious fraud trials in six cases. The emerging picture is as follows. The jury is deluged with a mountain of paper. In case after case the jury are asked to take eight or more volumes of documents to the jury room. Moreover, the jury is asked to listen to the evidence of vast numbers of witnesses testifying sometimes on somewhat peripheral issues. How can jurors be expected to master such a volume of documentary evidence and to remember the evidence of numbers of witnesses varying between 70 and 100? A judge and counsel can only master such a volume of evidence by constantly refreshing their memories. It is impracticable in a jury trial to afford to jurors such opportunities. Another feature of modern fraud trials which

---

[16] Devlin, *Trial by Jury* (1988), p. 164.

makes a jury trial unmanageable is the lengthy gaps in a jury trial. It is essential that a jury trial should, by and large, be continuous. In giving the judgment of the court in the Blue Arrows case Lord Justice Mann observed[17]:

> The awesome time-scale of the trial (more than a year), the multiplicity of issues, the distance between evidence, speeches and retirement and not least the two prolonged periods of absence by the jury (amounting to 126 days) could be regarded as combining to destroy a basic assumption. This assumption is that a jury determine guilt or innocence upon evidence which they are able as humans both to comprehend and remember, and upon which they have been addressed at a time when the parties can reasonably expect the speeches to make an impression upon the deliberation.

Nevertheless in subsequent serious fraud cases the trials have unavoidably been punctuated by repeated and lengthy absences of the jury during legal arguments and to accommodate difficulties of jurors, counsel and the judge, as well as to allow for reasonable holidays. How can the jury possibly be expected after such lengthy gaps to have in mind the evidence they have heard many months before? Without refreshing their memories a judge and counsel could not do it. Why should we pretend that jurors can do so? But ultimately the total length of fraud trials is the most telling factor. Trials of the order of a year have taken place a number of times. But there have been numerous trials lasting more than six months. For obvious reasons such trials place intolerable strains on jurors, and the quality of justice suffers. Moreover, while there are comparatively few serious fraud cases they swallow up 40 per cent of the legal aid budget. That is prejudicial to the legal aid system as a whole and is intolerable. The failure of the present system is not the fault of the prosecution, the defence, the judge or the jury. It is the result of the inherent unsuitability of the jury system in most complex fraud cases. Much tinkering with the system has been advocated and undertaken. More tinkering has been recommended. It will not work. The present system for the trial of serious fraud cases is irredeemably flawed. The rule of law itself requires us to create an effective and fair system to try such cases.

That brings me to possible solutions. I do not think the device of a special jury, drawn from the ranks of businessmen, will achieve anything. Drawing on my South African experience, I incline to the view that a judge and two assessors (perhaps an accountant and a lawyer) is the route forward. A consequence of such a system is, of course, a reasoned judgment and a more effective right of appeal than in the case of a jury trial. Some scepticism of South African models is understandable. But in the field of fraud trials the position was unaffected by the evils of the apartheid era. It was a successful system. The judge and the assessors would decide issues of fact by a majority if necessary: the law would be for the judge. I think that the accountancy profession would co-operate. Indeed it would probably be seen as an honour to be asked to sit as an assessor. Similarly, there should be no difficulty in

---

[17] *R. v. Cohen and Others*, C.A.C.D., July 14, 1992, unreported.

persuading advocates, barristers or solicitors, to act as assessors. It would, however, inspire confidence if it were provided that they must have the status of recorders. Such a system would be fair and efficient. It is true that the assessors would have to be remunerated. In the result, however, that would be a small cost compared to the huge sums of public money presently spent on such cases. If such a model is adopted, I would expect the consequences to be as follows. The absurdly long preliminary hearings in fraud cases would become virtually extinct. The length of trials would be dramatically curtailed. After all, with the assistance of an accountant, the scheme of the alleged fraud would usually be well understood by all from the inception of the trial. The focus would largely be on the question whether dishonesty is established. Pleas of guilty would become more common. The rate of convictions of the guilty would increase. The saving to the public purse would be enormous. It is surprising that the present system of trying complex fraud cases has been allowed to linger on so long. But I do not recommend yet another Criminal Justice Bill produced at breakneck speed. We should hasten slowly and get the necessary law reform right.

The summing up

Now I turn to another topic affecting jury trials. It is trite law that a judge must tell a jury in what circumstances they may convict and in what circumstances they must acquit. In my view a summing up should contain only such directions on the law as is essential in order to enable the jury to carry out their task. The jury need not to be told about purely legal reasoning. If a house has been ransacked by a burglar and the only issue before the jury is whether the defendant did it, the jury do not need an explanation on the ingredients of theft and burglary. It is purely sensible that judges avoid over-directing the jury by incorporating unnecessary legal material in a summing up. Unfortunately, as a result of the praiseworthy Specimen Directions of the Judicial Studies Board, as well as some judgments at appellate level, trial judges sometimes feel that the safer course is to discuss points of law which do not arguably arise on the evidence. In my view it is very important that judges should regard it as a vital part of their duty to simplify the task of the jury and to filter out superfluous law. And that necessarily involves that appellate courts must take full account of the way in which the issues were placed before the jury as explaining the parameters of the summing up. It is true that there are dicta in *Stonehouse v. D.P.P.* requiring the so called "general issue" to be left to the jury.[18] The view prevailed that a defendant has a right to a chance of a perverse verdict of acquittal. It is not self evidently a sound principle that directions should be framed so as to allow a jury to bring in a perverse verdict divorced from the facts and alleged facts of the case. The dicta in *Stonehouse* may discourage the pursuit of simplicity in a summing up. Possibly *Stonehouse* ought to be reconsidered. But in the meantime, I would hope that the shift will be towards

---

[18] [1978] A.C. 35; see note in [1977] Crim.L.R. at 549–550 and Edward Griew, "Summing Up The Law", [1989] Crim.L.R. 768.

a practice of eliminating unnecessary law from the directions of a trial judge.

In my view there is also a tendency for some trial judges to sum up the evidence in too great detail. A. P. Herbert's Mr Justice Swallow started his summing up as follows[19]:

> Gentlemen of the jury, the facts of this distressing and important case have already been put before you some four or five times, twice by prosecuting counsel, twice by counsel for the defence, and once at least by each of the various witnesses who have been heard; but so low is my opinion of your understanding that I think it is necessary, in the simplest language, to tell you the facts again.

In Scotland, where there is no opening by the prosecution, the evidence is usually led in a logical sequence: it enables the jury to follow the unfolding story and the issues. In Scotland the judge is not obliged in his charge to discuss the evidence. But if he does so the result in practice is usually a short charge on the facts compared to what we are accustomed to in England. I am not advocating that we adopt the same system as in Scotland. But I do think the experience in Scotland underlines the value of simplicity and brevity. By way of illustration only, I venture to suggest that a summing up of more than an hour and a half after a trial lasting, say, two weeks is too long. Unfortunately, it is not always easy for trial judges to be concise. The problem is that in judgments at appellate level standards of comprehensiveness are sometimes enunciated which make a succinct summing up impossible. Thus in *Lawrence* Lord Hailsham of Marylebone, L.C., observed that a summing up should include[20]:

> a correct but concise summary of the evidence and arguments on both sides, and a correct statement of the inferences which the jury are entitled to draw from their particular conclusions about the primary facts.

If trial judges are to comply with these requirements the sort of summing up which I advocate would often be impossible. For my part I much prefer the way in which Lord Morris of Borth-y-Gest summarized the duty of a trial judge in *McGeevy*. He observed[21]:

> It is not essential that the trial judge should make every point that can be made for the defence. If he were to do so and were also to follow each such point with the Crown's rebutting argument, he would run the risk of breaking up the defence case in such a way as to destroy its effect. There is no set formula for doing justice to the defence in the course of the charge: the fundamental requirements are correct directions in point of law, an accurate review of the main facts and alleged facts, and a general impression of fairness.

---

[19] *Uncommon Law*, Case No. 13.
[20] [1982] A.C. 510 at 519.
[21] 57 Cr.App.R. 424 at 430.

62 Public Law

Having cited contrasting observations in the House of Lords, I make clear that in my view this is a matter for the Court of Appeal and not the House of Lords. But I hope that a relatively short summing up on the facts will become the model recommended to trial judges by the Court of Appeal.

Miscarriages of justice

In conclusion, I turn to the question of miscarriages of justice. The number of such cases exposed during recent years is deeply disturbing. Some of those miscarriages of justice are relatively recent. Investigative journalism of a high quality exposed some of those miscarriages. Inevitably such exposures by journalists must be somewhat random. What can we do about this cancer in the system? I do not think there is any simple answer. But conscience demands that we take steps to identify and eliminate features of our system which might predispose to miscarriages of justice. For my part I would offer only three observations. First, if I am right in saying that, in common with the citizens of many democracies, an English citizen has a constitutional right to a fair trial, this ought to improve the culture of the criminal justice system. Secondly, in our system where the investigation process is controlled by the police the right to fair pre-trial disclosure is an indispensable part of the right to a fair trial. If there is one virtually constant theme in recent miscarriages of justice it is that there were lamentable failures to disclose critical documents and information. Too often the views of the police and prosecution about what documents should be disclosed have been shown to be seriously mistaken. It is therefore not enough to say that we must trust the police and prosecutors. The standard to be applied must be an objective one. And the court is and must remain the final arbiter. It is true that defence counsel sometimes ask for palpably unnecessary disclosure of documents. In doing so they may be abusing the system. To that problem there is only one answer: the trial judge must be fair and firm. Thirdly, there is the uncomfortable fact that miscarriages of justice have sometimes not been detected on a first appeal to the Court of Appeal. To some extent this may be due to the emergence of new evidence. But that is not a complete explanation. It seems too that the basis on which the Court of Appeal approaches the question whether, despite a material irregularity, a conviction is nevertheless safe, needs to be exported further. Given that the defendant has an absolute right to be tried by a jury, I think that the test applied by the Privy Council over many years is a salutary one. The question in such a case is whether in the absence of a material irregularity the jury would inevitably have convicted.[22] It is a stringent test. In my view it should be. In *Chalkeley* it was apparently held that section 2 (1) of the Criminal Justice Act 1995 mandates the Court of Appeal to apply a less stringent test, viz. to ask whether in the view of the Court of Appeal the conviction is "safe" irrespective of how unfairly the conviction may have been obtained.[23] Now is not the time

---

[22] *Anderson v. The Queen* [1972] A.C. 100 at 107D; *Mitchell v. The Queen* [1998] 2 W.L.R. 839 at 848.
[23] *R. v. Chalkeley*, [1998] 2 Cr.App.R. 79 at 98–99.

to explore in depth the correctness of decisions of the Court of Appeal. The language of the statute is general. And section 2 of the 1995 Act was passed by Parliament on the assurance of the Home Secretary that, despite the deletion of the words "or unsatisfactory" it restates the practice of the Court of Appeal.[24] The section may be open to more than one interpretation. It would be wrong for me to express a firm view on a point of supreme importance which may have to be considered by the House of Lords. But perhaps more important than the precise legal test is the frame of mind to be adopted, where there has been a material irregularity. The idea that "the spirit of liberty is the spirit that is not too sure that it is right" ought to be imprinted on the mind of every judge.[25] We have probably not heard the last of miscarriages of justice. But it would be appalling if we became habituated to accepting the inevitability of miscarriages of justice. There is no excuse for not doing our utmost to prevent them. In the sombre words attributed to William of Orange (1533–1584) "It is not necessary to hope in order to work, and it is not necessary to succeed in order to persevere."[26]

---

[24] See the note by Sir John Smith, Q.C., in [1998] Crim.L.R. at 482–483; and the discussion by Sir Louis Blom-Cooper, Q.C., in the Birmingham Six and other cases, [1997] Crim.L.R. 66–74.

[25] Those words were used by Justice Learned Hand in his speech in New York City's Central Park on May 21, 1944.

[26] Editorial note; on rights of audience and constitutional issues, see also S. Kentridge "Rights of Audience. A Quiet Revolution?" in *Counsel*, December 1998, p. 24.

[7]
The Value of Dissenting Judgments: *Fisher v Minister of Public Safety and Immigration**
[1998] A.C. 673, 686

LORD STEYN delivered the following dissenting opinion. A dissenting judgment anchored in the circumstances of today sometimes appeals to the judges of tomorrow. In that way a dissenting judgment sometimes contributes to the continuing development of the law. But the innate capacity of different areas of law to develop varies. Thus the law of conveyancing is singularly impervious to change. But constitutional law governing the unnecessary and avoidable prolongation of the agony of a man sentenced to die by hanging is at the other extreme. The law governing such cases is in transition. This is amply demonstrated by the jurisprudence of the Privy Council over the last 20 years. In 1976, and again in 1979, in unanimous judgments the Privy Council held that a condemned man could not complain about delay of his execution caused by his resort to appellate proceedings: *de Freitas v. Benny* [1976] A.C. 239; *Abbott v. Attorney-General of Trinidad and Tobago* [1979] 1 W.L.R. 1342. In 1983 cases involving delays of between six and seven years in the execution of condemned men in Jamaica came before the Privy Council: *Riley v. Attorney-General of Jamaica* [1983] 1 A.C. 719. The majority observed that "it could hardly lie in the applicant's mouth to complain" about delay caused by appellate proceeding (p. 724F). The ruling of the majority was in absolute terms: "whatever the reasons for or length of delay in executing a sentence of death lawfully imposed, the delay can afford no ground for holding the execution to be a contravention of section 17(1)" (p. 726H). Lord Scarman and Lord Brightman dissented from "the austere legalism" of the majority. That dissent helped to keep alive the idea that under a constitutional guarantee against inhuman or degrading treatment or punishment prolonged and unnecessary delay may render it unlawful to execute the condemned man. Ten years later the issue again came before the Privy Council in *Pratt v. Attorney-General for Jamaica* [1994] 2 A.C. 1. The Board observed that in Jamaica alone 23 prisoners had been awaiting execution for more than 10 years and 82 had been under sentence of death for more than five years (p. 17G). In *Pratt's* case the Privy Council, exceptionally consisting of seven members, departed from the earlier decisions of the Privy Council and held that prolonged and unacceptable delay, pragmatically set at periods in excess of five years, might be unconstitutional. And in important subsequent decisions the Privy Council ruled that the five-year period is not a rigid yardstick but a norm from which the courts may depart if it is appropriate to do so in the circumstances of a case: see *Guerra v. Baptiste* [1996] A.C. 397 and *Henfield v. Attorney-General of The Bahamas* [1997] A.C. 413. After a long struggle effect was given to the constitutional guarantee of human rights enshrined in article 17(1). But there are important unresolved questions. Now for the first time the important issue must be squarely faced whether prolonged and unacceptable pre-sentence delay may be taken into account to tilt the balance where the delay since sentence of death is $2\frac{1}{2}$ years thus falling short of the $3\frac{1}{2}$ years norm applicable on the authority of *Henfield's* case in The Bahamas. In these circumstances I must explain the reasons for my dissent from the majority judgment in some detail.

On a narrow view the issue before the Privy Council may appear to be confined to the question whether mere pre-sentence delay may as a matter of law be taken into account in deciding whether, by reason of the lapse of time between the imposition of the death sentence and the proposed date of execution, it would be a breach of article 17(1) of the Constitution of the Commonwealth of The Bahamas to allow an execution to proceed. But it is impossible to divorce the narrow question from related and contributory pre-sentence causes of the mental anguish of the condemned man, such as his detention in appalling conditions contrary to any civilised norm. In the present case there is a finding by the judge that while the conditions under which Fisher and other condemned prisoners were housed could be improved, the condition could not be described as falling below the evolving standards of decency that are a hallmark of a maturing society "having regard to security and financial constraints." So be it. But in other countries in the Caribbean death row conditions may not meet the criterion of minimum civilised standards. It is therefore necessary to consider the narrow question in the context of a broader perspective.

There is no binding authority compelling the Privy Council as a matter of precedent to decide the narrow question one way or the other. Indeed, as recently as October 1996 the Privy Council expressly left this question open for subsequent decision: *Henfield v. Attorney-General of The Bahamas* [1997] A.C. 413, 426–427. Their Lordships are not called upon to decide this question on the basis of their individual views of what is desirable in the interests of the administration of justice in The Bahamas. The question must be resolved on the basis of an evaluation of the strength of the competing arguments on the proper construction of article 17(1) of the Constitution. Their Lordships are mandated by the Constitution to afford to Fisher the full measure of protection of the rights enshrined in it.

Sir Godfray Le Quesne, who appeared on behalf of the respondents, made one of the most eloquent and powerful speeches that I have ever been privileged to hear. But perhaps I can be forgiven for saying that the longer he spoke the more convinced I became that he was urging on the Board a formalistic method of construction appropriate to the interpretation of a conveyancing statute. It is necessary to bear in mind the genesis of article 17(1). It was taken from article 3 of the European Convention for the Protection of Human Rights and Fundamental Freedoms (1953) (Cmd. 8969), which served as a model for the Constitutions of most of the Caribbean countries. In *Minister of Home Affairs v. Fisher* [1980] A.C. 319 Lord Wilberforce explained how such constitutional guarantees should be construed. Delivering the opinion of the Judicial Committee Lord Wilberforce observed in a classic judgment that such constitutional guarantees must not be subjected to the approach applicable to the interpretation of other legislation. What is needed is "a generous interpretation avoiding what has been called 'the austerity of tabulated legalism,' suitable to give to individuals the full measure of the fundamental rights and freedoms referred to" (p. 328H). It follows that article 17(1) ought to be interpreted so as to ensure that it affords meaningful and effective rights protecting individuals from, inter alia, inhuman treatment and punishment.

Turning from the general to the particular I draw attention to the wording of article 17(1) which comes within the category of constitutional guarantees described by Lord Wilberforce as "drafted in a broad and ample style which lays down principles of width and generality:" see *Fisher's* case [1980] A.C. 319, 328. Furthermore in the jurisprudence of the European Court of Human Rights three principles have emerged with important implications for the proper construction of article 17(1). First, article 3 of the European Convention is an unqualified and absolute guarantee of the human rights it protects: see *Ireland v. United Kingdom* (1978) 2 E.H.R.R. 25, 79, para. 163. In order to filter out insubstantial complaints the only qualification is that in order for conduct to be covered by the prohibition it must "attain a minimum level of severity." But there is no express or implied derogation in favour of the state: the prohibition is equally applicable during a war or public emergency. There is no derogation in favour of the state in order to enable it to fight terrorism or violent crime: *Tomasi v. France* (1992) 15 E.H.R.R. 1, 33, para. 115; see also Jacobs and White, *The European Convention on Human Rights*, 2nd ed. (1996), p. 49; Harris, O'Boyle and Warbrick, *Law of the European Convention on Human Rights* (1995), pp. 55–56; Lester & Oliver, *Constitutional Law and Human Rights* (1997), pp. 127–128, para. 124 and note 5. Similarly, in article 17(1) of the Bahamian Constitution there is no express or implied derogation in favour of the state. It is an absolute and unqualified constitutional guarantee of the relevant human rights which it serves to protect. What is the consequence of this general principle? There can under article 17(1) be no complaint about the inevitable consequences of the need to carry out a death sentence after the lapse of sufficient time to allow for appeal procedures, requests for clemency, and so forth. Such lapses of time are required in the interests of the condemned man. But in principle any substantial and serious suffering of an avoidable nature added to the anguish inevitably resulting from the death sentence may constitute inhuman or degrading treatment or punishment. The state may not superimpose upon the inevitable consequences of a death sentence further unnecessary agony and suffering. The second principle emerging from the jurisprudence of the European

Court of Human Rights is the principle of effectiveness, viz. that in interpreting the Convention the court seeks, given the provisions of the Convention, to give the "fullest weight and effect consistent with the language used and with the rest of the text:" see *Merrills, The Development of International Law by the European Court of Human Rights* (1988), p. 98. The third principle developed in the jurisprudence of the European Court of Human Rights is equally important in the present context. In judging cases under article 3 the court must consider the actual facts of the case in order to assess whether the treatment or punishment in its impact on the individual was inhuman or degrading. This is illustrated by observations of the court in *Soering v. United Kingdom* (1989) 11 E.H.R.R. 439 where the court held that it would be contrary to article 3 for a state to extradite a person where there were substantial grounds for believing that the person concerned, if extradited, would face a real risk of being subjected to inhuman or degrading punishment in the requesting country. The applicant faced a possible death sentence in the United States. The court's decision turned on a combination of the "conditions of detention," viz. the death row phenomenon, and the "personal circumstances" of the applicant who was 18 years old and somewhat immature. Accepting that the death sentence was a lawful punishment the court observed, at p. 474, para. 104:

> "The manner in which [the death penalty] is imposed or executed, the personal circumstances of the condemned person and a disproportionality to the gravity of the crime committed, as well as the conditions of detention awaiting execution, are examples of factors capable of bringing the treatment or punishment received by the condemned person within the proscription under article 3."

Taking into account the death row phenomenon, and "the personal circumstances of the applicant, especially his age" (see p. 478, para. 111) the court held that the extradition, if implemented, would give rise to a breach of article 3. Similarly, it follows that article 17(1) does not require the court to shut its eyes to realities of particular torment that a condemned man had undergone. It requires the court to take into account the actual impact of the infliction of illegitimate or unnecessary suffering on the individual: see *Jacobs and White, The European Convention on Human Rights,* pp. 55–56. Nothing of a substantial nature that is logically relevant to that question ought to be excluded from consideration.

I pause now to mention two arguments advanced by the respondents for the contention that pre-sentence delay is always irrelevant. They said that article 20 of the Constitution guarantees a fair hearing within a reasonable time, and that it enables a man awaiting trial to seek an order for the expediting of his trial or for a stay. That is so. But the existence of the due process remedy does not mean that the court in judging an issue of delay after the imposition of the death sentence must always ignore what had happened before he was condemned to death, e.g. that awaiting trial for murder for 10 years the individual was held in appalling conditions on death row itself. In constitutional interpretations one does not set off against inhuman treatment a failure of due process. That would be absurd. The respondents also argued that article 28(1) shuts out any possibility of taking into account pre-sentence delay. It provides that where there is

690

adequate means of redress "under any other law" the court may not allow constitutional redress. The reality is, however, that the appellant does not rely on unnecessary and unacceptable pre-sentence delay as an independent cause of action but merely as evidence tending to aggravate the inhuman or degrading treatment or punishment to which he would be subjected if he were now to be executed. The respondents' legalistic arguments are misconceived in the construction of a constitutional guarantee like article 17(1).

That brings me to the substantial question whether as a matter of constitutional construction article 17(1) compels the court to ignore any pre-sentence delay. The starting point is that under *Pratt v. Attorney-General for Jamaica* [1994] 2 A.C. 1 a lapse of five years between sentence of death and proposed execution presumptively makes it unlawful to proceed with the execution; under *Henfield's* case [1997] A.C. 413 that period is contracted to $3\frac{1}{2}$ years in the case of The Bahamas. But this does not mean that the actual circumstances affecting the condemned man may not be examined. On the contrary in *Henfield's* case Lord Goff of Chieveley stated, at p. 421:

> "In considering the effect of such delay, attention has been concentrated on the five-year period specified in *Pratt v. Attorney-General for Jamaica*. This period has been treated as the overall period which, in ordinary circumstances, must have passed since sentence of death before it can be said that execution will constitute cruel or inhuman punishment. It has not however been regarded as a fixed limit applicable in all cases, but rather as a norm which may be departed from if the circumstances of the case so require."

In other words, a shorter period may suffice depending on the circumstances of an individual case. This observation is in line with the earlier observation of Lord Goff in *Guerra v. Baptiste* [1996] A.C. 397 about a norm applying without "detailed examination of the particular case" (p. 415H). This approach is consistent with the approach adopted by the European Court of Human Rights in regard to article 3. Given this recognition that it is sometimes necessary to examine the actual circumstances of a particular case, I venture to suggest that it is self evident that evidence may be placed before a court that the mental suffering involved in the period between the imposition of the death sentence and the proposed execution may affect particularly severely a very immature young man, a mentally retarded man, and so forth. Moreover, one can imagine a case where it is proved that in order to terrify a condemned man prison officers regularly taunted him with the horrors of his meeting with the hangman, or subjected him to a mock reading of the death warrant or even a mock execution. Such cases occur: see Schabas, *The Death Penalty as Cruel Treatment and Torture* (1990), pp. 101–102. Plainly such circumstances would be relevant to the question whether a shorter period than five years or $3\frac{1}{2}$ years may justify the inference that it would be unlawful under article 17(1) to execute the condemned man. It is true of course that these examples are all special cases affecting a particular condemned man. But there then springs to mind the distinct possibility that in one or more Caribbean countries—not The Bahamas—the conditions under which condemned men are kept on death row are truly appalling. Echoing language of Lord Griffiths in *Pratt v. Attorney-General for Jamaica* I would say that a state that wishes to retain capital punishment must accept the responsibility of ensuring that condemned men are confined in conditions that satisfy a minimum standard of decency. In considering whether a lesser period than the five-year or 3½-year norms may be sufficient to render a proposed execution unlawful it must be permissible to take into account that the anguish of the condemned man has been greatly increased by his incarceration in appalling conditions. Our humanity permits no other answer to this question.

The theme of my reasoning so far is that article 17(1) requires the court to take into account the whole picture in so far it has an impact on illegitimate and unnecessary suffering inflicted on the individual. But Sir Godfray Le Quesne submitted that even if this proposition is correct all pre-sentence delay is irrelevant. The substantial argument he advanced is that delays before and after the sentence of death are qualitatively different in their impact on the individual. He said that the agony associated with a sentence of death only starts upon pronouncement of that sentence. That is not a realistic way of looking at the matter. A condemned man usually hopes that his appeals, and application for clemency, will succeed. The uncertainty attaching to those proceedings adds to his anguish. He also suffers the agony of not knowing when the death warrant will be read to him. Uncertainty looms large in the causes of his despair. It is true that in contrast the man still awaiting trial on a charge of murder is assailed by other uncertainties: he hopes to be acquitted. For him the spectre of the macabre meeting with the hangman is somewhat more distant. He has greater hopes of escaping death by hanging than a condemned man. But from the time of his arrest and charge, or at least from the time of his judicial committal for trial on a charge of murder, he is in real jeopardy of eventually being sentenced to death and hanged. And in cases like the present he will be held in prison conditions where he will be exposed to the terror of executions from time to time. Like a distinguished author in this field, who argues that pre-sentence delay is relevant, I too would say that "it is here that the horror of contemplating the sentence would normally begin:" Schabas, *The Death Penalty as Cruel Treatment and Torture*, pp. 133–134. There is undoubtedly a difference between the position of a man awaiting a trial at which he may be sentenced to death and a man already condemned to death. On the other hand, it is unrealistic to say either that there is no pre-sentence mental suffering or that it can be ignored in considering the broad question under article 17(1). If due to the failure of the state there is inflicted on the individual the agony of a prolonged delay of his trial on a charge of murder that must logically be relevant as a contributory and aggravating factor which, depending on the circumstances, may tilt the balance in a given case.

Article 17(1) does not mandate a rigid line being drawn between pre-sentence delay and delay after pronouncement of the death sentence. Instead it requires the court to assess the totality of the circumstances regarding the treatment and punishment which may make it inhuman or degrading to execute the condemned man. It is important also to bear in mind a major premise of *Pratt v. Attorney-General for Jamaica* [1994] 2 A.C. 1. Lord Griffiths explained, at p. 29:

> "There is an instinctive revulsion against the prospect of hanging a man after he has been held under sentence of death for many years. What gives rise to this instinctive revulsion? The answer can only be our humanity; we regard it as an inhuman act to keep a man facing the agony of execution over a long extended period of time."

Equally our humanity does not require us to exclude from consideration circumstances, even if they arose before sentence, if they significantly tend to aggravate the individual's suffering. Our sense of humanity and decency ought not to permit us to ignore the circumstance, if proved, that he has for several years before sentence been held in appalling conditions with a noose constantly dangling before his mind's eye; it ought not to permit us to ignore a deliberate decision by the state to delay bringing on his trial for several years; and it ought not to permit us to ignore an inexcusable failure to bring him to trial for many years. Moreover, on simple common sense grounds one must recognise the relevance of pre-sentence circumstances, e.g. it must be an aggravating circumstance if the state arranges to delay a murder charge in order to have an accused tried and flogged on a lesser charge before proceeding with the murder charge. Similarly, our common sense tells us that the interaction of pre-sentence delay and prison conditions, with the brooding horror of an awareness of executions going on, may add greatly to sapping the will and increasing the torment of the condemned man. Only by shutting one's eyes to reality can such circumstances be ruled out of consideration on a priori grounds.

Now I turn to a point of supreme importance. Neither in his written case nor his oral argument did Sir Godfray Le Quesne contend that it is open to their Lordships to exclude pre-sentence delay from consideration on the ground that to do so would cause practical difficulties for The Bahamas. The reason why he did not do so is plain. To admit as relevant such an argument necessarily imports an implied derogation in favour of the state under article 17(1). That would emasculate the absolute prohibition in article 17(1) and would be wrong. But, Sir Godfray Le Quesne was specifically asked to deal with the consequences for The Bahamas of a ruling in his case that pre-sentence delay may be relevant. In a written submission he then referred to the following observation in *Bell v. Director of Public Prosecutions* [1985] A.C. 937, 950 where Lord Templeman observed:

> "But by section 20(1) [of the Jamaican Constitution] the applicant is entitled to a fair hearing 'within a reasonable time,' albeit that, in considering whether a reasonable time has elapsed, consideration must be given to the past and current problems which affect the administration of justice in Jamaica."

The statement in *Bell's* case is irrelevant to the construction of article 17(1) and does not begin to suggest there is an implied derogation in favour of the state in article 17(1). With characteristic candour Sir Godfray Le Quesne conceded that the problems of the administration of justice in The Bahamas may be irrelevant. Substituting "are" for "may be" I agree.

The position is clear: if The Bahamas wishes to maintain the death sentence for murder it must ensure that murder trials are not unduly delayed.

That brings me to the proposition in the judgment of the majority that, although the possibility of taking into account serious pre-trial delay is not excluded, it is anticipated that it will only occur in exceptional circumstances. In my respectful view this ruling cannot be reconciled with article 17(1). It is at odds with constitutional language of width and generality. It fails to give effect to the full measure of the fundamental rights protected by article 17(1). It means that, unless a court judges that the threshold of exceptionality is passed, even substantial additional suffering caused by prolonged and unjustifiable pretrial delay caused by the state may not be taken into account in the ultimate decision. Such an exclusionary restriction on what may be considered is contrary to the language, purpose and spirit of article 17(1).

By way of conclusion I would summarise the position as follows. Nobody suggests that a time table must be provided for the conduct of murder trials in The Bahamas. On the other hand their Lordships were informed that in The Bahamas such trials are almost invariably concluded in a period of 18 months. In my view unjustifiable delay beyond 18 months of murder trials in The Bahamas may well be an aggravating circumstance which may entitle the court to depart from the norm.

This brings me to a consideration of the facts of the present case. Given a $2\frac{1}{2}$-year delay between the imposition of the death sentence and the reading of the death warrant, the case falls 12 months short of the $3\frac{1}{2}$-year norm applicable in The Bahamas. But a distinctive feature of this case is a wholly exceptional period of pre-sentence delay. The period between Fisher's arrest and the imposition of the death sentence was three years and seven months; the period between Fisher's committal and the death sentence was two years and eight months. It is necessary to consider how this came about. After his arrest Fisher pleaded guilty to possession of a firearm and was sentenced to two years' imprisonment. Two years and two months after his arrest, the prosecuting authorities put Fisher on trial on separate charges of attempted murder, armed robbery and possession of a firearm. After a trial he was convicted and sentenced to a total of 15 years' imprisonment. He appealed to the Court of Appeal but his appeal was dismissed. I am satisfied that this decision to proceed with lesser charges caused a delay in bringing Fisher to trial on the murder charge of about two years. And that period ties in with the undisputed proposition that criminal trials for murder are usually completed within 18 months in The Bahamas. The respondents rightly conceded that the course adopted by the prosecuting authorities in putting Fisher on trial for lesser offences was unprecedented and irregular. Why it happened remains obscure because the respondents say that the prosecutor concerned has left The Bahamas. In any event, in this case the reading of the death warrant was in the result put back by two years. And that was wholly due to the culpable conduct of the prosecuting authorities. Before I leave this aspect I would make clear that, if this exceptional delay had been caused by congestion in the courts of The Bahamas, I would still have regarded that explanation as one that does not assist the respondents. Given the constitutional guarantee in article 17(1), The Bahamas can only maintain the death sentence if persons charged with murder are not exposed to exceptional and abnormal pre-trial delays.

Now I turn to the impact on Fisher of the exceptionally long delay in bringing him to trial on the murder charge. He would have known that the only sentence for murder is death by hanging. He faced a strong prosecution case. In any event nine months after his arrest he was judicially committed for trial on the murder charge. He knew that he was in jeopardy of being sentenced to death and executed. And it is important not to lose sight of the circumstances in which he lived during that $3\frac{1}{2}$-year period. While I do not criticise the conditions of Fisher's pre-trial detention, it is necessary to face the stark picture that on undisputed evidence during the $3\frac{1}{2}$ years leading up to his sentence of death Fisher shared accommodation with condemned men and others awaiting serious charges. While the affidavits filed on Fisher's behalf are unsatisfactory, it is obvious that he was exposed for $3\frac{1}{2}$ years to the travails of condemned men and the horror of executions. Some delay in bringing on his trial was inevitable. But I am satisfied that the prosecuting authorities have added a period of about two years to Fisher's suffering on top of the $2\frac{1}{2}$ years that he has been condemned to death. It would be inhuman to execute him now. If ever there has been a case departing from a norm, this is it.

Mr. Owen Davies, who appeared on behalf of Fisher, persuaded me in a careful and balanced argument that it would be contrary to article 17(1) to allow Fisher to be executed. I would therefore advise Her Majesty that the sentence of death in Fisher's case be quashed and that a sentence of life imprisonment be substituted.

Note

By a majority of four to one the Privy Council dismissed Mr Fisher's appeal. He was hanged.

Part Two

Constitutional Law and Public Law

[8]
The Weakest and Least Dangerous Department of Government

The role of the judiciary in our democracy has recently been the subject of public debate. Judges exercise power. They take decisions which affect the lives and interests of people. They make judgments on matters that affect the way in which we are governed. Yet the judges are unelected. They cannot claim to have a mandate from the public for their decisions. It is, of course, possible to devise a system for the election of judges. But, as a matter of high principle, the idea of candidates for judicial office entering into electoral battle is hostile to the very concept of a neutral and impartial judiciary. So far as I know there is no support in this country for the idea that judges should be elected. But the question remains: How is the exercise of power by unelected judges to be reconciled with the democratic ideal? The premise is that judges are removed from the pressure of partisan policies. The justification for giving to such judges the power to make judicial decisions is that the judiciary as an arm of government is intended to buttress the democratic process and not to act contrary to it. That is a political premise upon which our democracy is based. But that is far from saying that the public should unquestioningly accept what the judges do and say. Rightly the public views the conduct of all arms of government—and the judiciary is one—with intense scepticism. A sceptical and ever watchful public opinion is the best guarantee of the quality of our democratic processes.

Alexander Hamilton, writing in the Federalist (No. 78), described the judiciary in a democracy as the weakest and least dangerous department of government. More than 200 years later I would argue that his statement accurately describes the role of the judiciary in the governance of our country. Adapting Hamilton's reasoning to contemporary conditions in Britain I would put the matter as follows. A neutral arbiter on disputes between citizens, and between citizens and the state, is essential to the working of the democratic system. An independent and impartial judiciary is therefore an indispensable part of our system. The reasons why the judges, despite the fact that they, like everybody else, are prone to error, pose no real danger to the public interest are to be found in a combination of factors. First, uniquely in our society, the

---

* This article is based on the 1996 Administrative Law Bar Association lecture, delivered at Lincoln's Inn on November 27, 1996.

judges seem to be the only public servants who do all their own work. The case is heard and decided by a judge, or a three or five member appellate court, without any aid or intervention by anybody else. The parties, and the public, can be confident that the decision has been taken not in a secret cabal but wholly and exclusively by the judge or judges who heard the evidence and the arguments. The second factor is that generally judges hear cases in open court in the searchlight of public opinion. This principle ensures, as Bentham observed, that the judge is constantly on trial. Any exceptions to this principle of open justice can only be justified by compelling countervailing considerations, *e.g.* the overriding interest of children. The third factor is that judges announce their decisions, and give their reasons, in open court. And it is important to bear in mind that English judgments are not written in the oracular style that characterises judgments of the European Court of Justice: in an English judgment the reasons including policy reasons for the decision are discursively but fully exposed. That facilitates constant public scrutiny of what is done in the name of justice. And, finally, in our system a judicial decision at any level of the judicial hierarchy can rapidly be overturned by Parliament. Compared to a sovereign Parliament, and an executive, which commands a majority in Parliament, the judiciary is relatively weak. And it is no part of my argument that the judiciary should not be relatively weak.

That leads me to consider the role of the judiciary in relation to the two other arms of government. The relationship between the judiciary and the legislature is simple and straightforward. Parliament asserts sovereign legislative power. The courts acknowledge the sovereignty of Parliament. And in countless decisions the courts have declared the unqualified supremacy of Parliament. There are no exceptions. Legally, and ignoring economic and political realities, Parliament may at any time by express enactment repeal the European Communities Act of 1972 and take Britain out of the European Union. Parliamentary sovereignty is the ultimate principle of our constitution. And the judiciary unreservedly respects the will of Parliament as expressed in statutes. The task of judges in a case involving a statute is simply to construe and apply the statute. But given the fact that in drafting perfect clarity is often not attainable the task of interpreting the will of Parliament is sometimes a complex one. And obviously the judges do not decide cases in a vacuum. We live in a democracy in the narrow sense that majority rule prevails. But, more importantly, we live in a liberal European democracy based on values of justice, liberty, equality and humanity. Judges are therefore entitled to assume, unless a statute makes crystal clear provision to the contrary, that Parliament would not wish to make unjust laws. Indeed, as the House of Lords made clear in the *Boucraa*, in the context of statutory interpretation legal reasoning may proceed on the initial premise that "simple fairness ought to be the basis of every legal rule".[1] That approach is perfectly consistent with the unqualified loyalty of the courts to the supremacy of Parliament. There is accordingly no tension in the relationship between the legislature and the judiciary.

---

[1] *L'Office Cherifien des Phosphates v. Yamashita Shinnion Steamship Co.* [1994] 1 A.C. 486, at 525 A-B.

That brings me to the relationship between the executive and the judiciary. In *M v. Home Office* Nolan L.J., (now Lord Nolan) neatly encapsulated the essentials of the relationship in the following words[2]:

> ... the proper constitutional relationship of the executive with the courts is that the courts will respect all acts of the executive within its lawful province, and that the executive will respect all decisions of the court as to what its lawful province is.

Those propositions can be expanded. First, the function of declaring what the law is rests with the courts. Moreover, the courts have a limited but essential function to make law in the gaps left by Parliament. Sometimes politicians seem surprised to hear that judges interstitially make law. The answer is that without that creative function of judges we would have no common law: the common law is entirely judge made law. Secondly, it is the constitutional duty of the courts on application by an aggrieved party to declare invalid the acts of the executive where the executive has acted unlawfully. In exercising this function the courts take into account that Parliament has entrusted the administrative discretion not to them but to the minister or other decision-maker; and that the executive must be accorded a reasonable space to govern or administer. But the courts do not defer to executive opinion: the acts of the executive are either lawful or not. Thirdly, as Nolan L.J. pointed out, the executive must carry out the law as declared by the courts. Fortunately, in our advanced democracy, the executive respects this fundamental rule. Given this constitutional relationship, and the complexity of carrying on the multifarious functions of government in a modern state, it is not surprising that the executive is regularly challenged in the courts. The vast majority of public law decisions go in favour of the executive, a relatively small percentage go against it. It is however a fact of life that ministers who are found by the courts to have acted unlawfully, sometimes find adverse decisions hard to stomach. So be it. The law is the sovereign mistress of us all. And only what Edmund Burke called the cold neutrality of impartial judges can stand guard over this fundamental requirement of a democracy.

Now I must try to examine the integrity of the administration of justice in the context of constitutional theory. Three constitutional principles interact: the rule of law, the principle of separation of powers and the principle of constitutionalism. By the rule of law we primarily mean the principle of legality, *viz.* that every exercise of governmental power must be justified in law. But the rule of law also comprehends in a broad sense a system of principles developed by the courts to ensure that the exercise of executive power is not abused. Under the pervasive influence of Dicey the rule of law has dominated constitutional thinking in England. The rule of law has played a vital part in the development of public law. It is still of great importance. But by itself the rule of law is an insufficient guarantee of the integrity of the administration of justice. The doctrine of the separation of powers and the principle of constitutionalism have necessary and complementary functions.

---

[2] [1992] 1 Q.B. 220, at 314–315A.

Turning first to the doctrine of separation of powers, eminent academic lawyers have argued that it has no place in our constitution.[3] They point to a number of substantial divergences from the concept of a separation of powers. The existence of divergences from the concept of separation of powers is undeniable, and in due course I will examine the different hats worn by the Lord Chancellor, the Attorney-General and the Home Secretary. It does not, however, follow from these exceptions to the doctrine of separation of powers that the concept is not a feature of our constitution. Lord Diplock, no mean constitutional lawyer, considered this point in *Hinds v. The Queen* in the context of constitutions of former colonies. Lord Diplock said[4]:

> All of them were negotiated as well as drafted by persons nurtured in the tradition of that branch of the common law of England that is concerned with public law and familiar in particular with the basic concept of separation of legislative, executive and judicial power as it had been developed in the unwritten constitution of the United Kingdom.

And in *Duport Steels Ltd v. Sirs*, Lord Diplock repeated that "it cannot be too strongly emphasised that the British Constitution, though largely unwritten, is firmly based on the separation of powers".[5] I respectfully agree with those observations. But, given that all members of the political executive are members of the legislature, the concept applies in a qualified form in this country. Tonight my interest is in the separation of powers between the executive and the judiciary. In that context the doctrine plays a large part in our constitutional practice and in institutional arrangements which separate executive and judicial functions. And it is right that it should be so because the principle of separation of powers is an essential constitutional safeguard of judicial independence, and the integrity of the administration of justice. It exists not to eliminate friction between the judiciary and the executive. It exists not to promote efficiency. It exists for one reason only: to prevent the rise of arbitrary executive power. But I confess immediately that I have every sympathy with those of you who are thinking that it is a bit rich for a serving Law Lord, a member of both the supreme court and the legislature, to be making these points about separation of powers.

That brings me to the principle of constitutionalism.[6] It is neither a rule nor a principle of law. It is a political theory as to the type of institutional arrangements that are necessary in order to support the democratic ideal. It holds that the exercise of government power must be controlled in order that it should not be destructive of the very values which it was intended to promote. It requires of the executive more than loyalty to the existing constitution. It is concerned with the merits and quality of constitutional

---

[3] See, for example, O. Hood Phillips, "A Constitutional Myth: Separation of Powers" (1977) 93 L.Q.R. 11.

[4] [1977] A.C. 195, at 212.

[5] [1980] 1 W.L.R. 142, at 157.

[6] I acknowledge my indebtedness to M. J. C. Vile, *Constitutionalism and the Separation of Powers*, 1967.

arrangements. In aid of political liberty it sets minimum standards of constitutional government. Two particular applications of this political theory must be noted. It suggests that it is insufficient that the holders of high office are public spirited men of great competence and honour. What matters is that the institutional arrangements must provide for effective control of executive power. The reason for this emphasis is the fact, as James Madison observed in the Federalist (No. 10), "Enlightened statesmen will not always be at the helm". The second feature is that absolute executive power ought to be avoided by a diffusion of authority. This can be achieved by nurturing independent centres of decision making. Such autonomous centres introduce checks and balances in a democratic system. Thus at the apex of our constitutional system there is the neutrality of the sovereign which is the indispensable pivot on which our entire unwritten constitution depends. A politically neutral civil service is a vital centre of autonomy. So is an independent police force. An authoritarian regime cannot easily tolerate a wholly independent body of advocates: it is a substantial check on absolute executive power. A free press, controlled by diverse interests, is the great servant of the cause of democracy.

Whatever the political complexion of a government the principle of constitutionalism is not usually high on its agenda of business. In an important and closely reasoned book published last year Mr Simon Jenkins, a former editor of *The Times* and now a distinguished columnist, argued that in recent years there has been a steady growth of centralisation, and the erosion of centres of accountability.[7] He described the phenomenon of centralisation in regard to the administration of justice. His examination of postwar experience led Mr Jenkins to call for a radical change in our constitution. He said:

> I am a convert to "written" constitutional entrenchment, to the code of superior statutes and a supreme court, and above all to limiting the spurious Sovereignty of Parliament, which means little more than the sovereignty of central government.

Similarly, in *A Bill of Rights for Britain*, 1990, Professor Ronald Dworkin called for an entrenchment of constitutional rights in our system. I am not persuaded. Great constitutional change should only be embarked on if it is truly essential. In any event, such changes usually only come about as a result of great historical events. I do not think an entrenchment of rights such as suggested is either practical or desirable. In particular I am not persuaded that it would be beneficial to replace our present system with a system based on a superior statute and a supreme court in the U.S. sense. It would tend to undermine the efficiency of our form of government. Moreover I am opposed to a substantial increase in judicial power. But it seems to me that some modifications of our constitutional arrangements are needed. I must be economical. I will concentrate on the existing arrangements regarding the three great offices of state which directly affect the administration of justice—the Lord Chancellor, the Attorney-General and the Home Secretary.

[7] *Accountable to None. The Tory Nationalisation of Britain*, 1995.

Unfortunately, it is necessary to spell out the obvious. I have no criticism whatever of the present and past holders of those three great offices. The present holders of these offices are all men of great honour and competence. So were their predecessors. My interest lies not in personalities but in principles, and in particular the desirability of the institutional arrangements presently in place. If personal considerations were relevant I would have to bear in mind that under three Lord Chancellors I as an obscure commercial lawyer was promoted beyond my just deserts. But personal considerations are totally irrelevant. After all, in the famous words of John Marshall, we must never forget that it is a constitution we are expounding.

The Lord Chancellor

There is a fundamental congruence of executive and judicial functions in the Lord Chancellor. He is a member of the Cabinet. He speaks for the government in the House of Lords and elsewhere. He is not the head of the judiciary in Scotland: the Lord President holds that office. He is not the head of the judiciary in Northern Ireland: the Lord Chief Justice of Northern Ireland holds that office. But, for historical reasons, in England the Lord Chancellor is President of the Supreme Court, an *ex officio* judge of the Court of Appeal and President of the Chancery Division. He sits in the House of Lords and the Privy Council and presides when he is able to and he chooses to sit. In England and Wales he is the head of the judiciary.

In recent years two Lord Chancellors explained in public lectures why a Lord Chancellor should be both a Cabinet member and the head of the judiciary in England. Lord Hailsham defended the status quo as follows[8]:

> To the student of Montesquieu and the American constitution the office of Lord Chancellor is thus an anomaly hard to explain, and, at first sight, impossible to defend. But an examination of his actual functions shows that in actual practice the anomaly wholly disappears. He is there not because the doctrine of the separation of powers can safely be disregarded, for it cannot be disregarded. In particular, the independence of the judiciary from political interference, to which it is almost always subject even in otherwise free countries, is a cardinal principle of liberty to be preserved at almost any cost and at the price, if necessary, of constant vigilance. . . . separation of powers is the primary function of the Lord Chancellor, a task which he can only fulfil if he sits somewhere near the apex of the constitutional pyramid, armed with a long barge pole to keep off marauding craft from any quarter.

This is an important argument: Why should we not rely on the Lord Chancellor to preserve the essentials of a separation of powers? But Lord

---

[8] "The Problems of a Lord Chancellor", The 1972 Presidential Address, The Holdsworth Club, Faculty of Law, University of Birmingham, pp. 3–5.

Hailsham acknowledged that having both an executive and judicial hat posed problems. He said:

> ... in matters involving policy as well as law (which most legal questions do) it is not possible for me even to speak candidly in public without prior consultation with sometimes a majority but always a significant proportion of different colleagues.

In 1995 the present Lord Chancellor vigorously defended his dual role.[9] He referred to the "rather esoteric and doctrinaire questions of separation of powers". The Lord Chancellor said that there are great advantages in the existing arrangements. He explained:

> I have often felt that when I am among judges I am a lone politician and when among politicians I am a lone judge. Yet I believe that far from undermining either the executive or the judiciary, this combination of roles requires the Lord Chancellor to be particularly sensible of the perspective of each one.

This is also a point: the Lord Chancellor's dual role enables him to interpret the views of the cabinet and the judges better.

Despite the firm expression of views by two eminent Lord Chancellors, it seems to me necessary to examine the contrary arguments. Undoubtedly, the dual functions of the Lord Chancellor are inconsistent with the constitutional principle of the separation of executive and judicial function. Constitutionally, the position seems prima facie undesirable. For my part the critical and pragmatic question is: What are the positive advantages of the present dispensation which outweigh any disadvantages? I am far from convinced that the interpretative process explained by Lord Mackay cannot continue if the Lord Chancellor merely ceased to be the head of the English judiciary. He would still retain all his other functions about appointments, law reform, statute law revision, legal administration, as legal and constitutional advisor to the government, and so forth. In any event, the Lord Chancellor's point was a limited one for what the judges wish to say to the executive, and what the executive wish to say to the judges, should be in the public domain. That leaves the fact that if the Lord Chancellor ceased to be head of the judiciary in England it would follow that he would not be able to sit in the House of Lords or Privy Council. In practice the Lord Chancellor seldom sits. The Lord Chancellor is a great lawyer. But all lawyers are dispensable and it would make little difference if he ceased to sit. On balance it seems to me that little of value would be lost if the Lord Chancellor ceased to be head of the judiciary in England.

Turning to the other side of the balance sheet, it seems to me that there are positive disadvantages in the Lord Chancellor being both a cabinet member and the head of the judiciary. A Lord Chancellor gives the appearance to the public of speaking as the head of the judiciary with the neutrality and impartiality so involved. The truth is different. Under governments of all

---

[9] Speech delivered by the Lord Chancellor to the Citizenship Foundation on July 8, 1996.

complexions the Lord Chancellor is always a spokesman for the government in the furtherance of its party political agenda. Even in respect of matters affecting the administration of justice he is as Lord Hailsham explained always subject to collective cabinet responsibility. In recent times the effect of financial constraints on the administration of justice has been a controversial issue. The Lord Chancellor as a cabinet member represents the voice of reform guided by the treasury perspective. The view of the judges is rather different. They do not wholeheartedly share the modern adoration of the deity of economy. On the whole they put justice first. That view can in our system best be put forward by the Lord Chief Justice. He should be the head of the judiciary in England and Wales. Why, I ask, rhetorically, should the man on the Underground be expected to understand the ambivalence of the Lord Chancellor's position? Why should the public gain the impression that the Lord Chancellor speaks on behalf of the judges? For my part the proposition that a cabinet member must be the head of our judiciary in England is no longer sustainable on either constitutional or pragmatic grounds.

The Attorney-General

The office of Attorney-General is a political one. Although the Attorney-General is not normally in the cabinet he is a member of the government. Yet the Attorney-General exercises superintendence over the initiation and continuance of criminal proceedings. The Director of Public Prosecutions is responsible to the Attorney-General who in turn is accountable to Parliament. The position is more complex in regard to the power of the Attorney-General to take civil proceedings. In 1986 in a parliamentary statement, which was intended to give authoritative guidance, Sir Michael Havers explained the position as follows:

> In civil proceedings a distinction is to be drawn between proceedings in which the Attorney-General is involved in a representative capacity on behalf of the Government, and action undertaken by him on behalf of the general community to enforce the law as an end in itself. In the latter capacity the Attorney-General again acts, whether ex officio or ex relatione, wholly independently of the Government. In the former he is by definition representing it. In this representative capacity the Attorney-General will assert the public interest as perceived by the Government as a whole.[10]

An example of proceedings on behalf of the general community is action taken by the Attorney-General against the media to enforce the law of contempt.

The power of the Attorney-General to take civil proceedings on behalf of the general community and his control over criminal prosecutions is quasi judicial. Yet he is also a political figure responsive to political pressures. It is

---

[10] H.C. Deb., December 8, 1986, *col.* 2.

argued that abuse is avoided by two constitutional conventions. First, in his quasi judicial function the Attorney-General is not subject to collective responsibility and he does not take orders from the Government. But he may seek the views of other ministers and they may volunteer their views. Secondly, it is said that the Attorney-General is not influenced by party political considerations. On the other hand, he may take into account public policy considerations. These conventions are weak. Their efficacy depends on Chinese walls in the mind of the Attorney-General. My view is that the independence of the Attorney-General should be strengthened. But I must make clear that I am not influenced in my views by the Scott report and public immunity certificates. I approach the matter generally and from the point of view of constitutional principle.

In his 1990 Hamlyn lectures Sir Harry Woolf (now Lord Woolf, Master of the Rolls) examined the traditional function of the Attorney-General to bring civil proceedings for protecting the public interest.[11] He said that in controversial cases involving the government it seems virtually impossible for the public or the media to identify when the Attorney-General is wearing his guardian of the public interest hat rather than his governmental hat. He added that it would be extremely difficult if not impossible for any Attorney-General to bring civil proceedings against a colleague or department of the very government of which he is a member. Lord Woolf concluded that it is not apt any longer for the Attorney-General to perform this important traditional role of his office. He called for reform by way of the appointment of an independent Director of Civil Proceedings. Tonight I go further than Lord Woolf was prepared to go in 1990. The same reasoning based on considerations of public confidence seem to me to apply to the Attorney-General's power over criminal prosecutions. How can there be public confidence in a decision by the Attorney-General to prosecute or not to prosecute in a politically sensitive case? How can the public have confidence that the Attorney-General is able to keep his political and public interest responsibilities in separate mental compartments? The present position is entirely inconsistent with constitutional principle. Nothing will be lost if the office of Attorney-General is removed from the political arena, as an independent office outside government. That is a model adopted by a number of former colonies.[12] Alternatively, the Attorney-General could be relieved of his functions in respect of criminal prosecutions and the power to take civil proceedings to enforce the law by entrusting those powers to independent public servants, such as, in the case of criminal justice, the Director of Public Prosecutions, and in the case of civil proceedings to an independent public servant such as Lord Woolf suggested, or such offices could be combined. And such independent public servants, or servant, could be made accountable to Parliament through the appropriate select committee.

---

[11] *Protection of the Public—A New Challenge*, (1990), pp. 103–113.
[12] Roberts-Wray, *Commonwealth and Colonial Law*, (1966), p. 354.

The Home Secretary

Newspapers have repeatedly said that there is a state of tension between the judges and the Home Secretary. The implication is that this is an undesirable state of affairs. That is a misconception. It is when there is a state of perfect harmony between the judges and the executive that citizens need to worry. A state of tension between the judges and the executive, with each being watchful of encroachment into their province, is the best guarantee the subject can have against the abuse of power.

I acknowledge that at present there is a pronounced uneasy relationship between the judges and the Home Secretary. I believe it came about because judges fear that fundamental values regarding justice are being imperilled. The criminal justice system exists to control crime. But in order to be effective it must be fair. In a speech made in the House of Commons Winston Churchill as Home Secretary explained his philosophy. He said:

> The mood and temper of the public in regard to the treatment of crime and criminals is one of the most unfailing tests of the civilisation of any country. A calm dispassionate recognition of the rights of the accused, and even of the convicted criminal, against the State—a constant heart-searching by all charged with the duty of punishment—. . . . These are the symbols, which, in the treatment of crime and criminal, mark and measure the stored-up strength of a nation, and are sign and proof of the living virtue in it.

That is how judges tend to approach matters of sentencing. That explains their view about minimum sentences. For my part that particular issue involves no constitutional dimension but only the wisdom or otherwise of putting sentencing into a straitjacket.

But there is one constitutional aspect. The Home Secretary still retains the power to set the tariff of the term of imprisonment to be served in the case of mandatory sentences of life imprisonment for murder. Sentencing for any crime is a judicial function. The function of determining the tariff in the case of mandatory life sentences ought to be performed in public by neutral judges. That function ought not to be performed by the Home Secretary. The present opaque arrangements are in conflict with the principle of the separation of powers and with open justice. It ought to be brought into line with the position in regard to discretionary life sentences which is recognised to be a judicial function. I would hope that we can put our own house in order in this respect rather than await a further ruling from the European Court of Human Rights.

Human rights

The idea underlying the human rights movement is a simple one. In 1933 J. B. Priestley set out on an English journey. He wrote a book called *English Journey*. He ended his account of his journey with the following remarks:

> Let us be too proud . . . to refuse shelter to exiled foreigners, too proud to do dirty little tricks because other people can stoop to them, too proud

to lose an inch of our freedom, too proud, even if it beggars us, to tolerate social injustice here, too proud to suffer anywhere in this country an ugly mean way of living. . . . We headed the procession when it took what we see now to be the wrong turning, down into the dark bog of greedy industrialism, where money and machines are of more importance than men and women. It is for us to find the way out again, into the sunlight.

Today, the existence of human rights is recognised in all advanced democracies. And for the U.K. the European Convention on Human Rights defines the fundamental rights recognised by our courts.

Given the recognition of those rights a practical question remains: How can those rights best be protected? For us in England two problems remain. First, there is the question whether the European Convention on Human Rights should be enacted as part of our domestic law. If I thought for one moment that such an enactment of the convention would entail a great transfer of political power to judges I would oppose it. It will mean nothing of the kind. It will simply mean that issues of alleged abuses of human rights law will be tried in our courts rather than in Strasbourg. It should be a matter of national pride for us to put our own house in order in the field of human rights. I therefore strongly favour the enactment of the convention as part of our law. But I do not have in mind some kind of superior law. The enactment of the convention should be subject to the overriding principle of parliamentary supremacy. In other words, after incorporation of the convention, Parliament would be able by express enactment to repeal the incorporating statute. But, of course, in a culture of liberty one can be tolerably confident that no such repeal would ever take place.

The second problem is a legal one. Should the principle of proportionality be recognised in aid of the protection of fundamental human rights? Undoubtedly, the human rights context is important. The more drastic the administrative inroad upon human rights, the more the court will require by way of justification before it can be satisfied that the decision is reasonable in the required sense. All this is elementary law. The real question is whether the principle of *Wednesbury* unreasonableness is adequate protection of human rights, or whether only a recognition of the principle of proportionality can adequately protect human rights. I would accept that there is a difference between the two concepts. A powerful case has been made by academic lawyers, practitioners and judges with great public law experience for recognition of the principle of proportionality in aid of the protection of fundamental human rights. Sooner or later the issue of proportionality will have to be considered by the House of Lords in the context of a case involving an alleged abuse of human rights. In advance of hearing the contrary arguments I do not intend to express a concluded view on this issue.

Conclusion

The legal issue of the recognition of the test of proportionality in cases involving fundamental rights will be settled in the courts. On the policy question of the enactment of the European Convention on Human Rights the arguments have been fully deployed. The time to decide the issue has come. On the questions regarding the separation of powers, as it affects the relationship between the executive and the judiciary, it seems to me that the debate has hardly begun. That academic lawyers will rise to the challenge I do not doubt. But I would hope that the legal profession, through the Bar Council and the Law Society, will take note of the constitutional issues. Bagehot said that Lord Eldon took the view that everything must remain as it always has been: Lord Eldon feared the danger of making anything more, the danger of making anything less. Today, the independent legal profession in our country can be a little more open-minded. If the points I have made have no merit, they can be ignored. But, if the arguments I have put forward are substantial, I would expect the legal profession to join a continuing constitutional debate on those issues. I am not willing to countenance the thought that the legal profession might be too absorbed with self-interest to care about the integrity and well-being of our constitution. Of course, they will speak if the issues demand it.

[9]
The Case for a Supreme Court

In 1867 in his book *The English Constitution* Walter Bagehot contrasted the close unity between the executive and the House of Commons (what he called the effective parts of our constitution) with the separation of the executive and legislature under the United States Constitution. Although he described the House of Lords as one of the "dignified" or "theatrical" parts of our constitution, he approved of it as a revising chamber. But he said[1]:

> "I do not reckon the judicial function of the House of Lords as one of its true subsidiary functions. First because it does not in fact exercise it, next because I wish to see it in appearance deprived of it. The Supreme Court of the English people ought to be a great conspicuous tribunal . . . ought not to be hidden beneath the robes of a legislative assembly."

In 2002 the highest court in the land is still a committee of the legislature. Since 1947 it has been called the Appellate Committee. It has the appearance of a subordinate part of the Upper House. The sittings of the Appellate Committee therefore take place in a Committee room in the Palace of Westminster, and the Law Lords work on the Law Lords' Corridor. The constitutional status of the Appellate Committee is underlined at the beginning of each legal year when it sits for a week in the chamber of the House of Lords. A regular reminder of its status is also the theatrical performance in the chamber of Law Lords making speeches when they give their opinions after prayers with the mace on the woolsack. When judgments were delivered in *Pinochet No. 1*[2] the crowded benches of the chamber apparently led foreign television viewers to believe that Lady Thatcher was part of the dissenting minority who opposed the extradition of General Pinochet! The fact that the Appellate Committee is a part of the House of Lords is the foundation of two striking anomalies in our constitutional arrangements, *viz.*, that the Lord Chancellor may participate in judicial business, and that serving Law Lords may speak and vote on legislative business in the House of Lords. Is there any principled, practical or pragmatic reason to retain the link between the legislature and the highest court? Do the existing arrangements have a present day value

---

[1] (Fontana Press, 1993), at p. 149. For this reference, and much else, I am indebted to Professor Robert Stevens' *Law and Politics: The House of Lords as a Judicial Body 1800–1976* (1979). I have also been assisted by Blom-Cooper and Drewry, *Final Appeal: A Study of the House of Lords in its Judicial Capacity* (1972) and Lord Bingham of Cornhill, *The Highest Court in the Land*, an unpublished lecture delivered at Grays Inn on October 24, 2000.

[2] *R. v. Bow Street Metropolitan Stipendiary Magistrate, ex p. Pinochet Ugarte* [2000] 1 A.C. 61.

or would it be better to strip away the legislative façade and create a true Supreme Court?

In this Hall I do not need to defend the proposition that experience has shown that democracy is a better form of government than any other. A distinctive feature of democracies is the classification of the departments of government in tripartite fashion, *viz.*, the legislature, executive and judiciary. In all democracies there is some principle of separation of powers, ranging from a strong principle, as in the United States, to a comparatively weak one, as in Britain, notably as between the legislature and the executive. I am, however, concerned only with separation of powers between, on the one hand, the legislature and executive, and on the other hand, the judiciary. In this respect our system is undoubtedly based on a constitutional principle of the separation of powers. In insulating the judicial function from the legislative and executive functions separation of powers in turn rests on the constitutional principles of judicial independence and the rule of law. Even this separation of powers is never absolute. It is thus usual for the legislative and executive branches of government to control judicial appointments, the funding of the courts and the removal of judges. On the other hand, once appointed, judges always have security of tenure and must distance themselves from partisan political affairs. But nowhere outside Britain, even in democracies with the weakest forms of separation of powers, is the independence of the judiciary potentially compromised in the eyes of citizens by relegating the status of the highest court to the position of a subordinate part of the legislature. And nowhere outside Britain is the independence of the judiciary potentially compromised in the eyes of citizens by permitting a serving politician to sit as a judge at any level, let alone in the highest court which fulfils constitutional functions.

The major obstacle to creating a Supreme Court is the privilege of the Lord Chancellor of sitting in the Appellate Committee of the House of Lords. I will argue that the Lord Chancellor's participation in judicial business in the highest court no longer serves a useful purpose and is contrary to the public interest. The privilege of serving Law Lords to participate in legislative business is no longer defensible. This is an obstacle of a lesser order: in reality it only exists to this day to keep afloat the Lord Chancellor's anomalous privilege of sitting in the Appellate Committee. And, due to the continuing process of the constitutionalisation of our public law and the fact that interventions by Law Lords in debate create the risk of challenges to them in Appellate Committee hearings, Law Lords now rarely speak in debate. In 2000 a Scottish Law Lord spoke three times. No other Lord of Appeal in Ordinary spoke in that year. In 2001 the same Scottish Law Lord spoke twice, both on debates on reports of the European Union Committee which he had chaired. In 2001 a English Law Lord made a maiden speech which enabled him to speak to the Hunting

Bill. No other Lord of Appeal *in Ordinary* spoke last year. Gradually the practice appears to be withering away. The Lord Chancellor's privilege is the only real obstacle to the creation of a Supreme Court.

The change can be brought about in stages. The Lord Chancellor can announce that he will no longer sit on the Appellate Committee or simply cease to do so. If he does so, the Law Lords will undoubtedly cease to take part in legislative business. Thereafter, severing the link between the legislature and our highest court and the setting up of a Supreme Court is a relatively simple matter in legislative terms. In Britain we do not need a final court with powers like that of the United States Supreme Court. The aim must be a Supreme Court independent of other branches of government, in the framework of our existing system in which the supremacy of Parliament is the paramount principle of our constitution. Such a court would in the eyes of the public carry a badge of independence and neutrality: it would be a potent symbol of the allegiance of our country to the rule of law. These are the arguments I will develop tonight. The Lord Chancellor is on record as saying that the Government takes the view that the case for the creation of a Supreme Court is not made out.[3] My respect and admiration for the Lord Chancellor cannot be allowed to deflect me from following the arguments and evidence to where they lead. It will be for you to judge whether the case for the creation of a Supreme Court is made out. If it is you may agree that the time for change has come.

That this topic has taken so long to come centre stage is not surprising. Until recent times constitutional law did not seem to matter much in Britain. There was a comforting sense of satisfaction with our existing constitutional arrangements. Sceptical questions about the shape of our unwritten constitution could be met with the argument that "it works". Historically that is unremarkable. Unlike many countries in Europe, England has had a long history of constitutional habits, and of evolutionary rather than revolutionary change. England had the enduring advantage of a well-developed common law, rooted in custom and usage, and a Westminster model of Parliamentary democracy, both of which were transplanted to many dominions, colonies and dependent territories. The break-up of the British Empire did not spell the end of English legal influence. On the contrary, as English became the principal language of international commerce and in practice the first language of international institutions, the spread of English legal culture continued. There was reason for satisfaction. And constitutional debate was not on the agenda. Now the landscape has changed. It has become possible to examine sceptically but constructively the arrangements affecting the apex of our legal system.

---

[3] Speech by the Lord Chancellor to the Third Worldwide Common Law Judiciary Conference: July 5, 1999, p. 19.

The causes of the change in legal culture can only be touched on briefly. Public law has been transformed over the last 30 years. The claim that the courts stand between the executive and the citizen, and control all abuse of executive power, has been reinvigorated and become a foundation of our modern democracy. The European dimension has played a large role. Subject to the principle of Parliamentary supremacy, our courts must set aside Acts of Parliament if they are inconsistent with directly effective European Community law. Since the creation of the right of petition to the European Court of Human Rights in 1966 the influence of the European Convention on Human Rights has increased year by year. Since October 2001 the Convention is effectively our constitutional Bill of Rights. The principles of judicial independence under Article 6 of the Convention now apply to all courts of law including the highest court. One consequence has been that it has been held that temporary sheriffs in Scotland do not satisfy the guarantee of independence,[4] which in turn necessitated giving part-time judges in England greater security of tenure. The incorporation of the Convention into our law has generally accelerated the constitutionalisation of our public law. A culture of justification now prevails. The renaissance in constitutionalism in democracies such as Australia, Canada, India, New Zealand and South Africa has not bypassed the United Kingdom. As citizens we may now ask the executive to justify, on public interest grounds, inroads on the rule of law, judicial independence and the separation of powers. Some historical baggage can now be put aside. The fog surrounding the figure of the Lord Chancellor, so vividly described in 1853 by Dickens in *Bleak House*, has not entirely lifted. A close analysis of the contemporary value of existing arrangements is necessary.

By convention the Lord Chancellor is a Cabinet Minister, and he is in charge of a large spending government department. For a long time the Lord Chancellor's predominantly political role has raised questions about the propriety of his subsidiary judicial role. In her important book *The Office of the Lord Chancellor* (2001) Professor Woodhouse has shown why these questions became more acute during the Lord Chancellorship of Lord Mackay of Clashfern (1989–1996) and even more so during the period in office of Lord Irvine of Lairg (1997 to date). She attributes this to the increasing politicisation of the office. She has described in detail the vast increase in the nature and extent of the present Lord Chancellor's executive responsibilities. He is responsible for formulating and implementing policies affecting the administration of justice, which are often a matter of party political debate. In addition he chairs Cabinet committees over a large range of policy issues beyond his departmental responsibility. He is at the centre of political power in a party political sense. In all these respects he is bound by the doctrine of collective responsibility. In his

---

[4] *Millar v. Dickson* 2001 S.L.T. 988: *Starrs v. Ruxton* 2000 S.L.T. 42.

legislative role he assumes some of the functions of the Speaker in the House of Commons; he takes part in debates; he speaks for the Government; and he votes. For historical reasons the Supreme Court Act 1981 provides that in England the Lord Chancellor is President of the Supreme Court, an *ex officio* judge of the Court of Appeal and President of the Chancery Division. These are symbolic functions. But under the Appellate Jurisdiction Act 1876 he may and does sit in the Appellate Committee of the House of Lords, and in the Privy Council. When he sits the Lord Chancellor automatically presides, with the attendant influence of doing so. He swears an oath to act impartially when he sits judicially. In England he is the head of the judiciary. His task is to protect the independence of the judiciary wherever the onslaughts on it may come from.

It is, of course, well known that constitutional conventions have played a substantial and benign role in the development of our institutions. One might have thought that there would be crystallised conventions governing the participation of the Lord Chancellor in judicial business of the Appellate Committee. When this point was probed during 1999 in questions in the House of Lords the Lord Chancellor confirmed expressly that there are *no* such conventions and in particular he rejected the idea that he should follow the advice of the Senior Law Lord or Law Lords collectively about his sitting.[5] He asserts an absolute right in his unfettered discretion to decide when to sit. The Senior Law Lord and individual Law Lords are not so privileged: they must bow to the collective will.

The Lord Chancellor also asserted that he "*delegates* to the Senior Law Lord the day-to-day management of judicial business, including the composition of committees".[6] He therefore asserts a right to intervene. A concession that the Senior Law Lord, and the Law Lords, are in control, would have breached the fragile edifice. It is, however, an astonishing proposition that a member of the executive claims to this day to have the right to decide who among the Law Lords should sit on a particular case. It is, however, by no means a theoretical point. If the Lord Chancellor has the legal power to dictate in a given case the composition of the highest court in the land, he will be entitled to exercise it and nobody will in practice know when the power has been exercised directly or indirectly. Not much legal certainty and transparency there.

The Lord Chancellor occasionally sits in the Appellate Committee. Behind that lies the work of the Law Lords in deciding what petitions for leave to the House or the Judicial Committee of the Privy Council should be granted. There are of the order of 300 petitions to the House a year: about 270 are determined on paper by committees of three and the remainder go to an oral hearing before three Law Lords. In the Privy

---

[5] *Hansard*, H.L. Deb., June 22, 1999, written answers, cols 77–78.
[6] *ibid*.

Council there are an average of 60 petitions a year and all require oral hearing by committees of three. This is work of great importance. The Lord Chancellor plays no role in it. Since he has been in office for almost five years it is possible to take stock of the present Lord Chancellor's role in the disposal of appeals. The context is that annually the Law Lords sit in about 65 appeals in the House and 60 appeals in the Privy Council. Since Lord Irvine of Lairg became Lord Chancellor in May 1997 he has sat in only one case in the Privy Council, *viz.*, a case about the licensing of motor launches in Gibraltar.[7] The case raised no point of major principle and the decision is unreported. The focus must be on the Lord Chancellor's role in the Appellate Committee. In all he has sat in eight cases. His first two cases were of considerable importance, and both involved the relationship between the executive and citizens. *Boddington v. British Transport Police*[8] concerned the issue whether a citizen may raise in the magistrate's court an issue that subordinate legislation was *ultra vires*. In *Director of Public Prosecutions v. Jones*[9] the issue was one of statutory construction, namely whether there is a right of peaceful demonstration on the highway. The decision was arrived at by a majority of three to two: the Lord Chancellor was in the majority. The Lord Chancellor's role in these two decisions was criticised in the House.[10] Since then the Lord Chancellor has sat in one important criminal law case, *B (A Minor) v. D.P.P.* where the issue involved the *mens rea* required in respect of a statutory sexual offence.[11] While all cases are important, and particularly cases in the House, I have to say that the remaining five cases in which the Lord Chancellor has sat were private law cases involving no major issues of legal principle.[12] It is also of interest that in 1999, the Lord Chancellor was challenged when he had decided to sit in the Appellate Committee which was due to hear an appeal concerning police liability for the suicide of a man in police cells. He had to stand down.[13] From this account one can fairly deduce two propositions. The range of cases in which the Lord Chancellor can now sit is shrinking to, in relative terms, less important cases. Certainly, it is unthinkable that he could now sit in any of the major cases which come before the Law Lords every year, such as cases involving constitutional law, public law, devolution, human rights, important points of statutory construction, and so forth. Secondly, the Lord Chancellor does not make a significant contribution to the judicial work of the House of Lords. From the point of view of the

---

[7] *Schiller v. H.M. Attorney-General for Gibraltar,* July 20, 1998 (unrep.).
[8] [1999] 2 A.C. 143.
[9] [1999] 2 A.C. 240.
[10] Lord Lester of Herne Hill. *Hansard,* H.L. Deb., October 28, 1988, col. 197.
[11] [2000] 2 A.C. 428.
[12] *Murray v. Foyle Meats Ltd* [2000] 1 A.C. 51; *Modahl v. British Athletic Federation, The Times,* July 23, 1999; *Carmichael v. National Power Plc* [1999] 1 W.L.R. 2042; *Uratemp Ventures Ltd v. Collins* [2002] 1 A.C. 301; *AIB Group UK Ltd v. Martin* [2002] 1 W.L.R. 94.
[13] Woodhouse *op.cit.* p. 127.

efficient despatch of judicial business by the Appellate Committee there will not be a ripple on the pond if he ceases to sit.

The practice of the Lord Chancellor and his predecessors of sitting in the Appellate Committee is not consistent with even the weakest principle of separation of powers or the most tolerant interpretation of the constitutional principles of judicial independence or rule of law. In *Hinds v. The Queen*, in the context of the relationship between the legislature and the judiciary under the constitution of Jamaica, the Privy Council held "that the British Constitution is firmly based on the separation of powers between the legislature, the executive and judiciary".[14] In *Duport Steels Ltd v. Sirs*, again in the setting of the relationship between the legislature and the courts, the House of Lords reiterated "that it cannot be too strongly emphasised that the British constitution, although largely unwritten, is firmly based on the separation of powers".[15] The same necessarily applies to the relationship between the executive and the courts. Initially Lord Irvine of Lairg took the same view.[16] In office he has become dismissive of the principle: his theme became "we are pragmatists, not purists".[17] It is therefore necessary to examine, in the context of the separation between, on the one hand, the legislature and the executive and, on the other hand, the judiciary, the value of separation of powers, judicial independence and the rule of law. Justice Brandeis said that separation of powers serves, not to promote efficiency, but to prevent the exercise of arbitrary power.[18] To allow a Cabinet Minister to take part in deciding cases introduces a risk of things going wrong which would otherwise not exist. The importance of this point is reinforced by the role of the judiciary in a modern democracy. The democratic ideal involves two strands. First, the people entrust power to the Government in accordance with the principle of majority rule. Secondly, basic values of liberty and justice for all and respect for human rights and fundamental freedoms are guaranteed. For protection citizens must look to the courts. Tensions between these ideals arise from time to time. The executive and the judiciary are not on the same side. How the balance should be struck is a task that can only be entrusted to the judgment of a wholly independent and impartial judiciary. Only such a system has democratic legitimacy. There is, however, another rationale for a wholly independent judiciary. The stability of democratic institutions ultimately depends on public confidence in the way in which the three co-ordinate branches of government carry out their functions. As the weakest of the three branches, the judiciary can effectively fulfil its role only if the public

---

[14] [1977] A.C. 195.
[15] [1980] 1 W.L.R. 142 at p. 157B. See also *R. v. Secretary of State for the Home Department ex p. Fire Brigades Union* [1995] 2 A.C. 513 at pp. 567D–568B (Lord Mustill, dissenting on the result).
[16] Speech to the Lord Mayor's Dinner for Majesty's Judges (Mansion House) London, July 23, 1997.
[17] *Hansard*, HL Deb., June 24, 1999, cols 1061–1062.
[18] *Myers v. U.S.* 272 U.S. 52 (1926) at pp. 292–295.

has confidence that the courts, even if sometimes wrong, act wholly independently. It is of paramount importance that the nation must have confidence in judges at every level as independent and impartial guardians of the rule of law. What must citizens make of the fact that in the highest court a member of the Government participates in judicial decision making? Surely it creates a risk of undermining in public perception the belief that our highest court is a neutral and impartial arbiter in our affairs. Drewry rightly said that the multiple roles of the Lord Chancellor have always entailed "a heroic piece of stage craft, one which requires a massive suspension of disbelief on the part of the spectator".[19]

Why is it axiomatic that, apart from the Lord Chancellor, no judge may have a connection with a political party or take part in party political debate? Why does our constitution guarantee to all judges, except to the Lord Chancellor, security of tenure? The answer is surely that these principles serve to make clear to the public that in judicial business there must not be a hint of a lack of independence and neutrality. How then can it be right to make an exception in favour of a powerful Cabinet Minister? And if such an exception is justified, by what logic is it denied to legally qualified Home Secretaries, like Mr Howard or Mr Straw, or the Attorney-General? After all the differences between the suitability of the Lord Chancellor, a Home Secretary and the Attorney-General as candidates to sit in the highest court are only matters of degree.

The case against the Lord Chancellor continuing to sit is powerful. But, I agree with the Lord Chancellor on one point: ultimately the question must be whether on pragmatic grounds, weighing all countervailing considerations, the public interest is served by him continuing to sit.

The Lord Chancellor and spokesmen for the Government have frequently explained the ground on which it is asserted that the existing practice is in the public interest. The most recent explanation was given in the House of Commons on December 4, 2001 when the Parliamentary Secretary to the Lord Chancellor's Department was asked to explain the Government's policy for reform of judicial functions of the House of Lords. It is worth reciting the exchanges[20]:

> "*Mr Heath* (a Liberal Democrat M.P.): Is it sustainable that the Lord Chancellor remains a member of the Executive, the legislature and the judiciary at the same time? Is not the highest court in the land compromised by its position in the legislature? Is it not time to establish a supreme court for this country that is clearly separate from the legislature—these Houses of Parliament?

---

[19] *Judicial Independence in Britain: Challenges Real and Threats Imagined* in *Constitutional Studies* (R. Blackburn ed., 1992), p. 15.
[20] *Hansard*, HC Deb., December 4, 2001, col. 155. The last paragraph repeats language previously used by the Lord Chancellor: Speech by Lord Chancellor to the Third Worldwide Common Law Judiciary Conference, July 5, 1999. para. 29.

Mr Wills: We have considered those questions exhaustively and extremely carefully, and we are content with the proposals that we have made; otherwise, we would not have made them.

The Hon. Gentleman rightly refers to the separation of powers. That is important, which is why we have that arrangement in this country, and we are keeping it because we believe that it works. I must point out that the Wakeham Royal Commission considered the arrangement under which the Law Lords sit in the House of Lords and concluded that it works. Because it works, we are going to keep it.

The Hon. Gentleman also referred to the position of the Lord Chancellor, and of course he is right: the office is unusual in the way that it combines different roles, but it is also unusually useful, because through it the judiciary has a representative in the Cabinet and the Cabinet has a representative in the judiciary. As such, we believe that the Lord Chancellor is well placed mutually to represent the views of each branch of our constitution to the other."

The reference to the Royal Commission chaired by Lord Wakeham requires explanation. The anomaly of the Lord Chancellor sitting in the Appellate Committee, and the creation of a Supreme Court, were subjects beyond the terms of reference of the Royal Commission. And they were not examined by the Royal Commission. The curiously truncated nature of the inquiry avoided the searchlight being turned on the Lord Chancellor's judicial role and the merits of the idea of creating a Supreme Court.[21]

The core of the explanation is that through the position of the Lord Chancellor "the judiciary has a representative in the Cabinet and the Cabinet has a representative in the judiciary" and that "the Lord Chancellor is well placed to represent tne views of each branch of the constitution to the other". This is the scaffolding which is said to support the Lord Chancellor's judicial role. At the outset one may ask how the Lord Chancellor's minimal sittings in the Appellate Committee can be said to promote these ends. The answer is apparently that the fact that the Lord Chancellor occasionally sits in the Appellate Committee increases his stature with his Cabinet colleagues and among the judges. Presumably the former know, and the judges certainly know, that the Lord Chancellor can rarely sit and only in relatively unimportant private law cases. It would be surprising if either side was particularly impressed with his judicial role. The very foundation of the argument is built on sand. But on wider grounds the argument is specious. The proposition that the Lord Chancellor represents the judiciary in the Cabinet reveals the fragility of the argument. The judiciary does not need a "representative" in the Cabinet. In no other constitutional democracy does the judiciary have a "representative" in the Cabinet. In any event, in respect of all matters discussed in Cabinet,

---

[21] *A House for the Future*, Royal Commission on the Reform of the House of Lords, Cm. 4534 (January 2000), para. 9.11.

including all aspects of policies in regard to civil and criminal justice, the Lord Chancellor is subject to collective responsibility. He cannot therefore act as a representative of the judiciary. The implied suggestion that the Lord Chancellor can act as an impartial arbiter between the Cabinet and the judiciary is constitutionally unsound and practically unattainable. And as in other democracies our judiciary is well capable, through the senior judiciary, of making known its views to the executive and if necessary directly to the public. Moreover, what the judiciary needs to say to the executive should always be in the public domain. It is, however, necessary to tease out a subtext of the Lord Chancellor's justification.

It is the suggestion that the Lord Chancellor can protect the administration of justice from periodic bouts of authoritarianism by the Home Office. This too is unnecessary. When after the last election the suggestion was made by Downing Street that supervision of the court system should be transferred to the Home Office the senior judiciary strongly objected. They did so by pointing out that it would be absurd for the Home Office, a regular party before the courts, to control the court system. It would have amounted to a flagrant breach of separation of powers. The idea was abandoned. The judiciary can and will speak when it is necessary to do so. In any event, it is unclear how this aspect can even arguably be a justification for the Lord Chancellor's judicial role.

That brings me to the second part of the explanation, namely that the Cabinet "has a representative in the judiciary". In *M v. Home Office* Nolan L.J. (subsequently Lord Nolan) observed that the proper constitutional relationship between the executive and the courts is that the courts will respect all acts of the executive within its lawful province, and that the executive will respect all decisions of the court as to what its lawful province is.[22] This is the constitutional principle of separation of powers in action. Allowing the executive, who is daily in dispute with citizens before the courts, to have a "representative" in the judiciary undermines the proper constitutional relationship. A moment's reflection will show that the type of legal issues in which the executive is particularly interested, such as criminal justice, law and order, civil justice, human rights, public law, and so forth, are par excellence matters on which it would be unacceptable for the Lord Chancellor, as representative of the Cabinet, to indicate in private discussions with judges the aims and wishes of the Government. After all, Government policy is not a source of law. If judges are to be informed of policy matters as background relevant to their decisions, it must be done in open court where the executive's views can be tested in adversarial debate. This part of the explanation is unfortunate. Already the very fact of the Lord Chancellor sitting from time to time in the Appellate Committee tends to emasculate the neutrality and independence of the

---

[22] [1992] 1 Q.B. 270 at pp. 314–315A.

highest court. But the explanation adds a further vice: it openly asserts that it is proper for the Lord Chancellor in his political function to inform the judiciary of the wishes of the Government of the day. The Lord Chancellor's professed role is hardly likely to promote in the eyes of citizens confidence in the absolute neutrality of the highest court.

The very grounds on which the Lord Chancellor seeks to justify his sitting on the Appellate Committee demonstrate that on principled and pragmatic grounds the practice is no longer defensible. The sooner it ceases the better. By gracefully accepting the inevitable, the Lord Chancellor, a principal architect of the Human Rights Act 1998, will render another great service to our law. If he does not do so, it can only be a matter of time until the issue arises whether his participation in a committee deprived it of the character of an independent tribunal under Article 6 of the European Convention. Such a case will cause embarrassment and damage to our highest court and our legal system. It should be unnecessary. But it may have to be faced. That issue will in the first place have to come before a differently constituted committee of Law Lords, as in *Pinochet No. 2*.[23] If that happens the issue will not be an abstract question of law. It will inevitably involve an intense Brandeis-type focus on the detail of the role and political activities of the Lord Chancellor. At stake will be the separate guarantee under Article 6 that every tribunal must be independent and impartial. Independence is the cornerstone, a necessary prerequisite, for judicial impartiality.[24] Article 6 requires institutional independence. European jurisprudence shows that in its primary application independence postulates effective insulation of courts from the executive.[25] How this central provision of the Convention must be approached was recently explained by Lord Hope of Craighead in the Privy Council in a Scottish devolution case. He said[26]: "Central to the rule of law in a modern democratic society is the principle that the judiciary must be, and must be seen to be, independent of the executive." As in *Pinochet No. 2* the question will be whether the Lord Chancellor is seen to be independent. That is how the Appellate Committee may approach such a challenge.

If such a challenge before the Appellate Committee were to fail, the next port of call will be Strasbourg. That court is likely to take account amongst other things of international developments reinforcing the principle of judicial independence. On November 29, 1985 the UN General Assembly endorsed Basic Principles of the Independence of the Judiciary and invited governments "to respect them and to take them into account within the

---

[23] *R. v. Bow Street Metropolitan Stipendiary Magistrate, ex p. Pinochet Ugarte (No. 2)* [2000] 1 A.C. 119.
[24] *Attorney-General v. Lippe* [1991] 2 S.C.R. 114 at p. 139, per Lamer C.J.
[25] *Ringeisen v. Austria (No. 1)* (1971) 1 E.H.R.R. 455 at para. 95.
[26] *Millar v. Dickson* 2001 S.L.T. 988 at p. 998L.

framework of their national legislation and practice".[27] The International Commission of Jurists has published international standards of judicial independence.[28] Even more pertinent is an initiative of the Council of Europe. The background to the initiative was the acute difficulties experienced by judges in countries in Central and Eastern Europe. The problems included and include direct and indirect political interference in the work of judges, uncomfortably close links between the prosecution and judges, and a general disinclination of judges to find against the state. As those Central and Eastern European countries were adapting to democratic structures the absence of experience of the role of an independent and impartial judiciary was a great obstacle. On October 13, 1994 the Committee of Ministers of the Council of Europe adopted a recommendation on the independence, efficiency and role of judges.[29] The text states that the aim of the Council of Europe is the evolution of constitutionally governed states, based on the rule of law, in order to achieve the promotion and protection of human rights and fundamental freedoms. It describes the independence of judges as one of the central pillars of the rule of law. It contains detailed proposals for the constitutional protection of the independence of judges. A draft European Charter of the Statute for Judges was then prepared. At a multilateral meeting of judges, again organised by the Council of Europe, held in July 1998, the text was discussed, amended and eventually approved. It was approved by the Council of Europe on July 8–10, 1998.[30] It was followed by the Universal Charter of the Judge, unanimously adopted in November 1999 by the International Association of Judges. Article 2 of this text provides that "Judicial Independence must be ensured by law creating and protecting judicial office that is genuinely and effectively independent from other state powers".[31] Throughout these texts there is a golden thread: the necessity of the independence of judges from the executive.

Standing back from these developments, one may legitimately ask what message would be sent across Europe if the European Court made a drastic exception to the principle of separation of functions between the executive and the judiciary in favour of the historical anomaly of the Lord Chancellor's position in Britain. Why should it not then be acceptable to have a Minister of Justice in the highest court of an Eastern European country? It seems to me probable that the European Court will want to

---

[27] A/RES/40/146, December 13, 1986.
[28] See *The Independence of Judges and Lawyers: a Compilation of International Standards*, Bulletin No. 25–26 (a special issue), published by the Centre for the Independence of Judges and Lawyers, April–October 1990.
[29] Recommendation No. R(94) 12. Compare also the fascinating account by Professor Jeffrey Jowell, *The Venice Commission: Disseminating Democracy through Law* [2001] P.L. 675.
[30] *Charte Europeéne Sur Le Stat des Juges.*
[31] The French text provides: "*L'indépendance du juge doit être garantie par une loi spécifique, lui assurant une indépendance réelle et effective à l'égard des autres pourvoirs de l'Etat.*"

apply minimum standards of judicial independence consistently across Europe. If that is so, there is much to be said for the prediction in 2000 of Sir William Wade Q.C. and Dr Forsyth that "any mixture of judicial with the legislative or executive functions ... is now likely to prove vulnerable, from temporary sheriffs in Scotland at one end of the scale to the Lord Chancellor himself at the other".[32]

The position of the Lord Chancellor as the head of the judiciary must now be considered. If this role, for historical reasons, was a purely symbolic and ceremonial one, there could be no sensible objection to it. But as presently understood it is a functional role in which the Lord Chancellor speaks on behalf of the judiciary. He is said to be uniquely qualified to defend the independence of the judiciary. This theory needs to be examined. The executive and the judges are not on the same side. Their functions, duties and perspectives are different. Inevitably there are sometimes tensions between the executive and the judiciary. It is not to be regretted: it is democracy working as it should. How then can a Cabinet Minister be a spokesman for the judges? Threats to judicial independence rarely come from citizens. Rather they come from a government irked by the judiciary fulfilling its traditional role of standing between the executive and the citizen. From the perspective of judges the activities of the Home Office and Lord Chancellor's Department require constant vigil. It is therefore curious for the Lord Chancellor to be the spokesman on behalf of the judges. Let me give the point concrete shape. In very recent times the Home Secretary has on occasions, when the Home Office lost cases, criticised the judges involved in terms that arguably tended to undermine public confidence in the judiciary.[33] The Lord Chancellor did not publicly rise to the defence of the judges. Realistically, he could not have done so. A Lord Chancellor can hardly be expected to join swords in public with a senior Cabinet colleague. By the very nature of his position as a Cabinet Minister the Lord Chancellor is unable to discharge the task of protecting judicial independence. Moreover, under governments of all complexions the Lord Chancellor is always a spokesman for the government in the furtherance of its party political agenda. That is so whether he speaks in the Chamber of the House or outside it. In my opinion it would be impossible for a group of distinguished constitutional lawyers, let alone the public, to identify the occasions on which the Lord Chancellor put aside his party political hat and spoke on behalf of the judiciary with the neutrality required of that function. One might think that at least when the Lord Chancellor speaks to the judges, he speaks as head of the judiciary. But when the Lord Chancellor spoke to the judges for the first time in 1997 he

---

[32] Wade and Forsyth, *Administrative Law* (8th ed., 2000), preface.
[33] Joshua Rozenberg. *The Daily Telegraph*, November 11, 2001.

criticised the Conservative Government—accusing Mr Major of "complacency" and "enervating insularity"—and he had considerable praise for the stance of New Labour.[34] Surely, the Lord Chancellor was not speaking as head of the judiciary. Lord Hailsham of St Marylebone frankly acknowledged the problems caused for him as Lord Chancellor by the wearing of both an executive and judicial hat. He said: "in matters involving policy as well as law (which most legal questions do) it is not possible for me even to speak candidly in public without prior consultation with sometimes a majority but always a significant proportion of different colleagues". Professor Oliver and Professor Drewry have also observed that "many aspects of the relationship between the Lord Chancellor and the judiciary are still shrouded in mystery, based on the mythology of judicial independence, which tends to undermine public confidence and inhibit parliamentary scrutiny".[35] All these problems would disappear if a Supreme Court is created. In that event the Lord Chief Justice would speak on behalf of the judiciary and would be the head of the judiciary. The public would then know by which branch of government ideas and policies are put forward and judge them accordingly. The democratic process would be better served.

It is now necessary to consider the impact on the Lord Chancellor's Department if the Lord Chancellor ceases to sit in the Appellate Committee and ceases to be the head of the judiciary. There is no need to dismantle it. There is no reason why the Lord Chancellor should not retain his other functions. In particular, for reasons already given, the power of appointment of judges should remain with the Lord Chancellor's Department. On the other hand, it is important that the process should become more transparent. Recent changes are widely and rightly seen to be damage limitation measures. A true Judicial Appointments Commission will have to come.[36]

The creation of a Supreme Court will require the repeal of the Appellate Jurisdiction Act 1876. About the consequential structural changes I propose to say very little. I would hope that the Supreme Court would not be larger than the existing figure of 12 Law Lords. The Senior Law Lord would obviously become the President of the Supreme Court. He would not be encumbered with the multifarious administrative duties of a Lord Chief Justice.

If the Lord Chancellor was to forego his privilege of sitting in the Appellate Committee the road would be clear for the creation of a truly independent Supreme Court. It will be necessary for our Supreme Court to be accommodated outside the House of Lords. It is possible that the

---

[34] Speech at Mansion House, London, on July 23, 1997.
[35] *The Law of Parliament* (1998), p. 41.
[36] Compare the Rt. Hon. Dame Brenda Hale, "Equality and the Judiciary: Why Should We Want More Women Judges?" [2001] P.L. 489.

absence of a suitable building to house a Supreme Court may be used as a pretext to delay the constitutional development. In a recent debate in the House of Lords the Lord Chancellor said[37]:

> "A new Supreme Court building of high architectural merit in the heart of London may be one of the most worthy of ambitions and is entertained by the senior Law Lord, but the Government have no plans for such a project . . . I plan or contemplate new court buildings, in various parts of the country, offering better facilities for victims and the disabled, not to mention much-needed improvements to the High Court in the Strand. New court buildings are planned for Sheffield, Bristol, Exeter and East Anglia and a new major court centre in the heart of Manchester is a strong gleam in my eye. I believe that all those matters are higher priorities than a new building for our Supreme Court."

Needless to say there could not be a seat for a Cabinet Minister in a Supreme Court. Does this explain the Government's present disinterest in the creation of a Supreme Court? But the creation of an independent Supreme Court does not have to be delayed until a suitable building is found. On the contrary, the sooner our highest court becomes truly independent the better. The heroic stagecraft, employed to support the Lord Chancellor's judicial role, can now be put to one side, thereby removing the only impediment to the natural and obvious development of a Supreme Court fit for a modern democracy. There is no legitimate excuse for procrastination.

I have not come to speak of buildings and facilities. But I have to say that in every constitutional democracy, large or small, the Supreme Court is accommodated in a dignified building fit for a co-ordinate branch of government. To accommodate our Supreme Court in an unsuitable building would be a signal to the world that the values of constitutionality, allegiance to the rule of law and equal justice for all are not held in high regard in our country. Given that I will not be a member of the Supreme Court, when it is created, I hope you will accept that in putting before you these views my concern is the welfare of our democracy.

---

[37] *Hansard*, H.L. Deb., November 8, 2001, col. 299.

* A Lord of Appeal in Ordinary. This is the text of the Neill Lecture, delivered at All Souls College, Oxford, on March 1, 2002, and is reproduced by kind permission of the Warden and Fellows.

I have had the advantage of detailed comments by Professor Jeffrey Jowell Q.C. on a draft of this lecture. The responsibility for the views expressed in it is entirely mine.

[10]
Creating a Supreme Court

The decision has been made to sever links between the highest court in the land and other branches of Government, and to create a Supreme Court. We ought to act together to ensure that the new arrangements are worthy of a modern constitutional democracy and civil society. Given this forward looking perspective, some may think that the reasons for creating a Supreme Court need no longer detain us. This would be a mistake. The reasons for the decision are relevant to the sort of Supreme Court that should be created.

The changing scene

In dynamic terms many causes led to the change. Three factors were pivotal. First, it was always unlikely that the existing arrangements, which involved a mixing of legislative, executive, and judicial functions, could survive the coming into effect in October 2002 of our bill of rights in the form of the European Convention on Human Rights.

Secondly, there has been a parallel domestic development of the emergence of a true constitutional state. Decisions of the House of Lords have contributed to this evolutive process: see, for example, *R (Anderson) v Secretary of State for the Home Department* [2002] 3 WLR 1800. A distinctive characteristic of such a state is that it has a wholly separate and independent Supreme Court, which is the ultimate guardian of the fundamental laws of the country.

Thirdly, the participation of the United Kingdom in the affairs of an expanding European Union is of supreme importance to our national interest. With the active support of this country the Council of Europe has been encouraging Eastern European countries to adopt constitutional structures which separate the functions of the judiciary and other branches of government. How then could

CONSTITUTIONAL CHANGE I

we credibly continue to defend the historical anomalies of the Lord Chancellor sitting as a judge and the Law Lords acting as legislators? The only route forward was to create a Supreme Court.

No more fudging

Learning the lessons of history, we must now create a Supreme Court fit for a modern liberal democracy. It must be institutionally and structurally wholly independent of the legislature and the executive. Old habits involving the fudging of the principle of the separation of powers will have to be unlearnt by all including the judiciary. The relationship between, for example, the Supreme Court and the Home Office will have to be transparent, measured and conducted in a way which encourages rather than undermines public confidence in the administration of justice.

Positively the new Supreme Court must have full powers to exercise an effective surveillance over the development of all branches of our law and to act as guardian of our unwritten constitution.

The announcement by the government of the decision to create a Supreme Court was accompanied by comments that a Supreme Court on the United States model with power to declare legislation unconstitutional would be created. Where this idea came from is not known. It was wide off the mark. The existing powers of the House of Lords are sufficient to enable the new Supreme Court to fulfil its proper role.

Constitutional symbol

So far the transformation of a committee of the House of Lords into a Supreme Court is largely a formal and technical matter. It is the easy part. But the government has a heavy duty to ensure that the new court will be able to discharge its functions effectively. If it fails in this duty, it will have done lasting damage to our constitutional system by the change. It is not clear from the relevant consultation paper that the government is fully aware of what is needed.

In every constitutional democracy, large and small, the Supreme Court is accommodated in a dignified building fit for a co-ordinate branch of government. This is not a matter of the prestige of individual members of the court. It would be a symbol to the world of the high regard in which values of constitutionality, allegiance to the rule of law and equal justice for all are held in our country. Such a building must be available and ready for occupation before the Law Lords leave the Law Lords corridor in the House of Lords. The idea of unsuitable but temporary accommodation for the new court (if it has occurred to anyone in government) would be totally unacceptable.

While it has been a great privilege for Law Lords to work in the historic splendour of the Palace of Westminster, with its wonderful ambiance, the accommodation available for the final court of appeal was not adequate. For example, there is only one conference room, which serves also as a small library; the space for secretaries is cramped; and there is only barely enough space for four judicial assistants.

The new building must have sufficient space for the members of the court, secretaries, judicial assistants, law reporters, an information bureau to serve the public, a press office to serve the media, as well as accommodation for the Registrar and staff answerable to the court.

It is also an indispensable requirement that the new Supreme Court must be properly equipped and resourced in every way. Its budget must be an independent one, structured so that any suspicion of political pressure is avoided.

An apex of 12

For historical reasons the number of members will probably be 12. That is already a large number. The number certainly does not

The judiciary a new regime

Steyn Counsel - a new Supreme Court - let your voice be heard

need to be increased in foreseeable circumstances. In my view eligibility to sit in the court should be restricted to the members of the court and possibly retired members who are still below the age limit. I make no apology for saying that it should be a small and elite group of men and women from diverse backgrounds at the apex of the legal system. Making it possible for others to have a chance to sit in the Supreme Court would be in disharmony with general international practice and would not contribute to the standing of the court.

The probability is that those who are serving Lords of Appeal in Ordinary at the time of the changeover will become the first members of the court. How the system for appointment of new members should be structured is the most difficult of all problems. I would like to reserve my opinion until I have heard all sides of the argument. I venture only preliminary views on a few points. Certainly, the new system will have to be more open and transparent than has so far been the case. A

CONSTITUTIONAL CHANGE

solution is a small Appointments Commission consisting of, say, seven members. It should be seen to be a neutral and impartial body. It must therefore be in no way identified with the government or civil service. On the other hand, it should also not be entirely dominated by judges. At this stage my view is that the members should include the two most senior judges of the court, the Chairman of the Bar Council, the President of the Law Society, an academic lawyer and a non-lawyer, leaving one gap. That gap, I repeat, should not be filled by a Permanent Secretary or anybody identified with the government, no matter how eminent. In my opinion the way the system would work is that the Appointments Commission would recommend (if necessary by majority vote) to the Prime Minister for submission to Her Majesty a candidate suitable for appointment. In the unlikely event of the candidate proving unacceptable, the process would have to start again.

This is in very broad terms a way in which the new system could be structured. Space has not allowed me to comment on how such a system would take account of any separate perspectives of Scotland and Northern Ireland. I would, however, emphasise that what is in contemplation is a Supreme Court for the United Kingdom.

What's in a name?

What the head of the new court, and the members of the court should be called, is not a major problem. Given that new members will not become Peers, I favour simplicity. The terminology that has currency internationally, viz Chief Justice or President and Justice, is good enough for me. Personally, I cannot see any problem in judges lower down the ladder using titles such a Lord Justice or Lady Justice. The prestige of the individual members of the court will depend not on formal titles but on the quality of the work of the court.

Head of the judiciary

I regard it as axiomatic that the Chief Justice or President of the Supreme Court of the United Kingdom will become the head of the judiciary, leaving it to him or her to delegate such administrative and representational functions to judges on a lower tier as he deems appropriate.

The role of the Bar

These are the individual views of one Law Lord. Others may have better ideas. The voice of the Bar on the making of a Supreme Court will be particularly important and its views should be put forward with clarity and vigour. ❖

[11]
Democracy Through Law

In his last case in the House of Lords Lord Cooke of Thorndon delivered the unanimous opinion of the Appellate Committee. On that occasion I said[1]:

> "... it is appropriate to pay tribute to [Lord Cooke's] massive contribution to the coherent and rational development of the law in New Zealand, in England and throughout the common law world. His opinion in the case before the House is characteristically lucid and compelling."

Like great cricketers great judges select themselves. Robin Cooke is in that small but select international band. A small country has produced a towering figure in the law. It is a great honour for me this evening to deliver the first Robin Cooke lecture under the auspices of Victoria University of Wellington. I have chosen what I hope you will regard as an important topic.[2] Lord Cooke will not agree with all I will say this evening. But on the testing ground of real cases I am reassured by the fact that when we sat together, as we often did, I almost invariably ended up on the same side as Robin.

It was however adventurous of the Dean to invite me to be the first lecturer in this series. He could not have been aware of my record. One example will suffice. Recently in *MacFarlane*[3] there was before the House of Lords a case of parents of an unwanted healthy child born as a result of negligent sterilisation advice. The parents wanted compensation for the cost of bringing up the child. Unanimously, but for different reasons, the House ruled against the claim. This decision was unpopular among barristers who conducted a profitable business in such cases. They invited the Law Lords to explain their decision. In cowardly fashion we all refused. But we could not

---

[1] *Delaware Mansions Ltd and others v. Lord Mayor and Citizens of the City of Westminster* [2002] 1 A.C. 321 at 324E.
[2] The title was suggested to me by Professor Jeffrey Jowell's article? "The Venice Commission: Disseminating Democracy Through Law" [2000] P.L. 675.
[3] *MacFarlane and another v. Tayside Health Board (Scotland)* [2000] 2 A.C. 59.

724 Democracy Through Law

escape ultimate scrutiny in legal journals. Professor Thompson savaged our reasoning.[4] He was very severe on my colleagues. He said that they had abandoned all principles of tort law. I thought he was going to say my judgment was a notable exception. Not a bit. He said that I had not only abandoned the law of tort but law itself.

The Democratic Ideal

In Britain the press frequently criticise the power exercised by unelected judges. It is suggested that it is anti-democratic. This is a fundamental misconception. The democratic ideal involves two strands. First, the people entrust power to the Government in accordance with the principle of majority rule. The second is that in a democracy there must be an effective and fair means of achieving practical justice through law between individuals and between the state and individuals. Where a tension develops between the views of the majority and individual rights a decision must be made and sometimes a balance has to be struck. The best way of achieving this purpose is for a democracy to delegate to an impartial and independent judiciary this adjudicative function. Only such a judiciary acting in accordance with principles of institutional integrity, and aided by a free and courageous legal profession, practising and academic, can carry out this task, notably in the field of fundamental rights and freedoms. Only such a judiciary has democratic legitimacy. The judiciary owes allegiance to nothing except the constitutional duty of reaching through reasoned debate the best attainable judgments in accordance with justice and law. This is their role in the democratic governance of our countries. At the root of it is the struggle by fallible judges with imperfect insights for government under law and not under men and women.

The Criminal Law

A primary function of the judiciary is, of course, to maintain the Queen's peace by enforcing the criminal law. How should the judiciary approach its task? Among judges a liberal view has gained the upper hand. The purpose of the criminal law is not punishment for its own sake. Its aim is to permit everyone to go about their daily lives without fear of harm to person or property. It promotes values of stability and order in which democracy can flourish for the benefit of all. It is the premise of our criminal justice systems that in the words of John Stuart Mill the only purpose for which power can be rightfully exercised over any member of a civilised community is to prevent harm to others. If this objective requires severe punishment, in a particular case, so be it. Above all, a modern judge must have in mind the values of the pluralistic, liberal and tolerant society of which he is a member, in the context of the triangulation of the interests of the accused, the victim and his family, and the public. Undoubtedly, a judge must be alive to the concerns of the public. The baying of a lynch mob, however it manifests itself in modern society, can be dismissed with what Burke called the cold neutrality of the impartial judge. But the concerns of fair-minded citizens are of critical importance because public confidence is the pivot on which the criminal and civil justice systems rest. The rule of law is undermined if communities come to fear that the criminal law offers them no protection. That is why in England in recent years civil

[4] Thompson, *Abandoning the Law of Delict*? [2000] Scots L.T. 43.

injunctions, backed up by criminal penalties, have been extensively used to buttress the criminal law, *e.g.* against young thugs who terrorise neighbourhoods. The practical advantage is, of course, that the hearsay rule does not apply in the civil proceedings for an injunction. On the other hand, expediency must not be allowed to prevail over justice. Sometimes there are tensions between competing values and intractable problems which one can identify but not entirely solve. Perhaps it is an illusion to think that all problems can be solved: sometimes one may have to settle for containment and the least bad choice.

Judicial Review

In my view judicial review is the ground on which the contours of a modern democracy are shaped. The theoretical underpinning of the principles of judicial review is important because it may affect their reach. The orthodox view in Britain is that the statute-based part of judicial review is legitimised by the *ultra vires* doctrine. With the agreement of other Law Lords I repeated this mantra in 1999 in *Boddington*.[5] Academic lawyers in England and New Zealand have argued persuasively that this theory is incomplete, formalist, contrived and fictional.[6] Britain has much to learn from New Zealand jurisprudence about the legal foundation of judicial review. I have found it instructive that by and large, your courts have not found it necessary to invoke the *ultra vires* doctrine. In *Peters v. Davison* your Court of Appeal put the matter quite simply by saying that "the judicial review powers of the High Court are based on the central constitutional role of the court to rule on questions of law".[7] As a department of state the judiciary is charged with the constitutional duty to control abuse of power by the state, its officials and emanations. In a democracy the rule of law itself legitimises judicial review. I now accept that the traditional justification in England of judicial review is no longer supportable. By overwhelming weight of reasoned argument the *ultra vires* theory has been shown to be a dispensable fiction.[8]

An examination of the architecture of judicial review requires consideration in particular of four matters, *viz.* the principle of the separation of powers, the rule of law, the principle of constitutionality or legality, and the reach of judicial review.

Separation of powers

In all democracies there is a division of the departments of government between the legislature, executive and judiciary. Invariably there is a principle of separation of powers, ranging from a strong principle, as in the United States, to a comparatively weak one as in Britain, notably as between the legislature and executive. I am, however, only concerned with separation of powers between, on the one hand, the legislature and executive, and on the other hand, the judiciary. Even in this respect the principle

---

[5] *Boddington v. British Transport Police* [1999] 2 A.C. 143.
[6] Jeffrey Jowell Q.C., "Beyond the Rule of Law: Towards Constitutional Review". [2000] P.L. 119. Phillip A. Joseph, *The Demise of Ultra Vires—Judicial Review in the New Zealand Courts* [2001] P.L. 354.
[7] [1999] 2 N.Z.L.R. 164 at 192.
[8] Bearing in mind the lesson of *R. v. Bow Street Metropolitan Stipendiary Magistrate, ex p. Pinochet (No. 2)* [2000] A.C. 119 I must insist that this view, and indeed all the views expressed in this lecture, are obviously subject to hearing further argument.

of separation of powers is not absolute. On the other hand, the insulation of the judicial role from the executive and legislature is reinforced by the constitutional principles of judicial independence and the rule of law. How the line could be drawn is illustrated by the evolving jurisprudence on the power of the Home Secretary to decide if and when life sentence prisoners should be released. As a result of decisions of the European Court of Human Rights the system was judicialised in 1991 for discretionary life sentence prisoners (the most dangerous category of life sentence prisoners) and in 1997 for young persons found guilty of murder and detained during Her Majesty's pleasure. The Home Secretary continued to exercise his traditional power over mandatory life sentence prisoners, *i.e.* adult murders. In May 2002 the European Court observed in *Stafford v. United Kingdom*[9]:

> "the continuing role of the Secretary of State in fixing the tariff and in deciding on a prisoner's release following its expiry, has become increasingly difficult to reconcile with the notion of separation of powers between the executive and the judiciary, a notion which has assumed growing importance in the case-law of the Court."

This issue returns to the House of Lords in November this year when, exceptionally, it will be decided by seven rather than five Law Lords.

In Britain there are still the historical anomalies of the Lord Chancellor sitting from time to time in the Appellate Committee of the House of Lords and the privilege of Law Lords to speak and vote in the legislative chamber. Save to say these anomalies are in the process of withering away in scope and importance before our very eyes, I will not on this occasion discuss the Lord Chancellor's dwindling judicial role.[10] It is, however, interesting to reflect that the probability is that rightly New Zealand will soon have its own Supreme Court and that in the United Kingdom the natural and obvious development of a Supreme Court is not presently high on the agenda of a government dedicated to constitutional reform.[11] What happens next in England may be dictated by events.

Threats to judicial independence usually come from governments irked by a judiciary fulfilling its traditional role of standing between the executive and the citizen. The observation of Nolan L.J. (subsequently Lord Nolan) in *M. v. Home Office and another*[12] is pertinent. He said that the proper constitutional relationship between the executive and the courts is that the courts will respect all acts of the executive within its lawful province, and that the executive will respect all decisions of the court as to what its lawful province is. This is the constitutional principle of separation of powers in action. In Britain it is sometimes necessary to add the elementary proposition that

---

[9] Judgment in Application No. 46295/99 given on May 28, 2002.
[10] I discussed this subject under the heading *"The Case for a Supreme Court"* in my 2002 Neill Lecture delivered at All Souls, Oxford: 118 L.Q.R. 382. Shortly afterwards Lord Bingham of Cornhill delivered a lecture entitled *A New Supreme Court for the United Kingdom* which was published by The Constitution Unit, London. Lord Cooke has argued to the contrary: *The Law Lords: An Endangered Heritage*.
[11] The Senior Law Lord, Lord Bingham of Cornhill, advocated such a development in the United Kingdom in his lecture mentioned in n. 10.
[12] [1992] 1 Q.B. 270 at 314–315A.

government policy is not a source of law. Unquestionably separation of powers is a cornerstone of judicial review.

The rule of law

From the time of Dicey to the present day the concept of the rule of law has been used in a number of different senses. The authors of a book called *The Noble Lie* observed that the "rule of law, elastic though it may be, comes as close as anything to signposting our unique compact".[13] There are two core meanings of the rule of law. The first is a jurisprudential concept. The rule of law is a norm of institutional morality. It conveys the idea of government under law. But that is not enough. Totalitarian regimes, such as Nazi Germany and South Africa in the apartheid era, often achieved their oppressive aims by scrupulous observance of legality. During the Second World War some Jews were in prison in Germany as a result of sentences imposed before the War broke out. The Gestapo did not touch them. When they had served their sentences the Gestapo waited for them at the gate. They were then taken to the death camps where they died. So the formal rule of law was observed.[14] The rule of law as a principle of institutional morality utterly rejects the instrumentalist conception of law that enables an oppressive government to attain its aims by the use of law. It addresses the moral dimension of public power. It contemplates a civil society under equal and just laws. This is the sense in which the rule of law is expressly mentioned in a preamble to the European Convention on Human Rights. It permeates the later, more comprehensive and more sophisticated international instrument ratified by New Zealand, namely the International Covenant on Civil and Political Rights 1966. In this sense the rule of law is a fundamental moulding force of democratic values.

In its second sense the rule of law is a principle of law. Justice Scalia called it a law of rules.[15] That is a rather impoverished concept. The rule of law means much more. It is an overarching principle of constitutional law. It has many applications. It captures the spirit of liberty which is a major theme of the common law. Whatever is not specifically forbidden, individuals and their enterprises are free to do. By contrast the Government and its agencies may only do what the law permits: what is done in the name of the people requires examination and justification. Since the Second World War the reach of the rule of law has been expanded by the lessons of the Holocaust and the growing recognition that human rights must be effectively protected. Where a human rights instrument proves inadequate to its task the rule of law is the safety net. Its terrain of application is closely linked with the values of a liberal democracy in which the pluralism of our societies is recognised and the rights of minorities are protected.

A central focus of the rule of law is to constrain the abuse of official power. An interesting example of the application of the rule of law is *Venables and Thompson* where the majority of the House of Lords quashed the Secretary of State's decision setting a tariff for the custodial term to be served by child murderers.[16] One factor was that the

---

[13] I. Harden and N. Lewis, *The Noble Lie: The British Constitution and the Rule of Law* (Hutchison, 1986).
[14] I owe this example to Aharon Barak, the President of the Supreme Court of Israel.
[15] *The Rule of Law as a Law of Rules* (1989) 56 Univ. Chicago L. Rev. 1175.
[16] [1998] A.C. 407.

728 Democracy Through Law

Secretary of State had based his decision on a press campaign for an increase in the tariff. The rule of law abhors arbitrariness. In *Wheeler v. Leicester City Council* a local authority withdrew the licence of a football club because some of their members had visited South Africa.[17] There was, however, no law prohibiting contact with South Africa. The local authority's decision was held to be contrary to the rule of law. Legal certainty is a fundamental requirement of the rule of law. It enforces minimum standards of substantive and procedural fairness through our public law.[18] It has been invoked by judges in many diverse circumstances.[19] There is no closed category of cases in which it may be applied.

The principle of constitutionality

The supremacy of Parliament no longer means what it did in the time of Dicey. It is a more complex concept. Subject to Parliament's power to legislate expressly to withdraw from the present 15-nation European Union—an unthinkable hypothesis—our membership created a divided concept of legal sovereignty. This is illustrated by the second *Factortame* case.[20] There was a clash between Community law and a later Act of the United Kingdom Parliament. Within the Community legal order, the Queen in Parliament is not sovereign. Community law is supreme. The House of Lords granted an injunction to forbid a Minister from obeying the Act of Parliament. The Act was disapplied. Only an express enactment of Parliament could terminate our membership of the European Union. The view may also prevail that arguments that the Human Rights Act 1998 was impliedly repealed by a later statute would not be upheld by the courts: it is a constitutional measure and only an express repeal may be recognised. Similarly, in regard to the legislation devolving powers to Northern Ireland, Scotland and Wales, the better view may be that there is no scope for an implied repeal. If Parliament wishes to abrogate a political settlement of a constitutional character, it will have to say so expressly. The Westminster Parliament has qualified its own sovereignty.

In the *International Tin Council* case the House of Lords held that treaties which are not incorporated into domestic law by Parliament, cannot give rise of rights or obligations.[21] This view is now being questioned. The rationale of the principle is that the executive must not be allowed to bypass Parliament and oppress citizens by entering into treaties which are not incorporated into domestic statute law. Human rights treaties ratified by the executive are untouched by this rationale. It is arguable that where the reason for the rule stops the reach of the rule may end. There is scope for the evolution of a more realistic notion, which may place in a special category decisions of international human rights tribunals to which a country submitted

---

[17] [1985] A.C. 1054.

[18] *R. v. Secretary of State for the Home Department, ex p. Pierson* [1998] A.C. 539 at 59. Compare also Karen Steyn, *Substantive Legitimate Expectations* [2001] J.R. 244.

[19] Compare Jeffrey Jowell, *The Rule of Law Today,* 57–77, in *The Changing Constitution,* ed. by Jowell and Oliver, 3rd ed.

[20] [1991] A.C. 603 at 658–9.

[21] *J. H. Rayner (Mincing Lane) Ltd v. Department of Trade and Industry* [1990] 2 A.C. 418.

pursuant to an unincorporated treaty. This issue has not yet been addressed. But there has been an important development. By resort to constitutional due process clauses the Privy Council in two recent cases held that condemned men in Caribbean countries could not be executed until the determination of their appeals to the Inter-American Human Rights Committee, the jurisdiction of which depended on an unincorporated treaty.[22] This development gnaws at the vitals of the doctrinaire reasoning in the *International Tin Council* case. Lawrence Collins has said that "it may be a sign that one day the courts will come to view that it will not infringe constitutional principle to create an estoppel against the Crown in favour of individuals in human rights cases".[23]

Where does this leave the relationship between Parliament and the courts? The traditional view is that Parliament has the power to pass any legislation other than legislation purporting to bind itself for the future. There has been a vigorous debate in which the supremacy of Parliament has been questioned. I take the traditional view. Parliament has the sovereign legal power to legislate as it thinks fit. The courts will give effect to the clearly expressed will of Parliament. The courts have said so on countless occasions. On the other hand, it is of fundamental constitutional importance that the courts must interpret and apply legislation on the assumption that Parliament does not write on a blank sheet. Parliament legislates for a modern liberal democracy. This gives rise to what Rupert Cross described as a presumption of general application which operates as a constitutional principle.[24] General words in a statute should not be allowed to abrogate fundamental rights. Yet until recently this principle remained dormant. In 1998 in *Pierson*[25] Lord Browne-Wilkinson and I in separate judgments tried to bring together the rich strands of authority in support of this principle. It was not however part of the ratio of the decision. Two years later in *Simms*[26] the House of Lords authoritatively restated the principle. In that case the rationale and reach of the principle was aptly described by Lord Hoffmann as follows:

> "Parliamentary sovereignty means that Parliament can, if it chooses, legislate contrary to fundamental principles of human rights. The Human Rights Act 1998 will not detract from this power. The constraints upon its exercise by Parliament are ultimately political, not legal. But the principle of legality means that Parliament must squarely confront what it is doing and accept the political cost. Fundamental rights cannot be overridden by general or ambiguous words. This is because there is too great a risk that the full implications of their unqualified meaning may have passed unnoticed in the democratic process. In the absence of express language or necessary implication to the contrary, the courts therefore presume that even the most general words were intended to be subject to the basic rights of the individual."

---

[22] *Thomas v. Baptiste* [2000] 2 A.C. 1; *Lewis v. Attorney-General of Jamaica* [2000] 3 W.L.R. 1785, PC.
[23] Foreign Relations and the Judiciary, July 2002, 51 I.C.L.Q. 485 at 496.
[24] Statutory Interpretation, 3rd ed., at 166.
[25] [1998] A.C. 539, at 575D.
[26] *R. v. Secretary of State for the Home Department, ex p. Simms* [2000] 2 A.C. 115.

730 Democracy Through Law

It is now firmly re-established in English law.[27] If this principle is followed by your courts, it will strongly reinforce the protection of fundamental rights in New Zealand.[28]

The reach of judicial review

The paradigm of judicial review is the exercise of public power under statute. It has however long been recognised that judicial review extends to trade unions, trade associations and corporations with *de facto* monopoly power.[29] But the reach of judicial review goes wider. In *R. v. Panel on Take-overs and Mergers, ex p. Datafin plc*[30] the Court of Appeal held that decisions of the Take-over Panel, which exercises its functions as part of a self-regulatory framework, are judicially reviewable. For the Court of Appeal the decisive factor was not the source of the power of the Take-over Panel but the nature of the functions it exercised. The Court of Appeal regarded the common law as the true foundation of this branch of public law. In *Electoral Commission v. Cameron*[31] the New Zealand Court of Appeal came to a similar conclusion. It is true that in some decisions in England a different test has been employed, namely whether it can be said that "were no self regulatory body in existence, Parliament would almost inevitably intervene to control the activity in question".[32] This is fiction run riot. Murray Hunt has convincingly explained[33]:

> "The test for whether a body is 'public', and therefore whether administrative law principles presumptively apply to its decision-making, should not depend on the fictional attribution of derivative status to the body's powers. The relevant factors should include the nature of the interests affected by the body's decisions, the seriousness of the impact of those decisions on those interests, whether the affected interests have any real choice but to submit to the body's jurisdiction, and the nature of the context in which the body operates. Parliament's non-involvement or would-be involvement, or whether the body is woven into a network of regulation with state underpinning, ought not to be relevant to answering these questions. The very existence of institutional power capable of affecting rights and interests should itself be a sufficient reason for subjecting exercises of that power to the supervisory jurisdiction of the High Court, regardless of its actual or would-be source."

---

[27] *R. v. Special Commissioner and Another, ex p. Morgan Grenfell & Co. Ltd* [2002] U.K.H.L. 21.
[28] Compare the observation of Elias L.J. and Tipping J. in *R. v. Pora* [2001] 2 N.Z.L.R. 37 at 50.
[29] Craig, *Constitutions, Property and Regulation* [1991] P.L. 538.
[30] [1987] Q.B. 815.
[31] [1997] 2 N.Z.L.R. 241, CA.
[32] *R. v. Chief Rabbi of the United Hebrew Congregations of Great Britain and the Commonwealth, ex p. Wachmann* [1993] 2 All E.R. 249, and see *R. v. Football Association Ltd, ex p. Football League* [1993] 2 All E.R. 833.
[33] *The Province of Administrative Law*, ed. Michael Taggart, Chapter 2, Constitutionalism and the Contractualisation of Government in the United Kingdom, at pp. 32–33; see also Lord Justice Sedley, *Freedom, Law and Justice*, Hamlyn Lectures, 1999, Chapter 2 (Law: Public Power and Private Power), p. 19.

In my view this is the correct approach. If this reasoning is correct, it calls into question the decision of the English Court of Appeal that the Jockey Club is not amenable to judicial review.[34] After all, those wanting to race their horses had no alternative but to subject themselves to the rules of the Jockey Club. Why should it be beyond the reach of judicial review? There is, however, a more important dimension. In an era when it is government policy to privatise public services, and to contract out activities formerly carried out directly by public bodies, it may be necessary to develop a functional test of reviewability in order to hold accountable entities who de facto perform public functions.[35]

The Evolution of Constitutional Rights

Britain has no written constitution. Nevertheless, the courts have recognised certain fundamental rights as constitutional. The courts protect as constitutional the right of participation in the democratic process, equality of treatment, freedom of expression, and religious freedom. Another constitutional principle is that all citizens (including prisoners convicted of heinous crimes) have a right of unimpeded access to courts. Even before the incorporation of the European Convention on Human Rights into English law the courts held that everybody has an absolute constitutional right to a fair trial which if breached must lead to the setting aside of the conviction.[36] By contrast considerations of proportionality apply to the requirements for the content of a fair trial.

What is the significance of classifying a right as constitutional? It is meaningful. It is an indication that added value is attached to the protection of the right. It strengthens the normative force of such rights.[37] It virtually rules out arguments that such rights can be impliedly repealed by subsequent legislation.[38] Generally only an express repeal will suffice. The constitutionality of a right is also important in regard to remedies. The duty of the court is to vindicate the breach of a constitutional right, depending on its nature, by an appropriate remedy.

The importance of the development of constitutional rights has not come to an end with the advent of the Human Rights Act. One illustration is sufficient. The anti-discrimination provision contained in Article 14 of the European Convention is parasitic inasmuch as it serves only to protect other Convention rights. There is no general or free-standing prohibition of discrimination. This is a relatively weak provision. On the other hand, the constitutional principle of equality developed domestically by English courts is wider. The law and the Government must accord to

---

[34] *R. v. Disciplinary Committee of the Jockey Club, ex p. Aga Khan*, [1993] 1 W.L.R. 909; *R. v. Football Association Ltd., ex p. Football League Ltd* [1993] 2 All E.R. 833.

[35] Part 54 of the Civil Procedure Rules speaks, *inter alia*, of the review of "a decision ... in relation to the exercise of a public function". Compare: *R. (on the application of Heather and others) v. Leonard Cheshire Foundation and another* [2002] 2 All E.R. 936. A comprehensive review of the pre-Human Rights Act case law is to be found in the judgment of Moses J. *R. v. Servite Houses, ex p. Goldsmith* (2000) 3 C.C.L. Rep. 354.

[36] *R. v. Brown (Winston)* [1994] 1 W.L.R. 1599; *R. v. Bentley* (2001) 1 Cr. App. Rep. 307. Now the absolute guarantee of a fair trial is governed by Article 6(1) of the European Convention: the relevant case law is reviewed in *Mills v. Lord Advocate (Scotland Act)*, July 22, 2002, PC.

[37] *Mohammed v. The State* [1999] 2 A.C. 111.

[38] *Thoburn and Others v. Sunderford City Council and Others* (February 18, 2002, DC).

732 Democracy Through Law

every individual equal concern and respect for their welfare and dignity. Everyone is entitled to equal protection of the law, which must be applied without fear or favour. Except where compellingly justified, distinctions must never be made on the grounds of race, colour, belief, gender or other irrational ground. Individuals are therefore comprehensively protected from discrimination by the principle of equality. This constitutional right has a continuing role to play. The organic development of constitutional rights is therefore a complementary and parallel process to the application of human rights legislation.

Bills of Rights

Ten years after your Bill of Rights came into force the United Kingdom first acquired a Bill of Rights in the modern sense. Time only allows me to comment on a few perspectives.[39] Values of liberty, equality and justice underlie Bills of Rights. In the decision of the Privy Council in *Matadeen v. Pointu*, Lord Hoffmann, giving the judgment of the Privy Council, said[40]:

> "What the interpretation of commercial documents and constitutions have in common is that in each case the court is concerned with the meaning of the language which has been used. As Kentridge AJ said in giving the judgment of the South African Constitutional Court in *State v. Zuma* (1995) 4 BCLR 401, 412: 'If the language used by the lawgiver is ignored in favour of a general resort to "values" the result is not interpretation but divination.'"

This is an important observation. So far as it goes it is also a valuable statement. But it has wrongly been pressed into service in aid of the austere argument that values are irrelevant to questions of interpretation of Bills of Rights in constitutions. That cannot be right. The strait-jacket of legal logic is not enough for a human rights system. Bills of Rights aim to promote the rule of law and standards of decency and justice in fair and tolerant democracies. Bills of Rights in Commonwealth countries are the progeny of the Universal Declaration of Human Rights (1948) and are a distillation of ethical values. An assessment of the weight of competing moral values, such as liberty and equality, or individualised justice and stability and order needed in a democracy, are of the essence of decision making under Bills of Rights.

The Human Rights Act 1998 has created, and will continue for sometime to create, changes in murkier areas of English law. It opened up a new landscape. Historically English lawyers have been sceptical about rights based legal reasoning. Nevertheless, in the last 20 years such a system has slowly evolved. Now there has been a decisive shift towards a rights based system. A legal culture of demanding justification for inroads on fundamental rights and freedoms now prevails. This re-examination of existing law is a profoundly valuable one for the United Kingdom. Its impact will

---

[39] A comprehensive and valuable review is to be found in two recent lectures given in New Zealand by Lord Lester of Herne Hill: *The Magnetism of the Human Rights Act 1998* [2002] J.R. 179; *Parliamentary Scrutiny of Legislation under the Human Rights Act 1998* [2002] E.H.R.L.R. 486. The first will also be published in the New Zealand Law Review; and the second in the Victoria University of Wellington Law Review.
[40] [1999] A.C. 98 at 108F.

extend beyond the limits of the statute. It did not create a separate regime. There is one legal system in which the common law, statute law and the 1998 Act coalesce. As English courts become used to applying the principle of proportionality in convention right cases, they are likely also to apply it in other cases whenever logically appropriate. In this sense the German Federal Constitutional Court has captured the right nuance by holding that the German Bill of Rights has a radiating effect throughout the legal system.[41] That does not mean that I would argue for a direct horizontal application of our Bill of Rights. I now turn briefly to this complex subject.

Bills of Rights apply vertically, *viz.* they protect fundamental rights of individuals against the State and its agencies. The question is whether a Bill of Rights also has direct horizontal application between private parties. Generalisations on this subject are unwise. It depends crucially on the terms of each instrument. There has been a vigorous debate on the point in England.[42] The importance of the point can be illustrated by the potential scope of guarantee of privacy in the Convention. English law knows no tort of privacy. Does the guarantee of privacy under the Convention empower the English courts to create a free-standing tort of privacy? The matter is still undecided and any view must be provisional. I am inclined to share the view of those who argue that the structure of our Act rules out direct horizontal application. If this is right, it is beyond the power of the English courts to develop a general tort of privacy. On the other hand, by its radiating effect the Act may indirectly lead to the incremental development of existing remedies which protect rights of privacy, *e.g.* based on a duty of confidentiality. Some may be disappointed by this unheroic stance. For my part, as I said in *Simms* with the agreement of a majority, freedom of expression in a democracy is the "primary right" and "without it an effective rule of law is impossible". Freedom of speech is the lifeblood of democracy. Lincoln's participatory democracy—government of the people, by the people, for the people—can only flourish if there is freedom of speech and, may I add, freedom of information.[43] Inroads on freedom of expression must therefore be carefully contained. Even the excesses of the tabloid press in England may have to be tolerated for the larger purpose of not undermining freedom of expression.

There are, of course, important structural differences between our bills of rights. The English model was framed with the benefit of experience of other Commonwealth models including the New Zealand Bill of Rights Act 1990. The strong interpretative obligation under section 3 of the Human Rights Act 1998, linked with the express power and duty under section 4 to make a declaration of incompatibility, affords stronger protection of fundamental rights than your system. On the other hand, my impression is that your Act has been successful in mandating constitutional adjudication. Your Court of Appeal has placed your jurisprudence on a secure foundation in

---

[41] B. S. Markesinis, *Always on the Same Path*, 2001, Vol. 2, Chapters 7 and 8.
[42] Sir William Wade Q.C., *Horizons of Horizontality*, (2000) 116 L.Q.R. 217 argued in favour of direct horizontality. Lord Lester of Herne Hill Q.C. and David Pannick Q.C., *The Impact of the Human Rights Act: The Knights Move* (2000) 116 L.Q.R. 380 explained the structural arguments against direct horizontality.
[43] *R. v. Secretary of State for Home Department, ex p. Simms* [2000] 2 A.C. 115 at 126.

734 Democracy Through Law

developing the doctrine of an implied remedial jurisdiction to issue declarations of inconsistency.[44] The good sense of this approach is anchored in democratic values. I am confident that the New Zealand Parliament would not wish to gather en passant in substantial judgments that it has passed legislation which is inconsistent with the 1990 Act. Rather it would wish your Court of Appeal to address the issue directly so that the public and Parliament know how the judicial branch of government views matters. Given this development, the divergence between our bills of rights is less marked than may at first glance appear. With some diffidence I would, however, suggest that New Zealand could profitably consider creating a Parliamentary Committee on Human Rights, like our Joint Committee on Human Rights which is empowered to consider matters relating to human rights in the United Kingdom, excluding individual cases. It may strengthen the scrutiny of legislation in New Zealand. It is my impression that this can be done without legislation under the Standing Orders of your Parliament.[45]

Inching Towards Becoming Constitutional States

Having sketched some steps along the road towards the constitutionalisation of public law, one may pose the question whether our countries can now be described as constitutional states. For England the answer at present must be no. But the landscape is changing. I mention three positive developments in Britain, ranging from the banal to the fundamental. First, by and large, English judges no longer refer to subjects: they speak about citizens. Secondly, historically in English law the State had no legal identity and the State was not a legal concept.[46] A reason may have been the idea encapsulated by the claim of Louis XIV that "L'etat c'est moi". Or perhaps the fact that the United Kingdom has four law districts—England, Wales, Northern Ireland, and Scotland—may have played a role. In any event, this mystification has now disappeared. The State has become a legal concept. Thirdly, the idea that injunctive relief could not be granted against Ministers of the Crown, or only exceptionally, lingered on in our system.[47] It was a relic of an age of deference towards Ministers of the Crown. In a recent case from Grenada the Privy Council has held that Ministers have no immunity or quasi immunity. The rule of law applies even to the most powerful holders of office.[48] This is a development of constitutional and symbolic significance. England can fairly claim to be inching towards becoming a constitutional state. And New Zealand is already thereabouts.

---

[44] *Moohen v. Film & Literature Board of Review* [2000] 2 N.Z.L.R. 9; *Poumaka* [2000] 2 N.Z.L.R. 37; compare *R. v. Pora* 2001 2 N.Z.L.R. 37: I have had the benefit of the examination of this subject by Philip A. Joseph, *Constitutional Law* [2000] N.Z.L.R. 301 at 313–319; and Andrew S. Butler, *Judicial Indications of Inconsistency—A New Weapon in the Bills of Right Armoury*? [2000] N.Z.L.R. 43.

[45] Compare the Companion to the Standing Orders and Guide to the Proceedings of the House of Lords, 2000, para. 3.31; paras 8.20–23; and para. 9.53. The second lecture of Lord Lester of Herne Hill referred to in n. 37 above is particularly illuminating.

[46] Patrick Birkinshaw, "The Main Features of British Constitutional Law", British Report published in *Die Entstehung einer europäischen Verfassungsordnung*, edited by J. Schwarze, 2000.

[47] *M. v. Home Office* 1994 A.C. 377.

[48] *Gairy v. The Attorney-General of Grenada*, June 19, 2001.

Constitutionalism

That brings me to the principle of constitutionalism.[49] It is neither a rule nor a principle of law. It is a political theory. It holds that the exercise of government power must be controlled in order that it should not be destructive of the very democratic values which it was intended to promote. It requires of the executive more than loyalty to the existing constitution. It is concerned with the merits and quality of institutional arrangements. In aid of political liberty it sets minimum standards of constitutional government. Two particular applications of this political theory are important. It is not sufficient that the holders of high office are public spirited men of great competence and honour. What matters is that the institutional arrangements must provide for effective control of the abuse of executive power. The second feature is that absolute executive power must be avoided by a diffusion of authority. This can be achieved by nurturing independent centres of decision making. Such autonomous centres introduce checks and balances in a democratic system. Thus at the apex of our constitutional system there is the neutrality of the sovereign which is the essential and indispensable constitutional pivot on which our entire unwritten constitution depends. A politically neutral civil service is a vital centre of independence. So is an independent police force. A wholly independent academic and practising legal profession is a substantial check on absolute executive power. A free press reflecting diverse points of view is a great servant of the cause of democracy.

Constitutionalism is not often at the top of the agenda of business of governments. But there has been progress. The Bank of England Act 1998 gave the Bank of England independence in the setting of interest rates. By legislation Parliament created a Scottish Parliament and Assemblies for Northern Ireland and Wales. The post of a Mayor for London was created. A plan to create Regional Assemblies in regions of England is far advanced. Following a number of public health scares, an independent Food Standards Agency has been set up under the Food Standards Agency Act. A Freedom of Information Act 2001 has been enacted. Unfortunately, it is a rather weak measure, notably because the information commissioner is given limited powers. Yet overall constitutionalism has been advanced.

The European Dimension and Comparative Law

The isolation of England from European legal culture has ended. The dominant influence has been our membership of the European Economic Community and the European Union. The direct impact on our substantive law has been enormous. By analogy general principles of community law have influenced the development of our public law, *e.g.* in regard to principles of non-discrimination, legal certainty, legitimate expectations, proportionality, and the variable intensity of judicial review depending on the interests at stake. The European Convention on Human Rights, and the jurisprudence of Strasbourg, has brought us into the mainstream of the Human Rights movement. Many multi-lateral treaties are incorporated into our law. Such treaties are products of a mixture of civil law and common law influences and techniques. Our universities teach not only community law but the modern *jus commune* of Europe. Our

---

[49] I have drawn on my article in [1997] P.L. 83. I repeat my acknowledgement of my indebtedness to M. J. C. Vile, *Constitutionalism and the Separation of Powers*, 1967.

736 Democracy Through Law

country is a European liberal democracy. In the words of the Treaty on European Union, as amended by the Amsterdam Treaty, the Union "is founded on" the principles of liberty, democracy, and respect for human rights and fundamental freedoms.[50] Those values must inevitably be the context against which judges will have to interpret statutes and develop the common law. The process of our integration into the legal culture of Europe through directives and regulations is irreversible and continuing. And it cannot but strengthen the constitutionalisation of our public law.

As a result of the European dimension, and the work of writers such as Professor Basil Markesinis Q.C. of University College, University of London, it is not too bold to say that comparative law has come of age. Our highest court expects, for example, that counsel should research the case law and literature of Australia, Canada and New Zealand and other countries in cases where the possibility of common problems exist. So in *MacFarlane* the Law Lords were taken on a tour d'horizon of the law and practice in many common law and civil law jurisdictions. This review showed that in most jurisdictions the cost of bringing up a healthy unwanted child is not recoverable. In New Zealand there is, of course, a no-fault compensation scheme. But we took account of two decisions of the Accident and Compensation Authority, which held that there is no causal connection between medical error and a cost of raising such a child. This case demonstrates that the discipline of comparative law does not aim at a poll of the solutions adopted in different countries. It has the different and inestimable value of sharpening our focus on the weight of competing solutions. In this way a judgment of the Canadian Supreme Court led the House of Lords recently to depart from earlier English authority and to rule that the owners of a boarding house may be vicariously responsible for the warden's sexual abuse of boys.[51] Making due allowance for cultural differences, however, it is in the field of constitutional law, public law and human rights law, that our system has profited most from comparative techniques. And for us in England the intellectually rigorous judgments of your powerful Court of Appeal have been of inestimable value.

Nowadays, the cross-pollination between international jurisdictions is accelerating. There is an international dialogue among appellate courts.[52] It is right that the appellate courts of our countries should play a full part in this process. When the link with the Privy Council has been cut, and you have your own Supreme Court, the time may be ripe for creating regular judicial exchanges between our two countries. I can assure you that my colleagues will queue up to visit this beautiful country.

---

[50] Articles 6–7 of the TEU. See also the commentary in Craig and De Burca, *EU Law: Text, Cases, and Materials*, 2nd ed. 1998, at pp. 332–333.

[51] *Lister and others v. Hesley Hall Ltd* [2002] 1 A.C. 215 and *Bazley v. Carry* (1999) 174 D.L.R. (4th) 45.

[52] Madam Justice L'Heureux Dube of the Canadian Supreme Court has eloquently described this process: *The Importance of Dialogue: Globalization And The International Impact of the Relinquish Court* (1998) 34 Tulsa Law Journal 15.

[12]
Constitutional Principle in Action: *R (Anufrijeva) v Secretary of State for the Home Department**
[2004] 1 A.C. 604, 618

LORD STEYN

21 My Lords, the question is how regulation 70(3A)(b)(i) of the Income Support (General) Regulations 1987 should be interpreted. The question is whether Parliament intended to authorise the withdrawing of income support by an internal note on a departmental file with legal effect from a date before notification of the decision. At first glance it may appear to be a rather technical issue. But the decision by the House may have a more general bearing on the development of our public law.

22 The background is as follows. On 31 August 1998 the appellant applied for asylum. On 4 September 1998 she claimed income support benefits, which were paid with effect from that date. Regulation 70(3A) of

the Income Support (General) Regulations 1987 provides for the payment of income support at the rate applicable for urgent cases (90% of the normal rate) to persons who are asylum seekers within the meaning of the same regulation. Regulation 70(3A)(b)(i) provides that a person ceases to be an asylum seeker (and thus loses the right to income support): "in the case of a claim for asylum which, on or after 5 February 1996, is recorded by the Secretary of State as having been determined (other than on appeal) or abandoned, on the date on which it is so recorded . . ." On 20 November 1999 a Mr Stuart Beaton signed an internal file note. It read:

"This woman has cited numerous mishaps throughout the 1990s and puts her woes down to an encounter her father had with a drunken solicitor in 1991. There is no credibility in any of this and no Convention reason anyway. For the reasons given in the letter aside, this application has failed to establish a well founded fear of persecution. Refusal is appropriate. Case hereby recorded as determined."

On 30 November 1999 the content of this file note was communicated to the Benefits Agency. It was not communicated to the appellant and the "letter aside" of 20 November 1999 containing the Home Secretary's reasons for refusal of asylum was not sent to the appellant.

23   By letter of 28 November 1999 the appellant was asked to attend an interview on 11 January 2000. On 9 December and 15 December 1999 the Benefits Agency asked for the return of the appellant's income support book. The appellant's income support was stopped without explanation with effect from 9 December 1999. On 17 December 1999 the solicitors now acting for the appellant asked the Home Office for a postponement of the interview fixed for 11 January 2000. On 23 December 1999 the Benefits Agency advised the appellant's solicitors that it had been informed by the Home Office that the appellant's claim for asylum had been refused on 20 November 1999. For this reason the Benefits Agency had stopped the income support payments with effect from 9 December 1999.   On 24 December 1999 the appellant's solicitors lodged an appeal with the Benefits Agency against the withdrawal of the appellant's income support. A further interview was arranged by the Home Office for 7 March 2000, which was subsequently refixed for 17 April 2000. The appellant was unable to comply because she was unable to obtain funds for the train fare. Under cover of a letter dated 25 April 2000 the decision rejecting the appellant's application for asylum and refusing her leave to enter was sent to her. The notice of refusal of leave to the appellant to enter the United Kingdom was signed by an immigration officer on 18 April 2000 and sent to the appellant. The notice of 18 April 2000 was accompanied by the reasons for refusal letter dated 20 November 1999.

24   The hearing at first instance before Sir Christopher Bellamy—to whose judgment I wish to pay tribute—took place under the shadow of the decision of the Court of Appeal in *R v Secretary of the State for the Home Department, Ex p Salem* [1999] QB 805. In *Ex p Salem* the Court of Appeal (Hobhouse, Brooke LJJ and Sir John Balcombe) held that for the purposes of regulation 70(3A)(b)(i) a person ceased to be entitled to income support from the date when his claim for asylum was recorded as determined on an internal file note in the Asylum Directorate in the Home Department, even though he had not yet been informed of the determination. The House

granted leave to appeal the decision in *Ex p Salem*. In the event, the matter did not proceed as Mr Salem was granted refugee status: see [1999] 1 AC 450. Reluctantly, Sir Christopher felt compelled to dismiss the appellant's application for judicial review. The Court of Appeal also regarded itself as bound by *Ex p Salem*. Having so decided the Court of Appeal had to dismiss the appeal of the present appellant. But the Court of Appeal voiced its concerns about the policy of the Secretary of State and the decision in *Ex p Salem* in clear terms. Schiemann LJ (with the agreement of Hale and Sedley LLJ) trenchantly observed about the factual matrix [2002] EWCA Civ 399, para 29:

> "We have also been told by leading counsel for the Home Secretary, Mr John Howell QC, that the delay of over four months between the preparation and the dispatch of the letter explaining why asylum has been refused was not accidental: it was a consistent practice. But for it, the present issue of law would have no significance. Mr Howell was wholly unable to explain it, let alone justify it. He was able to do no more than read us part of an affidavit which had been sworn in *Salem* which asserted that the implications of cost and effort if interim notifications were sent out were too great. When one bears in mind first that the asylum-seeker's ability to contest the refusal of asylum is entirely dependent on receipt of the Home Secretary's reasons for refusal, and secondly that the letter containing full reasons is already on file and that sooner or later the Home Office will have to put it in an envelope and post it, even the flimsy explanation we were given falls away. Since Mr Howell was able to tell us that the practice is now to send out a prompt notification (though he could not tell us whether it included reasons, and Mr Gill's instructions suggested that it did not), one is left wondering what the real reason was. Ms Anufrijeva's inability, her benefit having been stopped, to find £17 to travel to Gatwick for her 'reasons for refusal' interview gives little to be proud of."

In oral argument before the House counsel stated that the Secretary of State did not condone delay in notification of a decision on asylum. These were weasel words. There was no unintended lapse. The practice of not notifying asylum seekers of the fact of withdrawal of income support was consistently and deliberately adopted. There simply is no rational explanation for such a policy. Having abandoned this practice the Secretary of State still seeks to justify it as lawful. It provides a peep into contemporary standards of public administration. Transparency is not its hallmark. It is not an encouraging picture.

25 The Court of Appeal observed about the interpretation of the regulation, at para 30:

> "once an asylum seeker knows that her application has been refused, and that she is not to be given leave to enter the country on any other basis, and has the reasons for those decisions, she can reasonably be expected to make a choice: either to accept the decision and leave or to stay and fight but without recourse to state benefits. But she cannot reasonably be expected to make that choice before she knows of the decisions and the reasons for them. There is nothing in the material

before us to suggest that it is consistent with the declared purpose of the regulation to expect her to do so."

I would respectfully endorse this observation.

26 The arguments for the Home Secretary ignore fundamental principles of our law. Notice of a decision is required before it can have the character of a determination with legal effect because the individual concerned must be in a position to challenge the decision in the courts if he or she wishes to do so. This is not a technical rule. It is simply an application of the right of access to justice. That is a fundamental and constitutional principle of our legal system: *Raymond v Honey* [1983] 1 AC 1, 10G, per Lord Wilberforce; *R v Secretary of State for the Home Department, Ex p Leech*, [1994] QB 198, 209D; *R v Secretary of State for the Home Department, Ex p Simms* [2000] 2 AC 115.

27 What then is the relevance of this dimension for the present case? The answer is provided by Lord Hoffmann's elegant explanation of the principle of legality in the *Simms* case. He said, at p 131:

"Parliamentary sovereignty means that Parliament can, if it chooses, legislate contrary to fundamental principles of human rights. The Human Rights Act 1998 will not detract from this power. The constraints upon its exercise by Parliament are ultimately political, not legal. But the principle of legality means that Parliament must squarely confront what it is doing and accept the political cost. Fundamental rights cannot be overridden by general or ambiguous words. This is because there is too great a risk that the full implications of their unqualified meaning may have passed unnoticed in the democratic process. In the absence of express language or necessary implication to the contrary, the courts therefore presume that even the most general words were intended to be subject to the basic rights of the individual. In this way the courts of the United Kingdom, though acknowledging the sovereignty of Parliament, apply principles of constitutionality little different from those which exist in countries where the power of the legislature is expressly limited by a constitutional document."

This principle may find its primary application in respect of cases under the European Convention on Human Rights. But the Convention is not an exhaustive statement of fundamental rights under our system of law. Lord Hoffmann's dictum applies to fundamental rights beyond the four corners of the Convention. It is engaged in the present case.

28 This view is reinforced by the constitutional principle requiring the rule of law to be observed. That principle too requires that a constitutional state must accord to individuals the right to know of a decision before their rights can be adversely affected. The antithesis of such a state was described by Kafka: a state where the rights of individuals are overridden by hole in the corner decisions or knocks on doors in the early hours. That is not our system. I accept, of course, that there must be exceptions to this approach, notably in the criminal field, e g arrests and search warrants, where notification is not possible. But it is difficult to visualise a rational argument which could even arguably justify putting the present case in the exceptional category. If this analysis is right, it also engages the principle of construction explained by Lord Hoffmann in *Ex p Simms*.

29 In European law the approach is possibly a little more formalistic but the thrust is the same. It has been held to be a "fundamental principle in the Community legal order . . . that a measure adopted by the public authorities shall not be applicable to those concerned before they have the opportunity to make themselves acquainted with it": *Firma A Racke v Hauptzollamt Mainz* (Case 98/78) [1979] ECR 69, para 15; *Opel Austria GmbH v Council of European Union* (Case T-115/94) [1997] ECR II 39, para 124; Schwarze, *European Administrative Law* (1992), pp 1416–1420; Council of Europe Publishing, *The Administration and You, A Handbook* (1997) chapter 3, para 49.

30 Until the decision in *Ex p Salem* it had never been suggested that an uncommunicated administrative decision can bind an individual. It is an astonishingly unjust proposition. In our system of law surprise is regarded as the enemy of justice. Fairness is the guiding principle of our public law. In *R v Commission for Racial Equality, Ex p Hillingdon London Borough Council* [1982] AC 779, 787, Lord Diplock explained the position:

> "Where an Act of Parliament confers upon an administrative body functions which involve its making decisions which affect to their detriment the rights of other persons or curtail their liberty to do as they please, there is a presumption that Parliament intended that the administrative body should act fairly towards those persons who will be affected by their decision."

Where decisions are published or notified to those concerned accountability of public authorities is achieved. Elementary fairness therefore supports a principle that a decision takes effect only upon communication.

31 If this analysis is correct, it is plain that Parliament has not expressly or by necessary implication legislated to the contrary effect. The decision in question involves a fundamental right. It is in effect one involving a binding determination as to status. It is of importance to the individual to be informed of it so that he or she can decide what to do. Moreover, neither cost nor administrative convenience can in such a case conceivably justify a different approach. This is underlined by the fact that the bizarre earlier practice has now been abandoned. Given this context Parliament has not in specific and unmistakeable terms legislated to displace the applicable constitutional principles.

32 The contrary arguments can be dealt with quite briefly. Counsel for the Home Secretary submits that before a "determination" can be "notified" there must be a determination. This is legalism and conceptualism run riot. One can readily accept that in this case there must have been a decision as reflected in the file note. That does not mean that the statutory requirement of a "determination" has been fulfilled. On the contrary, the decision is provisional until notified.

33 Counsel for the Home Secretary relied strongly on some niceties of statutory language. He pointed out that in regulation 21ZA of the Regulations, as well as in section 6 of the Asylum and Immigration Appeals Act 1993, the draftsmen provided expressly for notification. In contrast regulation 70(3A)(b)(i) makes no reference to notification. The fact, however, that other provisions made the requirement of notification *explicit* does not rule out the possibility that notification was all along *implicit* in the concept of "the determination". For my part a stronger indication of

Parliamentary intent is provided by the Statement of Changes in Immigration Rules (HC 395), which were laid before Parliament on 23 May 1994 under section 3(2) of the Immigration Act 1971. The concept of a "refusal" of asylum to be found in rules 331, 333 and 348 plainly contemplates notification of an adverse decision. These rules are part of the contextual scene of regulation 70(3A)(b)(i). They support the argument that notification of a decision is necessary for it to become a determination. But the major point is that the semantic arguments of counsel for the Home Secretary cannot displace the constitutional principles outlined above.

34 For all these reasons I would reject the submissions of counsel for the Home Secretary and hold that *Ex p Salem* was wrongly decided. It follows that in my view the present appeal should be allowed.

35 My noble and learned friend, Lord Bingham of Cornhill, has observed that the Home Secretary was under a public law duty to give notice within a reasonable time but that breach of this duty cannot nullify or invalidate his decision. I would question this conclusion. It is important to bear in mind that the breach involved a deliberate policy decision by the Home Office not to comply with the public law duty. This amounts to an abuse of power and ought to preclude the Home Secretary from relying on his unlawful conduct until notification has taken place. While generally an estoppel cannot operate against the Crown, it can be estopped when it is abusing its powers: *HTV Ltd v Price Commission* [1976] ICR 170, 185G–H, per Lord Denning MR; *R v Inland Revenue Comrs, Ex p Preston* [1985] AC 835, 865D, per Lord Templeman; *Laker Airways Ltd v Department of Trade* [1977] QB 643, 707D–F, per Lord Denning MR, and 709A–E, per Roskill LJ. For this further reason I would reject the submissions made on behalf of the Home Secretary.

36 I recognise, of course, that in some ways the appellant's case does not merit great sympathy. But even in unprepossessing cases fundamental principles must be upheld. The rule of law requires it. In my view the appellant is entitled to recover income support until proper notification of the determination on 25 April 2000. I would therefore allow the appeal.

*Note

By a majority of four to one the House of Lords allowed the appeal. The *ratio decidendi* is reflected in my Judgment

Part Three

Human Rights Law

[13]
Human Rights: The Legacy of Mrs Roosevelt

Those who doubt the value of the human rights system would do well to ponder the story "The Kilikov Trial". I quote the central part of the story[1]:

> '... for not for its worldly qualities alone is Kilikov to be extolled, but it is to be praised for the judicial decisions of its judges. What are the decisions of its judges? It is told that once, during the Polish wars, a gentile killed his friend in Kilikov. Maliciously or accidentally? From the judgment it emerges that he was killed with malice. He was put in jail and convicted of killing, as a man is convicted when murdering another with malice.
>
> When the murderer was taken out to be hanged it was remembered that he was a blacksmith by profession and that in all Kilikov there was no other blacksmith. And indeed a city cannot cope without a blacksmith, who serves the needs of many.
>
> They investigated and found that in the city there were two tailors but that they could make do with one. The judges reconvened and said: instead of the blacksmith we shall hang one tailor and we shall let the blacksmith live, for the city cannot manage without a blacksmith but one tailor will suffice.
>
> They acquitted the blacksmith and brought him back from the hangman's house and in his stead they hanged one of the two tailors living in the city.

It was said that in this way the interests of the citizens of Kilikov were served and the rule of law was promoted by deterring others from committing vile crimes. And the wisdom of the judges became legendary. But one does not have to go to a satirical Polish story. Lord Denning, the greatest English judge of the twentieth century, refused to entertain the idea that the Birmingham Six might be not guilty. In 1980, when the Court of Appeal denied the Birmingham Six the right to sue the police in civil proceedings, Lord Denning

---

* Delivered as the Holdsworth Club lecture on November 30, 2001 at the School of Law, The University of Birmingham.

[1] I am indebted to Dr Shulamit Almog of the Faculty of Law, University of Haifa, Israel for the story: (1999) 1 *Interdisciplinary Literary Studies, A Journal of Criticism and Theory* 37.

said about the possible innocence of the men: "This is such an appalling vista that every sensible person in the land would say: it cannot be right that these actions should go further".[2]

The men remained in prison. Some 12 years later their convictions had to be quashed. It was a seismic shock for the English legal system. Nowadays we have come to realise that the risk of convicting the innocent is ever present: no system can eliminate the risk of a dishonest policeman or an incompetent scientist persuading a jury of the guilt of an innocent person. The idea became established that it is the duty of judges, where things have gone wrong in the justice system, to put it right. This is the context in which in 1999 in *R. v. Secretary of State for the Home Department, ex p. Simms*,[3] in the face of some 60 miscarriages of justice during the 1990s which were only exposed by investigative journalism, the House of Lords set aside Home Office instructions denying prisoners access to journalists in their efforts to get their convictions overturned.

In the aftermath of the terrible events of September 11, 2001 in New York, human rights are accorded a low value by some. In the fight against Al-Qaida, oppressed minorities in many parts of the world are sacrificed to the need for co-operation with oppressor states. Even in liberal democracies such as our own there are powerful voices demanding an abandonment of some fundamental rights. The creation of an International Criminal Court, the *Pinochet* case and the holding to account of Milosevic in The Hague, held out hope of an advance of human rights. Now the world may have changed.

It is an opportune time to ask why fundamental human rights must be respected. The first premise of the democratic ideal is, of course, that the people entrust power to the government in accordance with the principle of majority rule. Its second premise is that basic values of liberty and justice for all and respect for human rights and fundamental freedoms must be guaranteed. What is the foundation of the second premise? For my part there is a clear answer. It is morally right that states and their agencies should respect fundamental rights of individuals. Moreover, the observance of human rights is instrumentally valuable. It tends to promote conditions in which democratic systems can flourish for the benefit of people generally. Amartya Sen, the winner of the 1998 Nobel Prize for Economics, has graphically illustrated this truth. He wrote: "in the terrible history of famines in the world, no substantial famine has ever occurred in any independent and democratic country with a relatively free press".[4] After a review of the history of famines he added:

> Famines are easy to prevent if there is a serious effort to do so, and a democratic government, facing elections and criticisms from opposition parties and independent newspapers, cannot help but make such an effort. Not surprisingly, while India continued to have famines under British rule right up to independence (the last famine, which I witnessed as a child, was in 1943, four years before independence), they disappeared

---

[2] *McIlkenny v. Chief Constable of the Midlands* [1980] Q.B. 283, 000.
[3] [2000] 2 A.C. 115, 127D–E.
[4] "Democracy as a Universal Value" (1999) 10 *Journal of Democracy* 3, 7–8.

suddenly with the establishment of a multiparty democracy and a free press.

My starting point is therefore that the moral and practical case for democracy, and guarantees of fundamental human rights, is plain.

The roots of the human rights system are old. Our 1689 Bill of Rights, the 1776 American Declaration of Independence and the subsequent Bill of Rights, the 1789 French Declaration of the Rights of Man and the Citizen were events of great importance. But it is an undoubted fact that before the Second World War the assumption was widespread that however barbarously governments treated their citizens such matters were not properly the concern of other governments or international organisations. The Third Reich and the Holocaust forever changed that perception. During the Second World War the idea of guaranteeing fundamental human rights and irreducible minimum standards took root. In 1941 President Roosevelt identified as essential freedoms of speech and religion, and from want and fear. In 1945 the Nuremberg trial revealed that the Nazi regime had killed millions of Jews and forced into concentration camps gypsies, communists, labour unionists, Poles, Ukrainians, Kurds, Armenians, disabled people, Jehovah's Witnesses and homosexuals. The full horror of the Nazi era became apparent. And the Tokyo trials in the same year demonstrated brutal repression practised by Japan in the East.

On June 26, 1945, in San Francisco, the U.N. Charter was signed. The preamble of its Charter recited the determination by the "peoples of the United Nations . . . to reaffirm faith in fundamental rights, in the dignity and worth of the human person". Six other references to human rights in the Charter underlined the importance of the subject. On the other hand, the Charter contained the principle of non-interference in domestic affairs of member states.[5] Moreover, human rights were not defined. What was still needed was a text with international legitimacy which spelt out fundamental rights and freedoms. The differences between nations in culture, political systems and economic circumstances made agreement on any text, even if only aspirational in character, extraordinarily difficult to accomplish. Among many nations, and notably Stalinist Russia and its satellite nations, there was considerable hostility to such a project. And among western democracies there was opposition to the creation of legally enforceable human rights. On the other hand, there seemed to be a chance of achieving the promulgation of a set of universal minimum standards of political morality. But in such a great enterprise there were great problems to overcome.

Fortunately, in the years 1946 to 1948 before the onset of the Cold War there was a window of opportunity.[6] But a huge push was needed. In 1946 the U.N. Commission of Human Rights had been created. The four main

---

[5] Art. 2.7.
[6] For the history of the Universal Declaration of Human Rights I have relied in particular on Mary Ann Glendon, *A World Made New: Eleanor Roosevelt and the Universal Declaration of Human Rights* (Random House, 2001) and Glen Johnson and Janusz Symonides, *The Universal Declaration of Human Rights: A History of its Creation and Implementation 1948–1998* (UNESCO, 1998).

members of the U.N. Human Rights Commission undertook this task. Eleanor Roosevelt chaired the Commission during the period from April 1946 to December 1948 during which the Universal Declaration of Human Rights was drafted. How that came about is intriguing. In 1945 President Truman had assumed the Presidency of the United States. He wanted to keep the widow of the late president on board, so to speak, but to remove that indomitable campaigner from involvement in progressive domestic causes. He sent Mrs Roosevelt to the United Nations. The U.S. delegation was aghast. They decided to sideline her by relegating her to what was regarded as the unimportant Third Committee (Social, Humanitarian and Cultural). That led to her appointment to the Human Rights Commission. She was a famous figure in her own right, known to be devoted to the cause of human rights, and her election as chair of the Human Rights Commission was a formality. In that way she became the pivotal figure in the drafting of the Universal Declaration and in preparing the ground for its adoption. She was not a philosopher, lawyer or intellectual. But with a combination of grandmotherly tact, political realism and sublime courage she brought the project centre stage and eventually to a successful conclusion. By a happy coincidence the other members of the Steering Committee complemented her role. Dr P.C. Chang, a distinguished Chinese lawyer, was the Vice-Chair of the Commission. He ceaselessly reminded everyone that they were expounding universal values. His mastery of Confucian philosophy enabled him to suggest subtle drafting compromises which eased the adoption of the text. René Cassin, was a Frenchman and son of a Jewish merchant. His work in the human rights field was his very personal response to the Holocaust. He was a distinguished French lawyer and philosopher. He supplied the European perspective. And one must never forget that, despite the tragic history of Europe with repeated reversions to barbarism, the ideals such as political democracy, the rule of law and human rights which underlie the Universal Declaration are European in origin. He apparently produced an early handwritten draft, prepared over a weekend, which provided the structure of the Universal Declaration. The fourth member was Charles A. Malik who served as Rapporteur of the Commission. He was a philosopher trained at the American University of Beirut and he taught at that university for many years. He was a strong believer in the natural law basis of human rights, but the ultimate text did not ground human rights in natural law. Malik was, however, a strong personality. His contribution left a large imprint on the Universal Declaration. The four principal figures were assisted by an able secretariat, headed by John Humphrey, a tough and pragmatic Canadian international lawyer. He was responsible for a 408 page "Documented Outline" which became the principal working document in drafting sessions. This select cast played the decisive role in the development of the text of the Universal Declaration.

In early December 1948, after hundreds of drafting sessions and endless negotiations in New York, Geneva and Paris, the scene was set for the final act. There were last minute crises. For example, the Pakistani delegate declared her intention to vote against the Declaration because she believed the provision guaranteeing a right to change one's religion was contrary to the dictates of Islam. Mrs Roosevelt lobbied the head of the Pakistani delegation, Sir Mohammed Zaffrulah Khan. He ruled that while the delegate was technically correct the Koran also taught that hypocrisy was a more serious sin: people should therefore not profess a religion in which they did not believe. Pakistan's vote for the declaration was thus secured.

On December 10, 1948 in Paris the General Assembly by a unanimous vote of 48 with eight abstentions adopted the text. The members rose in a standing ovation for Mrs Roosevelt. The abstentions were by Russia and its satellite nations, Saudi Arabia and South Africa. The reasons for the abstentions are interesting. The communist bloc was motivated by fear of the loss of sovereignty in treating its citizens in any way that was thought desirable in the interest of the furtherance of communist ideology. Saudi Arabia could not tolerate the idea of a right to change one's religion. In passing I observe that few things have done more harm than the belief by groups, religious or otherwise, that only they are in possession of the truth and that those who do not believe in that truth are evil, a prejudice that still exerts its influence in the times in which we live. The rulers of South Africa realised that the Declaration was incompatible with the system of racial discrimination already prevailing in that country. The South African representative warned:

> [the Declaration] will undoubtedly be invoked as a source of moral rights and obligations, and may therefore lead not only to intensified internal unrest and agitation, but also to repeated embarrassment and agitation before the United Nations and their various organs.

Today the communist bloc no longer exists. Saudi Arabia is still rooted in the past. But in South Africa a combination of the liberation struggle, economic boycotts, the coming down of the Berlin Wall in 1989 and the subsequent collapse of communist regimes in Eastern Europe ultimately led to the release of Nelson Mandela, the end of the apartheid regime and a new constitutional dispensation in South Africa based squarely on the principles of the Universal Declaration. The passing of the Universal Declaration was a momentous achievement. In paying tribute to the leading role of Mrs Roosevelt, the President of the General Assembly described her as "the person who had raised to even greater heights ever so great a name: Eleanor Roosevelt, the representative of the United States of America".

The Universal Declaration was not intended to create legal rights: it was drafted as an aspirational text. It was intended that legally binding international treaties would follow. In fact it took some 18 years before that aim was achieved. But the moral force of the text was immediate and enormous. A brief reference to its elegant and logical structure is necessary. The preamble and proclamation, together with Articles 1 and 2 contain the general part. The first preamble recited that "the inherent dignity and . . . the equal and inalienable rights of all members of the human family is the foundation of freedom, justice and peace in the world". Its first Article proclaimed that "All human beings are born free and equal in dignity and rights". Next come Articles 3 to 11. They spell out rights to life, liberty, and personal security; bans on slavery and torture; right to legal recognition, equality before the law, effective remedies for violation of fundamental rights and freedom from arbitrary arrest and detention; guarantees of fair criminal procedures, presumption of innocence and the principle of non-retroactivity in criminal law. Then follows a section containing Articles 12 to 17 which are concerned with the rights of people in civil society. These rights include the right to be free of interference with one's privacy, family, home or correspondence and from arbitrary attacks upon one's honour and reputation; freedom of movement and the right to return; the right to seek and enjoy political asylum; the right to nationality; provisions on marriage and the family and the right to own property. Articles 18 to 21 are concerned with freedom of religion and belief; freedom of expression; freedom of assembly; and the right of participation in government. There follow the provisions of Articles 22 to 27 for new social, economic and cultural rights, which are described as "indispensable for (man's) dignity and for the full development of his personality". The last three Articles of the Declaration seek to secure the conditions that are necessary to protect the rights and freedom comprised in the Declaration. Importantly, there is a provision that everyone has duties to the community. The theme is universal: there is a common conception of human rights capable of commanding wide acceptance throughout the world despite huge differences in culture, political systems, geographical location and economic circumstances. The Universal Declaration also ushered in the belief that individuals are not mere subjects but have rights against the state and its agencies. It gave birth to the rights revolution.[7]

The Universal Declaration has been the inspiration, and point of departure, for all subsequent general, regional and specifically targeted human rights texts intended to secure fundamental rights which were adopted during the next half century. The general texts include the International Covenant on Economic, Social and Cultural Rights (CESCR), and the International Covenant on Civil and Political Rights (ICCPR), which were opened for ratification in 1966 but only came into force in 1976. These two instruments together with the Universal Declaration have pride of place as the International Bill of Rights. As at October 22, 2001 the CESCR has been ratified by 145 nations and the ICCPR by 147 nations.[8] The CESCR is monitored by the Committee on Economic, Social and Cultural Rights and the ICCPR by the Human Rights Committee. Under the Optional Protocol of the ICCPR there is a right of petition by individual claimants to the Human Right Committee. To date 99 states have ratified the Optional Protocol. The regional instruments include the European Convention on Human Rights (1950) as well as the American Convention on Human Rights (1969). The specifically targeted instruments include the 1979 U.N. Convention on the Elimination of All Forms of Discrimination Against Women, the 1984 U.N. Convention Against Torture

---

[7] Michael Ignatieff, *The Rights Revolution* (2000), p. 49.

[8] The ratification by the U.S. of the ICCPR is so hedged about with qualifications and reservations that it amounts to little. This is symptomatic of the lukewarm attitude of the U.S. to the human rights movement. It has also not acceded to the treaty creating the International Criminal Court of Justice. For the importance of this development, see Fen Hampson et al., *Madness in the Multitude: Human Security and World Disorder* (Oxford, 2002), Chap. 4.

and Other Cruel, Inhuman or Degrading Treatment or Punishment and the 1989 U.N. Convention on the Rights of the Child.

For us in the United Kingdom the most important descendant of the Universal Declaration is the European Convention on Human Rights (ECHR). Subject to the qualification that it did not include economic, social and cultural rights, the ECHR is in large measure based on the Universal Declaration. The United Kingdom ratified the ECHR in 1951. In 1953 its reach was extended to 42 territories for whose international relations the United Kingdom were responsible. In due course it became the model for codes of human rights which were inserted into the constitutions of the great majority of independent Commonwealth countries and dependent territories. In 1959 a European Court of Human Rights was created. But British citizens were not able to bring cases before the European Court until 1966 when the right of petition was conferred on them. Incorporation of the ECHR into domestic law was then a distant prospect. Nevertheless, the concepts of the ECHR gradually exerted greater and greater influence on the development of our law and the integration of our legal system in European legal culture accelerated. In the late 1960s and 1970s anti-discrimination legislation in the United Kingdom was testimony to a new attitude to human rights. And in the 1980s and 1990s judges transformed the judicial review system to measure up to the previously somewhat empty theme of judges standing between individuals and the executive. But it was only in 1998 that a New Labour government, in an initial burst of enthusiasm for moral causes, secured the passing of the Human Rights Act 1998.

What kind of human rights instrument has been incorporated into our law? The ECHR had two principal objectives.[9] The first was to maintain and further realise human rights and fundamental freedoms. The framers of the Convention recognised that it was not only morally right to promote the observance of human rights but that it was also the best way of developing pluralistic and just societies in which all can peaceably go about their lives. The second aim was to foster effective political democracy. This aim necessarily involves the creation of conditions of stability and order under the rule of law, not for its own sake, but as the best way of ensuring the well-being of the inhabitants of the European countries. After all, democratic government has only one raison d'être, namely to serve the interests of all the people. The inspirers of the ECHR among whom Winston Churchill played an important role, and the framers of the ECHR ably assisted by English draftsmen, realised that from time to time the fundamental right of one individual may conflict with the human right of another. Thus the principles of free speech and privacy may collide. They also realised only too well that a single-minded concentration on the pursuit of fundamental rights of individuals to the exclusion of the interests of the wider public might be subversive of the ideal of tolerant European liberal democracies. The fundamental rights of individuals are of supreme importance but those rights are not unlimited: we live in communities of individuals who also have rights. The direct lineage of this

---

[9] I have repeated much of what I said in *Brown v. Stott* [2001] 2 W.L.R. 817, 839–840.

ancient idea is clear: Article 29 of the Universal Declaration of Human Rights (1948) expressly recognised the duties of everyone to the community and the limitation on rights in order to secure and protect respect for the rights of others. It is also noteworthy that Article 17 ECHR prohibits individuals from abusing their rights to the detriment of others. Thus, notwithstanding the danger of intolerance towards ideas, the Convention system draws a line which does not accord the protection of free speech to those who propagate racial hatred against minorities: Article 10. This is to be contrasted with the categorical language of the First Amendment to the United States Constitution which provides that "Congress shall make no law . . . abridging the freedom of speech". The ECHR requires that where difficult questions arise a balance must be struck. Subject to a limited number of absolute guarantees, the scheme and structure of the Convention reflects this balanced approach.

I now turn to the Human Rights Act 1998. It is a carefully and subtly crafted instrument. It proceeds on the basis that parliamentary sovereignty is the paramount principle of our constitution. That principle remains intact. But Parliament, recognising the moral and instrumental values for our democracy, legislated to ensure that fundamental rights under the ECHR are observed. It enjoins ministers in charge of Bills to make statements of compatibility or—at a political cost—incompatibility of bills. It enjoins courts to interpret primary and subordinate legislation, so far as it is possible to do, in a way which is compatible with Convention rights. And, if such a reading down is impossible, it is the duty of the court to issue a declaration of incompatibility, leaving Parliament to legislate compatibly with the ECHR or face the political cost of not doing so. Contrary to what sectors of the press suggest, this is not judges seizing power: it is the obligations imposed on them by Parliament.

The statute is a constitutional measure which has created, and will continue for some time to create, changes in murkier areas of English law. This exercise is a profoundly valuable one for our country. The impact of the statute will extend beyond the strict limits of the statute. The 1998 Act did not create a separate regime. There is one legal system in which the common law, statute law and the 1998 Act coalesce. Thus as English courts become used to applying the principle of proportionality in Convention rights cases, they are likely also to apply it in other cases where that is logically appropriate. It is also possible that the privacy provision in Article 8 ECHR may lead to developments beyond its scope. I say possible because in general I regard privacy as subordinate to freedom of expression.

It needs to be emphasised that the ECHR is a product of its time, having been drafted at the very infancy of the modern human rights movement. By contrast the ICCPR of 1966 which the United Kingdom ratified in 1976 is a more comprehensive human rights instrument. For present purposes this point can be illustrated by the anti-discrimination provisions in the two texts. Article 14 ECHR provides:

> The enjoyment of the rights and freedoms set forth in this Convention shall be secured without discrimination on any ground such as sex, race, colour, language, religion, political or other opinion, national or social

origin, association with a national minority, property, birth or other status.

This is a parasitic provision: its protection is limited to the scope of the rights and freedoms secured by the Convention. There is no free standing anti-discrimination provision in this convention. In this respect the ECHR failed to measure up to the Universal Declaration, which proclaimed the centrality of equality in a human rights system.[10] In contradistinction the ICCPR contains such a provision. Article 26 provides as follows:

> All persons are equal before the law and are entitled without any discrimination to the equal protection of the law. In this respect, the law shall prohibit any discrimination and guarantee to all persons equal and effective protection against discrimination on any ground such as race, colour, sex, language, religion, political or other opinion, national or social origin, property, birth or other status.

The United Kingdom has not incorporated the ICCPR into our law. Moreover, the enforcement mechanism under the Optional Protocol does not avail individuals in the United Kingdom: the right of petition to the U.N. Human Rights Commission has not been extended to our citizens. The gap in the ECHR remains. Admittedly, in response to the ICCPR there is a protocol to the European Convention which creates a free-standing anti-discrimination provision.[11] It opened for signature in 1984. Our government has refused to ratify it.

A Cambridge-sponsored independent review conducted under the chairmanship of Professor Bob Hepple Q.C. recommended that there should be a single and comprehensive Equality Act in Britain.[12] The government's response was equivocal.[13] The prospect of the government inviting Parliament to enact an Equality Act is bleak. Fortunately, this is not the end of the story. There has been a renaissance of constitutionalism, notably in Australia, Canada, India, New Zealand and South Africa. It has not bypassed England. There is now a dialogue between Supreme Courts of constitutional democracies, notably in respect of human rights issues, in which the House of Lords participates. There has also been a process of constitutionalisation of our public law. One facet of it is that the weak anti-discrimination provision in the European Convention is now supplemented by the recognition by the courts of equality as a constitutional right.[14] I have summarised the strong content of this right in a published paper as follows[15]:

---

[10] Art. 7.
[11] Protocol 12.
[12] For a summary see "Equality: A New Framework" (2000) *The Source Public Management Journal*, September 4, 2000.
[13] H.L. Deb., col. 1423, April 25, 2001, which contains the government response by Baroness Howells of St Davids.
[14] Jeffrey Jowell, "Is Equality a Constitutional Principle?" (1994) 7 C.L.P. 1, 12–14; Lord Lester of Herne Hill, "Equality and United Kingdom Law: past, present and future" [2001] P.L. 77.
[15] "Common Law; Common Values: Common Rights: Common Law Principle for the 21st Century", London, July 17, 2001.

It is a fundamental tenet of democracy that both law and government accord every individual equal concern and respect for their welfare and dignity. Everyone is entitled to equal protection of the law, which should be applied without fear or favour. Law's necessary distinctions must be justified but must never be made on the grounds of race, colour, belief, gender or any other irrational ground. Individuals are protected by law from discrimination on those grounds.

This is a principle fit for a tolerant European liberal democracy. It is buttressed by the principle of constitutionality developed by the House of Lords in recent years. This principle is to the effect that, outside the Human Rights Act, Parliament cannot remove or dilute fundamental rights by general words: only a specific provision will suffice.[16]

This brings me to a more general point. A Bill of Rights cannot exist in a constitutional vacuum. It needs to fit into a constitutional structure of a democratic character. While we now have a written Bill of Rights, we have no written constitution as such. But I do suggest that we embark on such an ambitious project. Nevertheless, I venture to suggest that pragmatically we ought to re-examine our institutional arrangements with a view to answering the question: are all current practices and conventions necessary and do they serve the needs of a modern constitutional democracy? I am an optimist. I believe that we are inching towards becoming a constitutional state. The changed landscape can be illustrated by three developments, ranging from the banal to the fundamental:

(a) By and large English judges now speak not about subjects but about citizens or individuals. In the rights-based legal culture now prevalent that was inevitable.

(b) Perhaps due in part to the fact that the United Kingdom has four law districts—England, Wales, Northern Ireland and Scotland—the notion of a state was not known to our law. The mystification has now disappeared. It is now beyond doubt that individuals have rights against the state and its agencies.

(c) The idea that injunctive relief could not be granted against ministers of the Crown, or only exceptionally, lingered on in our system.[17] A very recent Privy Council decision in a case from Grenada has finally established that ministers have no immunity or quasi immunity. The rule of law applies to all.[18]

The 1998 Act has, of course, invigorated the process of constitutionalisation of public law. It has put on the agenda structural changes in our system. The Lord Chancellor is a Cabinet minister. Nevertheless, from time to time he sits in the Appellate Committee, admittedly rarely and only in the most unimportant private law cases. His right to do so is now controversial. Appellate Committees which include the Lord Chancellor may not fulfil the requirement

---

[16] *R. v. Secretary of State for the Home Department, ex p. Simms* [2000] 2 A.C. 115.
[17] *M v. Home Office* [1994] A.C. 377.
[18] *Gairy v. Att.-Gen. of Grenada* [2002] 1 A.C. 167.

of independence required by Article 6 ECHR. Following *Pinochet (No. 2)*,[19] the House may have to rule on the issue at any time. Even 10 years ago Law Lords participated in debate in the House of Lords freely and in large numbers. Now there is a change. The Law Lords rarely exercise this right. The sooner it withers away altogether the better. The Home Secretary's power to decide on terms to be served by young persons sentenced to be detained at Her Majesty's pleasure has been abolished. The remaining power of the Home Secretary to decide on terms to be served by *adult* mandatory life sentence prisoners will now have to be considered by the House of Lords. Furthermore, it is no longer acceptable that alone among constitutional democracies our country does not have a supreme court. Public confidence in the administration of justice would be enhanced and the public interest would be advanced if the highest court in the land ceased to be a committee of the legislature. What is required is a proper supreme court as an independent branch of government in our parliamentary democracy in which the final word rests with Parliament. The Lord Chancellor dismissed a proposal along these lines when it was put forward by Lord Bingham of Cornhill, the Senior Law Lord.[20] This is not surprising because such a step would necessarily mean that there is no place for the Lord Chancellor in the highest court. Powerful politicians do not readily give up power. But the march of events may compel what on practical and pragmatic grounds is now undoubtedly in the public interest. It would be impudent to suggest that in a Supreme Court there would be a place for émigré South African lawyers. But, given the massive contribution of past and present Scots Law Lords, it would be essential in any new constitutional arrangement to retain the presence of Scots lawyers.

In bringing my reflections to a close I return to the Universal Declaration of Human Rights. The chords of the Declaration should be our theme in good times and in bad times. Undoubtedly, democracies may defend themselves against those who wish to destroy them. But there are limits to the means which democracies ought to employ. In the context of terrorism President Barak of the Israeli Supreme Court recently expressed this idea as follows[21]:

> This is the destiny of democracy, as not all means are acceptable to it, and not all practices employed by its enemies are open before it. Although a democracy must often fight with one hand tied behind its back, it nonetheless has the upper hand. Preserving the Rule of Law and recognition of an individual's liberty constitutes an important component in its understanding of security. At the end of the day, they strengthen its spirit and its strength and allow it to overcome its difficulties.

In my view the suspension of Article 5 ECHR—which prevents arbitrary detention—so that people can be locked up without trial when there is no evidence on which they could be prosecuted is not in present circumstances

---

[19] [2000] 1 A.C. 119.
[20] Lord Bingham of Cornhill, "The Highest Court in the Land", a lecture delivered at Gray's Inn on October 24, 2000; see also the powerful criticism of the status quo by Lord Alexander of Weedon, Denning Society 2001 Lecture, October 30, 2001.
[21] *Public Committee Against Torture in Israel v. The State of Israel*, September 16, 1999.

justified. One recalls the words of Lord Atkin, dissenting in *Liversidge v. Anderson*,[22] at a time when this country faced its greatest peril:

> In this country, amid the clash of arms, the laws are not silent. They may be changed, but they speak the same language in war as in peace. It has always been one of the pillars of freedom, one of the principles of liberty for which on recent authority we are now fighting, that the judges are no respecters of persons and stand between the subject and any attempted encroachments on his liberty by the executive, alert to see that any coercive action is justified in law.

The second report of the Joint Select Committee on Human Rights has observed:

> Parliament should take a long view, and resist the temptation to grant powers to governments which compromise the rights and liberties of individuals. The situations which may appear to justify the granting of such powers are temporary—the loss of freedom is often permanent... Too many ill-conceived measures litter the statute book as a result of such rushed legislation in the past.[23]

In the language of a preamble of the Treaty the European Union is said to be founded upon "the principles of liberty, democracy and respect for human rights and fundamental freedoms" and we must uphold those values.

---

[22] [1942] A.C. 206, 244.
[23] 2001–02 H.L. 37/H.C. 372, paras 76 and 79.

[14]
The Case of Augusto Pinochet: A Breakthrough*
Reg. v. Bow Street Metropolitan Stipendiary Magistrate Ex parte Pinochet Ugarte
[2002] 1 A.C. 61, 111

LORD STEYN. My Lords, the way in which this appeal comes before the House must be kept in mind. Spain took preliminary steps under the Extradition Act 1989 to obtain the extradition of General Pinochet, the former head of state of Chile, in respect of crimes which he allegedly committed between 11 September 1973 and March 1990 when he ceased to be the President of Chile. General Pinochet applied to the Divisional Court for a ruling that he is entitled to immunity as a former head of state from criminal and civil process in the English courts. He obtained a ruling to that effect. If that ruling is correct, the extradition proceedings are at an end. The issues came to the Divisional Court in advance of the receipt of a particularised request for extradition by Spain. Such a request has now been received. Counsel for General Pinochet has argued that the House ought to refuse to admit the request in evidence. In my view it would be wrong to ignore the material put forward in Spain's formal request for extradition. This case ought to be decided on the basis of all the relevant materials before the House. And that involves also taking into account the further evidence lodged on behalf of General Pinochet.

In an appeal in which no fewer than 14 barristers were involved over six days it is not surprising that issues proliferated. Some of the issues do not need to be decided. For example, there was an issue as to the date upon which General Pinochet became the head of state of Chile. He undoubtedly became the head of state at least by 26 June 1974; and I will assume that from the date of the coup d'état on 11 September 1973 he was the head of state. Rather than attempt to track down every other hare that has been started, I will concentrate my observations on three central issues, namely (1) the nature of the charges brought by Spain against General Pinochet; (2) the question whether he is entitled to former head of state immunity under the applicable statutory provisions; (3) if he is not entitled to such immunity, the different question whether under the

112

common law act of state doctrine the House ought to declare that the matters involved are not justiciable in our courts. This is not the order in which counsel addressed the issues but the advantage of so considering the issues is considerable. One can only properly focus on the legal issues before the House when there is clarity about the nature of the charges in respect of which General Pinochet seeks to establish immunity or seeks to rely on the act of state doctrine. Logically, immunity must be examined before act of state. The act of state issue will only arise if the court decides that the defendant does not have immunity. And I shall attempt to show that the construction of the relevant statutory provisions relating to immunity has a bearing on the answer to the separate question of act of state.

The case against General Pinochet

In the Divisional Court Lord Bingham of Cornhill C.J. summarised the position by saying that the thrust of the warrant "makes it plain that the applicant is charged not with personally torturing or murdering victims or ordering their disappearance, but with using the power of the state to that end." Relying on the information contained in the request for extradition, it is necessary to expand the cryptic account of the facts in the warrant. The request alleges a systematic campaign of repression against various groups in Chile after the military coup on 11 September 1973. The case is that of the order of 4,000 individuals were killed or simply disappeared. Such killings and disappearances mostly took place in Chile but some also took place in various countries abroad. Such acts were committed during the period from 11 September 1973 until 1990. The climax of the repression was reached in 1974 and 1975. The principal instrumentality of the oppression was the Dirección de Inteligencia Nacional ("D.I.N.A."), the secret police. The subsequent re-naming of this organisation is immaterial. The case is that agents of D.I.N.A., who were specially trained in torture techniques, tortured victims on a vast scale in secret torture chambers in Santiago and elsewhere in Chile. The torturers were invariably dressed in civilian clothes. Hooded doctors were present during torture sessions. The case is not one of interrogators acting in excess of zeal. The case goes much further. The request explains:

> "The most usual method was 'the grill' consisting of a metal table on which the victim was laid naked and his extremities tied and electrical shocks were applied to the lips, genitals, wounds or metal prosthesis; also two persons, relatives or friends, were placed in two metal drawers one on top of the other so that when the one above was tortured the psychological impact was felt by the other; on other occasions the victim was suspended from a bar by the wrists and/or the knees, and over a prolonged period while held in this situation electric current was applied to him, cutting wounds were inflicted or he was beaten; or the 'dry submarine' method was applied, i.e. placing a bag on the head until close to suffocation, also drugs were used and boiling water was thrown on various detainees to punish them as a foretaste for the death which they would later suffer."

113

As the Divisional Court observed, it is not alleged that General Pinochet personally committed any of these acts by his own hand. The case is, however, that agents of D.I.N.A. committed the acts of torture and that D.I.N.A. was directly answerable to General Pinochet rather than to the military junta. And the case is that D.I.N.A. undertook and arranged the killings, disappearances and torturing of victims on the orders of General Pinochet. In other words, what is alleged against General Pinochet is not constructive criminal responsibility. The case is that he ordered and procured the criminal acts which the warrant and request for extradition specify. The allegations have not been tested in a court of law. The House is not required to examine the correctness of the allegations. The House must assume the correctness of the allegations as the backcloth of the questions of law arising on this appeal.

The former head of state immunity

It is now possible to turn to the point of general public importance involved in the Divisional Court's decision, namely "the proper interpretation and scope of the immunity enjoyed by a former head of state from arrest and extradition proceedings in the United Kingdom in respect of acts committed while he was head of state." It is common ground that a head of state while in office has an absolute immunity against civil or criminal proceedings in the English courts. If General Pinochet had still been head of state of Chile, he would be immune from the present extradition proceedings. But he has ceased to be a head of state. He claims immunity as a former head of state. Counsel for General Pinochet relied on provisions contained in Part I of the State Immunity Act 1978. Part I does not apply to criminal proceedings: see section 16(4). It is irrelevant to the issues arising on this appeal. The only arguable basis for such an immunity originates in section 20(1) of the Act of 1978. It provides:

> "Subject to the provisions of this section and to any necessary modifications, the Diplomatic Privileges Act 1964 shall apply to—(*a*) a sovereign or other head of state; (*b*) members of his family forming part of his household; and (*c*) his private servants, as it applies to the head of a diplomatic mission, to members of his family forming part of his household and to his private servants."

It is therefore necessary to turn to the relevant provisions of the Diplomatic Privileges Act 1964. The relevant provisions are contained in articles 31, 38 and 39 of the Vienna Convention on Diplomatic Relations which in part forms Schedule 1 to the Act of 1964. Article 31 provides that a diplomatic agent shall enjoy immunity from criminal jurisdiction in the receiving state. Article 38(1) reads:

> "Except in so far as additional privileges and immunities may be granted by the receiving state, a diplomatic agent who is a national of or permanently resident in that state shall enjoy only immunity from jurisdiction, and inviolability, in respect of *official* acts performed in the exercise of his functions." (My emphasis.)

114

Article 39, so far as it is relevant, reads:

> "(1) Every person entitled to privileges and immunities shall enjoy them from the moment he enters the territory of the receiving state . . . (2) When the functions of a person enjoying privileges and immunities have come to an end, such privileges and immunities shall normally cease at the moment when he leaves the country, or on expiry of a reasonable period in which to do so, but shall subsist until that time, even in case of armed conflict. *However, with respect to acts performed by such a person in the exercise of his functions as a member of the mission, immunity shall continue to subsist.*" (My emphasis.)

Given the different roles of a member of a diplomatic mission and a head of state, as well as the fact that a diplomat principally acts in the receiving state whereas a head of state principally acts in his own country, the legislative technique of applying article 39(2) to former a head of state is somewhat confusing. How the necessary modifications required by section 20 of the Act of 1978 are to be achieved is not entirely straightforward. Putting to one side the immunity of a serving head of state, my view is that section 20, read with the relevant provisions of the Schedule to the Act of 1964, should be read as providing that a former head of state shall enjoy immunity from the criminal jurisdiction of the United Kingdom with respect to his official acts performed in the exercise of his functions as head of state. That was the synthesis of the convoluted provisions helpfully offered by Mr. Lloyd Jones, who appeared as amicus curiae. Neither counsel for General Pinochet nor counsel for the Spanish Government questioned this formulation. For my part it is the only sensible reconstruction of the legislative intent. It is therefore plain that statutory immunity in favour of a former head of state is not absolute. It requires the coincidence of two requirements: (1) that the defendant is a former head of state (ratione personae in the vocabulary of international law) and (2) that he is charged with official acts performed in the exercise of his functions as a head of state (ratione materiae). In regard to the second requirement it is not sufficient that official acts are involved: the acts must also have been performed by the defendant in the exercise of his functions as head of state.

On the assumption that the allegations of fact contained in the warrant and the request are true, the central question is whether those facts must be regarded as official acts performed in the exercise of the functions of a head of state. Lord Bingham of Cornhill C.J. observed that a former head of state is clearly entitled to immunity from process in respect of some crimes. I would accept this proposition. Rhetorically, the Lord Chief Justice then posed the question: "Where does one draw the line?" After a detailed review of the case law and literature, he concluded that even in respect of acts of torture the former head of state immunity would prevail. That amounts to saying that there is no or virtually no line to be drawn. Collins J. went further. He said:

> "The submission was made that it could never be in the exercise of such functions to commit crimes as serious as those allegedly committed by the applicant. Unfortunately history shows that it has

115

indeed on occasions been state policy to exterminate or to oppress particular groups. One does not have look very far back in history to see examples of the sort of thing having happened. There is in my judgment no justification for reading any limitation based on the nature of the crimes committed into the immunity which exists."

It is inherent in this stark conclusion that there is no or virtually no line to be drawn. It follows that when Hitler ordered the "final solution" his act must be regarded as an official act deriving from the exercise of his functions as head of state. That is where the reasoning of the Divisional Court inexorably leads. Counsel for General Pinochet submitted that this conclusion is the inescapable result of the statutory wording.

My Lords, the concept of an individual acting in his capacity as head of state involves a rule of law which must be applied to the facts of a particular case. It invites classification of the circumstances of a case as falling on a particular side of the line. It contemplates at the very least that some acts of a head of state may fall beyond even the most enlarged meaning of official acts performed in the exercise of the functions of a head of state. If a head of state kills his gardener in a fit of rage that could by no stretch of the imagination be described as an act performed in the exercise of his functions as head of state. If a head of state orders victims to be tortured in his presence for the sole purpose of enjoying the spectacle of the pitiful twitchings of victims dying in agony (what Montaigne described as the farthest point that cruelty can reach) that could not be described as acts undertaken by him in the exercise of his functions as a head of state. Counsel for General Pinochet expressly, and rightly, conceded that such crimes could not be classified as official acts undertaken in the exercise of the functions of a head of state. These examples demonstrate that there is indeed a meaningful line to be drawn.

How and where the line is to be drawn requires further examination. Is this question to be considered from the vantage point of the municipal law of Chile, where most of the acts were committed, or in the light of the principles of customary international law? Municipal law cannot be decisive as to where the line is to be drawn. If it were the determining factor, the most abhorrent municipal laws might be said to enlarge the functions of a head of state. But I need not dwell on the point because it is conceded on behalf of General Pinochet that the distinction between official acts performed in the exercise of functions as a head of state and acts not satisfying these requirements must depend on the rules of international law. It was at one stage argued that international law spells out no relevant criteria and is of no assistance. In my view that is not right. Negatively, the development of international law since the second world war justifies the conclusion that by the time of the 1973 coup d'état, and certainly ever since, international law condemned genocide, torture, hostage-taking and crimes against humanity (during an armed conflict or in peace time) as international crimes deserving of punishment. Given this state of international law, it seems to me difficult to maintain that the commission of such high crimes may amount to acts performed in the exercise of the functions of a head of state.

116

The essential fragility of the claim to immunity is underlined by the insistence on behalf of General Pinochet that it is not alleged that he "personally" committed any of the crimes. That means that he did not commit the crimes by his own hand. It is apparently conceded that if he personally tortured victims the position would be different. This distinction flies in the face of an elementary principle of law, shared by all civilised legal systems, that there is no distinction to be drawn between the man who strikes, and a man who orders another to strike. It is inconceivable that in enacting the Act of 1978 Parliament would have wished to rest the statutory immunity of a former head of state on a different basis.

On behalf of General Pinochet it was submitted that acts by police, intelligence officers and military personnel are paradigm official acts. In this absolute form I do not accept the proposition. For example, why should what was allegedly done in secret in the torture chambers of Santiago on the orders of General Pinochet be regarded as official acts? Similarly, why should the murders and disappearances allegedly perpetrated by D.I.N.A. in secret on the orders of General Pinochet be regarded as official acts? But, in any event, in none of these cases is the further essential requirement satisfied, viz. that in an international law sense these acts were part of the functions of a head of state. The normative principles of international law do not require that such high crimes should be classified as acts performed in the exercise of the functions of a head of state. For my part I am satisfied that as a matter of construction of the relevant statutory provisions the charges brought by Spain against General Pinochet are properly to be classified as conduct falling beyond the scope of his functions as head of state. Qualitatively, what he is alleged to have done is no more to be categorised as acts undertaken in the exercise of the functions of a head of state than the examples already given of a head of state murdering his gardener or arranging the torture of his opponents for the sheer spectacle of it. It follows that in my view General Pinochet has no statutory immunity.

Counsel for General Pinochet further argued that if he is not entitled to statutory immunity, he is nevertheless entitled to immunity under customary international law. International law recognises no such wider immunity in favour of a former head of state. In any event, if there had been such an immunity under international law, section 20, read with article 39(2), would have overridden it. General Pinochet is not entitled to an immunity of any kind.

The act of state doctrine

Counsel for General Pinochet submitted that, even if he fails to establish the procedural bar of statutory immunity, the House ought to uphold his challenge to the validity of the warrant on the ground of the act of state doctrine. They argued that the validity of the warrant and propriety of the extradition proceedings necessarily involve an investigation by the House of governmental or official acts which largely took place in Chile. They relied on the explanation of the doctrine of act of state by Lord Wilberforce in *Buttes Gas and Oil Co v. Hammer* [1982] A.C. 888. Counsel for General Pinochet further put forward wide-ranging

117

political arguments about the consequences of the extradition proceedings, such as adverse internal consequences in Chile and damage to the relations between the United Kingdom and Chile. Plainly it is not appropriate for the House to take into account such political considerations. And the same applies to the argument suggesting past "acquiescence" by the United Kingdom Government.

Concentrating on the legal arguments, I am satisfied that there are several reasons why the act of state doctrine is inapplicable. First the House is not being asked to investigate, or pass judgment on, the facts alleged in the warrant or request for extradition. The task of the House is simply to take note of the allegations and to consider and decide the legal issues of immunity and act of state. Secondly, the issue of act of state must be approached on the basis that the intent of Parliament was not to give statutory immunity to a former head of state in respect of the systematic torture and killing of his fellow citizens. The ground of this conclusion is that such high crimes are not official acts committed in the exercise of the functions of a head of state. In those circumstances it cannot be right for the House to enunciate an enlarged act of state doctrine, stretching far beyond anything said in the *Buttes Gas* case, to protect a former head of state from the consequences of his private crimes. Thirdly, any act of state doctrine is displaced by section 134(1) of the Criminal Justice Act 1988 in relation to torture and section 1(1) of the Taking of Hostages Act 1982. Both Acts provide for the taking of jurisdiction over foreign governmental acts. Fourthly, and more broadly, the Spanish authorities have relied on crimes of genocide, torture, hostage-taking and crimes against humanity. It has in my view been clearly established that by 1973 such acts were already condemned as high crimes by customary international law. In these circumstances it would be wrong for the English courts now to extend the act of state doctrine in a way which runs counter to the state of customary international law as it existed in 1973. Since the act of state doctrine depends on public policy as perceived by the courts in the forum at the time of the suit the developments since 1973 are also relevant and serve to reinforce my view. I would endorse the observation in *American Law Institute, Restatement of the Law, The Foreign Relations Law of the United States,* 3d (1986), vol. 1, section 443, p. 370, to the effect that:

> "A claim arising out of an alleged violation of fundamental human rights—for instance, a claim on behalf of a victim of torture or genocide—would (if otherwise sustainable) probably not be defeated by the act of state doctrine, since the accepted international law of human rights is well established and contemplates external scrutiny of such acts."

But in adopting this formulation I would remove the word "probably" and substitute "generally." Finally, I must make clear that my conclusion does not involve the expression of any view on the interesting arguments on universality of jurisdiction in respect of certain international crimes and related jurisdictional questions. Those matters do not arise for decision.

I conclude that the act of state doctrine is inapplicable.

118

Conclusions

My Lords, since the hearing in the Divisional Court the case has in a number of ways been transformed. The nature of the case against General Pinochet is now far clearer. And the House has the benefit of valuable submissions from distinguished international lawyers. In the light of all the material now available I have been persuaded that the conclusion of the Divisional Court was wrong. For the reasons I have given I would allow the appeal.

Note

By a majority of three to two the House of Lords held that General Pinochet was not entitled to immunity. This decision was set aside on the ground that Lord Hoffman had not disclosed a connection with Amnesty International: *R v Bow Street Metropolitan Stipendiary Magistrate, Ex parte Pinochet Ugarte (No. 2)* [2000] 1 AC 119. On a rehearing the House upheld the first decision on immunity: *R v Bow Street Metropolitan Stipendiary Magistrate, Ex parte Pinochet Ugarte (No. 3)* [2000] 1 AC 147.

[15]
The New Legal Landscape[1]

It may be enough to say that it is morally right to respect human rights. They should be valued for their own sake. But the recognition and development of the human rights law is also the best guarantee there is of creating a world order in which countries, hopefully democratic, can flourish in peace, and the best guarantee of promoting a just and tolerant society in our pluralistic democracy. In support of this view I would cite Amartya Sen, the Nobel prize winner in 1998. He has pointed out that[1]:

> "... one of the remarkable facts in the terrible history of famines in the world is that no substantial famine has ever occurred in any country with a democratic form of government and a relatively free press. This applies not only to the affluent countries of Europe and America, but also to poor but broadly democratic countries (such as India, Botswana, Zimbabwe). Also, we have intertemporal evidence in the same direction when a country undergoes *transition* to democracy. For example, India continued to have famines right up to the time of independence in 1947 (the Bengal famine in 1943 killed between 2 and 3 million people,) and then it stopped quite abruptly with independence and the installation of a multi-party democratic system. No government can afford to face elections after a social calamity, nor can it deal easily with criticism from the media and opposition

---

[1] *Human Rights and Economic Achievements*, Chapter 3, The *East Asian Challenge for Human Rights*, at 92.

550 The New Legal Landscape

> parties while still in office. The incentive effects of these connections can be very powerful."

This is a most telling practical justification of human rights.

There has been a debate about the status of the Human Rights Act 1998. In the correspondence columns of *The Times* an experienced barrister recently expressed the view that in law the Human Rights Act has no higher status than the Dangerous Dogs Act 1991.[2] Given that the latter statute has been widely condemned as an appallingly drafted piece of legislation, this is a particularly trenchant point. Other commentators have also expressed the view that the Human Rights Act is no more than an ordinary statute. I would defend to the end the right of the proponents of this view to express it whilst recording my belief that it is wholly misconceived. Until the Human Rights Act came into force on October 2 this year the people of England had the benefit of the protections offered by the common law but they did not have the advantage of a Bill of Rights in any modern sense. True it is that there is a Bill of Rights going back to 1689 but that text was primarily concerned with establishing the rights of Parliament and members of Parliament. Now we have a true Bill of Rights, in the shape of the European Convention on Human Rights, incorporated into our law by the carefully and subtly crafted Human Rights Act 1998. It is a Bill of Rights akin to similar measures in many constitutions. In *Reynolds* I said that the Human Rights Act has a constitutional or higher legal order foundation.[3] The Human Rights Act 1998 is now part of what is otherwise an unwritten constitution.

One may then legitimately ask why does it matter whether the Human Rights Act has a constitutional or higher legal order status. It matters greatly. The fact that a right is entrenched in a Bill of Rights is compelling testimony that it is to be accorded a higher normative status than other rights. This will be particularly important in regard to the interpretation and application of the Convention and the Act. Constitutional adjudication needs to be approached generously in order to afford citizens the full measure of the protections of a Bill of Rights. By contrast, decisions taken day by day by commercial judges in respect of the meaning of, say, standard forms of letters of credit may sometimes employ relatively strict methods of construction. The Human Rights Act as a constitutional measure will influence not only the interpretation of statute law but also the development of common law. Decisions under it are not to be regarded as a separate stream of jurisprudence. The common law, statute law and the Human Rights Act coalesce in one unified legal system.

It is necessary to say something about the values of liberty, equality and justice which underlie the Human Rights Act and Convention. In the decision of the Privy Council in *Matadeen v. Pointu*, Lord Hoffmann, giving the judgment of the Privy Council, said[4]:

> "What the interpretation of commercial documents and constitutions have in common is that in each case the court is concerned with the meaning of the language which has been used. As Kentridge A.J. said in giving the judgment of the South African Constitutional Court in *State v. Zuma* (1995) 4 B.C.L.R. 401, 412:

---

[2] *The Times*, September 7, 2000.
[3] *Reynolds v. Times Newspapers* [1999] 3 W.L.R. 1010, at 1029H and 1030B.
[4] [1999] A.C. 94, at 108F.

'If the language used by the lawgiver is ignored in favour of a general resort to "values" the result is not interpretation but divination.' "

This is an important observation. So far as it goes it is also a valuable statement. But it has wrongly been pressed into service in aid of the austere argument that values are irrelevant to questions of interpretation of Bills of Rights in constitutions. That cannot be right. The Convention aims to promote the rule of law and standards of decency and justice in fair and tolerant democracies. As Francesca Klug has pointed out in her recent book, the Convention is the child of the Universal Declaration of Human Rights and is a distillation of ethical values.[5] An assessment of the weight of moral values, such as the dictates of individualised justice as against considerations of stability and order, will be of the essence of decision making under the Act.

It is also worth considering how the Convention will fit into our legal system. The differences in high technique between the common law and civilian system are well known. The case-by-case development of the common law has been the source of its strength. Judges have generally concentrated on practical justice in the case at hand, anchoring their decisions in custom and tradition, and at the same time exposing their reasoning processes in detail thereby facilitating the development of the law. This methodology is distinctively English in origin and is to be contrasted with the civilian tradition, influenced by systematic codes and cultural traditions favouring doctrine over pragmatism. Subject to giving proper effect to the Convention I do not foresee that English judges need to abandon pragmatism. The Convention readily fits into both the civilian and common law systems. This is hardly surprising. After all, English lawyers played a large part in drafting the Convention.

The spirit of liberty is the dominant theme of the common law. Whatever is not specifically forbidden, individuals and their enterprises are free to do. By contrast the government and its agencies may only do what the law permits; what is done in the name of people requires constant examination and justification. This theme too matches the aspirations of the Convention.

Given that the Convention does not deal exhaustively with human rights, three common law developments will remain of continuing relevance. First, generally statutes will be held to be "always speaking"; they must be interpreted in the light of the current conditions and in the light of their place within the system of norms currently in force.[6] Secondly, in accordance with the principle of legality, as authoritatively explained in *Simms*, general words will be insufficient to trench on basic rights.[7] And generally the legislature employs general words to achieve its objectives. Thirdly, it is important to bear in mind the backcloth of common law recognition of fundamental rights. Here the gradual recognition by our courts of some basic rights as constitutional in character is of great importance. I have in mind rights such as freedom of expression, the principle of equality, the absolute right to a fair trial, and access to justice for all. This process has not come to an end with the coming into operation of the Human Rights Act. Let me give one illustration. The anti-discrimination provision contained in Article 14 of the Convention is parasitic inasmuch as it serves only to

---

[5] *Values for a Godless Age: The Story of the United Kingdom's New Bill of Rights* (Penguin Books, 2000).
[6] *R. v. Ireland* [1998] A.C. 147, at 158D-G; *Cross Statutory Interpretation* (3rd ed., 1995), p. 83.
[7] *R. v. Secretary of State for the Home Department, ex p. Simms* [1999] 3 W.L.R. 328.

protect specific Convention rights. There is no general or free-standing prohibition of discrimination. This is a relatively weak protection. On the other hand, the constitutional principle of equality developed domestically by our courts is stronger. In our system the law and the government must accord to every individual equal concern and respect for their welfare and dignity. Everyone is entitled to equal protection of the law, which must be applied without fear or favour. Law's necessary distinctions must be justified but must never be made on the grounds of race, colour, belief, gender or other irrational ground. Individuals are protected by the domestic principle of equality from discrimination on those grounds. It has a continuing role to play. The organic development of constitutional rights is therefore a complementary and parallel process to the application of the Human Rights Act.

And, more broadly, there has been a renaissance constitutionalism in many countries including Australia, Canada, India, New Zealand and South Africa. Developments in those countries are of great importance to us. This renaissance of constitutionalism has not bypassed the United Kingdom. A culture of justification now prevails in our country: it requires constitutional arrangements which diverge from fundamental constitutional principle to be justified pragmatically as being in the public interest. It is strongly reinforced by the Human Rights Act. In this context *Wade and Forsyth* in the recently published edition of their book observed[8]: "Any mixture of judicial with legislative or executive functions, a familiar feature in our tolerant Constitution, is now likely to prove vulnerable, from temporary sheriffs in Scotland at one end of the scale to the Lord Chancellor himself at the other." Another topical matter relates to the Home Secretary. The Home Secretary no longer takes decisions on the length of detention of the most dangerous category of prisoners, namely persons sentenced to discretionary life sentences. In the *Venables and Thompson* case[9] the European Court of Human Rights decided that the Home Secretary's power to decide on the period of imprisonment of young persons detained during Her Majesty's pleasure does not satisfy the Convention standard of impartial decisions by an independent tribunal. A Bill is now before Parliament to judicialize the system in respect of young persons.[10] But, despite the reasoning of the European Court, the Home Secretary maintains that the position in regard to adult prisoners is different. The lawfulness of this position will undoubtedly have to be subjected to scrutiny.

The major focus will be on the application of the Human Rights Act across the spectrum of English law notably in a few of its murkier corners. This has caused some tabloid newspapers and some broadsheets to describe the Act as a recipe for chaos. They fear that traffic will be brought to a halt; that disciplinary proceedings will be rendered toothless; and that serious crime will go unpunished. It will apparently rain sulphur and brimstone. The premise of this hysteria is that the courts will accede to every impractical and implausible claim, ignoring the balance inherent to the Convention between individual rights and conditions of stability and order required even in a liberal democracy. This ignores the fact that the direct application of the Convention has caused no such chaos in other European democracies. The truth is that our highly trained, independent and impartial judiciary, carrying out its task in accordance with

---

[8] Preface.
[9] (2000) 30 E.H.R.R. 121.
[10] Criminal Justice and Court Services Bill, at clause 55.

principles of institutional integrity, will approach the more extravagant claims made in the name of human rights with the scepticism which they deserve. Common sense has not been banished.

Let me take, for example, the fair trial provisions of Article 6 of the Convention, which will no doubt be the most frequently invoked provisions of the Convention. Concentrating on the criminal law, the approach of the judges will perhaps be that purpose of the criminal law is not punishment for its own sake. Its aim is to allow everyone to go about their daily lives without fear of harm to person or property. It promotes values of stability and order in which democracy can flourish for the benefit of all. A basic premise may be that in the words of John Stuart Mill the only purpose for which power can rightfully be exercised over any member of the community is to prevent harm to others.

Three considerations will constrain the application of the fair trial provisions. First, technical arguments have no place in Convention jurisprudence. Only matters of real substance are within its scope. Alleged breaches must reach a minimum level of severity to be entertained. Secondly, since the object of the Convention is the promotion of practical justice, the fairness of the trial must be determined in the light of the proceedings as a whole. Attempts to have such issues determined before trial are likely to be discouraged. The challenges will generally have to be made after the completion of the trial. Thirdly, and ultimately, there may be a tension between fairness to the individual and the public interest, and the courts will have to perform a balancing exercising. Given this framework the predictions of chaos are wide off the mark. The courts will no doubt allow some meritorious claims but I would apprehend that the vast majority of arguments advanced will fail to pass the tests laid down by the Convention. The experience in Scotland is instructive: there have been 600 Convention challenges of which 20 have succeeded. In any event, English judges are intensely aware that public confidence in the administration of justice is the bedrock of our legal system. While they cannot always please everybody, public confidence can only be maintained by a pattern of fair, balanced and sensible decisions under the Act. In my view the England judiciary is well up to this task. And decisions of our courts will in future have a profound effect on Strasbourg jurisprudence.

Let me sound a further word of caution. There is apparently a view in the legal profession that the Human Rights Act will open the door to wide ranging discovery and cross examination of witnesses. If this were right, it would cause severe problems for our already over-stretched administration of justice. But it is an unrealistic expectation. The Convention is also applicable in civilian countries where the discovery process is far more limited than in England. Subject to the demands of fairness in particular cases I would apprehend that the courts will in respect of discovery and oral evidence approach such cases very much in the way of which public law cases have been approached in the past. The scope for discovery and oral evidence will be limited. I regard it as important that first instance judges should make this clear from the very start of the operation of the Act.

That brings me to the question whether we can now claim to have by and large a fully developed human rights law. The answer must be that the development of our human rights law still has some way to go. The European Convention is a product of an era when human rights law was in its infancy. It is true that it is established that the European Convention must be interpreted as a living instrument in contemporary

554 The New Legal Landscape

conditions. But there are limits to the creative interpretation of specific Convention rights. There are gaps in the Convention. Time allows me to mention only the most important gap. The right of freedom of expression is spelt out in Article 10 the European Convention. It is a strong provision: it is the primary right and exceptions to it must be convincingly justified. But the idea of a right vesting in citizens to know what is done in their name by the state and its agencies is not to be found in the Convention. This is unsurprising: the notion of a right to know post dates 1950. But we now understand more clearly than our predecessors that a fully participatory democracy —Lincoln's government *of* the people, *by* the people, *for* the people—is only possible if the people have the necessary knowledge or at least the means of acquiring that knowledge. Freedom of expression is the very lifeblood of democracy. But it is truly meaningful only if there is full and effective freedom of information. A comprehensive Freedom of Information Act is the most important piece missing from the jigsaw of our law. Let us hope that Parliament will supply it.

[16]
The Ethos of the European Convention on Human Rights: *Brown v Stott**
[2003] 1 A.C. 681, 706

LORD STEYN

I The central question

On 3 June 1999 a vehicle belonging to Miss Brown was parked in a car park of a supermarket in Dunfermline. In reliance on section 172(2) of the Road Traffic Act 1988 a police officer asked Miss Brown who had been the driver of her vehicle when it entered the car park. She answered: "It was me." The police asked her for a specimen of breath. She gave a specimen. The breath test was positive. A prosecution ensued. The issue arose whether the procurator fiscal could lead evidence of the admission which Miss Brown had been compelled by law to make under section 172(2). The High Court of Justiciary 2000 SLT 379 held that section 172(2) is incompatible with the implied right against self-incrimination under article 6 of the European Convention for the Protection of Human Rights and Fundamental Freedoms and is therefore unlawful. In coming to this conclusion the High Court of Justiciary relied strongly on observations by the European court of Human Rights in *Saunders v United Kingdom* 23 EHRR 313, 337–338, paras 68–69. In the leading judgment of the Lord Justice General (Lord Rodger of Earlsferry), given with the approval of Lord Marnoch and Lord Allanbridge, the essential reasoning was as follows, at p 391:

"In fact the Solicitor General's argument is incompatible with the actual approach of the court in *Saunders*. The court held that the general requirements of fairness contained in article 6, including the right not to incriminate oneself, apply to criminal proceedings in respect of *all* types of criminal offences without distinction, from the most simple to the most complex. The court's conclusion on this point can be derived simply from the generality of the wording of article 6 which applies to the determination of '*any* criminal charge'. If the right not to incriminate oneself is inherent in the right to a fair hearing under article 6, then it must apply to all criminal trials covered by the article. More importantly, however, the court's conclusion is justified by the very nature of the right. If, as the court held, it lies at the heart of the notion of a fair procedure, then it must be a central right which applies to any criminal trial. Moreover, it is hard to see how there could be gradations of fairness depending on the seriousness of the charges in any given case. In any event, any central right would necessarily apply to the trial of an offence, such as a contravention of section 5(1) of the 1988 Act, which carries a possible penalty of imprisonment. In my view therefore there is nothing in the circumstances of the present case which would justify a restrictive interpretation or application of the right conferred by article 6(1)."

This comes very close to saying that the privilege against self-incrimination is an absolute Convention right and that no interference with it could ever be justified. Indeed it is far from clear what space, if any, is left for treating the privilege against self-incrimination as not absolute.

II *The objectives of the Convention*

In the first real test of the Human Rights Act 1998 it is opportune to stand back and consider what the basic aims of the Convention are. One finds the explanation in the very words of the preambles of the Convention. There were two principal objectives. The first was to maintain and further realise human rights and fundamental freedoms. The framers of the Convention recognised that it was not only morally right to promote the observance of human rights but that it was also the best way of achieving pluralistic and just societies in which all can peaceably go about their lives. The second aim was to foster effective political democracy. This aim necessarily involves the creation of conditions of stability and order under the rule of law, not for its own sake, but as the best way to ensuring the well being of the inhabitants of the European countries. After all, democratic government has only one raison d'être, namely to serve the interests of all the people. The inspirers of the European Convention, among whom Winston Churchill played an important role, and the framers of the European Convention, ably assisted by English draftsmen, realised that from time to time the fundamental right of one individual may conflict with the human right of another. Thus the principles of free speech and privacy may collide. They also realised only too well that a single-minded concentration on the pursuit of fundamental rights of individuals to the exclusion of the interests of the wider public might be subversive of the ideal of tolerant European liberal democracies. The fundamental rights of individuals are of supreme importance but those rights are not unlimited: we live in communities of individuals who also have rights. The direct lineage of this ancient idea is clear: the European Convention (1950) is the descendant of the Universal Declaration of Human Rights (1948) which in article 29 expressly recognised the duties of everyone to the community and the limitation on rights in order to secure and protect respect for the rights of others. It is also noteworthy that article 17 of the European Convention prohibits, among others, individuals from abusing their rights to the detriment of others. Thus, notwithstanding the danger of intolerance towards ideas, the Convention system draws a line which does not accord the protection of free speech to those who propagate racial hatred against minorities: article 10; *Jersild v Denmark* (1994) 19 EHRR 1, 26, para 31. This is to be contrasted with the categorical language of the First Amendment to the United States Constitution which provides that "Congress shall make no law . . . abridging the freedom of speech." The European Convention requires that where difficult questions arise a balance must be struck. Subject to a limited number of absolute guarantees, the scheme and structure of the Convention reflects this balanced approach. It differs in material respects from other constitutional systems but as a European nation it represents our Bill of Rights. We must be guided by it. And it is a basic premise of the Convention system that only an entirely neutral, impartial, and independent judiciary can carry out the primary task of securing and enforcing Convention rights. This contextual scene is not only directly relevant to the issues arising on the present appeal but may be a matrix in which many challenges under the Human Rights Act 1998 should be considered.

III Article 6

The present case is concerned with article 6 of the Convention which guarantees to every individual a fair trial in civil and criminal cases. The centrality of this principle in the Convention system has repeatedly been emphasised by the European court. But even in respect of this basic guarantee, there is a balance to be observed. First, it is well settled that the public interest may be taken into account in deciding what the right to a fair trial requires in a particular context. Thus in *Doorson v The Netherlands* (1996) 22 EHRR 330, 358, para 70 it was held that "principles of fair trial also require that in appropriate cases the interests of the defence are balanced against those of witnesses or victims called upon to testify". Only one specific illustration of this balanced approach is necessary. Provided they are kept "within reasonable limits" rebuttable presumptions of fact are permitted in criminal legislation: *Salabiaku v France* 13 EHRR 379. Secondly, once it has been determined that the guarantee of a fair trial has been breached, it is never possible to justify such breach by reference to the public interest or on any other ground. This is to be contrasted with cases where a trial has been affected by irregularities not amounting to denial of a fair trial. In such cases it is fair that a court of appeal should have the power, even when faced by the fact of irregularities in the trial procedure, to dismiss the appeal if in the view of the court of appeal the defendant's guilt is plain and beyond any doubt. However, it is a grave conclusion that a defendant has not had the substance of a fair trial. It means that the administration of justice has entirely failed. Subject to the possible exercise of a power to order a retrial where appropriate such a conviction can never be allowed to stand.

IV The privilege against self-incrimination

It is well settled, although not expressed in the Convention, that there is an implied privilege against self-incrimination under article 6. Moreover, section 172(2) undoubtedly makes an inroad on this privilege. On the other hand, it is also clear that the privilege against self-incrimination is not an absolute right. While there is no decision of the European court of Human Rights directly in point, it is noteworthy that closely related rights have been held not to be absolute. It is significant that the basic right of access to the courts has been held to be not absolute: *Golder v United Kingdom* 1 EHRR 524. The principle that everyone charged with a criminal offence shall be presumed innocent until proved guilty according to law is connected with the privilege against self-incrimination. Yet the former has been held not to be absolute: *Salabiaku v France* 13 EHRR 379. The European court has also had occasion to emphasise the close link between the right of silence and the privilege against self-incrimination: *Murray v United Kingdom* 22 EHRR 29. In *Murray* the European court held that the right of silence is not absolute.

In these circumstances it would be strange if a right not expressed in the Convention or any of its Protocols, but implied into article 6 of the Convention, had an absolute character. In my view the right in question is plainly not absolute. From this premise it follows that an interference with the right may be justified if the particular legislative provision was enacted in pursuance of a legitimate aim and if the scope of the legislative provision is necessary and proportionate to the achievement of the aim.

V Section 172(2)

In considering whether an inroad on the privilege against self-incrimination can be justified, it is necessary to concentrate on the particular context. An intense focus on section 172(2) is required. It reads:

> "Where the driver of a vehicle is alleged to be guilty of an offence to which this section applies—(a) the person keeping the vehicle shall give such information as to the identity of the driver as he may be required to give by or on behalf of a chief officer of police, and (b) any other person shall if required as stated above give any information which it is in his power to give and may lead to identification of the driver."

The penalty for failing to comply with section 172(2) is a fine of not more than £1,000. In addition an individual may be disqualified from driving and endorsement of the driver's licence is mandatory. It is well established that an oral admission made by a driver under section 172(2) is admissible in evidence: *Foster v Farrell* 1963 JC 46.

The subject of section 172(2) is the driving of vehicles. It is a notorious fact that vehicles are potentially instruments of death and injury. The statistics placed before the Board show a high rate of fatal and other serious accidents involving vehicles in Great Britain. The relevant statistics are as follows:

	1996	1997	1998
Fatal and serious accidents	40,601	39,628	37,770

The effective prosecution of drivers causing serious offences is a matter of public interest. But such prosecutions are often hampered by the difficulty of identifying the drivers of the vehicles at the time of, say, an accident causing loss of life or serious injury or potential danger to others. The tackling of this social problem seems in principle a legitimate aim for a legislature to pursue.

The real question is whether the legislative remedy in fact adopted is necessary and proportionate to the aim sought to be achieved. There were legislative choices to be made. The legislature could have decided to do no more than to exhort the police and prosecuting authorities to redouble their efforts. It may, however, be that such a policy would have been regarded as inadequate. Secondly, the legislature could have introduced a reverse burden of proof clause which placed the burden on the registered owner to prove that he was not the driver of the vehicle at a given time when it is alleged that an offence was committed. Thirdly, and this was the course actually adopted, there was the possibility of requiring information about the identity of the driver to be revealed by the registered owner and others. As between the second and third techniques it may be said that the latter involves the securing of an admission of a constituent element of the offence. On the other hand, such an admission, if wrongly made, is not conclusive. And it must be measured against the alternative of a reverse burden clause which could without further investigation of the identity of the driver lead to a prosecution. In their impact on the citizen the two techniques are not widely different. And it is rightly conceded that a properly drafted reverse burden of proof provision would have been lawful.

It is also important to keep in mind the narrowness of the interference. Section 172(2) is directed at obtaining information in one category, namely the identity of the driver at the time when an offence was allegedly committed. The most important part of section 172(2) is paragraph (a) since the relevant information is usually peculiarly within the knowledge of the owner. But there may be scope for using (b) in a limited category of cases, e g when only the identity of a passenger in the car is known. Section 172(2) does not authorise general questioning by the police to secure a confession of an offence. On the other hand, section 172(2) does, depending on the circumstances, in effect authorise the police officer to invite the owner to make an admission of one element in a driving offence. It would, however, be an abuse of the power under section 172(2) for the police officer to employ improper or overbearing methods of obtaining the information. He may go no further than to ask who the driver was at the given time. If the police officer strays beyond his power under section 172(2) a judge will have ample power at trial to exclude the evidence. It is therefore a relatively narrow interference with the privilege in one area which poses widespread and serious law enforcement problems.

VI What deference may be accorded to the legislature?

Under the Convention system the primary duty is placed on domestic courts to secure and protect Convention rights. The function of the European court of Human Rights is essential but supervisory. In that capacity it accords to domestic courts a margin of appreciation, which recognises that national institutions are in principle better placed than an international court to evaluate local needs and conditions. That principle is logically not applicable to domestic courts. On the other hand, national courts may accord to the decisions of national legislatures some deference *where the context justifies* it: see *R v Director of Public Prosecutions, Ex p Kebilene* [2000] 2 AC 326, 380–381 per Lord Hope of Craighead; see also: Singh, Hunt and Demetriou, "Is there a Role for the 'Margin of Appreciation' in National Law after the Human Rights Act?" [1999] EHRLR 15. This point is well explained in *Lester & Pannick, Human Rights Law and Practice* (1999), p 74:

> "Just as there are circumstances in which an international court will recognise that national institutions are better placed to assess the needs of society, and to make difficult choices between competing considerations, so national courts will accept that there are some circumstances in which the legislature and the executive are better placed to perform those functions."

In my view this factor is of some relevance in the present case. Here section 172(2) addresses a pressing social problem, namely the difficulty of law enforcement in the face of statistics revealing a high accident rate resulting in death and serious injuries. The legislature was entitled to regard the figures of serious accidents as unacceptably high. It would also have been entitled to take into account that it was necessary to protect other Convention rights, viz the right to life of members of the public exposed to the danger of accidents: see article 2(1). On this aspect the legislature was in as good a position as a court to assess the gravity of the problem and the public interest in addressing it. It really then boils down to the question whether in adopting the procedure enshrined in section 172(2), rather than a reverse burden technique, it took more drastic action than was justified. While this is ultimately a question for the court, it is not unreasonable to regard both techniques as permissible in the field of the driving of vehicles. After all, the subject invites special regulation; objectively the interference is narrowly circumscribed; and it is qualitatively not very different from requiring, for example, a breath specimen from a driver. Moreover, it is less invasive than an essential modern tool of crime detection such as the taking of samples from a suspect for DNA profiling. If the matter was not covered by authority, I would have concluded that section 172(2) is compatible with article 6.

VII *Saunders v United Kingdom*

The decision of the European court in *Saunders v United Kingdom* 23 EHRR 313 gave some support to the view of the High Court of Justiciary. With due respect I have to say that the reasoning in *Saunders* is unsatisfactory and less than clear: see the critique in Andrews, "Hiding Behind the Veil: Financial Delinquency and the Law" (1997) 22 ELR 369; Eriksen and Thorkildsen, "Self-Incrimination, The Ban on Self-Incrimination after the Saunders Judgment" (1997) 5 JFC 182; Davies, "Do polluters have the right not to incriminate themselves?" (1999) 143 SJ 924. The European court did not rule that the privilege against self-incrimination is absolute. Surprisingly in view of its decision in *Murray* 22 EHRR 29 that the linked right of silence is not absolute it left the point open in respect of the privilege against self-incrimination: 23 EHRR 313, 339–340, para 74.

On the other hand, the substance of its reasoning treats both privileges as not absolute. The court observed, at p 337, para 68:

> "The court recalls that, although not specifically mentioned in article 6 of the Convention, the right to silence and the right not to incriminate oneself, are generally recognised international standards which lie at the heart of the notion of a fair procedure under article 6. Their rationale lies, inter alia, in the protection of the accused against improper compulsion by the authorities thereby contributing to the avoidance of miscarriages of justice and to the fulfilment of the aims of article 6."

The court emphasised the rationale of improper compulsion. It does not hold that *anything* said under compulsion of law is inadmissible. Admittedly, the court also observed, at para 68:

> "The right not to incriminate oneself, in particular, presupposes that the prosecution in a criminal case seek to prove their case against the accused without resort to evidence obtained through methods of coercion or oppression in defiance of the will of the accused. In this sense the right is closely linked to the presumption of innocence contained in article 6(2) of the Convention."

Again one finds the link with the non-absolute right of silence. In any event "methods of coercion or oppression in defiance of the will of the accused" is probably another way of referring to improper compulsion. This is consistent with the following passage, at p 338, para 69:

> "In the present case the court is only called upon to decide whether the use made by the prosecution of the statements obtained from the applicant by the inspectors amounted to an unjustifiable infringement of the right. This question must be examined by the court in the light of all the circumstances of the case. In particular, it must be determined whether the applicant has been subject to compulsion to give evidence and whether the use made of the resulting testimony at his trial offended the basic principles of a fair procedure inherent in article 6(1) of which the right not to incriminate oneself is a constituent element."

The expression "unjustifiable infringement of the right" implies that some infringements may be justified. In my view the observations in *Saunders* do not support an absolutist view of the privilege against self-incrimination. It may be that the observations in *Saunders* will have to be clarified in a further case by the European court. As things stand, however, I consider that the High Court of Justiciary put too great weight on these observations. In my view they were never intended to apply to a case such as the present.

VIII Conclusion on article 6

That brings me back to the decision of the High Court of Justiciary. It treated the privilege against self-incrimination as virtually absolute. That conclusion fits uneasily into the balanced Convention system, and cannot be reconciled with article 6 in all its constituent parts and the spectrum of jurisprudence of the European court on the various facets of article 6.

I would hold that the decision of the High Court of Justiciary on the merits was wrong. The procurator fiscal is entitled to lead the evidence of Miss Brown's admission under section 172(2).

IX The remaining issues

I am in complete agreement with Lord Hope of Craighead that a devolution issue has been raised and I would respectfully endorse his reasons. I too would prefer not to express a view on the third issue.

X Disposal

For these reasons, as well as the reasons given by Lord Bingham of Cornhill, I would allow the appeal and quash the declaration made by the High Court.

*Note

The Privy Council was unanimous in allowing the appeal and ruling that evidence given by Miss Brown under section 172(2)(a) of the Road Traffic Act 1988, that she had been the driver of her car, could be led at her trial.

[17]
The Centrality of the Right to Fair Trial as a Human Rights Norm

Human rights law must of necessity be a rights-based system. The basic premise is that in a democratic society government exists in order to protect and promote the interests of the people. To achieve this goal, the actions of government and its agencies must be constrained by law and citizens must be given enforceable and effective legal rights against the state. In the context of human rights this is the core meaning of the rule of law. In countries where this premise is accepted, human rights law has scope for developing. In countries where this premise is not accepted, human rights law must struggle on infertile ground. The reality is, however, less simple: many countries must be placed in a grey "in between" world. And it is in respect of those countries that human rights organizations can do their most useful work.

The rule of law requires that there should exist a fair and effective administration of justice. This in turn requires the existence of two minimum conditions in domestic law and in practical reality. First, it is a well-established human rights norm that every individual must have unrestricted and effective right of access to the courts to establish his or her rights against the state and its agencies. For example, when an individual is unlawfully arrested and detained by the police, the individual must be able to obtain his or her release by an urgent habeas corpus application. If in a particular country this right of unimpeded access to the courts does not in practice exist, the system in that country fails to satisfy a critical human rights norm. Secondly, it is a basic principle of human rights law that every individual has a right to a fair trial in civil and criminal cases before an independent and impartial court. The pedigree of the principle is part of the story of enlightened progress. But it is in the last fifty years that the centrality of the principle as a human rights norm has been recognized. The principle was affirmed in three basic international texts, in Article 10 of the Universal Declaration of Human Rights (1948), in Article 6 of the European Convention on Human Rights and Fundamental Freedoms (1950), and in Article 14 of the International Covenant on Civil and Political Rights (ICCPR) (1966).

It is important at once to outline the status of the right to a fair trial. It is a litmus test of how civilized we are: it requires that we do not allow any individual to be condemned unless he or she has been fairly tried in accordance with law. Domestic courts must unswervingly

64 • Lord Steyn

uphold this over-arching human rights norm. Only in this way can a right be vindicated which is fundamental to all citizens. Only by quashing a conviction obtained after an unfair trial can courts effectively affirm and vindicate the right to a fair trial. This is to be contrasted with cases where a trial has been affected by irregularities not amounting to denial of a fair trial. In such cases it is fair that a court of appeal should have the power, even when faced by the fact of irregularities in the trial procedure, to dismiss the appeal if in its view the defendant's guilt is plain beyond any doubt. It is a grave conclusion that a defendant has not had the substance of a fair trial. It means that the system of justice has failed. Subject to the possible exercise of a power to order a retrial, where appropriate, the conviction cannot stand. By contrast, there are other more specific human rights norms, such as a suspect's right of access to a lawyer before interrogation by the police, the breach of which does not necessarily and invariably lead to the exclusion of the confession or the quashing of a conviction based on it. In the hierarchy of human rights norms, the right to a fair trial ranks at the very top.

The right to a fair trial includes a right to a fair and public hearing within a reasonable time before an independent and impartial court, established by law and applying civilized notions of justice, and resulting in a publicly announced and reasoned judicial decision. It involves consideration of a familiar triangulation: the interests of the victim or victims, the accused and society. It is impossible to discuss all facets of the principle or the multiplicity of typical situations in which it is to be applied. But I propose to examine three problem areas:

- the independence and impartiality of the court;
- the requirement of equality of arms of the parties; and
- the requirement of minimum substantive and procedural standards for the trial.

These requirements apply equally to civil and criminal cases, but the focus of my remarks will be on criminal cases.

The independence and impartiality of the court

It is an indispensable condition for the existence of the rule of law in a country that the judiciary should be independent and impartial. In an authoritarian state there is no place for judicial independence. Thus, in Nazi Germany, the judges played an important role in the Holocaust. It is one of the most sordid and shameful chapters in the legal history of our century. On the other side of the political spectrum, the idea of the independence of judges and the idea that citizens had rights against the state were foreign to Stalin's Russia and its satellite states. Judges played their part in those brutal regimes.

There are, however, some less extreme examples. Following the *coup d'état* of September 1973 in Chile, thousands were arrested and tortured. The civilized and constitutionally based legal system of that country had not formally been altered, yet it was not possible to obtain from the courts any relief by way of orders of habeas corpus. Lamentable as in retrospect it may appear to us, the new totalitarian regime intimidated and compromised the judiciary. In some ways the example of the role of the judiciary in South Africa during the apartheid years is even more instructive. By passing legislation of a truly monstrous kind, the legislature distorted justice for the vast majority of citizens in every aspect of their daily lives. If the judges applied these laws, as they had to do while they remained judges, the Nationalist government attained all it set out to do. It did not need subservient judges; the laws passed removed the power to protect the liberties and freedoms of citizens.

Much has been written about the role of the judges in South Africa. At the magistrates' level (including regional magistrates with enlarged criminal jurisdiction) the bench was drawn from the ranks of state prosecutors. It was a largely complaisant bench. At the Supreme Court level the picture was far better. There were many judges who honourably carried out their tasks in a spirit of recognition of the fundamental values of liberty, equality and justice which are the birthright of every human being. Outstanding among these judges was Michael Corbett, who subsequently became Chief Justice. But even the efforts of such judges were overwhelmed by the laws passed by the South African Parliament. In any event, it is right to recognize a darker side at the highest level of the South African judiciary. It is now clearly established that during the tenure of office of Chief Justice Rabie in the 1980s he arranged for a small so-called "emergency team" to hear all cases arising from the successive emergencies declared in the 1980s. It is obvious that the criterion of selection was the "soundness", or, in that very English phrase, the "safe hands", of four or five members of the Court of Appeal. The result of this manipulation of the panels hearing such cases was that every single case arising from the emergencies was heard by the "emergency team" and was decided in favour of the government.

I have recounted the historical precedents of the failures of the judiciary in Nazi Germany, communist regimes, Chile and South Africa because they highlight, in different ways, the almost insurmountable problems of maintaining judicial independence in the contaminated moral environment created by totalitarian regimes. The question is: what can be done to bolster judicial independence and impartiality? In countries where an all-powerful executive and legislature is bent on repressive rule, the sombre conclusion is that little can be done. After all, the judiciary is a comparatively weak department of government and no match for the other arms of government. But there are countries, teetering on the divide between democracy and authoritarian rule, where something worthwhile may be accomplished. There is some scope for beneficial assistance to them by advocating institutional arrangements on a domestic level which will foster judicial independence.

On 29 November 1985, the United Nations General Assembly endorsed the Basic Principles on the Independence of the Judiciary and invited governments "to respect them and to take them into account within the framework of their national legislation and practice".[1] These guidelines are an important affirmation of the pivotal importance of judicial independence in a democracy.

---

[1] UN General Assembly Resolution 40/146 (13 December 1985).

66 • Lord Steyn

In the 1990s, there was an increase in attacks on judicial independence in many countries. This led to a plea by the UN Commission on Human Rights for the appointment of a Special Rapporteur to focus on ways of promoting the independence of judges worldwide. In April 1994, the UN appointed Mr Param Cumaraswamy as Special Rapporteur. He has worked ceaselessly to promote the Basic Principles on the Independence of the Judiciary. He has published four valuable reports. The report dated 12 February 1998 records how difficult his task has become as a result of action taken against him in Malaysia. It is right also to acknowledge the valuable work done by the International Commission of Jurists and by the International Federation of Lawyers to keep the problem of judicial independence under world-wide review and to publish governing principles.[2] In 1996, Commonwealth Law Ministers initiated a project to study the problem. Since then the Attorney-General's Department of Australia, to whom the principal task was assigned, has gathered and organized information in the form of a database. A preliminary report has been prepared. The Commonwealth Secretariat is in charge of the project and will prepare an updated report. All these efforts are, of course, valuable in keeping the topic on the international agenda. On the other hand, it is only fair to add that there is no real evidence of positive results.

What more can be done? A possible way forward has been demonstrated by a very concrete initiative undertaken by the Council of Europe to promote and strengthen judicial independence in the context of the fair trial guarantee in Article 6 of the European Convention on Human Rights. The background to the initiative was the acute difficulties experienced by judges in countries in Central and Eastern Europe. The problems included and include direct and indirect political interference in the work of judges, uncomfortably close links between the prosecution and judges, and the general disinclination of judges to find against the state. Unfortunately, financial corruption was and is also a fact of life. And the criminal justice systems are sometimes woefully under-funded. As those Central and Eastern European countries were adapting to democratic structures, the absence of experience of the role of an independent and impartial judiciary was a great obstacle.

On 13 October 1994, the Committee of Ministers of the Council of Europe adopted Recommendation R (94) 12 on the independence of judges. The text records that the aim of the Council of Europe is the evolution of constitutionally governed states, based on the rule of law, in order to achieve the promotion and protection of human rights and fundamental freedoms. The text describes the independence of judges as one of the central pillars of the rule of law. It contains detailed proposals for the constitutional protection of the independence of judges, the authority of judges, proper working conditions for them, the formation of judges' associations to protect judicial independence, the duties of judges to uphold the rule of law, and security of tenure of office. This recommendation led to a detailed examination of the problem by judges from a wide group of European states. On 25 October 1996, in Pärnu, Estonia, Presidents and Judges of Supreme Courts of countries of Central and Eastern Europe adopted a resolution supporting the initiative of the Council of Europe. This was followed by widespread consultation of judges about a European charter for judges. Multilateral meetings of judges

---

[2] See *The Independence of Judges and Lawyers: A Compilation of International Standards*, Bulletin No 25-26 (Special Issue), Centre for the Independence of Judges and Lawyers, April-October 1990.

organized by the Council of Europe took place in Warsaw and Slok from 23 to 26 June 1997, in Strasbourg from 9 to 11 July 1997 and in Neuchâtel from 8 to 10 September 1997. A draft European Charter on the Statute for Judges was prepared. At a multilateral meeting of judges, again organized by the Council of Europe, held between 8 and 10 July 1998 in the Ukraine, the text was discussed, amended and eventually approved. My purpose in describing the process of the drafting of this text on judicial independence is to emphasize the "grassroots" judicial input at all stages. It was prepared by judges steeped in the realities of the vulnerability of the administration of justice in countries where for decades there had been no judicial independence.

The text of the European Charter[3] is impressive in its detailed regulatory framework to secure the independence of judges. In respect of every decision affecting the selection, recruitment, appointment, career progress or termination of the office of a judge, the European Charter envisages the intervention of an authority, independent of the executive and legislative power, of which at least one half are to be judges elected by their peers. In the event of a perceived threat to his or her independence, a judge will have the right to refer the issue to the independent authority which will have power to adjudicate. Such proposals for institutional arrangements to promote judicial independence ought to be in the forefront of the work of those who seek to foster judicial independence. And, as a matter of high strategy, it would be sensible not to start entirely afresh but to use and build on the work initiated by the Council of Europe.

Unfortunately, realism compels me to end this section of my paper on a sceptical note. The nations of Central and Eastern Europe have a political incentive to reform: they wish to be part of the European Union. Elsewhere, practical difficulties in the way of reform may be much greater. Moreover, it is an indispensable requirement for the existence of an independent and impartial judiciary that there must be a free and independent legal profession. By free and independent I mean, of course, not directly or indirectly controlled by government. This point is not addressed in the European Charter. Similarly, a free press is the great servant of democracy and in particular of a fair and effective administration of justice. A free press guarantees that judges will constantly be on trial themselves at the bar of public opinion. That is how it should be. If a country does not have freedom of the press, it is difficult to imagine that it can have true judicial independence.

The requirement of equality of arms of the parties

It is well established in the jurisprudence of the European Court of Human Rights that the right to a fair trial requires observance of the principle of equality of arms. The prosecution and the defence must have equal rights before the court. Specifically, an accused in criminal proceedings must have a reasonable opportunity of presenting his or her case to the court under conditions which do not place him or her at a substantial disadvantage vis-à-vis his or her opponent. This principle is applicable in many different contexts. I would

---

[3] See appendix to this paper, *infra*, at 70.

68 • Lord Steyn

like to concentrate on one of the most vital areas, namely the duty of the prosecution to disclose to the defence in advance of the trial all relevant information which may arguably have a bearing on the guilt or innocence of an accused person. The importance of this norm in criminal justice systems arises directly from the fact that the criminal investigation is usually initiated and controlled by the police. They hold the cards and there can be no equality of arms if they do not put their cards on the table. It is true that there are significant differences in criminal procedures between states. In some countries the judicial involvement arises earlier than in common law jurisdictions. It can be argued that in such countries the role of the *juge d'instruction* or examining magistrate compensates for a more restricted duty of disclosure. After all, the magistrate's dossier is available to the defence. But even in such countries the police play a critical role and may be in possession of information not disclosed to the magistrate. And, in any event, there is no principled basis for withholding from the defence any information which may damage the prosecution case or assist the defence case. In my view, fair pre-trial disclosure ought to be recognized as a universal human rights norm. And it must not be left to the discretion of the prosecution to decide on disclosure. It must be part of the rights-based system. The court must be the final arbiter on the matter.

In the last 15 years a series of miscarriages of justice has been exposed in England. If there is one virtually constant theme in the judgments of the Court of Appeal setting aside the convictions after the accused had spent many years in prison, it is that there were lamentable failures to disclose critical information and documents. It is certainly true in the cases of Judith Ward, the Birmingham Six, the Guildford Four and the Bridgewater Three. One is entitled to ask how this happened? Careless lapses and errors of judgment could account for some failures. But it does not explain the scale of the non-disclosure. It has to be said the enthusiasm of the police for disclosing evidence and information to lawyers acting for an accused regarded by them as guilty is not always great. I am afraid that experience in England shows that it is insufficient to leave the matter of pre-trial disclosure to the discretion of the prosecution. I am not aware of any comparative research in other countries on the impact of non-disclosure in criminal cases. In the nature of things such research would be difficult to conduct. But we do know that the right to pre-trial disclosure in England is already much wider than in most countries. It may be a fair inference that the negative impact of non-disclosure in criminal cases in other countries with less developed rules of disclosure is quite widespread.

What can be done about this problem? Article 6 of the European Convention on Human Rights does not expressly create a right to fair pre-trial disclosure. The jurisprudence of the European Court of Human Rights recognizes that "it is a requirement of fairness under Article 6(1) ... that the prosecution authorities disclose to the defence all material evidence for or against the accused ...".[4] In deciding on the outcome of a case the European Court of Human Rights concentrates on prejudice resulting from breaches of the Convention. The scope for general statements and analysis of the norms underlying Article 6 is therefore limited. For example, fairness requires not only the disclosure of material evidence (in the

---

[4] See *Edwards v UK* (1993) 15 EHRR 417, at 431-2; Stewart Field and James Young, "Disclosure, Appeals and Procedural Traditions: Edwards v UK", [1994] Criminal Law Review 264.

sense of relevant and admissible evidence) but all information which may arguably assist the defence. Moreover, given the specific rights spelt out in Article 6, it seems to me that it is a gap in the European Convention that it does not expressly provide (subject to a tightly defined public interest exception) for a general right to fair pre-trial disclosure of all arguably relevant information as an inseparable part of the right to a fair trial. In my view that gap ought to be filled. The same points can be made about Article 14 of the ICCPR and the work of the Human Rights Committee. At stake is a norm of human rights law which ought to be given due prominence by express incorporation in international texts. After all, such international texts have a symbolic value which transcends judgments rooted in the facts of particular cases. But states ought also to be encouraged to include this specific norm in their domestic legislation in the context of the right to a fair trial, whether that right be contained in a written constitution or in a general criminal procedure statute. In this way, human rights organizations can attempt to address one of the most critical problems bedevilling criminal justice world-wide.

Minimum substantive and procedural safeguards

In conclusion, I touch on a general problem of daunting complexity. The European Convention on Human Rights, as amplified by protocols, as well as the ICCPR, as amplified by optional protocols, contain valuable statements of human rights norms in respect of criminal justice. But these instruments do not deal comprehensively with human rights norms applicable to criminal justice. They deal only in part with the problems occurring today in criminal justice systems world-wide and with already established human rights norms. For example, the principles governing non-retroactivity of statutes, maximum certainty in the definition of offences, no conviction without fault, no conviction of the mentally disordered, no imprisonment for civil debt, and so forth, are not contained in either the European Convention or the ICCPR. On the procedural side, neither instrument deals with important specific rights, such as the right of an accused to consult a lawyer before interrogation by the police; justifications for holding proceedings in camera; and the link between the presumption of innocence, the burden of proof and the right of silence. Nobody would wish such international texts to resemble a quantity surveyor's bill of quantities. On the other hand, there ought to be a debate on the restatement in more comprehensive form of minimum substantive and procedural safeguards in respect of criminal justice.[5] It is a long-term enterprise deserving of the attention of Interights.

---

5   See Andrew Ashworth, "The European Convention on Human Rights and English Criminal Justice", in Mads Andenas (ed), *English Public Law and the Common Law of Europe* (London: Key Haven, 1998), at 227-40, and commentary by Helen Fenwick at 215-26.

Part Four

Humanitarian Law

[18]
Guantanamo Bay: The Legal Black Hole[1]

The most powerful democracy is detaining hundreds of suspected foot soldiers of the Taliban in a legal black hole at the United States naval base at Guantanamo Bay, where they await trial on capital charges by military tribunals. This episode must be put in context. Democracies must defend themselves. Democracies are entitled to try officers and soldiers of enemy forces for war crimes. But it is a recurring theme in history that in times of war, armed conflict, or perceived national danger, even liberal democracies adopt measures infringing human rights in ways that are wholly disproportionate to the crisis. One tool at hand is detention without charge or trial, that is, executive detention. Ill-conceived rushed legislation is passed granting excessive powers to executive governments which compromise the rights and liberties of individuals beyond the exigencies of the situation. Often the loss of liberty is permanent. Executive branches of government, faced with a perceived emergency, often resort to excessive measures. The litany of grave abuses of power by liberal democratic governments is too long to recount, but in order to understand and to hold governments to account, we do well to take into account the circles of history.

Judicial branches of government, although charged with the duty of standing between the government and individuals, are often too deferential to the executive in time of peace. How then would the same judges act in a time of crisis? The role of the courts in time of crisis is less than glorious. On this side of the Atlantic *Liversidge v Anderson* (1942)[2] is revealing. The question before the House of Lords was a matter of the interpretation of Defence Regulation 18B which provided that the Home Secretary may order a person to be detained 'if he has reasonable cause to believe' the person to be of hostile origin or associations. A majority of four held that if the Home Secretary thinks he has good cause that is good enough. Lord Atkin chose the objective interpretation: the statute required the Home Secretary *to have* reasonable grounds for detention. Lord Atkin said: 'amid the clash of arms the laws are not silent' and warned against judges who 'when face to face with claims involving the liberty of the subject show themselves more executive minded

---

[1] This is the text of the Twenty-Seventh FA Mann Lecture, organized by the British Institute of International and Comparative Law and Herbert Smith and held in Lincoln's Inn Old Hall, 25 November 2003 with Sir Lawrence Collins in the chair.
[2] [1942] AC 206.

than the executive'. At the time the terms of Lord Atkin's dissent caused grave offence to his colleagues. But Lord Atkin's view on the interpretation of provisions such as Regulation 18B has prevailed: the Secretary of State's power to detain must be exercised on objectively reasonable grounds. To that extent *Liversidge v Anderson* no longer haunts the law.[3] I have referred to a case sketched on the memory of every lawyer because, despite its beguiling framework of a mere point of statutory interpretation, it is emblematic of the recurring clash of fundamentally different views about the role of courts in times of crisis. How far contemporary decisions match Lord Atkin's broader philosophy is far from clear. The theory that courts must always defer to elected representatives on matters of security is seductive. But there is a different view, namely that while courts must take into account the relative constitutional competence of branches of government to decide particular issues, they must never, on constitutional grounds, surrender the constitutional duties placed on them.[4]

Even in modern times terrible injustices have been perpetrated in the name of security on thousands who had no effective recourse to law. Too often courts of law have denied the writ of the rule of law with only the most perfunctory examination. In the context of a war on terrorism without any end in prospect this is a sombre scene for human rights. But there is the caution that unchecked abuse of power begets ever-greater abuse of power. And judges do have the duty, even in times of crisis, to guard against an unprincipled and exorbitant executive response.

Not every one will agree with the picture I have put before you. Let me therefore explain, with reference to Second World War experience, on both sides of the Atlantic, why I feel justified in what I have said. During the Second World War the United States placed more than 120,000 American citizens of Japanese descent in detention camps. There was no evidence to cast doubt on the loyalty of these people to the United States. The military authorities took the view, as a general put it, that 'a Jap is a Jap'. In due course it was recognized by the United States that a grave injustice was done. In 1988 Congress enacted legislation acknowledging that the 'actions were taken without adequate security reasons' and that they were largely motivated by 'racial prejudice, wartime hysteria and a failure of political leadership'.[5] Restitution was made to individuals who were interned. This is to the great credit of the United States. On the other hand, it must be remembered that an earlier opportunity arose in 1944 in *Korematsu v United States*[6] for the Supreme Court to redress the injustice. Korematsu was a Californian of Japanese ancestry. After

---

[3] *Nakkuda Ali v Jayaratne* [1951] AC 66.
[4] J Jowell, QC, 'Judicial Deference: Servility, Civility or Institutional Capacity?' [2003] PL 592. I deal with this point in my recent lecture *Dynamic Interpretation Amidst an Orgy of Statues*, The Brian Dickson Memorial Lecture, Ottawa, 2 Oct 2003.
[5] The Civil Liberties Act 1988.
[6] 332 US 214.

the bombing of Pearl Harbor he volunteered for the army but was rejected on health grounds. He obtained a defence industry job. In June 1942 he was arrested for violation of the internment orders. He challenged the constitutionality of the orders. The issue was whether military necessity was established. The court was divided. Delivering the opinion of the majority of the Court, Justice Black stated: 'To cast this case into outlines of racial prejudice, without reference to the real military dangers which were presented, merely confuses the issue.' Demonstrating significant deference to the executive, he concluded:

> the military authorities considered that the need for action was great, and time was short. We cannot—by availing ourselves of the calm perspective of hindsight—now say that at that time these actions were not justified.

Not many in the United States, in the moderate spectrum of views, would now defend this outcome, even viewed from the perspective of 1942. In any event, in 1984 a federal district court overturned Korematsu's conviction on the ground that the government had 'knowingly withheld information from the courts when they were considering the critical question of military necessity.'[7] In giving judgment Judge Patel observed that the case 'stands as a caution that in times of distress the shield of military necessity and natural security must not be used to protect governmental institutions from close scrutiny and accountability'.[8]

The second decision of the United States Supreme Court which I must mention is *Ex parte Quirin* (1942), the so-called 'Saboteurs case'.[9] It is a case of a very different kind and in many ways more understandable than *Korematsu*. It is cited by United States government spokesmen as authority for the detentions at Guantanamo Bay. In June 1942, when the United States was at war with Germany, eight Nazi agents, including one American citizen, arrived by submarine in the United States. They intended to commit acts of sabotage. Two among them revealed the plot. On 2 July 1942 President Roosevelt ordered the men to be tried by military commission for offences against the law of war and the Articles of War. The Proclamation also provided that they were to be denied access to the courts. On 8 July 1942 the trial commenced and proceeded in secret. Three weeks later the Supreme Court convened a special Summer session to consider petitions for habeas corpus made on behalf of the saboteurs. The saboteurs argued that they had a constitutional right of due process and that they were entitled to be tried before an ordinary civilian court. On 31 July 1942 the Supreme Court made a unanimous order that the military commission was legally constituted and the petitioners were lawfully detained. By 8 August 1942 all the saboteurs had been found guilty and six of the eight had been executed. The turncoats had their sentences commuted. Almost three months after the saboteurs were executed,

---

[7] *Korematsu v United States*, 584 F Supp (1984), at 1406 (ND Cal 1984).
[8] At 1420. [9] 317 US 1.

the Supreme Court made public a unanimous decision holding that Congress had validly authorised military commissions to try violations of the laws of war. The court did, however, hold that the exclusion of judicial review did not apply to habeas corpus. Secret trials without the usual guarantees of fair trial were, however, constitutionally acceptable. In the context of the detentions at Guantanamo Bay it will be necessary to return to this case.

Between 1939 and 1945 almost 27,000 persons were detained in Britain without charge or trial and 7,000 were deported. The danger facing Britain was, of course, immeasurably greater than that of the United States. In the circumstances the total figure does not seem excessive. But most detentions were probably not justified. Not all cases of detention ended as happily as that of the German born Michael Kerr who was detained in 1940 for 6 months, released to fly for the RAF during the rest of the war, and rose to become a Lord Justice of Appeal.[10] In his book *In the Highest Degree Odious*[11] Professor AW Brian Simpson concluded that the courts washed their hands enthusiastically of responsibility for the legality of detentions. He said:

> the courts did virtually nothing for the detainees, either to secure their liberty, to preserve what rights they did possess under the regulation, to scrutinize the legality of Home Office action, or to provide compensation when matters went wrong. The legal profession too, as a profession, did nothing; I am told that it was not easy to persuade lawyers to act for detainees at all. . . . So far as the government lawyers were concerned, the Treasury Solicitor's Department comes across as unattractive; its ethos was ruthless determination to win cases at the least possible cost. One cannot but be struck by the absence in the papers of any hint of sympathy to those who litigated, or any generosity of spirit to individuals none of whom had been charged or convicted of any crime. Of the Law Officers Somervell seems to have sailed very close to the wind, and both he and Jowitt changed their tune over the relationship between the courts and the regulation. I cannot but suspect that other examples of dubious conduct have been concealed by the accidental loss of Treasury Solicitor's files . . . (418–19).

The 'hands off' approach continued after the war. In *R v Secretary of State, Ex p Hosenball* from 1977, a deportation case, Lord Denning said:[12]

> There is a conflict between the interests of national security on the one hand and the freedom of the individual on the other. The balance between these two is not for a court of law. It is for the Home Secretary. He is the person entrusted by Parliament with the task.

Exhibiting great deference to the executive Lord Denning added:

> In some parts of the world national security has on occasions been used as an excuse for all sorts of infringements of individual liberty. But not in England. Both during the wars and after them, successive ministers have discharged their duties to the complete satisfaction of the people at large.

---

[10] M Kerr *As Far As I Remember* (Oxford Hart 2002).
[11] Oxford Clarendon Press 1994.   [12] [1977] 1 WLR 766, at 783.

Possibly we would now say that such instinctive trust in public servants, executive or judicial, has been replaced by a culture requiring in principle openness and accountability from all entrusted with public power.

During the Second World War a new idea took root. Previously there had been an assumption that however outrageously a government treated individuals, it was not properly the concern of other governments. The Third Reich and the Holocaust changed that perception. Out of the ashes of the war came the creation in 1945 of the United Nations, committed by its charter to uphold 'the dignity and worth of the human person'. The adoption on 10 December 1948 in Paris of the Universal Declaration of Human Rights—the legacy of Mrs Roosevelt—was a momentous event. It gave birth to the human rights movement and the rights revolution. Eighteen years later it became known together with the International Covenant on Social and Cultural Rights (1966) and the International Covenant on Civil and Political Rights (1966) as the International Bill of Rights. Central to these instruments is the dignity of the human person and the maintenance of the rule of law to protect that most fundamental of rights. A large number of treaties, regional and specific, the descendants of the Universal Declaration, enshrine the same principle. For present purposes the Convention Relative to the Treatment of Prisoners of War of 12 August 1947 (the Third Geneva Convention III) is relevant. It contained detailed provisions protecting prisoners of war. I am content to assume that the Taliban soldiers detained at Guantanamo Bay are on a literal interpretation not covered by the Third Geneva Convention because they did not wear uniforms on the battlefield. But Article 75 of the First Protocol Additional to the Geneva Conventions of 12 August 1949, dated 8 June 1977, contains more far-reaching provisions to protect prisoners captured during armed conflicts. Whatever their status, such prisoners are entitled to humane treatment. It is true that the United States has not ratified this Protocol. But it is generally accepted that Article 75 reflects customary international law.[13] Indeed when the United States government decided not to ratify the Protocol, it had before it expert advice that many Articles of the Protocol accurately reflect customary international law. Specifically it was advised that Article 75 was an Article which was already part of customary international law and therefore binding on the United States.[14] Many of the provisions of Article 75 are relevant. The use of torture and inhuman or degrading treatment is prohibited. The authorities are entitled to question a prisoner but there is no obligation on the prisoner to answer the questions put. Coercing a prisoner to confess is unlawful. Article 75(4) is particularly significant. It provides:

---

[13] C Greenwood, 'International Law and the "War Against Terrorism"', *International Affairs* 78, 2 (2002) 307, at 315.

[14] T Meron, *Human Rights and Humanitarian Norms of Customary Law* (Oxford Clarendon Press 1989), at 62–9.

> No sentence may be passed and no penalty may be executed on a person found guilty of a penal offence relating to the armed conflict except pursuant to a conviction pronounced by an impartial and regularly constituted court respecting the generally recognized principles of regular judicial procedure . . .

In the 1990s there were important developments. On 16 October 1998 Augusto Pinochet, the former President of Chile, was arrested in London in response to an arrest warrant issued by a Spanish court. Henry Kissinger has described him as 'a fashionably reviled man of the right'. Given what we now know the verdict of history may be a little more severe. In any event, the warrant alleged crimes of murder, torture and 'disappearances'. The final decision of the House of Lords was to the effect that crimes under international law, such as torture, could not be acts within the official capacity of a Head of State and that extradition proceedings could continue. Despite the fact that due to his mental state Pinochet could eventually not be tried, the decision of the House of Lords was an important breakthrough on immunities and universal jurisdiction.[15] Equally important was the creation of ad hoc international criminal tribunals in the case of Rwanda, Yugoslavia, and Milosevic to try defendants on war crimes.[16] Despite the negative role of the United States, the International Criminal Court was set up. To date 91 countries have ratified or acceded to the Treaty. The court is fully operational. Recently Madam Justice Arbour of the Canadian Supreme Court has eloquently summed up what this means. She said:

> We have witnessed a maturation process from the declaratory era of some 50 years ago, through a monitoring and denunciatory phase, and now into the modern era of efficient enforcement through personal criminal responsibility. This culture carries with it the expectations of millions of human rights holders who until very recently did not perceive themselves as such. But globalization of the culture of rights, combined with the spread of democracy, has irreversibly changed their sense of entitlement . . . [17]

There was great progress on the humanitarian front between 1948 and 2001.

Then came the horror of 11 September 2001. Using civilian aircraft as missiles, Al-Qaeda terrorists attacked and attempted to attack the great symbols of the United States government and nation. A military response was inevitable. Three days later President Bush declared a national emergency.[18] Congress rushed through the Patriot Act[19] which gave to the executive vast

---

[15] *R v Bow Street Stipendiary Magistrate, Ex P Pinochet (No 3)* [2000] 1 AC 147.

[16] The International Criminal Tribunal for Rwanda was created by Security Council resolution 955 of 8 Nov 1994; The International Criminal Tribunal for the former Yugoslavia ('ICTY') was established by resolution 827 of 25 May 1993 and the case of Milosevic was transferred to the ICTY on 29 June 2001.

[17] '*Is The Growth of International Criminal Law A Threat to State Sovereignty?*' Irving R. Segal Lecture, University of Pennsylvania, Philadelphia, PA, 24 Sept 2003.

[18] Proc 7463 '*Declaration of National Emergency by Reason of Certain Terrorist Attacks*'.

[19] USA PATRIOT Act 2001.

powers to override civil liberties. Congress promptly authorised the President to use all necessary force against, inter alia, those responsible for the terrorist attacks of 11 September to prevent further attacks.[20] On 7 October 2001 the air campaign against Afghanistan began. In military terms the action was successful. But now the region is left with a ravaged country which under its warlords has enormously increased its production of opium grown for the world market. Afghanistan was followed by the deeply controversial Iraqi war of 'shock and awe' which fractured the international legal order so carefully crafted in the crucible of Lake Success in 1945. It is easier to destroy than to develop international institutions. But tonight I must concentrate on Guantanamo Bay.

On 13 November 2001 the President issued an order providing for the trial by military commissions of persons accused of violations of the laws of war.[21] That order has been repeatedly amended.[22] Beginning in January 2002 some 660 prisoners have been transferred at first to Camp X-Ray and then Camp Delta at Guantanamo Bay. The number included children between the ages of 13 and 16 as well as the very elderly.[23] Virtually all the prisoners are foot soldiers of the Taliban. It has been reported that there are no 'big fish' among the prisoners.[24] Contemporaneous reports stated that the prisoners, who are Muslims, were compelled contrary to the tenets of their religion to shave off their beards.

By a blanket presidential decree all prisoners have been denied prisoners of war status. Before the armed conflict started, the Taliban government had been in effective control of Afghanistan. The vast majority of the prisoners were soldiers of the Taliban forces. Let me assume that at Guantanamo Bay there are also some prisoners who are Al-Qaeda terrorists. But if there are such prisoners, criminal outlaws as they may be, they are also in law entitled to the protection of humanitarian law.[25]

How prisoners at Guantanamo Bay have been treated we do not know. But what we do know is not reassuring. At Camp Delta the minute cells measure 1.8 m by 2.4 m. Detainees are held in these cells for up to 24 hours a day. Photographs of prisoners being returned to their cells on stretchers after interrogation have been published. The Red Cross described the camp as principally

---

[20] 'Authorization for Use of Military Force' Public Law 107–40, 115 Stat 224 18 Sept 2001.

[21] Military Order of 13 Nov 2001, 'Detention, Treatment and Trial of Certain Non-Citizens in the War Against Terrorism' 66 FR 57833 (16 Nov 2001) 'The Presidential Order'.

[22] *Trials Under Military Order: A Guide to the Final Rules for Military Commissions*, Lawyers Committee for Human Rights Briefing Paper, July 2003.

[23] United States of America, *The Threat of a Bad Example: Undermining international standards as 'war on terror' continues*, Amnesty International, 19 Aug 2003, at 21.

[24] *Call for release of 'low-level' Guantanamo inmates*, J Borger, The Guardian, 20 Aug 2002.

[25] George H Aldrich, *The Taliban, Al-Qaeda, and The Determination of Illegal Combatants*, 96 AJIL 891.

a centre of interrogation rather than detention.[26] The *Washington Post* suggested there has been a sweeping change in United States policy on torture since 11 September, despite public pronouncements against its use. It quotes Cofer Black, the former director of the CIA's counter-terrorist branch, as telling a congressional intelligence committee: 'All you need to know: there was a before 9/11, and there was an after 9/11 ... After 9/11 the gloves came off'.[27] The United States website records thirty-two attempted suicides committed by twenty-seven prisoners.[28] A report of 16 March 2003 reported officials as saying that the techniques of interrogation are 'not quite torture, but as close as you can get'.[29] It appears likely that 'stress and duress' tactics of disrupting sleep and forcing prisoners to stand for extended periods, which have been used by United States interrogators in Afghanistan, are also employed at Guantanamo Bay.[30] The purpose of holding the prisoners at Guantanamo Bay was and is to put them beyond the rule of law, beyond the protection of any courts, and at the mercy of the victors. The procedural rules do not prohibit the use of force to coerce prisoners to confess. On the contrary, the rules expressly provide that statements made by a prisoner under physical and mental duress are admissible 'if the evidence would have value to a reasonable person', ie, military officers trying enemy soldiers.[31] At present we are not meant to know what is happening at Guantanamo Bay. But history will not be neutered. What takes place there today in the name of the United States will assuredly, in due course, be judged at the bar of informed international opinion.

Having invoked a historical perspective, I must acknowledge that, despite the Magna Carta, in harsher times England resorted to the expedient of sending prisoners beyond the reach of the rule of law. One of the charges made against Edward Hyde, the First Earl of Clarendon, in his impeachment in 1667 was that he had attempted to preclude habeas corpus by sending persons to 'remote islands, garrisons, and other places, thereby to prevent them from the benefit of the law', that is by sending persons to places where the writ of habeas corpus would not be available. In 1679 this loophole was blocked by section 11 of the Habeas Corpus Amendment Act 1679.[32] For more than three centuries such stratagems to evade habeas corpus have been unlawful in England.

---

[26] C Girod quoted in *La Vigilance inquiète de la Croix-Rouge à Guantanamo*, P Jarreau. Le Monde, 18 Oct 2003.
[27] '*Stress and Duress' Tactics Used on Terrorism Suspects Held in Secret Overseas Facilities*. D Priest and B Gellman, Washington Post, 26 Dec 2002.
[28] *Suicide Attempts at Guantanamo Reach 32*, Associated Press, 26 Aug 2003.
[29] *Interrogation or torture: Blurred line?*, D Van Natta Jr, New York Times, 8 Mar 2003.
[30] The Amnesty report cited above, at 23.
[31] Presidential Order s 4(3).
[32] I am indebted to Lord Bingham of Cornhill for this reference. See his Romanes Lecture given on 15 Oct 2002 in Oxford, 52 ICLQ 2003, at 841–58.

The regime applicable at Guantanamo Bay was created by a succession of presidential orders. It can be summarised quite briefly. The prisoners at Guantanamo Bay, as matters stand at present, will be tried by military tribunals. The prisoners have no access to the writ of habeas corpus to determine whether their detention is even arguably justified. The military will act as interrogators, prosecutors, defence counsel, judges, and when death sentences are imposed, as executioners. The trials will be held in secret. None of the basic guarantees for a fair trial need be observed. The jurisdiction of the United States courts is excluded. The military control everything. It is, however, in all respects subject to decisions of the President as Commander-in-Chief even in respect of guilt and innocence in individual cases as well as appropriate sentences. It is an awesome responsibility. The President has made public in advance his personal view of the prisoners as a group: he has described them all as 'killers'.

At Guantanamo Bay arrangements for the trials are proceeding with great efficiency. A courtroom with an execution chamber nearby has apparently been constructed. But the British prisoners will not be liable to be executed. The Attorney General has negotiated a separate agreement with the Pentagon on the treatment of British prisoners. He has apparently received a promise that the British prisoners of war will not face the death penalty. This gives a new dimension to the concept of 'most favoured nation' treatment in international law. How could it be morally defensible to discriminate in this way between individual prisoners? It lifts the curtain a little on the arbitrariness of what is happening at Guantanamo Bay and in the corridors of power on both sides of the Atlantic.

The United States government seeks to justify its action by relying on the *Quirin* case. It is a case rooted in the circumstances of the Second World War. Humanitarian law was not yet developed. It is worth recalling that at Yalta, Churchill, a humane man, argued that the Nazi leaders should be shot after the war as soon as they were caught. Stalin, who knew a thing or two about trials, said that they should be tried before they were shot.[33] Roosevelt had no trouble with a trial as long as it was, in his words, 'not too judicial'. That was a long time ago. In any event, the circumstances of the Nazi saboteurs were very different from the position at Guantanamo Bay. Now there has been no declared war. Congress has not authorised the military commissions. The Guantanamo Bay prisoners are subject to military prosecution for violations never before considered war crimes. They are deprived of the right of confidential communications with their lawyers, access to all relevant evidence, and judicial review—all of which were afforded to the German saboteurs. Most importantly, the status of the German saboteurs as enemy aliens was beyond dispute, whereas the 660 prisoners at Guantanamo Bay are not enemy aliens, ie, citizens of a State at war with the United States, and in any event,

---

[33] M Gilbert, *Winston S. Churchill*, Vol VII, *Road to Victory, 1941–1945*, at 1201–2.

are not a homogeneous group since some were captured on the battlefield in Afghanistan and some elsewhere. They are deprived of any right to test the legality of their detention. The *Quirin* case does not therefore support the action taken at Guantanamo Bay. In any event, today it is widely regarded as a sordid episode in United States history. Legal scholars are agreed, as Professor Bellknapp put it, 'that the court had fallen into step with the drums of war'.[34] Professor Danelski described *Quirin* as 'an embarrassing tale of ... a prosecution designed to obtain the death penalty ... a rush to judgment and agonising effort to justify a fait accompli.' He ended by saying that if there is a lesson to be learned, 'it is that the court should be wary of departing from its established rules and practices, even in times of national crisis, for at such times the court is especially susceptible to co-optation by the executive.'[35] The reliance of the United States Administration on this discredited precedent ignores more than half a century of progress of humanitarian law, notably in response to prisoners captured during armed conflict.

The Court of Appeals for the District of Columbia Circuit has recently in consolidated cases ruled that, despite the fact that the United States has had exclusive control over Guantanamo Bay since 1903, the courts have no jurisdiction to examine the legality of the detention of the prisoners. The Court of Appeals decided that it has no jurisdiction to consider the claims by nationals of Kuwait, Australia and Britain, captured by United States military forces in Afghanistan or Pakistan.[36] The applicants were not enemy aliens. Each of the applicants denied that he had engaged in hostilities against America, sought an explanation for the indefinite detention and complained of the refusal of access to legal counsel. Judge A Raymond Randolph (for the three-judge panel) concluded that the American courts had no jurisdiction because the claimants were aliens, were captured during military operations abroad, were now detained outside the United States, and had never been present in the United States. Even evidence of torture by the military authorities, however compelling, may not be examined. In other words, the court ruled that the United States government might legally evade the jurisdiction of the United States courts in the case of foreign nationals by its choice of a place of imprisonment beyond American soil. But on 10 November 2003 the United States Supreme Court granted *certiorari* for the case to proceed to a substantive hearing on the question whether the lower courts were right to conclude that they had no jurisdiction to entertain habeas corpus applications. This will be the only issue on which the Supreme Court will rule.[37] That hearing will take

---

[34] 'The Supreme Court Goes to War: The Meaning and Implications of the Nazi Saboteur case' Military Law Review, vol 89, 59, at 95.

[35] *The Saboteurs' case*, Journal of Supreme Court History, vol 1, 61–82.

[36] *Al Odah v US* 321 F 3d 1124 (2003).

[37] The order reads as follows: 'The petitions for writs of certiorari are granted limited to the following Question: Whether United States courts lack jurisdiction to consider challenges to the legality of the detention of foreign nationals captured abroad in connection with hostilities and incarcerated at the Guantanamo Bay Naval Base, Cuba.' A powerful amicus curiae brief signed,

place in the Spring next year. When the matter is considered by the United States Supreme Court, it will have before it the considered view of our Court of Appeal. When an action was brought in British courts on behalf of a British citizen detained at Guantanamo, the Master of the Rolls, Lord Phillips of Worth Matravers, said:

> We find surprising the proposition that the writ of the United States courts does not run in respect of individuals held by the United States government on territory that the United States holds . . . under a long-term treaty.

He called it 'objectionable' that a prisoner had no opportunity to challenge the legitimacy of his detention before a court or tribunal.[38]

It is now necessary to bring some of the threads together. In doing so a distinction must be drawn between two principal features. First, on the basis of the decision of the Court of Appeals for the District of Columbia Circuit, the prisoners have no right of recourse to any courts to determine on an individual basis their status or to rule on the lawfulness of their treatment. Secondly, there is the failure of the procedures and rules governing trials before military tribunals at Guantanamo Bay to measure up to minimum international standards. I turn to the first aspect.

The United States has a long and honourable commitment to the Magna Carta and allegiance to the rule of law. In recent times extraordinary deference of the United States courts to the executive has undermined those values and principles. As matters stand at present the United States courts would refuse to hear a prisoner at Guantanamo Bay who produces credible medical evidence that he has been and is being tortured. They would refuse to hear prisoners who assert that they were not combatants at all. They would refuse to hear prisoners who assert that they were simply soldiers in the Taliban army and knew nothing about Al-Qaeda. They would refuse to examine any complaints of any individuals. The blanket presidential order deprives them all of any rights whatever. As a lawyer brought up to admire the ideals of American democracy and justice, I would have to say that I regard this as a monstrous failure of justice.

In English law the writ of habeas corpus protects citizens and aliens alike. That is how it should be because foreign nationals must obey our laws and therefore deserve the protection of our laws. The writ is available whenever the detained person enters territory under the control of the Crown. That is consistent with human rights law. In *Cyprus v Turkey* (1982), the European Court of Human Rights held that States are: 'bound to secure the said rights and freedoms of all persons under their actual authority and responsibility, whether that authority is exercised within their own territory or abroad'.[39] Let

---

inter alia, by Sir Sydney Kentridge QC, Colin Nicholls QC, and Timothy Otty on the law of habeas corpus has been placed before the United States Supreme Court.

[38] *R (Abbasi) v The Secretary of State for Foreign Affairs* [2002] EWCA Civ 1598.
[39] 1982 4 EHRR 482, at 586, para 8.

me illustrate the point. Reports have been published in the media and by human rights groups of the detention of suspected Al-Qaeda suspects at the United States military facility at Diego Garcia.[40] The British government has denied this allegation. One must accept this categorical assurance. But if the allegation had been true, the writ of habeas corpus would have been available in respect of prisoners at the United States military facility because this small island is part of British Indian Ocean Territory and is leased to the United States. It would have been sufficient that the British government controls the territory. Until 11 September the understanding of the law of habeas corpus would have been the same in the United States. Deference to the executive has so far eroded the cardinal principles of habeas corpus. By denying the prisoners the right to raise challenges in a court about their alleged status and treatment, the United States government is in breach of the minimum standards of customary international law. The importance of this right is underlined by the experience of the Gulf war when the military held about 1,200 hearings to assess the status of captured prisoners, and about two-thirds were found not to be combatants.[41] It is surely likely that in the chaos of the Afghanistan war and its aftermath the United States military forces picked up a great many who were not even combatants.

While my focus is on the prisoners at Guantanamo Bay, denial of justice to foreigners was bound to erode the civil liberties of citizens in the United States. It was said that the Patriot Act is largely targeted at foreign nationals. The background is that 20 million non-citizens living in the United States cannot vote. In a book published in May this year David Cole, Professor at Georgetown University Law Centre, has shown how oppressive treatment of foreign nationals paves the way for similar measures against American citizens.[42] In recent times the United States government has imposed military custody on two United States citizens. In *Hamdi* the prisoner had been arrested on the battlefield in Afghanistan. In January 2002 he was transported to Guantanamo Bay. In April 2002 he was moved to military detention at a military base in Norfolk, Virginia. The Court of Appeals for the Fourth Circuit upheld the indefinite military detention of the prisoner as an unlawful combatant.[43] Padilla is an American citizen arrested on American soil. In June 2002 he was transferred to a military brig in South Carolina. He challenged the lawfulness of his detention. A District judge held that 'the commission of a judge . . . does not run to deciding de novo whether Padilla is associated with

---

[40] *Questioning Terror Suspects in a Surreal World*, D Van Natta Jr, New York Times, 16 Mar 2003. *Wake-Up call to UK government on torture*, Amnesty International, 7 Mar 2003.
[41] D Cole, *Enemy Aliens: Double Standards and Constitutional Freedoms in the War on Terrorism.* 2003, at 42.
[42] (As n 37).
[43] *Hamdi v Rumsfeld* (ED Va 11 June 2002) (No 02 CV 439); (4th Cir 12 July 2002) (No 02-6895); (ED Va 16 Aug 2002) (No 2: 02 CV 439); (4th Cir 8 Jan 2003) (No 02-7338); (4th Cir 9 July 2003) (No 02-7228).

Al Qaeda and whether he should therefore be detained as an enemy combatant'.[44] Previously, there had been very little protest about the United States government's actions at Guantanamo Bay. But the action against United States citizens has caused a chorus of disapproval. Objectively these protests are justified but inherent in them are double standards which are deeply troubling. In a review of David Cole's book in the New York Review of Books Anthony Lewis commented:[45] 'We must respect the humanity of aliens lest we devalue our own. And because it is the right thing to do.' That observation is one that we, in the United Kingdom, ought also to heed.

Let me now turn to the second matter. The question is whether the quality of justice envisaged for the prisoners at Guantanamo Bay complies with minimum international standards for the conduct of fair trials. The answer can be given quite shortly: it is a resounding 'No'. The military commissions contemplated by the United States government have been described by Professor Ronald Dworkin as the type of trials one associates with utterly lawless totalitarian regimes.[46] David Pannick QC invoked Joseph Kafka's *The Trial* in which the great novelist describes how Kafka's advocate warns him of the difficulties of presenting a defence when 'the proceedings were not only kept secret from the general public, but from the accused as well.' But as David Pannick observed, Kafka could see his lawyer, however incompetent, and there was a court, however imperfect, making the decision.[47] The military commissions are not independent courts or tribunals. The term 'kangaroo court' springs to mind. It derives from the jumps of the kangaroo, and conveys the idea of a pre-ordained arbitrary rush to judgment by an irregular tribunal which makes a mockery of justice. Internationally military commissions at Guantanamo Bay will be so regarded. Trials of the type contemplated by the United States government would be a stain on United States justice. The only thing that could be worse is simply to leave the prisoners in their black hole indefinitely.

Does the United States Administration care about international opinion? In his dissenting opinion in *Atkins v Virgina*,[48] which was concurred in by the Chief Justice and Justice Thomas, Justice Scalia observed in a death penalty case: 'Equally irrelevant are the practices of the world "community", whose notions of justice are (thankfully) not always those of our people.' This isolationist approach may also be the response of the United States government to criticism about Guantanamo Bay. On the other hand, there may possibly be winds of change. On 26 June 2003 the Supreme Court by a majority decision in *Lawrence et al v Texas* overruled an earlier Supreme Court decision in

---

[44] *Padilla v Bush* (SDNY 4 Dec 2002) (No 01 Civ 4445 (MBM)).
[45] *Un-American Activities*, Anthony Lewis, New York Review of Books, Vol L, No 16, 23 Oct 2003, at 19.
[46] *The Threat to Patriotism*, New York Review of Books, 28 Nov 2002, 44.
[47] The Times, 25 Mar 2003, Law 4.
[48] 20 June 2002, 122 Supreme Ct 2242 (2002).

Bowers v Hardwick,[49] which had upheld Georgia's sodomy law as constitutional. For the first time in its history the court (as opposed to individual justices) relied on international human rights law and practice. Justice Kennedy observed:

> When homosexual conduct is made criminal by the law of the State, that declaration in and of itself is an invitation to subject homosexual persons to discrimination both in the public and private spheres. The central holding of *Bowers* has been brought into question by this case, and it should be addressed. Its continuance as precedent demeans the lives of homosexual persons.

Justice Scalia, with whom Chief Justice Rehnquist and Justice Thomas agreed, said that the majority had signed up to what he called the homosexual agenda. He observed:

> The court's discussion of these foreign views (ignoring, of course, the many countries that have retained criminal prohibitions on sodomy) is ... meaningless dicta. Dangerous dicta, however, since this court ... should not impose foreign moods, fads, or fashions on Americans.

The relevance of this ongoing debate about the place of United States law in a global world is, of course, that it may in time become possible in the United States to look at Guantanamo Bay in the context of human rights law and humanitarian law regarding the rights of captured prisoners. It is also just possible that the Supreme Court could be persuaded to rule that United States courts have jurisdiction to entertain habeas corpus applications from prisoners at Guantanamo Bay. That would be an important vindication of the rule of law, but it would leave the prisoners at Guantanamo Bay with a long struggle to attain (a) justice on the merits of their habeas corpus applications, and (b) fair trials before regular courts.

So far I have considered what is happening at Guantanamo Bay in largely legal terms. There is, however, a wider view. Looking at the hard realities of the situation, one wonders what effect it may have on the treatment of United States soldiers captured in future armed conflicts. It would have been prudent, for the sake of American soldiers, to respect humanitarian law. Secondly, what must authoritarian regimes, or countries with dubious human rights records, make of the example set by the most powerful of all democracies? In his recent John Galway Foster lecture, Professor Koh of Yale University has shown how many foreign governments, who want to free themselves of the restraints of human rights, have already directly invoked the United States policy in regard to the Guantanamo Bay prisoners as justification for their actions.[50] Thirdly, the type of justice meted out at Guantanamo Bay is likely to make martyrs of the prisoners in the moderate Muslim world with whom the West must work to ensure world peace and stability.

---

[49] 478 US 186 (1986).
[50] *The United States and Human Rights*, Oct 2003, London.

What other route could the United States have taken? The International Criminal Court could not be used to try the Guantanamo Bay prisoners because the Rome Treaty applies prospectively only, and the prisoners were captured before the Treaty came into force in July 2002. The United States courts could have assumed universal jurisdiction for war crimes. The prisoners would have received fair trials before ordinary United States courts. It would have been an acceptable solution. On the other hand, the Muslim world would probably not have accepted this as impartial justice. The best course would have been to set up through the Security Council an ad hoc international tribunal. That would have ensured that justice is done and seen to be done.

There is, of course, a dilemma facing democracies. Aharon Barak, President of the Supreme Court of Israel, presided in a case in which the court held that the violent interrogation of a suspected terrorist is not lawful even if doing so may save human life by preventing impending terrorist acts. He confronted the problem created for democracies by terrorism. He said:[51]

> We are aware that this decision does not make it easier to deal with the reality. This is the fate of democracy, as not all means are acceptable to it, and not all methods employed by its enemies are open to it. Sometimes, a democracy must fight with one hand tied behind its back. Nonetheless, it has the upper hand. Preserving the rule of law and recognition of individual liberties constitute an important component of its understanding of security. At the end of the day, they strengthen its spirit and strength and allow it to overcome its difficulties.

Such restraint is at the very core of democratic values.

It may be appropriate to pose a question: ought our government to make plain publicly and unambiguously our condemnation of the utter lawlessness at Guantanamo Bay?[52] John Donne, who preached in the Chapel of Lincoln's Inn, gave the context of the question more than four centuries ago:

> No man is an Island, entire of it self; every man is a piece of the Continent, a part of the main; . . . any man's death diminishes me, because I am involved in Mankind; And therefore never send to know for whom the bell tolls; it tolls for thee.

---

[51] The citation relies on the magisterial essay of President Aharon Barak, 'A Judge on Judging: The Role of a Supreme Court in a Democracy', Harvard LR vol 116, no 1 Nov 2002, at 148.

[52] I have been greatly helped in preparing this lecture by my wife, Susan, by Laura Johnson, my judicial assistant, and by Alex Glassbrook, my son-in-law.

Part Five

Contract and Tort Law

[19]
The Role of Good Faith and Fair Dealing in Contract Law: A Hair-Shirt Philosophy?

The aim of any mature system of contract law must be to promote the observance of good faith and fair dealing in the conclusion and performance of contracts. The first imperative of good faith and fair dealing is that contracts ought to be upheld. But there is another theme of good faith and fair dealing: the reasonable expectations of honest men must be protected. It occasionally requires that the law should treat contractual obligations as defeasible or that a discretionary remedy should be denied. In these broad terms the common law and the civil law have a shared view of the aim of the law of contract.

It is in the matter of high technique that the jurisprudence of common law and civil law countries sharply differ. The level of generality of legal rules lies at the heart of the difference. English law favours empirical and concrete solutions; the civil law proceeds deductively from broad first principles. This difference in approach extends to statute law. In England the prevailing legislative technique seeks to provide detailed and concrete regulation. In civil law countries the legislative technique of stating broad principles still has great appeal. In *New Zealand Shipping Co. Ltd* v. *A. M. Satherwaite & Co. Ltd.*,[1] Lord Wilberforce characterised English contract law as follows:[2]

> "English law, having committed itself to a rather technical and schematic doctrine of contract, in application takes a rather practical approach, often at the cost of forcing the facts to fit uneasily into the marked slots of offer, acceptance and consideration."

In *Interfoto Library Ltd.* v. *Stilleto Ltd.*,[3] Lord Justice Bingham drew attention to the fact that in many civil law systems the law of contract recognizes and enforces an overriding principle that in making and carrying out contracts parties should

---
* The Royal Bank of Scotland Lecture 1991, Oxford, published by arrangement with Mr Justice Steyn and the Royal Bank of Scotland.

1. [1975] Q. B. 154.
2. At p. 167.
3. [1989] 1 Q. B. 433.

act in good faith. He pointed out that it means a great deal more than that parties ought not to deceive each other. He added:[4]

"English law has, characteristically, committed itself to no such overriding principle but has developed solutions in response to demonstrated problems of unfairness."

In my view Lord Justice Bingham has encapsulated the distinctive features of the two great progenitors of national legal systems, the common law and the civil law.

This difference in technique between the common law and the civil law is linked with a fundamental difference in philosophical approach between the common law and the civil law. The common law requires consideration for the existence of an enforceable contract. The civil law requires only subjective *consensus ad idem*. The approach of English law to the formation of a contract is largely objective. In civil law regimes it is largely subjective. In England there is an objective theory of the interpretation of contracts, with a rigid exclusion of evidence of prior negotiations and subsequent conduct as an aid to interpretation. In civil law jurisdictions the approach is more subjective, and evidence of prior negotiations and subsequent conduct is treated as part of the logically probative material. Throughout the web of English contract law the criterion of the reasonable man's response predominates. In the civil law greater account is taken of subjective factors. This emphasis of English law on an objective approach to contractual issues tends to make England somewhat infertile soil for the development of a generalized duty of good faith in the performance of contracts.

It is interesting to reflect how greatly commercial cases, and in particular international trade cases, have contributed to the shaping of the distinctive features of our law of contract. The perceived needs of commerce have been decisive. The dominant view has been that concrete regulation best serves the needs of commerce. The vigour of this view has spilled over into the field of commercial arbitration. Generally speaking, civil law countries allow parties to an arbitration agreement to stipulate that the arbitrator shall settle their differences *ex aequo et bono* or by amiable composition. Indeed, the Model Law of Arbitration, which was published by the United Nations Commission on International Trade Law (UNCITRAL) in 1985, expressly authorizes such methods of dispute resolution if the parties have so agreed.[5] To this day the orthodox view in England is that all clauses giving an arbitrator the power to decide in accordance with good conscience rather than legal rules are devoid of legal effect. Significantly, this restriction on the freedom of parties is said to rest on English public policy. Enough has been said to demonstrate a certain distrust of the *aequum et bonum* in England.

4. At p. 439.
5. Art. 28(2).

THE ROLE OF GOOD FAITH AND FAIR DEALING IN CONTRACT LAW

It is no part of my thesis that the civil law of contract is a more logical system than the common law. Like any other system the common law has flaws. But it is by and large a coherent and logical system. It is, however, undoubtedly a system that favours concrete rather than general solutions. This can be illustrated by a few practical examples. In English law the doctrine of rectification had to be developed to deal with cases where an integrated written contract inaccurately reflects the true agreement of the parties. No such doctrine is needed in civil law jurisdictions because it would be contrary to good faith for a party to put forward as accurate a document which does not reflect the true agreement of the parties. The second example relates to the implication of contractual terms. There is a popular misconception that it is particularly difficult in English law to imply terms in a contract. Compared to the civil law, English law shows a considerable hospitality to implied terms. In civil law countries the existence of a generalized duty of good faith in the performance of contracts reduces the need for the implication of terms. In the absence of a doctrine of good faith English law has to resort to the implication of terms by reason of the nature of the contract (*e.g.*, an implied duty to cooperate where the contract cannot be performed without cooperation, as in *MacKay* v. *Dick*)[6] or by reason of special circumstances of a particular contract. The third example is the burgeoning field of estoppel by representation and by convention. In the absence of a generalised duty of good faith the specific and concrete rules of estoppel are needed to deal with demonstrated problems of unfairness.

I do not intend to examine the subject of my lecture historically. My purpose is simply to consider the question whether England has anything to learn from jurisdictions where, in the field of contract law, duties of good faith and fair dealing are of general application. Traditionally, English lawyers have been unreceptive to such ideas. The title of this lecture echoes the remarks of Lord Templeman in *Banque Financiere* v. *Westgate Insurance Co.*,[7] a case in the House of Lords in which my flirtation with notions of fair dealing, in a very different context, was conclusively and decisively rejected by the House of Lords. Lord Templeman said:[8]

"A professional should wear a halo but need not wear a hair shirt."

It is probably right to say that most English lawyers still adopt an equally jaundiced view of notions of good faith and fair dealing.

On the other hand, there are winds of change which may produce a climate more receptive to notions of good faith and fair dealing in England. Under the influence of civilian traditions the United States Uniform Commercial Code,[9] and the

---

6. (1881) 6 App. Cas. 251.
7. [1990] 3 W.L.R. 364.
8. At p. 374.
9. S1-203.

Restatement of Contracts, Second,[10] now explicitly provide that parties are obliged to observe good faith in the performance and enforcement of a contract. The United States has adopted a synthesis of common law and civil law traditions. Distinguished commentators have also pointed out that in Australia and New Zealand notions of good faith and fair dealing are gaining ground.[11] In the Australian High Court is has been stated that the rationale of estoppel is good conscience and fair dealing.[12]

But there are also internal signs that English contract law is not to be regarded as set in tablets of stone dating from the time of Lord Eldon. The doctrine of consideration has played a powerful role in the development of English contract law. In England consideration is not under siege. It has not been qualified out of existence. On the other hand, in the practice of the courts, particularly in commercial cases, it has receded in importance. It may be negative anecdotal evidence but I have no recollection of any claim in the Commercial Court failing for lack of consideration in recent years. Privity of contract used to be regarded as the cornerstone of the law of contract. The notion of an enforceable *stipulatio alteri* was a heresy to traditionalists. Yet now we find that the Law Commission is actively investigating the question whether the privity rule should be maintained in its present rigid form. Earlier in this lecture I referred to general observations of Lord Justice Bingham in the *Interfoto* case. It is also instructive to consider his approach to the decision to be made in that case. The issue before the Court was the application of the doctrine of notice of standard form contractual conditions. Lord Justice Bingham held:[13]

> 'The tendency of the English authorities has, I think, been to look at the nature of the transaction in question and the character of the parties to it, to consider what notice the party alleged to be bound was given of the particular condition said to bind him; and to resolve whether in all the circumstances it is fair to hold him bound by the condition in question. This may yield a result not very different from the civil law principle of good faith, at any rate so far as the formation of the contract is concerned."

Today, there is at our universities a keen awareness of the fact that the law of contract, tort and restitution ought to be seen as part of a coherent law of obligations: each knitting into the other and influencing the other. The recent decision of the House of Lords in *Murphy* v. *Brentwood District Council*[14] has heralded a remarkable contraction in the scope of the law of tort. No doubt the

---

10. S. 205.
11. H. K. Lucke, "Good Faith and Contractual Performance", in P. D. Finn (ed.), *Essays on Contract* (1986), pp. 18-21; P. D. Finn, "Commerce, the Common Law and Morality", *Melbourne University L.R.*, 17 (1989), p. 87.
12. *Walton's Stores (Interstate) Ltd.* v. *Maher* (1988) 62 A.L.J.R. 110, at p. 129.
13. *Supra* n. 3, at p. 455 B-C.
14. [1990] 3 W.L.R. 414.

pendulum will swing again. For the present, however, the policy of incrementalism rather than high principle reigns. But it is interesting to speculate whether the effect of the contraction of the law of tort will result in an extension of contractual techniques. Possibly we will hear more about collateral contracts in the next few years.

There are international portents of change in relation to notions of good faith and fair dealing. On 11 April 1980 the representatives of 62 states (including representatives of the United Kingdom) approved the United Nations Convention on Contracts for the International Sale of Goods. The Vienna Sales Convention, as it is commonly called, required ratification by at least 10 states. It duly came into force on 1 January 1988. By the end of April 1991, 30 states had ratified the Vienna Sales Convention. Seven states are engaged in the process of ratification. It is believed that the number of ratifications may increase to 50 in the next two years. Within the European Economic Community, France, Italy and Germany have ratified the convention. In the common law family of states the United States and Australia have ratified the convention. Clearly, the international market place is voting for the convention. No international convention will ever completely satisfy all countries. But the text of the Vienna Sales Convention represents a satisfactory compromise between contrasting points of view.[15] Hopefully, there will shortly be a ministerial announcement that the United Kingdom will ratify the convention. If the will to ratify this convention now is absent, our businessmen will be placed at a disadvantage in international commerce. The Vienna Sales Convention bears the badge of neutrality, and it will prove popular among businessmen worldwide. If the United Kingdom does not ratify the convention now, commercial realities will compel ratification later. What, you may ask, does this have to do with my paper? The answer is that it underlines three points which are worth making. In the first place the convention demonstrates convincingly that in sales law the principles of the civil law and the common law can be blended into a coherent text. Secondly, if this country is to play a positive and influential role in the harmonization of international trade law, an insular attachment to the unsullied purity of the common law is not the best way forward. Thirdly, Article 7(1) provides:

"In the interpretation of this convention, regard is to be had to its international character and to the need to promote uniformity in its application and the observance of good faith in international trade."

Here one has a classic compromise which enabled the experience of the common law and the civil law to be blended into a generally acceptable international convention. The convention does not create a duty to observe good faith in the conclusion and performance of contracts. Article 7(1) only requires the observance

---

15. B. Nicholas, "The Vienna Convention on International Sales Law", (1989) 105 L.Q.R. 201.

of good faith in the interpretation of the convention itself. Nevertheless, if England ratifies the convention, English lawyers and judges will become used to employing the criterion of good faith in the wide process of interpretation of the convention.

The impact of the EEC on English contract law is a matter for a future generation of legal historians. Provisionally, it is my impression that the technique of the civil law is bound to play a major role in the decision making processes of EEC institutions, and that it is unlikely that the traditional technique of English contract law will remain unaffected. There is opportunity here for only one example. In September 1990, the European Commission published a Proposed Directive for submission to the Council of the European Communities. The purpose of the Proposed Directive is to facilitate the establishment of a single internal market by December 1992 by ensuring harmonized consumer protection laws in EEC countries. It applies to every contract between a consumer and a party acting in the course of trade, business or profession. It prohibits the use of unfair terms, and renders such terms void if used in contravention of the prohibition. The Proposed Directive is not limited to exception and limitation clauses: it extends to all contractual terms. It spells out that a term is unfair, *inter alia*, if:

"it is incompatible with the requirements of good faith."

If the Proposed Directive becomes law, it will be incumbent on the United Kingdom to give effect to its terms. The criterion of good faith will then come to play an important policing role over contractual terms in our consumer law. On the other hand, it is important to note that the Proposed Directive does not create a duty of good faith in the performance of contracts. Prohibiting unfair terms, and creating a positive duty of good faith in the performance of contracts, are very different things.

The philosophy of *caveat emptor* rather than notions of good faith and fair dealing has dominated English contract law. In *Bell* v. *Lever Bros.*[16] it was stated to be a principle of universal validity. Yet the notions of good faith and fair dealing have left some imprint on English contract law. Apart from special fiduciary relationships, contracts of insurance, suretyship, salvage and partnership are categorized as contracts of the utmost good faith. On the other hand, the scope of the duty of disclosure under a contract of insurance is very different from the scope of the duty of disclosure under contracts of suretyship, salvage and partnership. Later I will turn briefly to insurance contracts. Rules of equity regarding contractual penalties, unconscionable bargains and the limited remedy of relief from forfeiture also provide a refrain reminiscent of good faith notions. A classic instance of the notions of good faith and fair dealing prevailing over *caveat emptor* is provided by the rule that a party is not entitled to "snap up" an offer which he

16. [1932] A.C. 161, at p. 227.

THE ROLE OF GOOD FAITH AND FAIR DEALING IN CONTRACT LAW

knows to have been made under a mistake.[17] Sometimes duties of good faith are implied in particular contracts. In every contract of employment there is a term that the employer will not, without reasonable and proper cause, conduct himself in a manner calculated to destroy or seriously damage the relationship of confidence between employer and employee.[18] This term has been held to be an implied obligation of good faith.[19] Bearing in mind that an implied term must be clear and workable, the implication of an implied term of good faith in employment contracts must count as some acknowledgement of the utility of the concept of good faith in English contract law. Another thread is provided by cases where the contract expressly provides that the question whether a particular condition is fulfilled will depend on the unilateral approval of one of the parties. The interpretation of such a clause, depending on the language and context, will almost invariably be either that the decision making party must have reasonable grounds for his decision or that he need only act in good faith.[20] This is an example of English courts introducing the concept of good faith in a contractual context by a process of construction.

Our legislature has also on occasions adopted the technique of setting statutory standards of fair dealing. Three examples will be sufficient. A defence of fair dealing has existed under the Copyright Acts of 1911, 1956 and 1988. Until 1988 the defence applied only to literary, dramatic or musical copyright. In 1988 that defence was extended to broadcasts. Then there is the Unfair Contract Terms Act 1977. Although the Act does not expressly use the terminology of good faith and fair dealing, nevertheless it adopts a similar technique by requiring certain contractual terms to run the gauntlet of a criterion of reasonableness. By and large, however, the scope of the Act is restricted to exception and limitation clauses. Another illustration is to be found in the Consumer Credit Act 1974. It provides that if the Court finds a credit bargain extortionate it may reopen the credit agreement so as to do justice between the parties. It is expressly provided that a credit bargain is extortionate if it grossly contravenes ordinary principles of fair dealing. I do not, of course, suggest that by using the analogy of statutes judges may create new legal rights and obligations. But often judges have to choose between equally feasible solutions, and statutes can then legitimately be invoked as demonstrating the good sense or workability of a particular solution.

Taking stock of the position, my conclusion is that good faith and fair dealing have so far played a limited role in English contract law. But there are signs that the English legal culture may become (or may have to become) more receptive to such notions.

How much difference does it make whether a legal system is based on a patchwork of concrete legal rules, or uses the technique of an generalised duty of

17. *Hartog* v. *Colin and Shields* [1939] 3 All E.R. 566.
18. *Woods* (1981) IRL.R. 347.
19. *Imperial Group Pension Trust Ltd.* v. *Imperial Tobacco Ltd.* [1991] 2 All E.R. 597, at p. 606b.
20. *Niarchos (London) Ltd.* v. *Shell Tankers* [1961] 2 Lloyd's L.R. 496.

good faith? In a seminal article published in 1956, Professor Raphael Powell stated his provisional answer as follows.[21] First, he said that quite often the foreign court, using the medium of a rule requiring good faith, arrives at the same conclusion as an English Court which has used another rule or a more roundabout route. Relying on such limited practical experience as I have in the resolution of international trade disputes, governed by different laws, I would change the emphasis slightly by saying that an identical result by a different route is the general pattern. Secondly, Professor Powell said that in a number of cases a rule requiring good faith has enabled the foreign court to adjust relations between the parties more equitably than an English court in similar circumstances. My impression is that this proposition is correct to this day. But any judge's unconcious bias in favour of the justice and the merits of the case tends to reduce the incidence of different results.

Having indulged in too many generalities, it is now necessary to consider a case where one would expect a general duty of good faith in the performance of a contract to generate fair subsidiary rules. I select the example of an insurance contract which in the theory of English law imposes duties of the utmost good faith on both parties to the contract. In *Carter* v. *Boehm*,[22] decided in 1766 by Lord Mansfield, it was ruled that the *uberrima fides* principle, as it is sometimes called, imposes reciprocal duties of good faith on the insured and insurer. Lord Mansfield said that this principle extends to all contracts. This view was soon rejected but in relation to contracts of insurance the principle of *uberrima fides* has survived. My reason for selecting this example is twofold. First the contract of insurance is of great importance to commercial users and consumers alike. Secondly, this example will illustrate that what matters is not whether a contract is characterised as one giving rise to duties of good faith but whether the reality matches the nomenclature.

The rules governing non-disclosure under a contract of insurance sometimes compel a court to reach unfair results.[23] A minor and innocent non-disclosure may entitle the insurer to avoid. In *Container Transport Inc.* v. *Oceanus Mutual Underwriting Association (Bermuda) Ltd.*,[24] the Court of Appeal stated the law in terms which are starkly at variance with notions of good faith. First, the Court of Appeal ruled that in relation to the materiality of the matter not disclosed the only relevant yardstick was the probable reaction of a prudent insurer if it had been disclosed: it is irrelevant what the actual insurer's reaction would have been. Secondly, the Court of Appeal ruled that the proper test as to materiality is not whether the matter in question would have influenced the judgment of a prudent insurer in deciding whether to take the risk or in fixing the premium. The question

---

21. "Good faith in Contracts", [1956] *C.L.P.* 16.
22. 3 Burr. 1905.
23. See R. A. Hasson, "The Doctrine of *Uberrima Fides* in Insurance Law – a Critical Evaluation", (1969) 32 *M.L.R.* 615.
24. [1984] 1 Lloyd's L.R. 476.

is simply whether the matter not disclosed would have been taken into account by the underwriter in his decision making process. Since the *Container Transport* case related to marine insurance, the proper construction of the Marine Insurance Act 1906 played a major role in the reasoning of the court. But the Act, although not exhaustive, was a restatement of the common law. And, like cases ought to be decided alike. This decision is therefore equally applicable outside marine insurance law.

While the correctness of the *Container Transport* decision is not in issue, one can legitimately ask whether the law as stated in this case is satisfactory. It is difficult to understand why an underwriter should be able to avoid a contract for non-disclosure, when he would have written the risk anyway. If he would have chosen not to act as a prudent underwriter would have done, because he was seeking to create a new book of business, why should he be able to avoid? Moreover, how can avoidance on the grounds of a non-disclosure, which was causally irrelevant as far as the actual underwriter is concerned, be squared with the proposition that the parties owe each other reciprocal duties of the utmost good faith? Under the general law of misrepresentation proof of actual inducement is necessary. Why should an insured's position under a contract of the utmost good faith be less favourable?

The second point is also important. In the *Container Transport* case the trial judge had held that the test of materiality is whether the non-disclosure would have influenced the judgment of a prudent underwriter in accepting the risk or fixing the terms. As a result of the decision in the Court of Appeal the law is now that it is sufficient if the underwriter would have taken the matter into account albeit that he would thereafter have dismissed it from his mind as unimportant. This statement of the law is not in accord with the general law regarding misrepresentation. A party who seeks to avoid a contract on the ground of misrepresentation must show on a balance of probabilities that he was induced. It is easy for an insurer, upon rummaging through the documents an insured has disclosed upon discovery, to find grounds for raising defences of non-disclosure. Is this rule fair? Assume a fire insurance where a shopkeeper failed to disclose a small fire 10 years ago since when the shopkeeper introduced additional fire precautions. Conceivably, the evidence might show that if the matter had been disclosed a prudent underwriter would have written the risk on exactly the same terms. But it will in practice be easy to find an underwriter to testify that he would have taken the earlier fire into account. Does it accord with good faith and fair dealing, that the insurer should be able to avoid on such flimsy grounds?

Accepting the law as stated in *Container Transport* to be correct, it seems to me that the rules regarding non-disclosure under a contract of insurance are unfairly tilted in favour of the insurers. The only justification for this state of law is a premise that makes the insurers the judges in commercial causes in which they stand to lose money. The traditional argument is: insurers act responsibly and would only rely on a technical non-disclosure if there is good reason to suspect deliberate misconduct by the insured. It is a specious argument. This part of English insurance law is not easy to reconcile with duties of good faith and fair dealing.

It is also of some interest to consider the policy of our legislature in relation to insurance contracts. The insurance policies currently in use in England contain many unfair conditions and exceptions. Yet the Unfair Contract Terms Act 1977 provides that such contracts are wholly excluded from the scope of the Act. In this respect our Act is different from corresponding legislation in some other E.E.C. countries. The fact that the contract is a contract of the utmost good faith ought surely to be an incentive to prohibit, or control, unfair conditions and exceptions in contracts of insurance. Why are contracts of insurance excluded from the scope of this legislation? No ground of public interest suggests itself. There is only one answer: the astonishing strength of the insurance lobby secured the exemption.

Returning now to the question in the title of this paper, my answer is that good faith and fair dealing is in no sense a hair shirt philosophy. On the contrary, it has been demonstrated in the hard school of litigation and international commercial arbitration to be a perfectly workable and sensible technique for the imposition of legal duties in many legal systems, and in parts of our own system. Undoubtedly, contract law should strive to attain certainty of rights and predictability of results. But I regard as unproven the assertion that the pragmatic approach of our law necessarily leads to greater certainty and predictability than the more general methods of the civil law. But there is no need to abandon our legal heritage. Our methods have by and large served us tolerably well. Moreover, I am not persuaded that generalised duties of good faith are useful across the spectrum of contractual relations. There are so many varieties of contract. In some contexts good faith and fair dealing have no significant role to play. Such is the case, for example, in many commercial contracts where one is not concerned with fault but simply with an allocation of the risks of a particular undertaking or enterprise.[25] On the other hand, as our legal culture becomes more familiar with notions of good faith and fair dealing, it may be that in some areas there will be greater scope for using principles of good faith and fair dealing. Here I particularly have in mind consumer law. We live in a consumer society of mass production, distribution and consumption in which the nineteenth century premise of freedom of negotiation is a myth. But even in this field there may be a powerful case for the law to be developed by using the traditional techniques of the common law. My rather lame verdict is that there is no one self-evidently right answer on this point.

But I do firmly believe that if principles of good faith and fair dealing are to gain wider acceptance in consumer law, it will be important not to give to such principles too abstract a moral content. While a definition of good faith and fair dealing is impossible, it seems to me that the law ought not to set its sights too high.

---

25. Prof. G. Treitel, "Fault in the Common Law of Contract", in *Liber Amicorum for Lord Wilberforce* ed. M. Bos and I. Brownlie (1987), p. 185 *et seq.*.

THE ROLE OF GOOD FAITH AND FAIR DEALING IN CONTRACT LAW

These notions ought to reflect not the response of a moral philosopher but the responses and usages of ordinary right thinking people. But I would willingly forego such a development, provided that in using the high technique of common law the closest attention is paid to the purpose of the law of contract, *i.e.*, to promote good faith and fair dealing. After all, it is right that academic lawyers, practitioners and judges should constantly consider whether rules of law under consideration serve the purpose which led to their formation. Or, putting it more simply, we must never lose sight of Lord Reid's observation in *Cartledge* v. *E. Jopling & Sons Ltd.* that "The common law ought never to produce a wholly unreasonable result...".[26]

Nothing is more important than that the next generation of lawyers should approach the activities of Parliament, and the decisions of judges at every level with open-minded scepticism. Vigorous criticism is one of the great shaping forces of the common law. And we must never underestimate the continued capacity of the common law for disciplined growth in accordance with its own traditions.[27]

---

26. [1963] A.C. 758, at p. 772.
27. Mr J. Beatson, a Law Commissioner, read a draft of this lecture and made a number of suggestions which I have incorporated in the final text. The flaws in it are entirely my responsibility.

Contract Law: Fulfilling the Reasonable Expectations of Honest Men*

A thread runs through our contract law that effect must be given to the reasonable expectations of honest men. Sometimes this is made explicit by judges; more often it is the implied basis of the court's decision. I would like to examine what this means, and to relate it to some parts of English contract law. It is an important subject for the future development of English contract law.

The modern view is that the reason for a rule is important. The rule ought to apply where reason requires it, and no further. But often the real purpose of a rule is debatable. The question can then only be solved by rational argument, and a judgment by an impartial judge. Once the purpose of a rule has been identified by effective and proper adjudication, it is an important and legitimate matter to enquire whether the rule as formulated fulfils that purpose. If it appears not to fulfil the purpose, it is potentially defective. At the very least a judge, and particularly an appellate court, is then entitled to re-examine the law to make doubly sure that the law indeed commands that a rule must be applied that does not make sense. Usually, it will be found, on conscientious and rigorous re-examination, that the common law solution is one which is meaningful and in accord with common sense. In that process of re-examination a judge is entitled to take into account that simple fairness ought to be the basis of every legal rule and, in a common law case, that the presumption in favour of the fair solution is powerful. These considerations are the framework in which one must approach the proposition that in contract law effect must be given to the reasonable expectations of honest men.

That leads me to a preliminary distinction. It is a defensible position for a legal system to give predominance to the subjective intentions of the parties. Such a policy can claim to be committed to the ideal of perfect individualised justice. But that is not the English way. Our law is generally based on an objective theory of contract. This involves adopting an external standard given life by using the concept of the reasonable man. The commercial advantage of the English approach is that it promotes certainty and predictability in the resolution of contractual disputes. And, as a matter of principle, it is not unfair to impute to contracting parties the intention that in the event of a dispute a neutral judge should decide the case applying an objective standard of reasonableness. That is then the context in which in English law one should interpret the proposition that effect must be given to the reasonable expectations of honest men.

---

* This is a revised text of the Eleventh Sultan Azlan Shah Lecture delivered by Lord Steyn in Kuala Lumpur on October 24, 1996.

It is possible to refine the meaning of the proposition. Once one uses the external standard of reasonableness the reference to honest men adds little. Although the hypothetical reasonable man pursues his own commercial self-interest he is by definition not dishonest. The proposition can therefore be re-defined simply to say that the law must respect the reasonable expectations of the contracting parties. That brings me to consider what the reasonable expectations of the parties means. The expectations that will be protected are those that are, in an objective sense, common to both parties.[1] The law of contract is generally not concerned with the subjective expectations of a party. The law does not protect unreasonable expectations. It protects only expectations which satisfy an objective criterion of reasonableness. Reasonableness is a familiar concept and no definition is necessary. But it is, of course, right to stress that reasonableness postulates community values. It refers not to the standards of Lord Eldon's day. It is concerned with contemporary standards not of moral philosophers but of ordinary right thinking people. Sometimes those standards will receive their distinctive colour from the context of a consumer transaction, a business transaction or even a transnational financial transaction. And the usages and practices of dealings in those disparate fields will be prime evidence of what is reasonable.

It is of some relevance to consider the status of our proposition. It is certainly not a rule of law. It is possible to argue that it is a general principle of law, such as, for example, the principle that no man may benefit from his own wrongdoing. I prefer to regard it as the central objective of the law of contract. The function of the law of contract is to provide an effective and fair framework for contractual dealings. This function requires an adjudication based on the reasonable expectations of parties. It is right to acknowledge, however, that the reasonable expectations of parties cannot always prevail. Sometimes they must yield to countervailing principles and policies. For example, other values enshrined in law and public policy may render the contract defeasible. Nevertheless, the aim of protecting reasonable expectations remains constant.[2]

It is now possible to examine how the English law of contract measures up to this policy. Inevitably, I will have to be selective. But I hope to look at topics that are of considerable practical importance. The first relates to the formation of contracts.

The classical doctrine is that a contract can only come into existence by the congruence of a matching offer and acceptance. As a general proposition this makes sense. But it does not solve all cases satisfactorily. Take, for example, the so-called battle of the forms cases, notably in the

---

[1] Reiter and Swan, "Contracts and the Protection of Reasonable Expectations," in *Studies in Contract Law* ed. Reiter and Swan (1980), 1 at p. 7.
[2] Reiter and Swan, *op. cit. supra* at p. 6.

field of negotiations for the conclusion of building and engineering contracts. Each party insists on contracting only on his own standard conditions. In the meantime the work starts. Payments are made. Often it is a fiction to identify an offer and acceptance. Yet reason tells us that neither party should be able to withdraw unilaterally from the transaction. The reasonable expectations of the parties, albeit that they are still in disagreement about minor details of the transaction, often demand that the court must recognise that a contract has come into existence. The greater the evidence of reliance, and the further along the road towards implementation the transaction is, the greater the prospect that the court will find a contract made and do its best, in accordance with the reasonable expectations of the parties, to spell out the terms of the contract.[3]

That brings me to a serious blemish in the English law of contract. Some eighty years ago, in *Dunlop Pneumatic Tyre Co. Ltd v. Selfridge Co. Ltd*[4] the House of Lords held that English law does not recognise a contract for the benefit of a third party. This rule was re-affirmed by the House of Lords in *Midland Silicones Ltd v. Scruttons Ltd.*[5] Subsequently, in *Kepong Prospecting Ltd v. Schmidt*, in an appeal from Malaysia the Privy Council held that the doctrine of privity of contract is separate from consideration. The Privy Council said[6]:

> "But it was suggested that the law of Malaysia differed from the law of England in admitting the principle of *jus quaesitum tertio*. Their Lordships are of opinion that the appellant company failed to make good this contention. Their Lordships were not referred to any statutory provision by virtue of which it could be said that the Malaysian law as to contracts differs in so important a respect from English law. It is true that section 2(*d*) of the Contracts Ordinance gives a wider definition of 'consideration' than that which applies in England particularly in that it enables consideration to move from another person than the promisee, but the appellant was unable to show how this affected the law as to enforcement of contracts by third parties, and it was not possible to point to any other provision having this effect."

Despite the condemnation by many judges and academic writers the privity rule still lingers on. The rule was laid down as being a self evident proposition of logic. But the logic was flawed. It is indeed obvious that a bilateral contract cannot impose a burden on a stranger. But if for commercial or other good reasons two parties agree that one will confer a benefit on a third party, and the latter accepts the benefit, no legal logic demands that the stipulation be denied effect. Certainly, the doctrine of

---

[3] *G. Percy Trentham Ltd v. Archital Luxfer Ltd* [1993] 1 Lloyd's Rep. 25.
[4] [1915] A.C. 847.
[5] [1962] A.C. 446.
[6] [1968] A.C. 810 at p. 826.

consideration poses no problem: ex hypothesi the stipulation for the benefit of a third party is part of an agreement involving an exchange of promises between the contracting parties. The ruling in *Dunlop Pneumatic* is inconsistent with the prime function of the law of contract, which is to facilitate commercial dealings. It ignores the fact that parties in good faith rely on the agreement for the benefit of a third party. It fails to take into account that businessmen, for sensible reasons, sometimes wish to enter into such promises in favour of third parties. Confidence in promises is the lifeblood of commerce; and there can be no confidence if parties are not obliged to perform their promises. The privity rule causes particular difficulties where main contractors, subcontractors and consultants are linked in a network of contracts. The privity rule also frequently prevents a party to a bilateral contract from taking out an insurance policy for the benefit of a third party. Where there is no statutory inroad on the privity rule such a stipulation is unenforceable. Take also the common example of a buyer of goods from a distributor. As part of the distributorship agreement between the manufacturer and distributor a manufacturer's warranty is given for the benefit of the buyer. No consideration passes from the buyer to the manufacturer. The manufacturer's warranty is a classic contract for the benefit of a third party. It would be a serious defect in our contract law if businessmen were precluded by legal doctrine from conferring such benefits on third parties. Not surprisingly, judges display much ingenuity in inventing exceptions to the rule to avoid the inconvenience and unfairness of the rule. It is also noteworthy that a contract for the benefit of a third party is recognised in the legal systems of most European countries, as well as in much of the common law world, including the United States, New Zealand and parts of Australia. In an excellent report the English Law Commission has recommended that the rule be reversed by statute.[7] Given decades of procrastination one would hope that the proposed legislation will now be enacted speedily. It is to be noted, however, that the Bill provides that the legislation should not be construed as preventing judicial development of third party rights. That is important because the legislation may not be comprehensive. The Law Commission's proposals require identification of the third party by name, as a member of a class or as answering a particular description. It may not give a remedy in all cases. It may therefore still be desirable for the House of Lords to review *Dunlop Pneumatic* in a suitable case.

This brings me to the related topic of consideration. The classic model of English contract law is a bargain: and a bargain postulates an exchange. Consideration is therefore historically a fundamental doctrine of English law. Almost 90 pages are devoted to it in the ninth and latest edition of

---

[7] *Privity of Contract: Contracts for the Benefit of Third Parties*, Law Com. No. 242, Cm. 3329 (1996).

Professor Treitel's book on contract law. At first glance it seems a highly technical doctrine. The question may be asked why the law should refuse to sanction a transaction for want of consideration where parties seriously intend to enter into legal relations and arrive at a concluded agreement. If the court refuses to enforce such a transaction for no reason other than that the parties neglected to provide for some minimal or derisory consideration, is it not arguably a decision contrary to good faith and the reasonable expectations of the parties? Some of these considerations may have led Lord Goff of Chieveley in *The Pioneer Container* to say that it is now open to question how long the principles of privity of contract and consideration will continue to be maintained.[8] In my view the case for abandoning the privity rule is made out. But I have no radical proposals for the wholesale review of the doctrine of consideration. I am not persuaded that it is necessary. And great legal changes should only be embarked on when they are truly necessary. First, there are a few cases where even in modern times courts have decided that contractual claims must fail for want of consideration. On the other hand, on careful examination it will usually be found that such claims could have been decided on other grounds, *e.g.* the absence of an intention to enter into legal relations or the fact that the transaction was induced by duress. Once a serious intention to enter into legal relations and a concluded agreement is demonstrated in a commercial context there is virtually a presumption of consideration which will almost invariably prevail without a detailed search for some technical consideration.[9] On balance it seems to me that in modern practice the restrictive influence of consideration has markedly receded in importance. Secondly, it seems to me that in recent times the courts have shown a readiness to hold that the rigidity of the doctrine of consideration must yield to practical justice and the needs of modern commerce. The landmark case is the decision of the Court of Appeal in 1990 in *Williams v. Roffey Bros. & Nicholls (Contractors) Ltd.*[10] The important question arose whether there is sufficient consideration where one contracting party promised to pay an additional sum to the other contracting party simply in return for a further promise by the latter to perform his already existing contractual obligations. The orthodox view would have been that there was no consideration. But the Court of Appeal unanimously held that the defendants were bound by their promise since there was consideration in the form of the practical benefit inherent in the transactions. The court was obviously concerned that the doctrine of consideration should not restrict the ability of commercial contractors to make periodic consensual modifications, and even one-sided modifications, as the work under a construction contract proceeded. The

---

[8] [1994] 2 A.C. 324 at p. 335; see also *White v. Jones* [1995] 2 A.C. 207 at pp. 262–263; *The Makhutai* [1996] A.C. 650 at pp. 663–665.
[9] See *The Eurymedon* [1975] A.C. 154 at p. 167.
[10] [1991] 1 Q.B. 1.

reasonable expectations of the parties prevailed over technical and conceptualistic reasoning.

Next I turn to the approach of English law to the concept of good faith. In the new *jus commune* of Europe there is a general principle that parties must negotiate in good faith, conclude contracts in good faith and carry out contracts in good faith. The important point to note is that in exercising his rights and performing his duties each party must act in accordance with good faith and fair dealing. And the parties may not exclude this duty.[11] The Principles of International Commercial Contracts published by Unidroit also provide that in international trade parties must act in accordance with good faith and fair dealing, and that they may not exclude or limit this duty.[12] In the United States the influential Uniform Commercial Code is explicitly and squarely based on the concept of good faith. Elsewhere in the common law world, outside the United Kingdom, the principle of good faith in contract law is gradually gaining ground. It is the explicit basis of many international contracts. Since English law serves the international market place it cannot remain impervious to ideas of good faith, or of fair dealing. For my part I am quite confident that businessmen and indeed people on the Underground have no problem with the concept of good faith, or fair dealing. They understand very well what bad faith means. But English lawyers remain resolutely hostile to any incorporation of good faith principles into English law. The hostility is not usually bred from any great familiarity with the way in which the principle works in other systems. But it is intense. My impression is that the basis of the hostility is suspicion about what good faith means. If it were a wholly subjective notion, one could understand the scepticism. If it were an impractical and open-ended way of fastening contractual liability onto parties, it would deserve no place in international trade. But it is none of these things. While I accept that good faith is sometimes used in different senses I have in mind what I regard as the core meaning. Undoubtedly, good faith has a subjective requirement: the threshold requirement is that the party must act honestly. That is an unsurprising requirement and poses no difficulty for the English legal system. But good faith additionally sets an objective standard, *viz.*, the observance of reasonable commercial standards of fair dealing in the conclusion and performance of the transaction concerned. For our purposes that is the important requirement.[13] Used in this sense judges in the greater part of the industrialised world usually have no great difficulty in identifying a case of bad faith. It is not clear why it should

---

[11] *Principles of European Contract Law, Part 1: Performance, Non-Performance and Remedies*, prepared by the Commission on European Contract Law, ed. Lando and Beale (1995), Art 1.106 (p. 53).

[12] Art. 1.7 (pp. 16–17).

[13] Farnsworth, "Good Faith in Contract Performance", in *Good Faith and Fault in Contract Law* ed. Beatson and Friedmann (1995), 154–190.

perplex judges brought up in the English tradition. It is therefore surprising that the House of Lords in *Walford v. Miles* held that an express agreement that parties must negotiate in good faith is unenforceable. Lord Ackner observed that the concept of a duty to carry on negotiations in good faith is inherently repugnant to the adversarial position of the parties when involved in negotiations.[14] As the Unidroit principles make clear it is obvious that a party is free to negotiate and is not liable for a failure to reach an agreement. On the other hand, where a party negotiates in bad faith not intending to reach an agreement with the other party he is liable for losses caused to the other party. That is a line of reasoning not considered in *Walford v. Miles*. The result of the decision is even more curious when one takes into account that the House of Lords regarded a best endeavours undertaking as enforceable. If the issue were to arise again, with the benefit of fuller argument, I would hope that the concept of good faith would not be rejected out of hand. There is no need for hostility to the concept: it is entirely practical and workable. Indeed from July 1995 the E.C. Directive on Unfair Terms in Consumer Contracts has been in operation in England.[15] The Directive treats consumer transactions within its scope as unfair when they are contrary to good faith. It is likely to influence domestic English law. Given the needs of the international market place, and the primacy of European Union law, English lawyers cannot avoid grappling with the concept of good faith. But I have no heroic suggestion for the introduction of a general duty of good faith in our contract law. It is not necessary. As long as our courts always respect the reasonable expectations of parties our contract law can satisfactorily be left to develop in accordance with its own pragmatic traditions. And where in specific contexts duties of good faith are imposed on parties our legal system can readily accommodate such a well tried notion. After all, there is not a world of difference between the objective requirement of good faith and the reasonable expectations of parties.

That brings me to the interpretation of written contracts. Disputes about the meaning of contracts is one of the largest sources of contractual litigation, notably in respect of international contracts. The reason is, in the words of Oliver Wendell Holmes, that a word is not a transparent crystal. Clarity is the aim but absolute clarity is unattainable. And it is impossible for contracting parties to foresee all the vicissitudes of commercial fortune to which their contract will be exposed. Moreover, and quite understandably, business bargains have to be struck under great pressure of events and time. In passing I add that it is therefore particularly tiresome for judges to expatiate on the quality of draftsmanship of commercial contracts. Judges must simply do the best they can with the raw materials

---

[14] [1992] 2 A.C. 128 at p. 138E. See Sir Patrick Neill Q.C. (1992) 108 L.Q.R. 405.
[15] Unfair Terms in Consumer Contracts Regulations, S.I. 1994 No. 3159.

they are given. Given the intractable nature of problems of construction, the solution of English law is not to ask what the parties subjectively intended but to ascertain what in the context of the contract the language means to an ordinary speaker of English. By and large the objective approach to questions of interpretation serves the needs of commerce. It tends to promote certainty in the law and predictability in dispute resolution. But I must examine the matter in a little more detail. There is the rule that the court is not permitted to use evidence of the pre-contractual negotiations of the parties or their subsequent conduct in aid of the construction of written contracts even if the material throws light on the subjective intentions of the parties. Logically, these rules follow from the primary rule that the task of the court is simply to ascertain the meaning of the language of the contract. And the rationality of the law is important. But, if these rules were absolute and unqualified the primary rule would sometimes defeat the reasonable expectations of commercial men. Pragmatically, it has been decided that if pre-contractual exchanges show that the parties attached an agreed meaning to ambiguous expressions that may be admitted in aid of interpretation.[16] That is a substantial inroad into the primary rule in aid of the protection of the reasonable expectations of the contracting parties. More importantly, the courts have resorted to estoppel to temper the rigidity of orthodox rule regarding the inadmissibility of subsequent conduct. Thus in the *Vistafjord* the Court of Appeal authoritatively held that a party may be precluded by an estoppel by convention from raising a contention contrary to a common assumption of fact or law (including the interpretation of a contract) on which the parties have acted.[17] The operation of the estoppel is flexible: it only prevails so far as it would be unjust if one of the parties resiled from the agreed assumption. By this means the reasonable expectations of parties can fairly be met. This is simply one of many examples of the percolation of promissory estoppel into contract law. Promissory estoppel is often used to soften the rigidity of classical contract law solutions in order to give effect to the reasonable expectations of parties.

The general approach of courts to problems of interpretation has undergone a substantial change in the last twenty-five years. There has been a shift away from a black-letter approach to questions of interpretation. The literalist methods of Lord Simonds are in decline. The purposive approach of Lord Reid and Lord Denning, M.R, has prevailed. Two questions can be posed. First, what is literalism? This is easy. The tyrant Temures promised the garrison of Sebastia that no blood would be shed if they surrendered to him. They surrendered. He shed no blood. He

---

[16] *The Karen Oltmann* [1976] 2 Lloyd's Rep. 708. See McLauchlan (1997) 113 L.Q.R. 237.
[17] [1988] 2 Lloyd's Rep. 343.

buried them all alive.[18] That is literalism. It has no place in modern law. Second, the significance of the trend towards purposive construction must be considered. It does not mean that judges now arrogate to themselves the power to rewrite contracts for parties. It signifies an awareness that a dictionary is of little help in solving problems of construction. Often there is no obvious or ordinary meaning of the language under consideration. There are competing interpretations to be considered. In choosing between alternatives a court should primarily be guided by the contextual scene in which the stipulation in question appears. And speaking generally commercially minded judges would regard the commercial purpose of the contract as more important than niceties of language. And, in the event of doubt, the working assumption will be that a fair construction best matches the reasonable expectations of the parties.

That brings me to the implication of terms. In systems of law where there is a general duty of good faith in the performance of contracts the need to supplement the written contract by implied terms is less than in the English system. In our system, however, the implication of terms fulfils an important function in promoting the reasonable expectations of parties. Three categories of implied terms can be identified. First, there are terms implied by virtue of the usages of trade and commerce. The assumption is that usages are taken for granted and therefore not spelled out in writing. The recognition of trade usages protects the reasonable expectations of the parties. Secondly, there are terms implied in fact, *i.e.* from the contextual scene of the particular contract. Such implied terms fulfil the role of ad hoc gap fillers. Often the expectations of the parties would be defeated if a term were not implied, *e.g.* sometimes a contract simply will not work unless a particular duty to co-operate is implied. The law has evolved practical tests for the permissibility of such an implication, such as the test of whether the term is necessary to give business efficacy to the contract or the less stringent test whether the conventional bystander, when faced with the problem, would immediately say "yes, it is obvious that there is such an implied term". The legal test for the implication of a term is the standard of strict necessity. And it is right that it should be so since courts ought not to supplement a contract by an implication unless it is perfectly obvious that it is necessary to give effect to the reasonable expectations of parties. It is, however, a myth to regard such an implied term as based on an inference of the actual intention of the parties. The reasonable expectations of the parties in an objective sense are controlling: they sometimes demand that such terms be imputed to the parties. The third category is terms implied by law. This occurs when incidents are impliedly annexed to particular forms of contracts, *e.g.* contracts for building work, contracts of

---

[18] This example is given in *The Works of William Paley* (1838 edn.) Vol. III, 60. Paley's moral philosophy influenced thinking on contract in the last century.

sale, hire, etc. Such implied terms operate as default rules.[19] By and large such implied terms have crystallised in statute or case law. But there is scope for further development. In such new cases a broader approach than applied in the case of terms implied in fact must necessarily prevail. The proposed implication must fit the generality of cases. Indeed, despite some confusion in the authorities, it is tolerably clear that the court may take into account considerations of reasonableness in laying down the scope of terms to be implied in contracts of common occurrence.[20] This function of the court is essential in providing a reasonable and fair framework for contracting. After all, there are many incidents of contracts of common occurrence which the parties cannot always be expected to reproduce in writing. This type of supplementation of contracts also fulfils an essential function in promoting the reasonable expectations of the parties.

By way of conclusion I would acknowledge that the English law of contract is far from perfect. There is never a last and definitive word on the law. Yet there has been progress. In a more formalistic era courts sometimes neglected to consider the reason for a rule. But formalism is receding. Modern judges usually have well in mind the reason for a rule and in a contract case that means approaching the case from the point of view of the reasonable expectations of the parties. Where contract law is still deficient it will usually be found that the cause is that the reasonable expectations of the parties have been ignored or given inadequate weight. The most serious structural defect in English contract law is the privity rule. Otherwise English contract law is generally capable of safeguarding the reasonable expectations of parties by its own pragmatic methods. It is therefore not surprising that English standard form contracts are widely used in international transactions. Even more important is the fact that English proper law clauses are widely used in international trade. Businessmen tend to be knowledgeable and they vote for the legal system of their choice with proper law clauses. They recognise that the English law of contract is admirably designed to cope with the challenges of a modern and changing business world. It draws its strength and vitality from a close adherence to the reasonable expectations of the contracting parties.

---

[19] There is an excellent discussion of terms implied by law by Rakoff, "Implied Terms: Of 'Default Rules' and 'Situation Sense'", in *Good Faith and Fault in Contract Law*, ed. Beatson and Friedmann (1995), 191.

[20] *Liverpool City Council v. Irwin* [1977] A.C. 239; *Scally v. Southern Health and Social Services Board* [1991] 1 A.C. 294.

* A Lord of Appeal in Ordinary.

[21]
Written Contracts: To What Extent May Evidence Control Language?

All judges are prone to error. And one of the principal causes of judicial error is a lack of knowledge of the environment of the critical decision. Such an environment may be, in a general common law case, the impact of the decision on other areas of the law; in a judicial review case, the historical and social context of a statute; in a commercial case, the way in which a particular trade or market works; and many other examples spring to mind. But the law sometimes sets limits to the extent to which a judge may be informed of, and take into account, the broad environment against which his decision will be made. My concern is with the extent to which a judge, who is confronted with a problem of the interpretation of an integrated written contract as opposed to an issue of contract formation, may allow evidence of the broader environment to control the language of the contract, and therefore to influence the answer to the question to be decided. The interesting question is not what evidence may be admitted but the substantive question of the extent to which evidence may ultimately be allowed to influence the answer to the question of interpretation. Since all language is imprecise, and the vicissitudes of contractual relations are unpredictable, even Sir James Murray's great dictionary will seldom provide the answer. Some evidence, or agreement as to the relevant facts, will always be necessary.

The critical question is: Where is the line to be drawn? The answer to that question varies greatly between different legal systems. It is interesting to contrast the approaches of the common law and the civil law. The common law classifies all issues of interpretation as questions of law. The common law rules are based on an objective approach to the interpretation of contracts. The question is not what the parties subjectively intended but what

24 Written Contracts

meaning would be given to the language of the contract by an ordinary speaker of the English language, who is placed in the position of the parties at the time when they made their contract. English law therefore adopts an external standard and subordinates the equity of the particular case to the policy of striving for legal certainty in the generality of cases. Proceeding from this starting point English law readily arrives at the conclusion that evidence may only be used in aid of the interpretation of contracts in limited circumstances.

The civilian approach is diametrically opposite: the purpose is to determine what the parties actually intended when they made the contract. The meaning of contracts is generally regarded as a question of fact. It is a subjective theory of interpretation. The starting point is the language of the contract. But, if there is uncertainty about the meaning of the language, or a dispute about the intention of the parties, a civilian court will take into account all material which arguably throws light on the intention of the parties.

The superiority of the English system, and the desirability of maintaining it, should not be presumed. A number of factors combine to suggest that a re-examination may not be out of place. First, the jurisprudence of the European Court of Justice in relation to the interpretation of contracts is squarely based on the civilian approach. Secondly, the practice of the common law countries is not uniform: in the case law of the United States there has been a radical departure from the common law rules as developed by the English courts, with the result that in this area of the law the United States straddles the middle ground between the traditional common law and civilian approaches. Thirdly, in relation to wills and statutes, exclusionary rules as to the use of extrinsic material in aid of interpretation have been relaxed to some extent: in the case of wills by a 1982 statute[1] to broaden the categories in which an otherwise meaningless will may be construed in the light of evidence of a testator's intention, and in the case of statutes by House of Lords' decisions[2] which have made clear that statutes passed to give effect to unenacted treaties must nevertheless, when ambiguous, be construed in the light of the treaty and its *travaux preparatoires*. Finally, even in the framework of our own system, there have been attacks on the traditional approach, and attempts to circumvent it. The time is therefore ripe to take a critical look at our rules.

There are three classes of evidence which no sensible system of law can ignore. The first is identificatory evidence. It is self-evident that evidence ought always to be admitted to relate the terms of a contract to the external world, *i.e.* to identify persons, things and concepts. Such evidence is used not in order to construe the contract but only to ascertain whether a given factual situation comes within the words of the contract. So far there is nothing to excite controversy. But one has to add that identificatory evidence may itself give rise to difficulties of interpretation in the form of a latent ambiguity, and that qualification brings me to the second uncontroversial class of evidence.

In everyday life words receive their colour from their context. Samuel Johnson illustrated that in his dictionary by defining "oats" as—

> "A grain, which in England is generally given to horses, but in Scotland supports the people."

Time, place and circumstances are relevant to the process of selecting the appropriate meaning. And our law does recognise this reality. The purpose for which such evidence is admitted is to place the court in the same contextual scene as the parties were when they signed the contract or, in the conventional idiom, "The court must ... place itself in thought in the same factual matrix as that in which the parties were."[3] The advocate who urges the admission of seemingly inadmissible material, as a factor capable of arousing sympathy for his client's favoured interpretation, almost invariably says, "it is part of the factual matrix." But catchphrases tend to obscure the true nature of legal principles. Two questions arise. The first is *when* evidence of surrounding circumstances may be called in aid of interpretation. The second is *what* evidence may be used for this purpose. It used to be said that evidence of surrounding circumstances may only be used when there is an ambiguity in the language of the contract, or an ambiguity revealed by admitting identificatory evidence. In *Reardon Smith Line Ltd.* v. *Yngvar Hansen-Tangen*[4] the House of Lords held that in all commercial cases it is right that the court should know the commercial purpose of the contract which, it was said, presupposes knowledge of the genesis of the transaction, the background, the context and the market in which the parties are operating. But, if sufficient certainty as to the meaning of the contract can be gathered from the language alone, it would clearly not be right to reach a different result by drawing inferences from evidence as to the surrounding circumstances. In such a case the verdict must be that the resort to surrounding circumstances has proved unnecessary. It is helpful to concentrate not on what evidence a judge ought to admit as a matter of the rules of evidence, because under this heading he will admit what is arguably relevant, but on what use he may make of such material in selecting, as between contending interpretations, the appropriate one. No adequate generalised proposition is possible. All one can say is that the use which a judge may make of such materials will depend on how far the language is capable of stretching.[5] In other words, it depends on the different meanings which the language itself will let in. And it has rightly been said:

> "Language is a labyrinth of paths. You approach from one side and know your way about; you approach from another side and no longer know your way about."[6]

Where the uncertainty of the language of the contract is such that it is necessary and right to draw inferences from surrounding circumstances, it still remains to be considered what evidence of the objective setting of the contract may be allowed to influence the decision. It used to be said that the purpose of the rule is to allow recourse to objective matters and circumstances which were probably present to the minds of the parties when they contracted. If the rationale of the rule were allowed so to circumscribe the classes of evidence, which may be used in aid of the construction of contracts, a great deal of useful contextual material would be excluded. In *Reardon Smith Line Ltd.* v. *Yngvar Hansen-Tangen*,[7] a more flexible approach was adopted. It was held that when one is speaking of extrinsic evidence of aim, or object, or commercial purpose, one is speaking objectively of what reasonable persons would have in mind in the situation of the parties. In other words, the judge, who is faced with a question of interpretation, should consider all classes of evidence which arguably forms part of the objective setting in which a contract is to be construed. And it is no answer to say that the parties, or one of them, ignored the objective setting.

Given the fact that the sometimes amorphous objective setting of a contract may be allowed to influence its interpretation, the case for allowing a crystallised custom or usage to do so is overwhelming. A distinction must be drawn between custom and usage. The role of custom is deeply rooted in our legal history. It was one of the formative influences in the development of our commercial law. Today, that role has greatly diminished. Custom has played other roles: in localities where a custom was observed it enabled and still enables a court to annex incidents to a contract or to give a secondary meaning to contractual language. In order to establish a custom stringent requirements have to be met: a custom must be lawful, not inconsistent with the contract, reasonsable, notorious, certain and universally acquiesced in. The stringency of these requirements is such that the role of custom in the interpretation of written contracts is nowadays of marginal importance only. But in the course of time a more flexible doctrine, permitting the use of evidence of trade usage falling short of custom, became established. The good sense of the development is clear: it is the assumption that usages are mostly taken for granted and therefore not spelled out in writing. To ignore such usages would be to defeat the reasonable expectations of parties. When will it be right for a judge to allow such a usage to control the issue of interpretation? Negatively, it is easy to agree on the proposition that trade usage ought not to be encumbered with the stringent requirements of custom. For example, in the last few years the financial pages of our national newspapers have recorded the emergence of a number of new and orderly financial and commodities' markets, with a regularity of observance of usages, which ought to be recognised in the process of interpretation. In what seems to me a maze of irreconcilable precedent, I have been unable to find any coherent analysis of the circumstances in which a trade usage as opposed to a custom may be allowed to control an issue of interpretation. Here is a task still to be performed; it will require separate and special study. All I can tentatively suggest is that in the meantime the despairing judge may not go too far wrong if he adopts the simple and liberal solution of the United States Uniform Commercial Code.[8] It defines a trade usage as "any practice or method of dealing having such a regularity of observance in a place, vocation or trade as to justify an expectation that it will be observed with respect to that transaction." But it also provides that a trade usage will only bind a person if, when he contracted, he knew of it or should have known of it. Given the doubt that exists about the precise boundaries of trade usage, it is obvious in principle that any sensible legal system must allow recourse to it in aid of interpretation of written contracts.

Two classes of evidence mark the great divide between the common law and civilian systems, *viz.* evidence of prior negotiations and subsequent conduct of the parties. In civilian systems the search is for the subjective *consensus ad idem* of the parties. The concept of rectification of a written contract is not known. Pre-contractual exchanges are freely admitted as evidence of the parties' actual intentions. But it is probably right to say that the clearer the language of an integrated written contract the less likely it is that the court will ultimately allow evidence of the negotiations to control the interpretation. And, if the parties have contracted on standard-form terms, it is in practice difficult to persuade a civilian court to depart from the ordinary meaning of the language on the basis of inferences from the evidence of the negotiations. In England the rule is different. Pre-contractual negotiations are let in by a plea of rectification. But if that plea fails the judge may not allow his interpretation of the contract to be influenced by evidence of negotiations.[9] The rule is that evidence of the parties' intentions, or negotiations, may not be received as an aid to interpretation. This rule was clearly established by the decision of the House of Lords in *Prenn* v. *Simmonds*.[10] Lord Wilberforce, who gave the leading judgment, explained the rationale of the rule. He said that the reason for the rule is not a technical one or even one mainly of convenience. Such evidence is unhelpful because the positions of the parties change until final agreement. If earlier documents use different expressions, that does not help. If the same expressions are used, nothing is gained by looking back. And, the words used may and often do represent a formula which means different things to each side, yet are accepted because that is the only way to get agreement. Lord Wilberforce also referred to the judgment of Cardozo J. in *Utica City National Bank* v. *Gunn*[11] to dispel, as he said, "the idea that English law is some island of literal interpretation." He said that the New York Court of Appeals "followed precisely the English line." But in that case the great American judge was considering the admissibility of evidence of "the genesis and aim of the transaction," and not of evidence of pre-contractual negotiations. And it is tolerably clearly established in the United States, despite its multiplicity of jurisdictions, that pre-contractual negotiations are admissible in aid of the interpretation of contracts.[12] The terrain of the debate in the United States was apparently whether an ambiguity must be shown before such evidence may control the decision. In the Restatement Second of Contracts[13] Corbin's liberal view prevailed over Williston's more restrictive view. The law of the United States has therefore developed along very different lines.

But it is necessary to examine Lord Wilberforce's pragmatic justification of the rule. It would clearly not be right to say that evidence of negotiations is always unhelpful in the search for the subjective consensus of the parties. If it were, the practice of civilian courts, and of courts in the United States would be different. All one can safely say is that in the real world such evidence seldom reveals material which satisfactorily establishes the subjective consensus of the parties at the time of the making of their contract. The real reason for the exclusion of such evidence is the philosophical starting point of English law: the purpose of the process of interpretation is not to find what the parties intended but to determine what the language of the contract would signify to an ordinary speaker of English, who is properly informed as to the objective setting of the contract. In relation to that enquiry evidence of the actual intentions of the parties, or of their pre-contractual communications, is unhelpful.

Leaving aside the case of rectification, the question arises whether the exclusionary rule is subject to any exceptions. One hesitates to add to the burgeoning field of application of the doctrine of estoppel, but it seems conceivable that in pre-contractual exchanges an unequivocal representation as to the meaning of a word or expression may be made by one party, and that the other party may sign the contract in reliance on it, thus giving rise to an estoppel. But that must be a fairly rare case. A judgment given in the Commercial Court, appeared to form the basis of another potentially more virile exception to the general rule. In *Karen Oltmann*[14] the court used pre-contractual telex exchanges as an aid to the interpretation of an ambiguous word on the basis that the exchanges revealed that the parties had negotiated on an agreed basis. It was said that the parties had given to the word the same dictionary meaning. And this conclusion was reached despite the fact that the judge held that there was no basis for rectifying the contract, or for finding that an estoppel operated. It is an exception which could easily swallow up the rule. That has, however, not happened so far and this decision can perhaps be regarded either as justified on the orthodox basis of an estoppel or as depending on its own rather special facts. So, the rule appears to be intact.

That brings me to the next category of evidence which is in the controversial area where the solutions of civilian and common law legal systems differ, *i.e.* evidence of the conduct of the parties during the performance of the contract which reveals how they understood words and expressions in the contract. An example will illustrate the point. An exporter negotiates a revolving credit line for two years with his bank to finance his export transactions at an historic rate of interest. The limit is £1,000,000. He uses the facility repeatedly; on two occasions he repays the entire sum due to the bank; thereafter he uses the facility again. Then during the two-year period a rise in interest rates makes the transaction unprofitable for the bank. The exporter wishes to use the facility again. The bank then says "once you have repaid the entire sum the facility is at an end." The merchant says "But you did not say that when the market was in your favour." To the lay mind, and in particular a businessman, such evidence is not only relevant but of great persuasive value. In civilian systems such evidence is regarded as an important source of reliable information as to the true intention of the parties. In the United States such evidence is called "practical construction," and is given great weight as an aid to construction.[15] In England, on the other hand, such evidence is inadmissible as an aid to construction. If such evidence is admitted on the basis of pleas of variation or estoppel, and the pleas fail, the evidence as to subsequent conduct must be ignored. In the seventies the House of Lords was on two occasions asked to reconsider the rule.[16] But on each occasion the traditional rule was reaffirmed. It may be useful, however, to explore the reason for the exclusionary rule. For Lord Simon of Glaisdale in *Schuler A.G.* v. *Wickman Machine Tool Sales Ltd.* the principal reason was that subsequent conduct is equally referable to what the parties meant to say as to the meaning of what they said.[17] Lord Wilberforce stated the objection as follows:—

> "The general rule is that extrinsic evidence is not admissible for the construction of a written contract; the parties' intentions must be ascertained, on legal principles of construction, from the words they have used. It is one and the same principle which excludes evidence of statements, or actions, during negotiations, at the time of the contract, or subsequent to the contract, any of which to the lay mind might at first seem proper to receive."[18]

It cannot be doubted that such evidence may be helpful if the object of the enquiry is to determine the subjective consensus of the parties. Given that English contract law eschews that as an object of interpretation but instead seeks to determine the ordinary meaning of the language, in its objective setting, the result inevitably follows that such evidence cannot be allowed to influence interpretation. Evidence of the subsequent conduct of the parties, like evidence of prior negotiations, could only become admissible as an aid to construction if the objective theory to the interpretation of contracts was abandoned.

In taking stock of the merits and demerits of the different approaches, one has to accept that in a hard case the decision of a Continental and an English judge may be different.[19] Which is the better system? The disinterested idealist would probably say that the civilian approach represents a search for complete and perfect justice between the parties, and is therefore to be preferred. He would say that contractual disputes ought to be resolved in the light of all the facts of the case, and that the self-denying ordinance prescribed by the objective theory of interpretation results, from time to time, in a denial of justice. And he would probably say the English approach must occasionally result in an interpretation which neither party put forward. The answer of the English lawyer is pragmatic: he seeks to justify the objective approach on practical grounds. He points out that as between the parties to the contract the English approach tends to make the resolution of issues of interpretation more predictable, and, he would add, predictability is a matter of the greatest importance in commerce. He says that in an increasingly complex commercial world, a written contract between two parties is frequently linked with other contracts, and often forms the basis of other dealings. Third parties must necessarily take written contracts at face value. The interests of trade are therefore advanced by the objective theory. He says the resolution of contractual disputes is rendered less time-consuming and costly under the English system of allowing only limited resort to extrinsic evidence. Justice is more important than time and money. But the administration of civil justice cannot sensibly be organised on the basis that time and money do not matter. Moreover, the English lawyer says that it is an entirely defensible philosophical stance to say that under our system, the parties to a contract assume the risk of the interpretation which an impartial court or arbitral tribunal may place on their words. And, finally, he points to the popularity of English standard forms of contract in international commerce and to the remarkably high incidence in international transactions of an express choice of English law as the proper law of the contract and, in other cases, of the inclusion of a London arbitration clause. The English commercial lawyer says, and I agree, that the English approach has been vindicated in the international market-place, as well as in the hard school of international commercial litigation and arbitration.

NOTES

[1] Administration of Justice Act 1982, s.21(2)(a).
[2] *Fothergill* v. *Monarch Airlines Ltd.* [1981] A.C. 251; *Gatoil International Inc.* v. *Arkwright–Boston Manufacturers Insurance Co. Ltd.* [1985] A.C. 255.
[3] *Reardon Smith Line Ltd.* v. *Yngvar Hansen-Tangen* [1976] 1 W.L.R. 989 at 997C, *per* Lord Wilberforce.
[4] *Supra* at 995H, *per* Lord Wilberforce.
[5] *Fustis Mining Co.* v. *Bear* 239F. 976.
[6] Wittgenstein, *Philosophical Investigations* (1953), para. 203.
[7] *Supra* at 996E–F, *per* Lord Wilberforce.

[8] Section 1–205. See also Joseph H. Levie, "Trade Usage and Custom under the common law and the Uniform Commercial Code" 40 N.Y.U.L.R. 1101.

[9] On the other hand, it may be permissible to have recourse to pre-contractual exchanges for the limited purpose of identifying the objective setting of the contract. See *Prenn* v. *Simmonds*, [1971] 1 W.L.R. 1381 at 1385A, *per* Lord Wilberforce.

[10] *Supra.*

[11] (1918) 118 N.E. 607.

[12] Farnsworth, *Contracts*, 1982.

[13] s.212.

[14] [1976] 2 Ll.L.R. 708. See also *Polaris Aktieselskap* v. *Unilever Ltd.* 39 Com.Cas. 1 at 9, *per* Lord Atkin.

[15] Farnsworth, *op. cit.*, s.7.13.

[16] See *Whitworth Street Estates (Manchester) Ltd.* v. *James Miller & Partners* 1970 A.C. 583; *Schuler A.G.* v. *Wickman Machine Tool Sales Ltds.* 1974 A.C. 235.

[17] *Supra*, at 263F.

[18] *Supra*, at 261B.

[19] One is alive to the dangers of generalising about foreign legal systems. Fortunately, I had the advantage of the comments of Dr. Albert Jan van den Berg, a distinguished Dutch lawyer, on a draft of this lecture.

[22]
A Kind of Esperanto?

THERE is bound to be some hostility among English lawyers to the ratification of the U.N. Convention on Contracts for the International Sale of Goods, 1980. Such hostility is not simply the result of the conservatism of those who practise law: it is an aversion to what are conceived to be impractical and theoretical solutions offered in the name of misguided internationalism. Anthony Trollope explained this inclination of English lawyers in Orley Farm through the views of an experienced barrister of Lincoln's Inn. The passage reads as follows:[1]

'Mr Furnival, with many others—indeed, with most of those who were so far advanced in the world as to be making bread by their profession—was of opinion that all this palaver that was going on in the various tongues of Babel would end as it began—in words. 'Vox et praeterea nihil'. To practical Englishmen most of these international congresses seem to arrive at nothing else.'

The judgement of 'practical Englishmen' must be read in the context of Trollope's description of Lord Boanerges, a congenital law reformer and attender of international conferences. It has been suggested that Victorians would immediately have thought of Lord Brougham.[2] His full title was Baron Brougham and Vaux. A contemporary joke was apparently to say, unfairly, that he was *Vox et praeterea nihil*.

The Hague Rules received the force of law by the Carriage of Goods by Sea Act 1924. The Hague Rules were embodied in a convention adopted at an international conference. The Rules placed substantial limitations on the freedom of contract of shipowners. There was fierce opposition from English lawyers to the proposed ratification of the convention. The eleventh edition of Scrutton on Charterparties was edited by Lord Justice Scrutton and by the future Lord Justice MacKinnon. It was published in 1923, the year before the enactment of the Carriage of Goods by Sea Act. The editors of this influential textbook criticized the enactment of the Hague Rules in extreme language. They described the intended change in the law as 'a terrifying prospect'.[3] The objection of these eminent lawyers was to the very conception of the enactment of a multi-lateral international convention which interfered with the freedom of contract of citizens of this country. An acknowledged master of shipping law and its history, Lord Roskill, has explained that the United Kingdom's enactment of the Carriage of Goods by Sea Act 1924 was the result of the acceptance by the Government and shipowners in 1923 that Britannia no longer ruled the waves, and that her shipowners were no longer able to dictate terms to the traders of the world.[4] Today, nobody would seriously defend the position taken by Scrutton and MacKinnon. They were demonstrably wrong in what Lord Roskill described as hysterical opposition to the enactment of the Hague Rules. But it *is* important to remember that they spoke at the time for 'practical Englishmen', and for a legal profession confident that an international multi-lateral convention should not be allowed to detract from rights accorded by the common law.

It must not be thought that this hostility to international conventions was restricted to judges and practising lawyers. Based on a study of official papers released under the socalled thirty year rule, and with reference to the period to the middle fifties Dr Patrick Polden has commented as follows:[5]

'Most of the Lord Chancellors of this period, and their permanent secretaries, shared with the majority of judges and lawyers a profoundly insular outlook towards the law which made them instinctively hostile towards almost any proposition which might trench on the sovereignty of the English courts. Bilateral treaties to facilitate the enforcement of private rights might be tolerated, though seldom encouraged, but multilateral treaties and conventions were anathema.'

A good illustration is to be found in the field of international commercial arbitration. The Geneva Protocol of 1923 had two objectives. The first was to ensure that arbitration clauses would be enforceable internationally. The second was to ensure that arbitration awards made pursuant to such arbitration agreements would be enforced in the territory of the states in which they were made. Although the Geneva Protocol was limited in its application, it proved a highly successful convention. The Geneva Convention of 1927 broadened the field of application of the Geneva Convention of 1923. These two conventions provided the backbone of the New York

---

[1] Chapter XVII.
[2] Mullen, *Anthony Trollope, A Victorian in his World*, 1990, 484, footnote.
[3] Introduction, v.
[4] (1992) 105 L.Q.R. 501.
[5] *Guide to the Records of the Lord Chancellors Department*, Chapter 10. The Guide was published in 1988.

A Kind of Esperanto?

Arbitration Convention of 1958, which must rank as a great success story in the field of international conventions. But it is now clear from official papers released under the thirty year rule that the Lord Chancellor, Lord Cave, and the Permanent Secretary, Sir Claud Schuster, bitterly opposed the ratification of the Geneva Protocol of 1923. The flavour of the opposition appears from a letter written by Sir Claud Schuster in 1924. The Permanent Secretary referred to the birth of the Protocol. He then stated:[6]

'I was most unfortunately present at that birth. I protested in season and out of season against any such protocol being entered into. When it had been entered into, in spite of my opposition, there was not much object in attempting to obstruct the passage of the Bill.

The then Lord Chancellor (Lord Cave) was also opposed to the making of the protocol. Unfortunately the whole thing took place when he was ill, and his opposition, therefore, was greatly hampered ... I do not see what more we can do. I think we had better await the catastrophe which will undoubtedly follow and only hope that the officious persons who hatched this senseless document will then have to bear the consequences of their misdeed.'

This hostility to international conventions did not cease in 1923. A period of seventeen years elapsed before this country ratified the New York Arbitration Convention of 1958. It would be naive to suppose that the antipathy of English lawyers multilateral conventions had disappeared. But the success of the 1958 convention, the accelerating rate of ratifications, and the fact that the United Kingdom was being left out in the cold in international commercial arbitration, compelled ratification. And belated ratification of this convention in 1975 has been of enormous benefit to the United Kingdom.

Recently, there has been another manifestation of such antipathy towards international conventions. It concerns the Vienna Sales Convention. It took the form of a detailed note in a prestigious law journal under the heading 'International Conventions and Commercial Law: The Pursuit of Uniformity'.[7] The author was Sir John Hobhouse, an immensely experienced and most distinguished High Court Judge who sits in the Commercial Court. Apart from the Vienna Sales Convention the author specifically considers the following conventions and draft texts: U.N. Convention on the limitation period on the International Sale of Goods, New York, 1974; EEC Convention on the Law Applicable to Contractual Obligations, Rome, 1980; UNIDROIT Convention on Agency in the International Sale of Goods, Geneva, 1983. For present purposes I am only concerned with the writer's views on the Vienna Sales Convention. The writer poses the question whether the Vienna Sales Convention serves a useful purpose in the field of commercial law or provides a satisfactory basis for municipal legislation. He argues that the sole objective of the Vienna Sales Convention is the 'achievement of a stark uniformity'. He contends that the very concept of the convention is subversive of certainty which is the first and paramount requirement of a sound commercial law. He says that the convention is 'an inadequate legal tool without compensating gain'. He objects to the fact that the convention is in mandatory form. He likens the 'utopian ideal', which led to the adoption of the convention, to the movement for the adoption of Esperanto as a universal language. In conclusions he says:

'What should no longer be tolerated is the unthinking acceptance of a goal of uniformity and its doctrinaire imposition on the commercial community. Only conventions which demonstrably satisfy the well proven needs of the commercial community should be ratified and legislation should only be agreed to if it is demonstrably fit to be enacted as part of the municipal law of this country."[8]

As far as I am aware the arguments of Mr Justice Hobhouse have not been answered or critically examined. That is my only justification for venturing to express disagreement in print with the views of an esteemed colleague. But having abandoned any self-denying ordinance it is right that I should express my contrary views as clearly and forthrightly as Mr Justice Hobhouse expressed his views.

B. The Quality of the Text of the Convention

Given the controversy about the acceptability of the Vienna Sales Convention for incorporation into our municipal law, it is necessary to assess the quality of the text of the convention. This is the threshold question. It is important, however, to approach this qualitative enquiry realistically. The convention is not a rival text, domestically inspired and drafted, to the Sale of Goods Act. The convention was adopted on 11 April 1980 by 62 states. Thirty-four states have deposited instruments of ratification, accession, etc. It is therefore to be judged as an international text which has already received wide currency.

The subjectmatter of the convention is the international sale of goods. It is difficult to think of any good reason why the international sale of goods should intrinsically be less suitable as the subjectmatter of an international convention than, say, carriage of goods by sea. Domestically, the sale of goods was regarded as a suitable subjectmatter for

---

[6] Letter dated 25.10.1924 to Chitty. I am indebted to Mr V. V. Veeder, Q.C., for drawing my attention to this material.

[7] (1990) 106 L.Q.R. 530.
[8] op. cit., 535.

codification as long ago as 1893. And in international terms, although there is a substantial divergence in sales regimes of different nations, there is also sufficient common ground to make it a suitable subjectmatter for an international convention. I will not struggle with the point. The very fact that a convention was adopted by 62 nations, and ratified, acceded to, etc, by 34 nations to date, makes it impossible to argue that international sale of goods is intrinsically not a suitable subjectmatter for an international convention.

That brings me back to the quality of the particular text which was adopted. The drafting style of the convention is not that favoured by English Parliamentary draftsmen. I suspect that many English judges, who have to grapple with English statutes, would not regard this point as fatal to the intrinsic merits of the text of an international convention. I agree with the assessment of Mr Glower W. Jones that the Vienna Convention is expressed in the simple phraseology of commerce: it should be comprehensible to traders and lawyers alike.[9]

The delegates to the Vienna conference had to make compromises. The text is a blend of the techniques of the common law and the civil law. The nature of the compromises is usually clear. Occasionally, there is ambiguity. In international contract negotiations parties often leave a draft contract in ambiguous form in order to achieve agreement. The reasoning is: 'If we insist on our meaning being spelt out in the agreement the transaction will be lost. We will take the risk that a neutral judge or arbitrator will uphold our view if there is a dispute'. Similarly, in the drafting of an international convention studied ambiguity is a standard technique employed to achieve a consensus. Professor Nicholas gives a good illustration of this process at work in respect of the Vienna Sales Convention.[10] Article 16 (2) of the convention provides that an offer cannot be revoked

'(a) if it indicates, whether by stating a fixed time for acceptance or otherwise, that it is irrevocably; or
(b) if it was reasonable for the offeree to rely on the offer and being irrevocable and the offeree has acted in reliance on the offer.'

The provision in (a) is ambiguous. It has been pointed out that for the common lawyer, stating a fixed time for acceptance is *prima facie* no more than an indication that after that time the offer, unless revoked, will lapse. On the other hand, for the civil lawyer it indicates that the offer is irrevocable until that time. Professor Nicholas points out that at the Vienna conference a United Kingdom amendment designed to clarify the text in the common law sense was rejected, as was a West German amendment in the opposite sense. The ambiguity was recognized. Deliberate ambiguity is a fact of life in the negotiation of an international conventions. And in character it is not all that different from the occasion when Parliamentary draftsmen, acting on departmental instructions, simply say 'No. We will not clarify that point. We will leave it to the courts.' Making due allowance for this feature in the Vienna Sales Convention, it is important not to exaggerate its importance.

From an English point of view the intrinsic merits of the text have been examined and analyzed in depth by Mr J D Feltham[11] and Professor Nicholas,[12] who were delegates of the United Kingdom to the vienna conference. They have also explored the material differences between the convention rules and English law. Mr Feltham's ultimate verdict was as follows:

'given the difficulty of achieving agreement across a large number of nations, common law and civil law, capitalist and socialist, developed and developing, the code is probably as good as can be expected.'[13]

Writing several years later Professor Nicholas was prepared to delete 'probably'.[14]

It does not seem to me that it would be a useful exercise for me to attempt a comprehensive assessment of the merits of particular aspects of the text. But from the point of view of English law I will comment at this stage on three matters which are regarded as significant in the continuing debate on the convention. The first relates to Article 7. It reads as follows:

(1) 'In the interpretation of this Convention, regard is to be had to its international character and to the need to promote uniformity in its application and the observance of good faith in international trade.

(2) Questions concerning matters governed by this Convention which are not expressly settled in it are to be settled in conformity with the general principles on which it is based or, in the absence of such principles, in conformity with the law applicable by virtue of the rules of private international law.'

Impact of the Vienna Convention in Drafting International Sales Contracts, International Business Lawyer, September 1992, 421.
[10] Nicholas, (1989) 105 L.Q.R. 203, at 215.
[11] [1981] J.B.L. 346; (1991) J.B.L. 413.
[12] (1989) 105 L.Q.R. 203.
[13] op. cit., 361.
[14] op. cit., 243.

A Kind of Esperanto?

The concept of duty of good faith plays a restricted role in the common law.[15] In civil law systems there is an overriding principle that in the making and carrying out of contracts parties should act in good faith. Article 7 (1) creates no such duty. It merely spells out a canon of construction of the convention.[16] That seems to me a limited provision which ought to cause no concern to a common lawyer. It is true, of course, that the national courts of some civil law countries may hold that in the convention system there is a duty of good faith in the making and performance of the contract. If such a difference emerges it seems to me perfectly tolerable and not one which need imperil the success of the convention. The resort under Article 7 (2) to 'the general principles' on which the convention is based may seem strange to a common lawyer. But it makes good sense in a convention. For example, Article 13 provides that for the purposes of the convention 'writing' includes 'telegram and telex'. Facsimile exchanges were not yet in use when the convention was drafted. The application of 'the general principles' on which the convention is based make it easy to conclude that writing includes facsimile exchanges.

The second point relates to documentary sales. The convention, like the Sale of Goods Act 1979, does not contain special provisions spelling out the incidents of documentary sales. If the absence of such provisions in the convention make the conclusion and performance of C.I.F. and F.O.B. contracts, and other documentary sales, more difficult that would be a most serious reproach to the draftsmen of the convention. But it is important to remember that documentary sales are not uniquely English institutions. Such sales have their origin in trade usages and are accommodated in legal systems world wide. Article 9 reads as follows:

(1) 'The parties are bound by *any usage* to which they have agreed and by any practices which they have established between themselves.

(2) The parties are considered, unless otherwise agreed, to have impliedly made applicable to their contract or its formation a usage of which the parties knew or ought to have known and which in international trade is widely known to, and regularly observed by, parties to contracts of the type involved in the particular trade concerned. (My emphasis)

This provision ensures that documentary sales can be accommodated in the convention system.

In the third place I would refer to Article 49 (1). It reads as follows:

(1) The buyer may declare the contract avoided:
   (a) if the failure by the seller to perform any of his obligations under the contract or this Convention amounts to a fundamental breach of contract; or
   (b) in case of non-delivery, if the seller does not deliver the goods within the additional period of time fixed by the buyer in accordance with paragraph (1) of Article 47 or declares that he will not deliver within the period so fixed.

It seems to me that paragraph (b) contains a notion that would be perfectly acceptable to English contract lawyers. It has been said that the notion of 'fundamental breach' in paragraph (a) is new. That is true. But it seems to me a more satisfactory provision that our triple classification of terms as conditions, warranties and innominate terms. It is true that the convention does not expressly provide for terms with which strict compliance is required, i.e. conditions in English legal terminology. It is also true that such conditions sometimes have a useful role to play. But parties are, of course, free under the convention to require by the terms of their agreement strict compliance with particular terms.

No international convention will ever satisfy all countries. But from an English point of view I regard the Vienna Sales Convention as providing an acceptable basis for the negotiation and performance of international sale of goods as well as for resolution of disputes arising from such transactions.

C. The Objections in Principle

Mr Justice Hobhouse considered that the sole objective of the Vienna Sales Convention was the achievement of a stark uniformity. That observation seems to me an inadequate description of the objective of this trade law convention. The uncontroversial premise must be that the promotion of international trade is a desirable goal. One of the impediments to transnational trade is the differences between the commercial laws of different countries. And perhaps more important than objective divergences in national laws is uncertainty as to what the laws of different countries are. Uncertainty as to the nature and scope of legal risks is bad for trade. No convention can eliminate such differences: national courts may apply the convention differently. No convention can

---

[15] I explored this theme elsewhere: The Role of Good Faith and Fair Dealing in Contract Law: A Hair-Shirt Philosophy?, 1991 Denning Law Journal 131.

[16] Article 31 (1) of the Vienna Convention on the Law of Treaties, 1969, provides that a treaty shall be interpreted in good faith.

eliminate uncertainties in its application. But a convention such as the Vienna Sales Convention will tend to reduce differences and to eliminate uncertainty. Such considerations are the rationale of the convention rather than a simplistic notion of uniformity for its own sake.

The argument is, however, that a convention like the Vienna Sales Convention will by its nature 'introduce uncertainty where no uncertainty existed before'. The argument is that certainty is a hallmark of our sales code, which is based on legislation nearly 100 years old. That is not a generalization which should readily be conceded. For example, the English distinction between conditions, warranties and innominate terms still leads to considerable uncertainty in commercial practice. Our sales law is in other ways far from perfect. For example, the right to reject goods on the ground of a minor breach of a statutorily implied term is hardly a satisfactory rule.[17] Not surprisingly, judges often struggle to avoid the rigidity of the rule by doing justice in accordance with the merits of the individual dispute.

It seems to me that the argument against the ratification of the Vienna Sales Convention based on the importance of certainty in commercial dealings rests on a false premise. It appears to assume that English traders will always be able to insist that English sales law shall govern the contract. That assumption is wrong. This country is still an important trading nation but it is no longer in a dominant position in the international marketplace for the sale of goods. For every international sale of goods in respect of which an English trader is able to insist that English law must govern the transaction, there will be one where the English trader has to concede the applicability of a foreign legal system, which will usually have a different sales regime and, unfortunately, in the case of some developing countries will involve sales regimes which are little more than embryonic.

But that still leaves for consideration the assertion that the very concept of a multi-lateral convention like the Vienna Sales Convention is likely to be productive of uncertainty. The argument falls into the category of 'the sky will fall down' type of advocacy. In the field of trade law conventions it is also nothing new. Similar arguments were put forward by Scrutton and MacKinnon about the proposed enactment of the Hague Rules when they gave evidence to

the joint committee of the two houses presided over by Lord Sterndale, the Master of the Rolls. Lord Justice Scrutton told the committee:

'If you are going to make one contract which everybody must adopt, for Heaven's sake make it an intelligible one.'[18]

Both Scrutton and MacKinnon questioned the intelligibility of the Hague Rules with detailed references to the Rules. Lord Roskill has given the verdict of history about those predictions. He said:

'They gave dire and in the event wholly unwarranted warnings of the problems which would arise as to their construction with uncertainty and endless litigation replacing what they saw as the clarity of the existing law based upon freedom of contract. In truth, as every commercial lawyer knows, it is remarkable how few cases there have been in this country upon the construction of the Rules.'[19]

There is in my view no reason to think that the interpretation of the Vienna Sales Convention will give rise to significantly greater problems than were thrown up by the Hague Rules.

There is another policy argument based on certainty which must be considered. Article 8 (3) of the convention provides as follows:

'In determining the intent of a party or the understanding a reasonable person would have had, due consideration is to be given to all relevant circumstances of the case including *the negotiations*, any practices which the parties have established between themselves, usages and *any subsequent conduct* of the parties.' (My emphasis)

Mr Derek Wheatley, Q.C., who shares the views of Mr Justice Hobhouse on the Vienna Sales Convention, has argued that the certainty of our own law of contract would be undermined if the provisions of Article 8 (3) becomes part of such law.[20] He had in mind the rules of English law (a) that pre-contractual negotiations are not admissible in aid of the interpretation of a contract (the rule in *Prenn* v. *Simmonds*)[21] and (b) that the subsequent conduct of parties in the performance of a contract are also not admissible in aid of the interpretation of the contract (the rule in *Schuler* v. *Wickman*).[22] But English law is not quite so simple. Dealing first with the rule in *Prenn* v. *Simmonds* it is of some importance to note that in the *Karen Oltman*[23] the court rules that pre-contractual telex exchanges are admissible in aid of interpretation of an ambiguous word in a contract on the basis that the parties had contracted on an agreed basis. On this basis pre-contractual exchanges are

---

[17] Law Commission, No 160: Sale and Supply of Goods (1987).
[18] Parliamentary Papers, 1923, V, 836.
[19] (1992) 105 L.Q.R. 501.
[20] *The Times*, 27 March 1990. A riposte to Mr Wheatley's article by Professor Roy Goods was published in *The Times* on 22 May 1990.
[21] [1971] 1 WLR 1381.
[22] [1974] A.C. 235.
[23] [1976] 2 Ll.L.R. 708.

A Kind of Esperanto?

regularly adduced in relation to disputes about the interpretation of contracts. The rule in *Wickman* v. *Schuler* is also subject to an important qualification. It is now established that if parties have acted on a common assumption as to the meaning of a provision in a contract, then subject to considerations of justice and equity, a party may be precluded from relying on the true interpretation.[24] This qualification permits evidence of 'practical construction', as it is called in the United States, to be introduced in English courts. Despite these qualifications it is probably true that extrinsic evidence in aid of the c construction of contracts is more readily admitted in civilian systems than in England. But the concession in Article 8 (3) to civilian jurisprudence hardly threatens the fabric of English contract law. In my view it will be a fairly rare case in which the admission of such material, which is not at present admissible under English law, will lead to different results.

A further objection in principle, which was canvassed by Mr Justice Hobhouse, is the fact that the Vienna Sales Convention, if ratified, will have mandatory effect. I readily accept that it is not a sufficient answer to this objection say that parties may by agreement exclude the application of the convention. It is also true that it would have been possible to draft a Model Law of the International Sale of Goods, akin to UNCITRAL's Model Law of Arbitration, leaving it to countries to decide whether to adopt it as part of their municipal systems. Such a course was necessary in the field of arbitration because of the drastic difference in national arbitration laws which made the adoption of a convention beyond the scope of the 1958 New York Convention impractical. But in the field of sales law a convention was a feasible preposition, as the extent of the ratification of the Vienna Sales Convention has already demonstrated. But, in any event, a model law, if enacted, also represents a mandatory regime. Similarly, to the extent that a trade law convention is adopted it simply replaces the existing mandatory sales regimes of ratifying countries. This objection in principle attacks the very conception of the utility of a trade law convention, and it does so on the false premise that it introduces for the first time mandatory sales regimes. There is a very good reason why the Vienna Sales Convention has mandatory effect. It has mandatory effect because it provides solutions in transnational transactions which parties have failed to solve in their contract. In my view this objection in principle is not warranted.

Mr Justice Hobhouse raised another objection to the ratification of the convention. He referred to the difficulty of amending and updating them. This point applies to all international conventions and cannot by itself be a good reason for abandoning such international initiatives. The law must not set its sights too high. If a trade law convention can play a productive role in facilitating trade over a few decades that is a great success.

D. The case for ratification

In evaluating the case for ratification by the United Kingdom of the Vienna Sales Convention it is essential to take into account the extent to which the convention has gained currency. The convention has already been ratified by 34 nations. Within the European Economic Community the convention has been ratified by Germany, France, Italy, Netherlands, Denmark, Spain and Greece. In the common law family of states the United States, Canada, Australia and Singapore have ratified the convention. There is also the undoubted prospect of further ratifications in the next few years.

Another relevant aspect of the contextual scene is the relative strength of the United Kingdom in international trade. If Britannia still ruled the waves in international trade—to quote again Lord Roskill's phrase—it would have been possible to argue that our traders should generally be able to insist on English law applying to transactions entered into by them and that there is no compelling need for the United Kingdom to ratify the convention. Sadly, however, the decline of our position in international trade has been considerable. Britain's share of the world trade in manufacture has apparently declined, from about 40 per cent in 1880, to less than 7 per cent a century later.[25] And the inexorable downward trend since 1945 is particularly noteworthy.[26] It is idle to pretend that our position in the international marketplace for the sale of goods is stronger than that of other medium sized trading nations. This factor is one of the principal reasons which led the Law Commission, in response to the Consultative Document issued in June 1989 by the Department of Trade and Industry, to recommend that the United Kingdom should ratify the convention.[27]

The consequences of the decline in the United

---

[24] *Norwegian American Cruises A/S* v. *Paul Mundy Ltd* (*The Vistafjord*) [1988] 2 Ll.L.R. 343, at 350-53.
[25] Smith, *The British Economic Crisis: Its Past and Future*, Penguin Books, 1989, 55.
[26] *The British Economy since 1945*, edited by Craft and Woodward, Clarendon Press, 1991, 148 (Fig. 5.4).
[27] Law Commission memorandum submitted to the Department of Trade and Industry under cover of a letter dated 30 October 1989; Law Commissions Twenty-Sixth Annual Report 1991, par. 2.6.

Kingdom's position in international trade are obvious. It means that for every contract, subject to English law, which an English trader is able to negotiate, there will be another contract governed by foreign law. Looking at the matter from the point of view of English traders the argument based on the asserted superiority of English law over the convention therefore breaks down. Frequently, our traders will be confronted with an irresistible demand by the other Party that his law or the law of a neutral country must apply. The content of that foreign law may not always be easy to ascertain: in the case of developing countries the law may be skeletal in the extreme. These considerations are an impediment to the successful conclusion of the transaction. On the other hand, the Vienna Sales Convention has the badge of neutrality and tends to facilitate the conclusion of transnational transactions. There is another aspect of the problems presently confronting our traders which is worth considering. A prudent trader faced with a demand to contract subject to a foreign law will often take advice on the legal risks involved. Taking advice on foreign legal systems is time consuming: the transaction may be lost before the advice is received. Moreover, the taking of advice on foreign law is a costly business. The convention therefore tends to reduce the costs of business transactions.[28]

It is also necessary to consider what happens if a dispute arises. If the contract is governed by a foreign law, it is often necessary to call expert witnesses to prove the relevant foreign law. A substantial part of the Commercial Court's time is taken up by the hearing of such disputes. The need to prove foreign law tends to delay the disposal of cases, and adds enormously to the cost of litigation. On the other hand if the convention is ratified and the convention rules apply, the court will not need expert evidence. And that will be so even if a party wishes to refer to decisions of foreign courts as persuasive authority on the interpretation of the convention.

E. Conclusion

The right questions seems to me to ask whether it is in the best interests of the United Kingdom as a trading nation to ratify the Vienna Sales Convention. Like the Law Commission I take the view that the United Kingdom ought to ratify the convention.[29] At present our traders are at a disadvantage in the international market place. In my view it is important that ratification should not be delayed. But I am far from sanguine that anything will be done until the march of events, and acceleration of ratifications, absolutely compels it. Even in the face of overwhelming evidence that it is in the best interests of this country to ratify the convention, the antipathy of lawyers towards mandatory multi-lateral conventions may well delay what needs to be done for many years. Having started with a quotation from Trollope, I will end with another which dwells on the prejudice of English lawyers against learning from international experience. The reflection of an English lawyer was as follows:

'It would be useless at present, seeing that we cannot bring ourselves to believe it possible that a foreigner should in any respect be wiser than ourselves. If any such point out to us our follies, we at once claim those follies as the special evidences of our wisdom. We are so self-satisfied with out own customs, that we hold up our hands with surprise at the fatuity of men who presume to point out to us their defects.'[30]

Mr Wheatley's article in *The Times* was headed 'Why I oppose the wind of change'. Sadly, I doubt that there is yet much of a wind of change. Possibly there is still an educational task to be performed in demonstrating where the best interests of our country lie. But whatever we do the Vienna Sales Convention is a reality and its influence can only increase.

---

[28] Ndulo, (1989) 38 I.C.L.Q.R.1, 24–5.
[29] The Law Commission recommended that a declaration excluding Article 1 (1) (b) should be made under Article 95. I respectfully agree.

[23]
Perspectives of Corrective and Distributive Justice in Tort Law

It is a great privilege and honour to deliver a lecture in memory of John Maurice Kelly before such a distinguished audience. And I am delighted that Mrs Delphine Kelly is in the audience.

It was however adventurous of the Dean to invite me to speak on this occasion. Perhaps he was not aware of my dubious credentials. I restrict my disclosure to two matters. Some years ago when I was in the Court of Appeal I gave with the agreement of my colleagues a judgment in a case called *Elguzouli-Daff v Commissioner of Police*[1]. Relying on policy grounds we held that a prosecutor does not owe a duty of care to a defendant. In a recent book Professor Markesinis[2], the distinguished comparative lawyer, has said that our decision caused moral outrage even among hardened lawyers[3]. Moral outrage in the commercially minded Temple: that is quite something. My second antecedent is even more telling. Last year in *MacFarlane*[4] the House of Lords decided that parents are not entitled to recover compensation for the cost of bringing up an unwanted healthy child born as a result of negligent sterilisation advice. This decision was not very popular at the section of the Bar which conducted a profitable business in such cases. They invited the Law Lords to come and explain their decision. In very cowardly fashion we all refused. But we could not avoid ultimate scrutiny in legal journals.

---

* A Lord of Appeal in Ordinary.
1 [1995] 2 WLR 173.
2 *Tortious Liability of Statutory Bodies: A Comparative and Economic Analysis of Five English Cases*, B.S. Markesinis, (Hart Publishing, (1999)).
3 *Tortious Liability of Statutory Bodies*, 1999, at p.90.
4 *MacFarlane and Another v Tayside Health Board (Scotland)* [2000] 2 AC 59.

Perspectives of Corrective & Distributive Justice in Tort Law

Professor Thompson savaged our reasoning.[5] He was very severe on my colleagues. He said that they had abandoned all principles of tort law. I thought he was going to say my judgment was a notable exception. Not a bit. He said that I had not only abandoned the law of tort but law itself.

In England tort law is in flux. It is at the cross roads. In the new legal culture created by the Human Rights Act 1998 sacred cows may have to be culled. Let me start by giving three examples of the potential impact of the European Convention on Human Rights on tort law. Very recently the European Court of Human Rights, in the context of a sharp increase in night flights at Heathrow since 1993, held that English public law concepts did not allow the necessary consideration whether the increase in night flights was justifiable in the light of the right to respect for the private and family lives of those who live in the vicinity of Heathrow airport. The Strasbourg Court upheld a complaint which has been dubbed by the press as 'the right to sleep': see *Hatton and Others v The United Kingdom*, Application No. 36022/97, Judgment, 2 October 2001. As a resident in Fulham in West London, not terribly far from the flight paths, I felt like opening champagne. But as a judge I was troubled by the creativity of the Strasbourg Court in an area regulated by statute and in which local judges are perhaps best placed to weigh countervailing considerations. In any event, the *Hatton* case shows how considerations under the Human Rights Act may in future affect private nuisance cases. Secondly, the well known decision of the Strasbourg Court in *Osman*[6] appeared to call for a review of important decisions of the Court of Appeal and the House of Lords in respect of liability of public authorities for the negligent provision of services. Thirdly, the arguments about a right of privacy must now be addressed in the context of article 8 of the European Convention which does enshrine a qualified right to privacy. It is difficult to foresee how things will develop. One is reminded that when Chouen-Lai, the Chinese leader, was asked

---

[5] 'Abandoning the Law of Delict', 2000 Scots L.T. 43.
[6] *Osman v UK* (2000) 29 EHRR 24.

Perspectives of Corrective & Distributive Justice in Tort Law

what the consequences of the French Revolution were, his answer was that it was too early to tell. Nevertheless, it is an opportune time to reflect on the proper place of the law of tort in our legal system, and perhaps to pose the question whether our tort law is broadly set on the right course or whether we ought to yield to those who argue for a substantially expanded law of tort. During the last twenty years English society has changed greatly. We now have a consumerist society in which people are intensely aware of their rights. That is in principle a healthy development. But there may be a resulting social phenomenon of people looking for compensation for every misfortune. The impact of lawyers, who advertise in the media for clients, on the expectations of potential claimants is significant. Is there a danger that we may become a litigation driven society expecting a remedy for every loss suffered? Is this a policy consideration which judges may take into account?

It is almost banal to start with the observation that the contours of tort law are directly affected by its place in the law of obligations. We have a severely restricted theory of contract law. Seriously made promises, relied on by a promisee, may be unenforceable for lack of consideration. Benefits contractually arranged for the benefit of third parties are generally unenforceable. It could strongly be argued that these are structural defects in our contract law. In *The Pioneer Container* Lord Goff of Chieveley said that these principles may have to be reviewed.[7] What does this have to do with tort law? A great deal. A legal system with a wide theory of contract law, such as German law, can draw the boundaries of tort law more narrowly. A legal system with a restricted theory of contract law, such as ours, must look to tort law, the general law, to fill spaces which demand the recognition of rights and remedies. The classic illustration is the landmark decision of the House of Lords in *White v Jones*[8]. You will recollect that by a majority of 3:2 the House of Lords upheld a claim for loss suffered by a beneficiary as a result of the negligent preparation of a will by a solicitor. In German law the solution

---

7 [1994] 2 AC 324, at 335.
8 [1995] 2 AC 207.

would have been contractual. The privity doctrine debarred that solution in England. Hence the great conceptual difficulties encountered by the House. It is my impression that practical justice, and the reasonable expectations of the public, carried the day. Such reasoning is the enduring legacy of Lord Denning. The judicial oath requires a judge to do justice according to law: he is a servant of the law but his task is also to do justice whenever possible. And that is no longer so challenging a statement as it was in the days of Viscount Simonds. Indeed today the ever more knowledgeable public would be astonished if they thought that judges did not regard the attainment of practical justice as their main task.

In the broadest sense tort law fulfils two purposes. First it aims to compensate victims who have suffered loss as a result of civil wrongs. Secondly, it aims to keep wrongdoing under control and in that way to supplement the criminal law. The latter is a central but much overlooked function of tort law. What technique should the law adopt in translating these broad objectives into a coherent system of civil wrongs? Almost ninety years ago Salmond addressed this question and posed the question as follows:[9]

> 'Does the law of torts consist of a fundamental general principle that it is wrongful to cause harm to other persons in the absence of some specific ground of justification or excuse, or does it consist of a number of specific rules prohibiting certain kinds of harmful activity, and leaving all the residue outside the sphere of legal responsibility?'

The technique adopted by advanced legal systems differ greatly. At one extreme a few short articles of the Code Napoleon[10] unambiguously adopted the first theory:

---

[9] *Torts* (2nd ed. 1910) pp. 9-8.
[10] 'National, Supranational and International Tort Law Scope of Protection', Walter van Gerven, Hart Publishing (1998) at p. 31.

Perspectives of Corrective & Distributive Justice in Tort Law

Article 1382 Tout fait quelconque de l'homme, qui cause à autrui un dommage, oblige celui par la faute duquel il est arrivé, à le réparer.

(Anyone who, through his act, causes damage to another by his fault shall be obliged to compensate the damage.)

Article 1383 Chacun est responsable du dommage qu'il a causé non seulement par son fait, mais encore par sa négligence ou par son imprudence.

(Everyone is responsible for the damage caused not only by his act but also by his negligence or carelessness.)

The majestic French of the Code Napoleon, said by Stendhal, the writer of *Le Rouge et le Noire*, to have been the model for his elegant and precise style, is the starting point of the French law of civil wrongs. However, in the real life of the French courts policy considerations have created many limitations. Thus the Cour de Cassation has ruled out claims by parents for the cost of bringing up an unwanted healthy child after a failed abortion.[11]

By contrast we have a pragmatically arranged system which recognises specific torts only. In England the second theory is dominant. Harmful conduct beyond the scope of the specific torts is not the subject matter of legal responsibility. This is a point of great importance: while it does not rule out development of tort law it is a considerable check on the expansionist tendencies of the tort system. The Australian High Court in *Beaudessert Shire Council v Smith*[12] flirted with the overarching principle that independently of specific torts 'a person who suffers harm or loss as the inevitable consequence of the unlawful, intentional and positive acts of another is entitled to recover damages from the other.' In 1995 the Australian High Court reversed this decision and has now abandoned this idea[13]. And it

---

[11] Cass. Civ. Ire, 25 June 1991. Summary in publication at footnote 10, at p. 123.
[12] (1996) 120 CLR 145.
[13] See *Northern Territory v Mengel* (1995) 129 ALR 1.

Perspectives of Corrective & Distributive Justice in Tort Law

never took root in England. In 1982 the Privy Council refused to follow it[14]. English law therefore does not subscribe to the *prima facie* tort theory prevalent in the United States 'whereby the intentional infliction of temporal damages is a cause of action, which, as a matter of substantive law . . . requires a justification if a defendant is to escape'. On the other hand, the tort of a conspiracy to injure is well established. It however requires the acting in concert of two persons. The English approach sometimes puzzles our colleagues elsewhere. Why, they say, should harmful conduct become tortious because two conspire to act but not when a powerful individual undertakes it on his own? For example, if two newspaper proprietors combine to drive a third newspaper proprietor out of business by cutting the cost of their papers to an uneconomic level there may, depending on the circumstances, arguably be a case in tort. If one newspaper magnate undertakes such action the prevailing view is that he would be acting lawfully. I do not know the answer to such problems but perhaps persons acting in concert to cause harm is generally more harmful than one individual acting on his own.

It is important to be clear about the general aim of the law of tort because it will influence our thinking about concrete problems. The primary aim of tort law is the pursuit of corrective justice. It requires somebody who has harmed another without justification to indemnify the other. There is, however, another perspective, namely considerations of distributive justice. It concentrates on the place of the plaintiff and the defendant in society. It was first explained by Aristoteles in relation to Athenian society. While one thinks of an innocent plaintiff and a wrongdoing defendant one instinctively thinks in terms of corrective justice. If one shifts the focus to an enquiry whether the plaintiff should recover from the National Health Service (or ultimately the taxpayer) one's perception of the dictates of fairness may change. Not surprisingly, our courts have not shut their eyes to such considerations: the insurance position of parties has sometimes been treated as relevant. For example, in deciding that

---

[14] *Dunlop v Woollahra Municipal Council* (1982) AC 158.

a classification surveyor employed by shipowners did not owe a duty of care to cargo interests the House of Lords was influenced partly by the incidence of insurance.[15] In *Frost v Chief Constable of South Yorkshire Police*[16] the majority of the Appellate Committee expressly invoked such reasons. Having denied a remedy for psychiatric loss to bereaved relatives in *Alcock*[17] the majority in *Frost* felt that it would be morally indefensible to allow the claims of the police officers. I said:[18]

> 'The claim of the police officers on our sympathy, and the justice of the case, is great but not as great as that of others to whom the law denies redress'

Lord Hoffmann expressly invoked notions of distributive justice and said:[19]

> '(The ordinary man) would think it wrong that policemen, even as part of a general class of persons who rendered assistance, should have the right to compensation for psychiatric injury out of public funds while the bereaved relatives are sent away with nothing.'

Lord Browne-Wilkinson agreed with Lord Hoffmann and myself. You may or may not agree. It is a hard case. But reasons of distributive justice were decisive. An even more striking example is *MacFarlane*[20], the failed sterilisation case. Negligent advice about sterilisation caused the financial loss of the parents. Corrective justice required a remedy. In most jurisdictions such claims are denied. Why? The answer must lie in considerations of distributive justice. Many couples cannot have children.

---

[15] *March Rich v Bishop Rock Marine* [1996] AC 211, at 241.
[16] [1999] 2 AC 455.
[17] *Alcock and others v Chief Constable of South Yorkshire Police* [1992] 1 AC 310.
[18] at 498E.
[19] at 510F.
[20] *Supra*, p. 1.

Perspectives of Corrective & Distributive Justice in Tort Law

Others have the sorrow and burden of looking after a disabled child. Compensation for financial loss in respect of the upbringing of a child would necessarily have to discriminate between rich and poor. Parents may be put in a position of arguing in court that the unwanted child, which they accepted and care for, is more trouble than it is worth. Instinctively, there is a reasonable view that the law of tort has no business to provide legal remedies consequent upon the birth of a healthy child, which all of us regard as a valuable and good thing. It is this reasoning which in *MacFarlane* in diverse guises in a multiplicity of judgments led to a denial of a remedy for the cost of bringing up the unwanted child. On the other hand, the mother was allowed to recover compensation for pain, suffering and discomfort associated with pregnancy which she was advised could not happen. I will return to this aspect. These are not isolated illustrations of considerations of distributive justice. Recently in *Lister v Hesley Hall Limited*[21] the House of Lords held that when a warden sexually abused boys in a boarding school under his direct supervision the owners of the school were vicariously liable. Tort victims prefer to sue the employer, rather than the employee. The former has the larger purse and usually carries insurance. And vicarious liability encourages employers to take steps to ensure that employees are properly trained to be aware of risks and to avoid them as far as possible. It may well be right to say that the principle of vicarious liability of employers for torts committed in the course of employment by employees ultimately rests on grounds of distributive justice. Yet a controllable principle must be identified. In *Lister* the House of Lords enunciated a test of close connection between the torts and the employment. Standing back from the particular instances, the position appears to be that tort is not underpinned by a single overarching rationale. It is a mosaic of interwoven principles of corrective and distributive justice.

---

[21] [2001] 2 WLR 1311.

Perspectives of Corrective & Distributive Justice in Tort Law

The tort of negligence, moulded by *Donoghue v Stevenson*[22] into a general principle of civil liability, has dominated the landscape of tort law. Next in importance is *Hedley Bryne & Co Ltd v Heller & Partners*[23] which recognised liability on the basis of an assumption of responsibility for inaccurate statements, giving rise to a duty of care to a plaintiff who suffered economic loss by relying on the assumption of responsibility. After *Henderson v Merritt Syndicates*[24] this became the technique of English law for creating liability for the negligent provision of services. It has been powerfully argued by professor Hepple that the technique of assumption of responsibility is often based on a fiction.[25] It may also be said to be a fifth wheel on the coach since negligent provision of service may be said to be independently and without further ado a source of tort liability.[26]

In law taxonomy is important. It is necessary to ask and address the right questions and in the right order. Nowadays the debate on tort concentrates to a large extent on four critical questions about which I would comment briefly:

1. *Are all interests equally worthy of protection?*

The answer is No. The explanation given by Holmes is still the best[27]. He said:

'The life of the law has not been logic: it has been experience. The felt necessities of the time, the prevalent moral and political theories, intuitions of public policy, avowed or unconscious, even the prejudices which judges share with their fellow-men, have had a good deal more to do than the syllogism in determining the rules by which men should be governed.'

---

[22] [1932] AC 562.
[23] [1964] AC 465.
[24] [1995] 2 AC 145.
[25] 'Negligence: The Search for Coherence', 50 Current Legal Problems, 1997, at 86 *et seq.*
[26] *Phelps v Hillingdon Borough Council* [2000] 3 WLR 776, at 791F.
[27] 'Review of A Selection of Cases on the Law of Contracts . . .' 2nd ed by Christopher C. Langdell, American Law Review 1A (1880) 233.

Perspectives of Corrective & Distributive Justice in Tort Law

On the one hand, it would be an unusual case in which a defendant is not liable where his act has caused physical damage to the plaintiff or his property. On the other hand, claims for recovery of economic loss are accorded a lower value. This distinction throws up many problems. The contours of this ongoing debate are familiar to all and I say no more about it. Until the coming into force of the Human Rights Act 1998 the traditional view in England was that interests of privacy were unprotected.[28] Not all judges accepted the prevailing view. Thus Laws J. said in *Hellewill v Chief Constable of Derbyshire*[29]:

> 'If someone with a telephoto lens were to take from a distance and with no authority a picture of another engaged in some private act, his subsequent disclosure of the photograph would, in my judgment, as surely amount to a breach of confidence as if he had found or stolen a diary in which the act was recounted and proceeded to publish it. In such a case, the law would protect what might reasonably be called *a right of privacy,* although the name accorded to the cause of action would be breach of confidence.'

This was an interesting idea. Now in 2001 English courts are able to address issues of privacy in a radically different legal culture. Privacy is a directly protected interest under article 8 of the European Convention on Human Rights. Some say that the courts will now allow actions for breach of privacy on a large scale. Certainly many claims will be put forward. The idea appears to be gaining ground that commercial companies, such as McDonald's, have a right to privacy about their operations.[30] It has also been held that film stars who have sold publicity rights about their wedding to a magazine are potentially entitled to claim

---

[28] *Kaye v Robertson* [1991] FSR 62.
[29] [1994] 1 WLR 804.
[30] Compare *Reg v Broadcasting Standards Commission Ex parte British Broadcasting Corporation* [2000] 3 WLR 1325. Curiously the petition for leave to appeal to the House of Lords was refused by a committee of which I was a member.

against a rival magazine which published photographs of their wedding.[31] Subject to hearing further argument, I wonder whether it may not be the best interpretation of the right of privacy under the European Convention to restrict claims to individuals in their private lives. After all, we are talking about fundamental human rights. And by extending their ambit we risk diminishing the moral authority under-pinning human rights. That would not inhibit the development of the breach of confidence concept. In any event, *prima facie* breaches of privacy may often be justified by the countervailing right of freedom of expression. It is the lifeblood of our democracy. It may not always trump privacy but it will often do so. For ministers, judges and captains of industry who complain of invasions of privacy, the protection offered by the right of privacy under the European Convention may not be very great.

2. *Do certain persons or classes of persons enjoy a greater degree of protection than others?*

This is the territory of the duty of care. And the answer is emphatically Yes. Our law distinguishes between primary and secondary victims of a negligently caused accident, e.g. the onlooker who suffers psychiatric harm will not be compensated. The law's distinctions would not satisfy a moral philosopher and they displease tort law expansionists. I do not suggest that the law will not develop. Nevertheless, the distinctions based on a crude perception of immediacy and physical contact are likely to continue to exert a dominant influence on the English law of tort.

3. *Can any behaviour, act or omission, lead to tort liability?*

Generally English law does not impose liability for what are called pure omissions. Harsh as this principle is it is deeply embedded in English law. The rationale is 'that I must not harm

---

[31] *Douglas and Others v Hello Ltd* [2001] 2 WLR 992.

Perspectives of Corrective & Distributive Justice in Tort Law

my neighbour (misfeasance) but I am not required to save him (non feasance)'[32] Tony Weir explains:

> 'You need not tell a complete stranger that he is about to fall over a cliff – unless it is your cliff. If it is your cliff, you as an occupier will be in a special relationship with the visitor, which generates liability for unreasonable failure to inform.'[33]

Absent special circumstances there is no duty to prevent others suffering damage as a result of the deliberate wrong doing of third parties. By contrast affirmative duties are more widely recognised in continental systems. In 1988 the Cour d'Appel of Lyon[34] held that the organiser of a football match is under a duty to take adequate security measures to combat hooliganism. It had to pay compensation in respect of injury suffered by spectators as a result of a breach of this obligation. It was treated as an obligation *de moyens* as opposed to an obligation *de resultat* – we would call it an obligation to use reasonable endeavours to prevent harm. At first glance one might say that English law would treat such a case as a pure omission and deny a remedy. But I am not so sure. It may be an area in which the law of tort could be enlisted to impose community standards on those best capable of taking measures against football hooliganism. I think football clubs may have a responsibility which may arguably be treated as a case leading to liability for failing to take reasonable care to prevent the infliction of personal injury to spectators. Football clubs may find that they have more than just civic responsibilities.

4.   *Are all tortfeasors subject to the same rules?*

The answer is No. A public servant is not liable in negligence for carelessness in refusing a licence. He may be liable

---

[32] Winfield & Jolowicz on Tort by W.V.H. Rogers (15th edition (1998) Sweet & Maxwell) at p. 117.
[33] *A Casebook on Tort*, 8th ed.
[34] *L'Olympique Lyonnais v Fuster, Lyon*, 16 December 1988, JCP 1990. 11. 21510.

Perspectives of Corrective & Distributive Justice in Tort Law

under the tort of misfeasance in public office. That requires proof of the exercise of public power in bad faith, which requires at least subjective recklessness. Why are the limits of this tort drawn so narrowly? Tort law has a role to play in constraining the abuse of public power. On the other hand, public servants act for us, the people, and if they are assailed by unmeritorious suits they cannot carry out their tasks properly. The reconciliation of these imperatives explain why, rightly or wrongly, the House of Lords drew the lines in *Three Rivers*[35] as they did. On the other hand as I acknowledged in my judgment in *Three Rivers* the mental element required for the tort of misfeasance in public office means that it is not an effective remedy to deal with state liability for breaches of Community law.[36] Any gap must be filled by Community law. This illustrates the interplay between Community law and domestic law.

Even more pertinent is the position of public bodies who have failed to deliver services which could have prevented loss. In a series of decisions in the 1980s and 1990s the House of Lords and the Court of Appeal have held that a careless failure to deliver such services does not ground an action in negligence. The theory behind these cases is that the victim is no worse off if the services had not been provided in the first place. And it is justified on budgetary and efficiency grounds. Considerations of distributive justice underlie these decisions. Examples that spring to mind are *Murphy v Brentwood LBC*[37] on building inspection services, *Hill v Chief Constable of West Yorkshire*[38] on police services; *Elguzouli Daff v Commissioner of Police*[39] on prosecution services; *X (Minors) v Bedfordshire County Council*[40] on social services; *Stovin v Wise*[41] on highway improvements; *Capital and Counties*

---

35 *Three Rivers District Council & Ors v Governor & Co. of the Bank of England sub nom Same v Same* (No. 3) (2000) 2 WLR 1220.
36 at 1235H-1236A.
37 [1991] 1 AC 398.
38 [1989] AC 53.
39 *Supra*, p. 1.
40 [1995] 2 AC 633.
41 [1996] AC 923.

*plc v Hampshire County Council*⁴² on fire services; and *O'Rourke v Camden LBC*⁴³ on housing the homeless. It may, however, be that the decision by a seven member panel of the House of Lords in *Phelps v Hillingdon Borough Council*, in the context of the liability of local education authorities, runs counter to the trend of earlier decisions.⁴⁴

The *Osman*⁴⁵ decision in the European Court of Human Rights has raised questions about this line of decisions. You will appreciate that I must be somewhat circumspect about that decision since the House has not finally pronounced on it. What I can say is that the English procedure of permitting the striking out of unsustainable claims may not have been fully understood, and in particular the European Court may not have realised that a claim may only be struck out after a fair hearing and then only after a reasoned decision which may be appealed. But this point may not go to the core of *Osman*. Moreover, the distinction between an immunity and tort principles governing the existence of a duty of care was not fully appreciated. And the European Court may have made a judgment about the definition of tort liability of public bodies without a full appreciation of the cultural background of our particular social welfare system and its safety net provisions. But in its decision in *Z v UK* announced on 10 May 2001, the European Court accepted by a majority that at least in part that *Osman* was based on a wrong understanding of English law.⁴⁶

Nevertheless, the line of House of Lords' decisions, or some of them, are controversial. Professor Todd, a New Zealand tort writer, has argued that there is or may be an error in approach in some of the cases⁴⁷. He states that it has been assumed that

---

⁴² [1997] 3 WLR 331.
⁴³ [1997] 1 WLR 956.
⁴⁴ [2000] 3 WLR 776.
⁴⁵ *Osman v UK* (2000) 29 EHRR 245.
⁴⁶ *Z v UK* [2001] 10 BHRC 384.
⁴⁷ *The Law of Torts in New Zealand* edited by Stephen Todd (3rd ed, Brookers Ltd. (2001) at p. 350.

whether a statutory duty gives rise to a private cause of action is a question of construction, requiring an examination of the policy of the statute to decide whether it was intended to confer a right to compensation for breach. He argues that this tends to confuse the action for negligence with the action for breach of statutory duty, where the legislative intention is determinative. He concludes that the nature of the inquiry that needs to be undertaken is better expressed in terms of whether a duty of care is consistent with what the statute requires or empowers the public body to do. In some of the cases the problem may have been approached from the wrong angle. This is an important argument. The decisions on the liability of public bodies are certainly contrary to principles of corrective justice. The policy considerations, and in particular the pessimistic budgetary arguments underlying them, have been challenged. The argument that negligence suits against the police will lead to a diversion of resources from prevention of crime to the defence of law suits has been questioned. The view that to allow negligence suits against local authorities for failing to make roads safe enough will cause them to divert funds from education and social services has been criticised. In his book,[48] Professor Markesinis has shown that on similar facts French and German courts have rejected the policy grounds on which English courts have relied. The experience of these countries is important. No doubt there are some cultural differences. But Professor Markesinis has done a public service by enabling us in future to examine such problems in a more rigorous and informed way. This is one of the most intractable problems facing the modern law of tort. It will rumble on. As a serving Law Lord I have said more than enough about this subject.

I would now like to say something about the moulding forces of the law. I take the liberty of reading to you a passage from Benjamin Cardozo's *The Nature of the Judicial Process*[49] – one of the most profound books in American legal literature. He said:

---

[48] *op. cit.; passim.*
[49] Yale University Press: London: Humphrey Milford, 1921.

'My analysis of the judicial process comes then to this, and little more: logic, and history, and custom, and utility, and the accepted standards of right conduct, are the forces which singly or in combination shape the progress of the law. Which of these forces shall dominate in any case must depend largely upon the comparative importance or value of the social interests that will be thereby promoted or impaired. One of the most fundamental social interests is that law shall be uniform and impartial. There must be nothing in its action that savours of prejudice or favor or even arbitrary whim or fitfulness. Therefore in the main there shall be adherence to precedent. There shall be symmetrical development, consistently with history or custom when history or custom has been the motive force, or the chief one, in giving shape to existing rules, and with logic or philosophy when the motive power has been theirs. But symmetrical development may be bought at too high a price. Uniformity ceases to be a good when it becomes uniformity of oppression. The social interest served by symmetry or certainty must then be balanced against the social interest served by equity and fairness or other elements of social welfare. These may enjoin upon the judge the duty of drawing the line at another angle, or staking the path along new courses, of making a new point of departure from which others who come after him will set out upon their journey.'

Cardozo's view was that the ultimate test of a legal rule is not how well it fits into some abstract theory but how well it performs in the real world.[50]

---

[50] Judith Kaye, the Chief Justice of the Court of Appeals of the State of New York, who now sits in Cardozo's old seat, discusses *The Nature of the Judicial Process* in a magisterial review of Kaufmann's 'Cardozo: A Law Classic', 112 Harvard L.R. 1026.

Perspectives of Corrective & Distributive Justice in Tort Law

I hope you will forgive me a digression. What is the explanation for the truly magnificent legal prose of Holmes, Brandeis, Cardozo and Learned Hand? Perhaps it is a quirk of fate. On the other hand, they wrote when there were no word processors: what they had instead was a profound knowledge of history, literature, moral philosophy and constitutional theory from Athens to their day. Well, that is my theory. Like most theories it is probably wrong.

The basic tools of the common law are reasoning by analogy from decided cases, or deductive reasoning from established principles. The law must take into account changes in society: it must be responsive to the contemporary world. It is therefore necessary for the common law to be developed. On the other hand it has rightly been said that while engaged on the process of developing the law a judge is best advised to take his runs in singles rather than in fours. And a new rule must fit into the coherent structure of the law. Thus in *Gregory*[51] the House of Lords declined to extend the tort of malicious prosecution to disciplinary proceedings on the basis that the generality of such cases are already satisfactorily covered by other torts. Policy considerations are, of course, of vital importance as is shown by the line of cases on the liability of public bodies. A further illustration is *Arthur J.S. Hall & Co (a firm) v Simons*[52] where a divided House of Lords held that public policy no longer supported an immunity of suit in favour of trial advocates in civil and criminal cases. The case turned squarely on the Law Lords' weighing of countervailing considerations of social advantage.

Morality is a vital force in judicial decision making. It is, however, not the judge's personal values that are relevant but his perception of prevailing community standards. In this sense law and morality are inextricably interwoven. It would be strange if this were not so. A good illustration of the relevance of moral

---

51 *Gregory v Portsmouth City Council* [2000] 1 AC 419.
52 [2000] 3 WLR 543.

Perspectives of Corrective & Distributive Justice in Tort Law

considerations is *Smith New Court Ltd. v Scrimgeour Vickers*[53] where the House justified a wider liability for fraudulent misrepresentation than for negligent misstatements on purely moral grounds. I return to the comments of Professor Thompson about the sterilisation case. He confused one of the greatest of all the moulding forces of the law, morality, with legal principle. Then he went on to say that our decision to deny recovery of the cost of bringing up the child was right on policy grounds. Cardozo would have agreed so far. Then the professor argued that we were wrong to allow the claim for compensation of the mother, that being for a modest sum for pain and suffering. He said it was a typical compromise, inelegant and illogical. There is however a broader horizon. The law is only a means of ordering a civilised society, and we live in a complex world with all the tensions and untidy compromises involved. In any event, the reasons of morality militating against recovery of the main claim in respect of the cost of bringing up the unwanted child did not apply to the mother's modest claim for pain and suffering. There was therefore in fact no compromise of principle. The limited recovery allowed was eminently just. It was also supported by a comparative review placed before the House of Lords.

So far I have concentrated entirely on substantive tort law. John Fleming taught us that the law must be seen in its historical and practical framework.[54] He showed how distinctive procedural rules in the United States influenced the development of tort law.[55] Two features have particularly contributed to what seems to be a very expansive tort system. The first was the rule that the successful defendant in a tort case can by and large not recover costs from the losing plaintiff, and the rule which permit attorneys to undertake litigation on a contingency fee basis, the lawyers taking one third or substantially more of the damages awarded. The economic incentives for lawyers to advertise for

---

53 *Smith New Court Securities Ltd v Scrimgeour Vickers (Asset Management) Ltd.* [1997] AC 254.
54 *The American Tort Process*, 1988, chapters 5 and 6.
55 *The Law of Torts*, 8th ed.

clients and take on speculative litigation are enormous. Conflicts of interest are endemic in the system. The second feature is the system of class actions.[56] The procedure allows some individuals (class representatives) to sue on behalf of themselves and class members who are similarly situated. If the class representatives succeed, the defendant will be liable to each member in the class. If the defendant wins, the judgment binds all the members of the class. In order for a case to proceed as a class action the trial court must certify that it may do so. This procedure has been employed in so called mass torts. These procedural rules together with the jury system have played a huge role in making the U.S. tort system what it is. The scale of jury awards is simply staggering. But I note that there was only a seven figure award to an armed bank robber who slipped on the marble floor of the bank which he tried to rob. In any event, the legal culture and practice in the United States explains why U.S. tort awards are not recognised in England and Europe generally.

Let me now explain the context in a little more detail. The tobacco litigation in the United States is illustrative of class actions which did not come to trial and resulted in meagre recoveries by individual claimants yet resulted in outrageous sums being earned by lawyers. I quote a few examples.

9 December 1999 – The Baltimore Sun

'In a bitter battle of former allies over legal fees, Maryland Attorney General J. Joseph Curran Jr. sued Peter G Angelos yesterday, accusing the prominent Baltimore attorney of breach of contract and asking the court to protect the state's tobacco payout.

Angelos, who contends that the state owes him more than $1 billion for handling its tobacco lawsuit, meanwhile placed a lien on the first payment of Maryland's $4.7 billion share of the national tobacco settlement, said Deputy Attorney General Carmen M. Shepard.'

---

56 Christopher Hodges, 'Factors Influencing the Incidence of Multiple Claims', 1999 J.P.I.L. 289.

Perspectives of Corrective & Distributive Justice in Tort Law

7 March 1999 – The Houston Chronicle

'Of all the suspicious dealings associated with the Texas tobacco lawsuit, perhaps none is so blatant as Houston attorney Marc Murr's claim against Texas taxpayers for $260 million.'

'the same scrutiny needs to be applied to the $3.3 billion in fees awarded to the other five plaintiffs' attorneys, the "Tobacco Five." Like Murr, these lawyers are seeking $130,000 plus per hour legal fees for a case that never went to trial.'

4 January 1999 – Business Dateline

'Lawrence B Kraus, president of the U.S. Chamber of Commerce Institute for Legal Reform called a recent agreement for $8.2 billion to be paid lawyers in three states an 'unconscionable money grab that should outrage all Americans.' He said these anti-tobacco lawyers in Texas, Mississippi and Florida "have hit the lottery --- becoming instant billionaires without creating one new job or otherwise contributing to the American economy.'

13 September 1998 – Pittsburgh Post-Gazette

'The system of contingency fees – in which lawyers take 30 to 50 per cent of settlements, but only if they win, and get nothing if they lose a case – has resulted in a few celebrated instances of billings equivalent to $30,000 an hour for their work.'

The stock argument in the United States is that class actions are the great equaliser between consumers and the corporate would. Has it benefited United States' society? Judge Posner touched on this in his 1995 Clarendon Law lectures at Oxford University:[57] He avoided a definitive answer. But he points out several salient facts: the death rate from accidents in the U.S. is nearly twice that in the U.K. despite far greater American damage awards in accident cases. And he notes: 'In the

---

[57] Richard A. Posner *Law and Legal Theory In England and America*. (Clarendon Law Lectures Series 1997, Oxford University Press), at p.112.

intangibles of life such as safety, longevity, freedom from violence and civility – all of which are components of social welfare in a broad, but accurate, sense – the UK may actually be ahead of the U.S.'

It is being urged by the United States law firms and some commentators that European countries, and England in particular, ought to adopt the United States system of class actions in order to meet the needs of claimants affected by major catastrophes, accidents, etc. I would strenuously oppose its introduction in England. Our own system of allowing a nominated judge to take charge of the management of group claims, in accordance with Civil Procedure Rules (1998), as amended in 2000, satisfies the needs of our country.[58] My view is that class actions have and should have little future in Europe.

Fortunately, so far we have been spared a contingent fee system under which lawyers receive a percentage of the damages recovered. I hope that rumours that it is under consideration by the Lord Chancellor's Department are unfounded. What about the conditional fee system involving a percentage uplift on costs depending on a successful outcome which replaced the legal aid system? Access to justice is a basic right. Will the conditional fee system deliver justice? For my part the jury are still out on the conditional fee system. If it does not deliver comprehensive and effective access to justice we will have allowed justice itself to be undermined notably for the poorest members of society. The untried system requires open and independent monitoring. There is no such monitoring system at present. Next one would like to know more about the level of fees which lawyers will earn from the system. What the scale of fees will be in large-scale representative actions I do not know. But I suggest that this aspect of the operation of the system must also be open and transparent. It also needs the closest independent monitoring to ensure that lawyers do not earn fees which the public would regard as scandalous. Unfortunately, one can no longer assert with

---

[58] Hodges, Multi-Party Actions, 2001, *passim*.

complete conviction that the practice of law is in all respects an honourable profession. For many it has become a business. And, if there is merit in this pessimistic assessment, it must come as no surprise to the practising profession if their conduct of legal business is put under the searchlight more and more in the years to come.

Drawing my reflections to a close, I would say that in England there is a perception among many judges, in this respect possibly reflecting public opinion, that the tort system is becoming too expansive and wasteful. There may also be an unarticulated but nevertheless real conviction among many judges that a determined effort must be made to prevent our social welfare state from becoming a society bent on litigation. These considerations, even if relevant, are controversial. And, in the wake of *Pinochet No. 2*,[59] I must insist that they are subject to hearing further argument.

---

[59] *R v Bow Street Stipendiary Magistrate, Ex parte Pinochet* (No. 2) [2000] 1 AC 119.

[24]
Immunity of Suit of Advocates: *Arthur J.S. Hall Co. v Simons**
[2002] 1 A.C. 615, 675

20 July **LORD STEYN** My Lords, there are three appeals before the House from orders of the Court of Appeal in a building case and in two cases involving family proceedings. Clients raised claims in negligence against firms of solicitors. In response the solicitors relied on the immunity of advocates from suits in negligence. In all three cases judges at first instance ruled that the claims against the solicitors were unsustainable. The circumstances of these cases and the disposals are set out in the judgment of the Court of Appeal, ante, p 623H, given by Lord Bingham of Cornhill CJ. In effect the Court of Appeal ruled in all three cases presently before the House that the claims were wrongly struck out. The solicitors now appeal. The results of the appeals are of great importance to the parties. But transcending the importance of the specific issues arising on the appeals there are two fundamental general questions, namely: (1) ought the current immunity of an advocate in respect of and relating to conduct of legal proceedings as enunciated by the House in *Rondel v Worsley* [1969] 1 AC 191, and explained in *Saif Ali v Sydney Mitchell & Co* [1980] AC 198, to be maintained in England? (2) What is or ought to be the proper scope in England of the general principle barring a collateral attack in a civil action on the decision of a criminal court as enunciated in *Hunter v Chief Constable of the West Midlands Police* [1982] AC 529? The position in Scotland was not the subject matter of argument on these appeals.

These questions before the House affect both branches of the legal profession. Your Lordships have had the benefit of careful arguments from

676

three sides. First, by counsel for the appellant solicitors who were supported by the Solicitors Indemnity Fund. Secondly, by counsel for the Bar Council who was given leave to intervene and played a particularly helpful part in the appeal. Thirdly, by counsel for the individual litigants who put forward the contrary argument. Having studied the detailed written arguments and heard the oral arguments of counsel for the appellants, the interveners, and the respondents, your Lordships are now in as good a position to form a judgment on the principal issues as is achievable.

It is necessary to explain the scheme of my opinion. There is a direct link between the two general questions. How the law deals with the problem of relitigation of matters already decided, as identified in the *Hunter* case, is an important aspect of any reconsideration of the immunity of advocates. It will be necessary to examine the two issues together. Secondly, although the cases before the House involve actions against solicitors and not against barristers, the reality is that the immunity of barristers is of longer standing and underpinned to some extent by arguments not available to solicitors. It will therefore be convenient first to concentrate by and large on the position in regard to barristers and then to consider whether the conclusions arrived at also apply to solicitors.

The existing immunity of barristers

For more than two centuries barristers have enjoyed an immunity from actions in negligence. The reasons for this immunity were various. It included the dignity of the Bar, the "cab rank" principle, the assumption that barristers may not sue for their fees, the undesirability of relitigating cases decided or settled, and the duty of a barrister to the court: Roxburgh, "Rondel v Worsley: The Historical Background" (1968) 84 LQR 178; and Roxburgh, "Rondel v Worsley: Immunity of the Bar" (1968) 84 LQR 513. In 1967 when the House decided *Rondel v Worsley* the dignity of the Bar was no longer regarded as a reason which justified conferring an immunity on advocates whilst withholding it from all other professional men. In *Hedley Byrne & Co Ltd v Heller & Partners Ltd* [1964] AC 465 the rule was established that irrespective of contract, if someone possessed of a special skill undertakes to apply that skill for the assistance of another person who relies upon such skill, a duty of care will arise: at pp 502–503. The fact that the barrister did not enter into a contract with his solicitor or client ceased to be a ground of justification for the immunity. Nevertheless, in a unanimous decision the House in *Rondel v Worsley* [1969] 1 AC 191 upheld the ancient immunity on considerations of "public policy [which are] not immutable:" at p 227B, per Lord Reid. It is worth recalling that in that case the appellant had obtained the services of the respondent to defend him on a dock brief, and alleged that the respondent had been negligent in the conduct of his defence. It is undoubtedly right, as counsel for the solicitors submitted and nobody disputed, that the principal ground of the decision is the overriding duty of a barrister to the court. The House thought that the existence of liability in negligence, and indeed the very possibility of making assertions of liability against a barrister, might tend to undermine the willingness of barristers to carry out their duties to the court. Lord Morris of Borth-y-Gest encapsulated the core idea by saying, at p 251D: "It would be a retrograde development if an advocate were under pressure unwarrantably to subordinate his duty to the court to his duty to the client." Other members of the Appellate Committee expressed similar views: see p 231E, per Lord Reid; pp 272B–273F, per Lord Pearce; pp 283E–283G, per Lord Upjohn; and p 293E, per Lord Pearson. This factor is the pivot on which in 1967 the existence of the immunity hinged. But for it the case would probably have been decided differently. There were however supporting reasons. Perhaps the most important of these was the undesirability of relitigating issues already decided: see p 230B–F, per Lord Reid and pp 249A–250B, per Lord Morris of Borth-y-Gest. Another factor to which some weight was attached was the "cab rank" rule, which imposed (and still imposes) upon barristers, but not solicitors, the obligation to accept instructions from anyone who wishes to engage their services in an area of the law in which they practised. In the year after *Rondel v Worsley* was decided Sir Ronald Roxburgh (formerly Roxburgh J) said that "the pressures for putting barristers on the same footing as other professional men ... are already strong, and may grow stronger": 84 LQR 513, 527.

Eleven years later in *Saif Ali v Sydney Smith Mitchell & Co* [1980] AC 198 the House revisited this topic. On this occasion the immunity established in *Rondel v Worsley* was not challenged and was not directly in issue. The existence of the debate on the merits of the immunity was not reopened. The terrain of the debate centred on the scope of the immunity. Except for Lord Diplock, the members of the House accepted the rationale of *Rondel v Worsley*, which Lord Wilberforce said, at p 213C, was that "barristers ... have a special status, just as a trial has a special character: some immunity is necessary in the public interest, even if, in some rare cases, an individual may suffer loss." About a barrister's overriding duty to the court Lord Diplock observed, at p 220:

"The fact that application of the rules that a barrister must observe may in particular cases call for the exercise of finely balanced judgments upon matters about which different members of the profession might take different views, does not in my view provide sufficient reason for granting absolute immunity from liability at common law. No matter what profession it may be, the common law does not impose on those who practise it any liability for damage resulting from what in the result turn out to have been errors of judgment, unless the error was such as no reasonably well-informed and competent member of that profession could have made. So too the common law makes allowance for the difficulties in the circumstances in which professional judgments have to be made and acted upon. The salvor and the surgeon, like the barrister, may be called upon to make immediate decisions which, if in the result they turn out to have been wrong, may have disastrous consequences. Yet neither salvors nor surgeons are immune from liability for negligent conduct of a salvage or surgical operation; nor does it seem that the absence of absolute immunity from negligence has disabled members of professions other than the law from giving their best services to those to whom they are rendered."

Lord Diplock did, however, think that the immunity could be justified on two other grounds. The first is the analogy of the general immunity from civil liability which attaches to all persons in respect of the participation in proceedings before a court of justice, namely judges, court officials, witnesses, parties, counsel and solicitors alike: p 222A–C: The second was

678

the public interest in not permitting decisions to be challenged by collateral proceedings: pp 222D–223D. There matters rested for a time.

The next development was the introduction by statute of a power enabling the court to make wasted costs orders against legal practitioners: see section 51 of the Supreme Court Act 1981 as substituted by section 4 of the Courts and Legal Services Act 1990. Not surprisingly barristers are occasionally guilty of wholly unjustifiable conduct which occasions a waste of expenditure. The Bar argued that because of the immunity of barristers no such orders ought in principle to be made against barristers. The Court of Appeal ruled to the contrary: *Ridehalgh v Horsefield* [1994] Ch 205. And that decision was accepted by the Bar. It operates satisfactorily. It has not been detrimental to the functioning of the court system or indeed the interests of the Bar.

As Roxburgh predicted in 1968 the pressure for a re-examination of *Rondel v Worsley* mounted. There has been considerable academic criticism of the immunity. In a detailed and balanced discussion Peter Cane (*Case, Tort Law and Economic Interests,* 2nd ed (1996), pp 233–238) found that, even taken together, the justifications adduced for the immunity do not support it strongly: see also similar effect Jonathan Hill, "Litigation and Negligence: A Comparative Study" (1986) 6 Oxford Journal of Legal Studies 183, 184–186. In an area where one is bound to a considerable extent to rely on intuitive judgments, the criticism of the immunity by two outstanding practising barristers is significant. In *Advocates* (1992), pp 197–206, Mr David Pannick examined the case for and against the immunity in detail. While accepting that there is some substance in some of the arguments for an immunity, he found that on balance the immunity is not justified. He added, at p 206: "This issue will not go away. English law will, in the future, have more to say on this topic." Recently, Sir Sydney Kentridge QC expressed the view, making use of his experience as an advocate in South Africa and in England, that the "gloomy speculations" on which the immunity of barristers in England is based are wide off the mark: see *Tortious Liability of Statutory Bodies,* edited by B S Markesinis (1999), Foreword, p ix. But even more important are the observations in the present case by Lord Bingham of Cornhill CJ, Morritt LJ and Waller LJ. They clearly considered that, while the principle against collateral challenge as enunciated in the *Hunter* case ought to be maintained, nevertheless there was a substantial case for the sceptical re-examination of the immunity of barristers.

It is now possible to take stock of the arguments for and against the immunity. I will examine the relevant matters in turn. First, there is the ethical "cab rank" principle. It provides that barristers may not pick and choose their clients. It binds barristers but not solicitor advocates. It cannot therefore account for the immunity of solicitor advocates. It is a matter of judgment what weight should be placed on the "cab rank" rule as a justification for the immunity. It is a valuable professional rule. But its impact on the administration of justice in England is not great. In real life a barrister has a clerk whose enthusiasm for the unwanted brief may not be great, and he is free to raise the fee within limits. It is not likely that the rule often obliges barristers to undertake work which they would not otherwise accept. When it does occur, and vexatious claims result, it will usually be possible to dispose of such claims summarily. In any event, the "cab rank" rule cannot justify depriving all clients of a remedy for negligence causing them grievous financial loss. It is "a very high price to pay for protection from what must, in practice, be the very small risk of being subjected to vexations litigation (which is, anyway, unlikely to get very far)": *Cane, Tort Law and Economic Interests*, p 236. Secondly, there is the analogy of the immunities enjoyed by those who participate in court proceedings: compare however Cane's observation about the strength of the case for removing the immunity from paid expert witnesses: at p 237. Those immunities are founded on the public policy which seeks to encourage freedom of speech in court so that the court will have full information about the issues in the case. For these reasons they prevent legal actions based on what is said in court. As Pannick has pointed out this has little, if anything, to do with the alleged legal policy which requires immunity from actions for negligent acts: ibid, at p 202. If the latter immunity has merit it must rest on other grounds. Whilst this factor seemed at first to have some attractiveness, it has on analysis no or virtually no weight at all.

The third factor is the public policy against relitigating a decision of a court of competent jurisdiction. This factor cannot support an immunity extending to cases where there was no verdict by the jury or decision by the court. It cannot arguably justify the immunity in its present width. The major question arises in regard to criminal trials which have resulted in a verdict by a jury or a decision by the court. Prosecuting counsel owes no duty of care to a defendant: *Elguzouli-Daf v Comr of Police of the Metropolis* [1995] QB 335. The position of defence counsel must however be considered. Unless debarred from doing so, defendants convicted after a full and fair trial who failed to appeal successfully will from time to time attempt to challenge their convictions by suing advocates who appeared for them. This is the paradigm of an abusive challenge. It is a principal focus of the principle in *Hunter v Chief Constable of the West Midlands Police* [1982] AC 529. Public policy requires a defendant who seeks to challenge his conviction to do so directly by seeking to appeal his conviction. In this regard the creation of the Criminal Cases Review Commission was a notable step forward. Recently in *R v Secretary of State for the Home Department, Ex p Simms* [2000] 2 AC 115, 127–128, there was uncontroverted evidence before the House that the Commission is seriously under-resourced and under-funded. Incoming cases apparently have to wait two years before they are assigned to a case worker. This is a depressing picture. The answer is that the functioning of the Commission must be improved. But I have no doubt that the principle underlying the *Hunter* case must be maintained as a matter of high public policy. In the *Hunter* case the House did not, however, "lay down an inflexible rule to be applied willy-nilly to all cases which might arguably be said to be within it": *Smith v Linskills* [1996] 1 WLR 763, 769, per Sir Thomas Bingham MR. It is, however, prima facie an abuse to initiate a collateral civil challenge to a criminal conviction. Ordinarily therefore a collateral civil challenge to a criminal conviction will be struck out as an abuse of process. On the other hand, if the convicted person has succeeded in having his conviction set aside on any ground, an action against a barrister in negligence will no longer be barred by the particular public policy identified in the *Hunter* case. But, in such a case the civil action in negligence against the barrister may nevertheless be struck out as unsustainable under the new flexible CPR rr 3.4(2)(a) and 24.2. If the *Hunter* case is interpreted

680

and applied in this way, the principal force of the fear of oblique challenges to criminal convictions disappears. Relying on my experience of the criminal justice system as a presiding judge on the Northern Circuit and as a member of the Court of Appeal (Criminal Division), I do not share intuitive judgments that the public policy against relitigation still requires the immunity to be maintained in criminal cases. That leaves collateral challenges to civil decisions. The principles of res judicata, issue estoppel and abuse of process as understood in private law should be adequate to cope with this risk. It would not ordinarily be necessary to rely on the *Hunter* principle in the civil context but I would accept that the policy underlying it should still stand guard against unforeseen gaps. In my judgment a barrister's immunity is not needed to deal with collateral attacks on criminal and civil decisions. The public interest is satisfactorily protected by independent principles and powers of the court.

The critical factor is, however, the duty of a barrister to the court. It also applies to every person who exercises rights of audience before any court, or who exercises rights to conduct litigation before a court: see sections 27(2A) and 28(2A) of the Courts and Legal Services Act 1990 as inserted by section 42 of the Access to Justice Act 1999. It is essential that nothing should be done which might undermine the overriding duty of an advocate to the court. The question is however whether the immunity is needed to ensure that barristers will respect their duty to the court. The view of the House in 1967 was that assertions of negligence would tend to erode this duty. In the world of today there are substantial grounds for questioning this ground of public policy. In 1967 the House considered that for reasons of public policy barristers must be accorded a special status. Nowadays a comparison with other professionals is important. Thus doctors have duties not only to their patients but also to an ethical code. Doctors are sometimes faced with a tension between these duties. Concrete examples of such conflicting duties are given by Ian Kennedy, *Treat Me Right; Essays in Medical Law and Ethics* (1988). A topical instance is the case where an Aids infected patient asks a consultant not to reveal his condition to the patient's wife, general practitioner and other healthcare officials. Such decisions may easily be as difficult as those facing barristers. And nobody argues that doctors should have an immunity from suits in negligence.

Comparative experience may throw some light on the question whether in the public interest such an immunity of advocates is truly necessary. In 1967 no comparative material was placed before the House. Lord Reid did, however, mention other countries where public policy points in a different direction: [1969] 1 AC 191, 228E. In the present case we have had the benefit of a substantial comparative review. The High Court of Australia followed *Rondel v Worsley*: *Gianarelli v Wraith* (1988) 165 CLR 543; see also *Boland v Yates Property Corpn Pty Ltd* (1999) 74 ALJR 209. In New Zealand the Court of Appeal has taken a similar course: *Rees v Sinclair* [1974] 1 NZLR 180. It is a matter of significance that the High Court of Australia and the Court of Appeal of New Zealand came to the conclusion that a barristers immunity from actions in negligence is required by public policy considerations in those countries. On the other hand, in countries in the European Union advocates have no immunity. It is true that there is a difference in that the control of a civilian judge over the proceedings is greater than is customarily exercised by a judge in England: see *Ralph Graef, Judicial Activism in Civil Proceedings* (1996), passim. But with the advent of the Woolf reforms this difference is reduced to some extent in civil cases: see CPR Pt 1, r 1.1 (the overriding objective). On the other hand, I accept that in the field of criminal procedure the role of a judge in England is far more passive than in European Union countries: see *Van Den Wyngaert, Criminal Procedure Systems in the European Community* (1993), passim. I am also willing to accept that, although an advocate in a civilian system owes a duty to the court, it is less extensive than in England. For example, in Germany there is apparently no duty to refer the court to adverse authorities as in England. Despite these differences the fact that the absence of an immunity has apparently caused no practical difficulties in other countries in the European Union is of some significance: *Tortious Liability of Statutory Bodies*, edited by B S Markesinis (1999), p 80. In the United States prosecutors have an immunity. In a few states the immunity is extended to public defenders. But otherwise lawyers have no immunity from suits of negligence by their clients: *Ferri v Ackermann* (1979) 444 US 193. While the differences between the legal system of the USA and our own must be taken into account, the United States position cannot be altogether ignored. In Canada an advocate had no immunity from an action in negligence before *Rondel v Worsley* was decided. In 1979 the question was re-examined in great detail as a result of the decision of the House of Lords in *Rondel v Worsley*: see *Demarco v Ungaro* (1979) 95 DLR (3d) 385. In Canada trial lawyers owe a duty to the court. After a detailed and careful review the court found there was no evidence that the work of Canadian courts was hampered in any way by counsel's fear of civil liability. The *Demarco* case has been consistently followed by Canadian courts: see *Karpenko v Paroian, Courey, Cohen & Houston* (1980) 30 OR (2d) 776; *Pelky v Hudson Bay Insurance Co* (1981) 35 OR (2d) 97; *Garrant v Moskal* [1985] 2 WWR 80, affirmed [1985] 6 WWR 31; *M Hodge & Sons Ltd v Monaghan* (1985) 51 Nfld & PEIR 173. I regard the Canadian empirically tested experience as the most relevant. It tends to demonstrate that the fears that the possibility of actions in negligence against barristers would tend to undermine the public interest are unnecessarily pessimistic.

There would be benefits to be gained from the ending of immunity. First, and most importantly, it will bring to an end an anomalous exception to the basic premise that there should be a remedy for a wrong. There is no reason to fear a flood of negligence suits against barristers. The mere doing of his duty to the court by the advocate to the detriment of his client could never be called negligent. Indeed if the advocate's conduct was bona fide dictated by his perception of his duty to the court there would be no possibility of the court holding him to be negligent. Moreover, when such claims are made courts will take into account the difficult decisions faced daily by barristers working in demanding situations to tight timetables. In this context the observations of Sir Thomas Bingham MR in *Ridehalgh v Horsefield* [1994] Ch 205 are instructive. Dealing with the circumstances in which a wasted costs order against a barrister might be appropriate he observed, at p 236:

> "Any judge who is invited to make or contemplates making an order arising out of an advocate's conduct of court proceedings must make full allowance for the fact that an advocate in court, like a commander in

battle, often has to make decisions quickly and under pressure, in the fog of war and ignorant of developments on the other side of the hill. Mistakes will inevitably be made, things done which the outcome shows to have been unwise. But advocacy is more an art than a science. It cannot be conducted according to formulae. Individuals differ in their style and approach. It is only when, with all allowances made, an advocate's conduct of court proceedings is quite plainly unjustifiable that it can be appropriate to make a wasted costs order against him."

For broadly similar reasons it will not be easy to establish negligence against a barrister. The courts can be trusted to differentiate between errors of judgment and true negligence. In any event, a plaintiff who claims that poor advocacy resulted in an unfavourable outcome will face the very great obstacle of showing that a better standard of advocacy would have resulted in a more favourable outcome. Unmeritorious claims against barristers will be struck out. The new Civil Procedure Rules 1999, have made it easier to dispose summarily of such claims: rules 3.4(2)(a) and 24.2. The only argument that remains is that the fear of unfounded actions might have a negative effect on the conduct of advocates. This is a most flimsy foundation, unsupported by empirical evidence, for the immunity. Secondly, it must be borne in mind that one of the functions of tort law is to set external standards of behaviour for the benefit of the public. And it would be right to say that while standards at the Bar are generally high, in some respects there is room for improvement. An exposure of isolated acts of incompetence at the Bar will strengthen rather than weaken the legal system. Thirdly, and most importantly, public confidence in the legal system is not enhanced by the existence of the immunity. The appearance is created that the law singles out its own for protection no matter how flagrant the breach of the barrister. The world has changed since 1967. The practice of law has become more commercialised: barristers may now advertise. They may now enter into contracts for legal services with their professional clients. They are now obliged to carry insurance. On the other hand, today we live in a consumerist society in which people have a much greater awareness of their rights. If they have suffered a wrong as a result of the provision of negligent professional services, they expect to have the right to claim redress. It tends to erode confidence in the legal system if advocates, alone among professional men, are immune from liability for negligence. It is also noteworthy that there is no obligation on the barrister (or for that matter the solicitor advocate) to inform a client at the inception of the relationship that he is not liable in negligence, and in practice the client is never so informed. Given that the resort to litigation is often one of the most important decisions in the life of the client, it has to be said that this is not a satisfactory position. Moreover, conduct covered by the immunity is beyond the remit of the Legal Services Ombudsman: section 22(7)(b) of the Courts and Legal Services Act 1990. In combination these factors reinforce the already strong case for ending the immunity.

My Lords, one is intensely aware that *Rondel v Worsley* [1969] 1 AC 191 was a carefully reasoned and unanimous decision of the House. On the other hand, it is now clear that when the balance is struck between competing factors it is no longer in the public interest that the immunity in favour of barristers should remain. I am far from saying that *Rondel v*

Worsley was wrongly decided. But on the information now available and developments since *Rondel v Worsley* I am satisfied that in today's world that decision no longer correctly reflects public policy. The basis of the immunity of barristers has gone. And exactly the same reasoning applies to solicitor advocates. There are differences between the two branches of the profession but not of a character to differentiate materially between them in respect of the issue before the House. I would treat them in the same way.

That brings me to the argument that the ending of the immunity, if it is to be undertaken, is a matter for Parliament. This argument is founded on section 62 of the Courts and Legal Services Act 1990. It reads:

> "(1) A person—(a) who is not a barrister; but (b) who lawfully provides any legal services in relation to any proceedings, shall have the same immunity from liability for negligence in respect of his acts or omissions as he would have if he were a barrister lawfully providing those services. (2) No act or omission on the part of any barrister or other person which is accorded immunity from liability for negligence shall give rise to an action for breach of any contract relating to the provision by him of the legal services in question."

The background to this provision is, of course, the judicially created immunity of barristers, which in 1967 was held by the House to be founded on public policy. And it will be recollected that Lord Reid observed that public policy is not immutable. Against this background the meaning of section 62 is clear. It provides that solicitor advocates will have the same immunity as barristers have. In other words, the immunity of solicitors will follow the fortunes of the immunity of barristers, or track it. Section 62 did not either expressly or by implication give parliamentary endorsement to the immunity of barristers. In these circumstances the argument that it is beyond the power of the House of Lords, which created the immunity spelt out in *Rondel v Worsley*, to reverse that decision in changed circumstances involving a different balance of policy considerations is not right. Should the House as a matter of discretion leave it to Parliament? This issue is more finely balanced. It would certainly be the easy route for the House to say "let us leave it to Parliament". On balance my view is that it would be an abdication of our responsibilities with the unfortunate consequence of plunging both branches of the legal profession in England into a state of uncertainty over a prolonged period. That would be a disservice to the public interest. On the other hand, if the decision is made to end the immunity now, both branches of the profession will know where they stand. They ought to find it relatively easy to amend their rules where necessary and to adjust their already existing insurance arrangements in so far as that may be necessary.

My Lords, the cards are now heavily stacked against maintaining the immunity of advocates. I would rule that there is no longer any such immunity in criminal and civil cases. In doing so I am quite confident that the legal profession does not need the immunity.

The Hunter case

So far as the *Hunter* case involves a separate question before the House I would refer to my discussion of this topic under the heading of immunity of barristers.

684

The disposal of the appeals

Given the conclusion that the immunity no longer exists, it follows that the appeals must fail. I would dismiss the three appeals.

Note

The outcome was that it was unanimously held that there was no immunity from suit for advocates in civil proceedings, and by a majority of four to three that there was no such immunity in criminal proceedings.

Part Six

Arbitration

[25]
England's Response to the UNCITRAL Model Law of Arbitration[1]

ENGLAND'S RESPONSE to the challenge of UNCITRAL's Model Law on International Commercial Arbitration has been to use it as a yardstick by which to judge the quality of our existing arbitration legislation and to improve it. After a gestation period, which has been elephantine in its proportions, a draft Arbitration Bill has now been prepared and when a consultation paper has been completed the consultation process will start. The single most important influence in the shaping of the Bill has been the Model Law.

The genesis of the Model Law was the idea that trading nations would benefit by having available an international text as a basis for harmonizing national legislation by adopting the text *en bloc* or by revising national laws in accordance with desirable features of it. It was an ambitious project, notably because arbitration is concerned with the procedure of dispute resolution and the relationship between arbitration and national courts. The divergences between national laws on arbitration are great. And it is usually more difficult to achieve harmonization of national laws in procedural as opposed to substantive matters. That was the principal reason why the technique of a model law as opposed to a convention was adopted.

The Model Law text was settled in 1985 after many lengthy sessions spread over several years. 32 states were represented by delegations. The United Kingdom delegation included Lord Justice Mustill (now Lord Mustill). A further 20 states sent observers. So did 14 international organizations. Lord Wilberforce represented the Chartered Institute of Arbitrators. Mr Martin Hunter was the delegate of the International Bar Association. All contributed in an active way in discussions. Inevitably, there had to be compromises between common law and civil law points of view, and the concerns of other legal cultures had to be taken into account. No international text ever satisfies everybody. But the Model Law was a remarkable achievement by UNCITRAL, ranking in importance with the New York Convention of 1958. The text is arranged in logical order, and its provisions are expressed in simple language, which will be readily comprehensible to international users of the arbitration process. Substantively, the solutions adopted by the

---

[1] This article reproduces the author's 1993 Freshfields Arbitration Lecture.

working Group reflect a widespread consensus as to what is practical and feasible in international commercial arbitration. It is therefore not surprising that 16 states have already based new legislation on the Model Law.[2] Germany and New Zealand may follow the same route. And other states are revising their arbitration laws in the light of the Model Law.

I. THE DECISION NOT TO ADOPT THE MODEL LAW

It is pertinent to ask why the Departmental Advisory Committee on Arbitration Law (the DAC) recommended that England should not adopt the Model Law. Cynical foreign observers say that the decision is in character with Britain's role in the process of harmonization of international trade law. Typically, they say, the United Kingdom is voluble at international congresses in promoting common law solutions in the framing of a convention and, having achieved significant success in that pursuit, it then rejects the convention as being inferior to native English law. This criticism is obviously too extravagant in its scope. But it is not entirely groundless. The Vienna Sales Convention has been ratified by 34 nations, including almost all the member countries of the European Economic Community, and most of the major trading nations of the world. My understanding is that Belgium, Japan, and New Zealand will also ratify. Yet the United Kingdom delays. I believe the reason is to be found in the deep seated antipathy of English lawyers towards multilateral conventions. The purity of the common law prevails over the needs of international commerce, and our own trading position. Moreover, as Professor Barry Nicholas, a United Kingdom delegate at the Vienna working sessions, pointed out earlier this year, it is vital that the United Kingdom should ratify the Convention quickly, so that the experience of English lawyers and of the Commercial Court can influence the way in which the Convention is interpreted and applied.[3] I would argue, however, that the decision of the DAC to recommend that England should not adopt the Model Law was justified on special grounds. And it is right to point out that the committee took this decision under the chairmanship of Lord Justice Mustill and after a most detailed and rigorous examination of the merits and demerits of the Model law as compared with English law.

Not all the reasons put forward in 1989 for not adopting the Model Law seem as compelling today as they did then. The committee stated:[4]

> The arguments in favour of enacting the Model Law in the interests of harmonization, or of thereby keeping in step with other nations, are of little weight. The majority of trading

---

[2] Legislation based on the Model Law has been enacted in Australia, Bermuda, Bulgaria, Canada, Cyprus, Hong Kong, Mexico, Nigeria, Peru, Russian Federation, Scotland, Tunisia and, within the United States of America, California, Connecticut, Oregon and Texas.

[3] The United Kingdom and the Vienna Sales Convention: Another case of splendid isolation? March 1993, *Centro di studi e ricerche di diritto comparato e straniero*, No. 9. In a paper under the heading "The Vienna Sales Convention: A kind of Esperanto?" which was presented at an All Souls seminar in April 1993 I considered the arguments for and against England ratifying the Vienna Sales Convention.

[4] 2, para. 89.

nations, and more notably those to which international arbitrations have tended to gravitate, have not chosen thus to keep in step.

That was a judgment made four years after the publication of the Model Law. Today one would have to revise that judgment. Less than a decade after its first publication the Model Law has proved popular internationally and has become a benchmark by which the quality of national arbitration laws is judged. Nevertheless, in my view, the decision taken in 1989 was right for England. I say that for two reasons. First, although our principal statute, the Arbitration Act 1950, is of poor quality, England already has a well developed and comprehensive arbitration system which, since the watershed of the Arbitration Act 1979, has by and large proved satisfactory domestically and popular among international users of the arbitration process. In comparison the Model Law quite understandably is more skeletal in its treatment of the arbitration process. It contains many gaps which would have to be filled. Secondly, much of arbitration law is concerned with the relationship between arbitration and national court systems, and in the English system that relationship involves greater supervision of the arbitral process than is envisaged by the Model Law. Subject to two qualifications to which I will turn later, the prevailing domestic view has been that England has found the right balance between party autonomy and judicial scrutiny of the arbitral process. In combination these two factors justified the decision taken in 1989 not to adopt the Model Law.

II. THE WAY FORWARD

In its 1989 report the Mustill committee recommended that a new statute should be drafted which would 'comprise a statement in statutory form of the more important principles of the English Law of arbitration, statutory and (to the extent practicable) common law'.[5] The committee advised that[6]

> Consideration should be given to ensuring that any such new statute should, so far as possible, have the same structure and language as the Model law, so as to enhance its accessibility to those who are familiar with the Model Law.

The government accepted this advice.

The initiative to translate the idea of a new statute into action came from Mr Arthur Marriott. It involved the privatized drafting of a new statute. It was founded by a large group of law firms, barristers' chambers and arbitration institutions. The Marriott Group engaged the services of Mr Basil Eckersley, a distinguished barrister and arbitrator. That was an inspired choice. He produced an Arbitration Bill and a Commentary. It was a *tour de force* and a convincing refutation of the notion that only a lawyer trained in the office of the Parliamentary Draftsman is capable of drafting a statute.

---

[5] Para. 108.
[6] *Ibid.*

Nevertheless the DAC resolved that the new statute should be drafted by somebody trained as a parliamentary draftsman. That decision puzzled many experienced observers. It was yet further testimony to the astonishing awe in which Whitehall holds Parliamentary Draftsmen. As Sir William Dale pointed out, legislative drafting in England is endowed with a mystique which it does not possess in civil law countries.[7] The decision of the DAC was the outcome of *realpolitik*. The DAC was advised by the Department of Trade and Industry that it was essential, in view of a crowded legislative agenda, to obtain government support for the new measure and that such support would not be forthcoming if the bill was not drafted by a lawyer trained as a parliamentary draftstman. The DAC was motivated by one desire only: that England should have the best possible new arbitration statute as soon as possible. The committee accepted the advice it was given, as it had to.

The Marriott Working Group instructed a former parliamentary draftsman to prepare a Bill. Unfortunately, his draft failed the threshold requirement of following the structure of the Model Law. The committee rejected it as a basis for future work. The Group instructed another former parliamentary draftsman. The committee accepted her first draft as a working draft. The committee then advised on successive drafts of the Bill.

Until 1992 the project had been financed and directed by the Marriott Working Group. By April 1992 it had become clear to all concerned that it would be more sensible for the project to become a public one. The DAC recommended that the Department of Trade and Industry should take over responsibility for work on the Bill and it should be carried forward as a Government Bill. The government accepted this recommendation.[8] That is the basis on which the DAC has advised on the drafting and redrafting of the Bill. Nevertheless the work of the Marriott Group, and Mr Eckersley's draft, proved of immense value in the second and public phase of the project. Without that work we would not today have an Arbitration Bill. And the DAC has been able to draw on the very extensive experience of the Marriott Group because two leading members of the Group, Mr Arthur Marriott and Mr Anthony Bunch, generously agreed to join the committee.

III. THE STRUCTURE OF THE BILL

The Bill looks very different from the existing arbitration legislation. The structure is different. For example, the draftsman of the 1950 statute thought

---

[7] *Legislative Drafting: A New Approach* (1977) p. 339.
[8] In the course of his lecture 'The Competitive Society', the 1993 Combar lecture given on 18 May 1993, the President of the Board of Trade explained the Government's approach as follows: 'We do very well in the arbitration field. But our law, built up over years, is becoming incomprehensible to the people who want to use it. Other countries have updated and clarified their law. Others are in the process of doing so. If we do not do the same, and keep abreast of them, we will lose business. I am pleased to be able to say that, having had the arguments put to me, I was able to agree to my Department taking on responsibility for preparing a new Arbitration Bill. This is being done in full cooperation with the Committee and others with direct interest'.

it right to start the statute with a provision on the revocation of the mandate of the arbitrator, and to scatter provisions about the challenge to arbitrators across the statute. Generally the structure of the 1950 statute was illogical and confusing. The Bill has a clear and logical structure taken from the Model Law. This is an important point because it was a prime objective of the DAC that the bill should improve the accessibility of our arbitration legislation to domestic and international users alike. The 1950 statute repeatedly uses the drafting technique of deeming provisions, which provide that 'unless a contrary intention is expressed therein, every arbitration agreement shall, be deemed to include a provision that...'. Like the draftsmen of the Model Law the DAC ultimately put its faith in simplicity. The deeming provisions have been replaced by straightforward prescriptive statements, sometimes mandatory in character and sometimes not. Another new feature is that the Bill emphasizes the principle of party autonomy. It also seems to me that generally the language in which the Bill has been expressed has been improved and that it is likely to be reasonably intelligible to laymen.

IV. SOME MAJOR ISSUES

It will not be possible to discuss the Bill in detail. But it might be useful to consider briefly a few features of the Bill, which either involve or might arguably involve important changes in the law, as well as certain major issues which are not at present affected by the Bill but nevertheless lie at the heart of the current debate. The matters which I propose to discuss are:

(a) *Kompetenz/Kompetenz* and the separability of the arbitration agreement;
(b) Evidence;
(c) Procedure;
(d) Immunity of arbitrators;
(e) The relationship between the courts and arbitration:
 (i) Special categories;
 (ii) Remission
(f) Equity clauses.

(a) *Kompetenz/Kompetenz and the separability of the arbitration agreement*

The doctrine of *Kompetenz/Kompetenz*, that is the question whether arbitrators may decide on their own jurisdiction, causes difficulties in some countries. In England the position is straightforward. Arbitrators are entitled, and indeed required, to consider whether they will assume jurisdiction. But that decision does not alter the legal rights of the parties, and the court has the last word. The new Bill does not change the law. It merely contains a provision declaratory of the common law position. Given the fact that the Commercial Court has the capacity to decide such preliminary issues speedily, the DAC took the view that the existing practice in England is probably satisfactory. Accordingly, the Bill contains no provisions comparable to Article 16(2) of the

Model Law, which requires a denial of jurisdiction to be raised not later than when the defence is served, and Article 16(3), which requires an application to a court challenging the arbitrators' decision to be made within 30 days. If the consultation process reveals strong support for corresponding provisions in our legislation, the committee will have to think again.

Until recently the doctrine of the separability of an arbitration clause contained in an integrated written agreement was not fully developed in England. Thus it was thought that a dispute whether a written agreement reflected the true intention of the parties and can be rectified always fell outside the scope of the arbitration clause in the contract. In 1987 in *Ashville Investments Ltd.* v. *Elmer Contractors Ltd*[9] the Court of Appeal finally laid to rest this absurd notion. The judgments in that case were a notable contribution to the development of the doctrine of the separability of the arbitration agreement. But there was still a problem. The orthodox view was that disputes as to whether a contract was invalid or illegal *ab initio* always fell outside the scope of an arbitration clause in that contract. Earlier this year *Harbour Assurance Co. (UK) Ltd* v. *Kansa General International Assurance Co. Ltd*[10] the Court of Appeal held that an arbitration agreement in a written contract could confer jurisdiction on an arbitrator to decide on the initial validity or illegality of the written contract provided that the arbitration clause was not directly impeached. I respectfully applaud the judgments in the Court of Appeal in *Harbour Assurance*. England has now adopted the approach of the Model Law. Article 16(1) of the Model Law reads as follows:

> An arbitration clause which forms part of a contract shall be treated as an agreement independent of the other terms of the contract. A decision by the arbitral tribunal that the contract is null and void shall not entail *ipso jure* the invalidity of the arbitration clause.

That provision is the most compelling evidence of the workability and desirability of a fully developed separability doctrine. Given that the relevant law has now been satisfactorily developed and settled in *Harbour Assurance*, some may think that there is no need for legislation. It is true that there will be no appeal to the House of Lords in *Harbour Assurance*. But there is the risk that the point may come before the House of Lords in another case. And the infallibles may say that it is all far more difficult than the Court of Appeal realized, and they may reverse the beneficial development of the law. That has been known to happen. In order to guard against that risk the Bill contains in clause 3(2) a separability provision squarely based on Article 16(1) of the Model Law.

(b) *Evidence*

In recent times it has been assumed by authors that arbitrators are bound by the technical rules of evidence unless the parties expressly or implied agree

---

[9] [1989] Q.B. 488.
[10] [1993] 3 All ER 897; [1993] 3 WLR 42; [1993] 1 Lloyd's Rep. 455.

otherwise.[11] This assumption is understandable since in enacting the Civil Evidence Act 1968 Parliament assumed that the technical rules of evidence apply to arbitrations.[12] That was, however, a mere assumption and it has no prescriptive force. If there is any such rule, it must therefore be found in the case law. Here I am fortunate. In an important paper Mr Richard Buxton QC, a Law Commissioner, (now Mr Justice Buxton) examined the relevant case law with great care.[13] His conclusion was that, contrary to what was generally believed to be the position, there is no binding authority which holds that the technical rules of evidence are applicable in arbitrations. And there are *dicta* the other way. That is a view which I respectfully share.

Looking at the matter more broadly it is difficult to see why the technical rules of evidence should apply to arbitrations. A term to that effect cannot be implied in the arbitration agreement. If there is such a rule, it must therefore be a rule of positive law. But what can be the rationale for such a rule? It can only be that the rules of law governing court proceedings and arbitrations must in all respects be the same. But that is a false premiss because one of the purposes of arbitration is to avoid the over-elaborate procedure of Court proceedings and the technical rules of evidence. It is also difficult to see why, in the thousands of domestic arbitrations conducted every year by architects, engineers, surveyors and other laymen, the arbitrators should have to master technical rules of evidence which sometimes baffle the House of Lords. Moreover, in international commercial arbitrations, where the parties have selected London as the venue because of the quality of our international arbitrators and the quality of our substantive law, it is difficult to justify the application of our technical rules of evidence. And where London is imposed on the parties by the decision of the International Chamber of Commerce, or another arbitral institution, the absurdity of applying our technical rules of evidence is even greater. It is true that most institutional rules expressly exclude the rules of evidence. It is also right that the rules of evidence are usually ignored in arbitrations. These are not, however, reasons for maintaining such a rule: these are added reasons for abolishing it. Lastly, it is relevant to note that the technical rules of evidence are under siege even in the court system. The centrepiece of the technical rules of evidence is the hearsay rule. That is the rule which led the House of Lords to conclude in *Myers*[14] that the factory records containing the engine block number of cars cannot be used as evidence to identify the cars since it was hearsay evidence. The fact that such evidence was rationally superior in quality to any evidence given by employees did not help. The statutory reversal of the particular decision in *Myers* has left unaffected the impact of the hearsay rule on many classes of rationally

---

[11] Mustill and Boyd, *Commercial Arbitration*, (2nd ed.) p. 352; *Russell on Arbitration* (20th ed), p. 273.
[12] S. 18(1) (*b*).
[13] 'The Rules of Evidence as Applied to Arbitrations'. *The Journal of the Chartered Institute of Arbitrators* (1992), Volume 58. p. 229.
[14] [1965] AC 1001.

superior evidence. Since Mr Buxton's paper was delivered, the Law Commission has convincingly demonstrated that the hearsay rule has no place in a modern court system and recommended that in civil proceedings evidence should not be excluded on the ground that it is hearsay.[15] There is, however, a risk that a court may convert the *communis error* that the technical rules of evidence apply to arbitrations into the *ratio decidendi* of a case. It is the unanimous view of the DAC that the inapplicability of technical rules of evidence to arbitrations should be made plain by legislation. Clause 11(1) of the Bill provides:

> the tribunal shall determine all procedural matters including the admissibility, relevance, materiality and weight of any evidence.

This provision is taken verbatim from Article 19(1) of the Model Law. If it becomes law it ought to remove any suspicion that in splendid isolation England insists on applying the technical rules of evidence to arbitrations.

That leaves one loose end under the heading of evidence. The losing party in an arbitration, who can identify no true question of law, frequently applies for leave to appeal under section 1 of the Arbitration Act 1979 on the ground that there was no evidence to support a finding of fact. The argument is that such a question is a question of law under section 1. To the best of my knowledge such submissions never succeed. But does the supposed rule exist? Mustill and Boyd have argued that the rule has not survived the changes introduced by the reforming measure of 1979.[16] I respectfully agree. But this relic from the last century, which was invented to control the decisions of illiterate juries, is still around and provides a convenient basis for attacking arbitrators' decisions on matters of pure fact.[17] The Bill does not expressly deal with this point. One would hope that with the final demise of the idea that arbitrators are bound by the technical rules of evidence this related rule would also perish. But one can imagine counsel arguing that the rule should be adjusted to provide that the issue whether there is relevant evidential material, as opposed to technically admissible evidence, in support of a finding of fact is a question of law. In drafting legislation one cannot, however, guard against every absurd argument. On balance I am confident that, if clause 11(1) of the Bill is enacted, it should put an end to all arguments that it is a question of law whether there is material to support a finding of fact.

(c) *Procedure*

It has been a conventional wisdom of English arbitration law that there is a rule of law requiring an arbitrator to conduct a reference in an adversarial as opposed to inquisitorial fashion unless the parties have agreed otherwise. In

---

[15] Law Com. No. 216 (Cm. 2321).
[16] *Commercial Arbitration*, (2nd ed) p. 596.
[17] In *The Baleares* [1993] 1 Lloyd's Rep: 215, at pp. 228 and 231–232, I explained in some detail why in my view this supposed rule should now be rejected.

obiter dicta Lord Roskill[18] and Lord Donaldson of Lymington[19] have said so. Distinguished authors have also said so.[20] But there appears to be no binding precedent containing a ruling to that effect. Moreover, the powers vested in arbitrators by section 12(1) of the Arbitration Act do not appear to be tied to the adversarial system. It contemplates that the arbitrator will examine the parties to the dispute, and presumably also their witnesses. Moreover, in sweeping terms section 12(1) provides that the parties shall 'do all other things which during the proceedings on the reference the arbitrator... may require'. That hardly looks like a legislative prescription for a rule requiring arbitrators to conform strictly to the adversarial model of the court process.

It seemed to me that the point should be researched. Here too I have been fortunate. I have had the advantage of meticulous historical and legal research done by Claire Blanchard.[21] A good starting point is to ask why English civil court proceedings acquired their distinctive adversarial character. Historically, the general mode of trial was by a judge and jury. The dynamics of a jury trial required one predominantly oral hearing, and involved a relatively passive judge, who left the deployment of the evidence and arguments to the lawyers.[22] There was no reason why this procedural framework should be imposed on arbitration as a matter of law. On the other hand, it is easy to see that historically the habits of the courtroom would often have been carried over into arbitration. Between 1694 and 1889 a number of textbooks were published on arbitration law. These books stated that the procedural powers of arbitrators are wider than those of judges; that arbitrators are not bound by rules of practice; and that arbitrators may in their discretion either examine the parties and their witnesses or leave it to the lawyers.[23] The contemporary case law provides an inconclusive picture. One must, of course, put to one side cases concerning court arbitrators, who were the predecessors of official referees. Clearly, it was only natural that such arbitrators would follow the same procedure as the court from which it received its authority. Subject to this qualification, and subject to the further qualification that arbitrators must always obey the principles of natural justice, there is nothing in the decided cases to show that there was an established rule requiring arbitrators to adopt an adversarial procedure. In 1889 the Arbitration Act provided by paragraph (f) of its First Schedule as follows:

> The parties to the reference... shall, subject to any legal objection, submit to be examined by the arbitrators... and shall, subject as aforesaid, produce before the arbitrators... documents within their possession or power respectively which may be required or called for,

---

[18] *Bremer Vulkan Schiffbau und Maschenenfabrik* v. *South India Shipping Corpn. Ltd.* [1981] AC 909.
[19] *Chilton and Another* v. *Saga Holidays plc.* [1986] 1 All ER 841, at p. 844.
[20] Mustill and Boyd, *op cit.*
[21] A barrister practising in 4 Essex Court, Temple, London EC4 (my former chambers).
[22] Lord Wilberforce, 'Written briefs and oral advocacy', (1989) 6 *Arbitration International.*, p. 348.
[23] Cleeve, *The Law of Arbitration* (1694), p. 18; Kyd, *The Law of Awards* (2nd ed., 1799), p. 96; Caldwell, *The Law of Arbitration*, (2nd ed., 1825) p. 53; Watson, *The Law of Arbitration and Awards* (3rd ed., 1846) p. 117; Redman, *The Law of Arbitrations and Awards* (1st ed.) p. 88; Russell, *The Power and Duty of an Arbitrator and the Law of Submissions and Awards* (3rd ed., 1864) p. 183.

and do all other things which during the proceedings on the reference the arbitrators or umpire may require.

That provision was the forerunner of section 12(1) of the Arbitration Act 1950. It did not impose an adversarial framework on arbitrators. On the contrary, its language contradicts the notion that arbitrators are rigidly tied to adversarial procedures. Given these statutory provisions, it is not surprising that there is no binding precedent requiring arbitrators as a matter of law to follow the adversarial procedure of the White Book. It is realistic, however, to accept that throughout this century lawyers trained in civil court proceedings in fact allowed that experience to govern arbitral procedure. And it is a fact that arbitrators and lawyers generally assume that they are bound to adopt adversarial procedures.

Under the Model Law system arbitrators have wide procedural powers to proceed in accordance with adversarial or inquisitorial methods or in accordance wth a mixture of both methods. Article 19 provides as follows:

(1) ..., the parties are free to agree on the procedure to be followed by the arbitral tribunal in conducting the proceedings.
(2) Failing such agreement, the arbitral tribunal may, subject to the provisions of this Law, conduct the arbitration in such manner as it considers appropriate.

The DAC unanimously took the view that it would benefit English arbitration to make clear that, subject to the terms of the arbitration agreement and to the overriding principles of natural justice, arbitrators may adopt inquisitorial powers. It does not at all follow that the essentially oral character of contested hearings will be dramatically changed if our proposal is adopted. On the other hand, such a provision may be a useful weapon in the uphill fight against ever longer and costlier hearings. In order to achieve this policy objective, clause 11(1) of the Bill in substance enacts the Model Law provision.

Before I leave the subject of procedure, there are two qualifications which ought to be mentioned. First, if an arbitrator exercises inquisitorial powers, the risk of him committing technical misconduct will become greater. After all, it is easier for an arbitrator to hold the scales fairly if matters are left to the parties. But our arbitrators would not be assuming unique burdens. After all, the adversarial system is unknown in half of the industrialised world. Secondly, my impression is that in sectors of the construction industry the idea is gaining ground that arbitrators are entitled to exercise procedural powers contrary to the wishes of the parties. That is wrong. The principle of party autonomy requires the tribunal to respect any agreement of the parties whenever it may be concluded and however informal it may be. It is enshrined in clause 11(1) of the Bill.

(d) *Immunity of arbitrators*

In a collection of comparative law essays edited by Dr Julian Lew it is demonstrated how widely national laws differ on the immunity of arbitrators.[24] During the sessions of the Working Group, which led to the adoption of the Model Law, Canada proposed that the Model Law should confer immunity from liability for negligence on arbitrators.[25] It proved to be a highly controversial proposal. The draftsmen of the Model Law were seeking common ground. It is therefore not surprising that the Canadian proposal was rejected.

In England the question whether under the common law arbitrators are immune from actions in contract or tort alleging breach of a duty of reasonable care is probably still an open one.[26] The question before the DAC was whether a statutory immunity should be conferred on arbitrators. This subject was a very controversial issue in the discussions of the DAC. The opposition to such a provision took various forms, covering outright rejection of the idea as a matter of principle, difficulties of definition and the pragmatic view that in a complex area of the law the matter is best left to development by the courts. By a very narrow majority the DAC recommended that an immunity provision should be included in the draft Bill. It seems to me that the better view might be that under the common law arbitrators, because of the judicial character of their duties, already have the benefit of an immunity from liability for negligence. I would also not oppose the enactment of a statutory immunity in favour of arbitrators. On the other hand, I do not regard this aspect as one of the critically important parts of the new legislation.

(e) *The relationship between the courts and arbitration*

The supervisory jurisdiction of English courts over arbitration is more extensive than in most countries, notably because of the limited appeal on questions of law and the power to remit. It is certainly more extensive than the supervisory jurisdiction contemplated by the Model Law. Nevertheless the Sub-committee on Arbitration Law of the Commercial Court Committee, which was chaired by Mr Justice Mustill and reported in October 1985, recorded that in an extensive consultation process it received no representations for a change in the law. Similarly, the Mustill Committee, which was appointed in 1985 and reported in 1989, received no proposals for a change in the law. In its second report of May 1990 the DAC endorsed the earlier decision to maintain the *status quo*. But eventually it became clear that further thought had to be given to the so-called special categories under section 3 of the Arbitration Act 1979 and to the ambit of the power to remit under section 22(1) of the Arbitration Act 1950.

(i) *Special categories*

Section 3 of the Arbitration Act 1979 recognises the contractual freedom of parties under non-domestic arbitration agreements to exclude at any time

---

[24] *The Immunity of Arbitrators* (1990).
[25] Holzmann and Neuhaus, *A Guide to the UNCITRAL Model Law on International Commercial Arbitration: Legislative History and Commentary* (1989) p. 1148.
[26] *Arenson* v. *Arenson* [1977] A.C. 405.

appeals on questions of English law to the High Court under sections 1 and 2 of the Arbitration Act 1979. That contractual freedom is restricted by section 4(1) of the Act. It provides that an exclusion agreement made before the commencement of the arbitration shall have no effect if the question of English law arising under the award or in the course of the reference relates to any of three special categories, namely maritime, insurance and commodities disputes. Section 4(3) of the Act provides that the Secretary of State may either limit or remove these special categories by statutory instrument.

The only justification for the restriction of the freedom of contract of commercial men engaged in shipping, insurance or commodities was that it was needed to protect the standing of our commercial law. In the debates in the House of Lords, Lord Diplock made clear that the special categories were intended to apply for an 'experimental period during which it will be possible to see how the section works'.[27] After some 14 years it seemed right to review the matter. There was also considerable criticism from commentators. They argue that the standing of our commercial law is secure enough not to need the protection enshrined in the special categories provision. The DAC recently issued a consultation paper in order to invite comment on the desirability of maintaining the special categories. On this occasion that process has been specially targeted on users of the arbitration process. The DAC will want to pay the closest attention to the wishes of the markets.

(ii) *Remission*

Section 22(1) of the Arbitration Act 1980 provides in sweeping terms that the court 'may from time to time remit the matters referred, or any of them, to the reconsideration of the arbitrator'. On the face of it section 22(1) creates an entirely open textured discretion permitting a court to order the re-opening of the arbitration in circumstances where an appellate court would not be empowered to order the re-opening of High Court proceedings. Since judicial intrusion in arbitration proceedings should be less extensive than the full appellate process applicable to court proceedings such an unlimited power of remission would be surprising. And the imperative of protecting the finality of awards militates strongly against it. Not surprisingly such a wide power of remission does not exist in most countries. And the draftsmen of the Model Law rejected such a wide power of remission.[28]

A jurisprudence grew up in England which in practice restricted the power of remission to four grounds: (1) error of law on the face of the award which is now of academic importance only; (2) 'misconduct' by the arbitrator: (3) the

---

[27] House of Lords debates, 15 February 1979, 1477.
[28] Article 34(4) of the Model Law does, however contain a narrow point of remission. It reads as follows: 'The court, when asked to set aside an award, may, where appropriate and so requested by a party, suspend the setting aside proceedings for a period of time determined by it in order to give the arbitral tribunal an opportunity to resume the arbitral proceedings or to take such other action as in the arbitral tribunal's opinion will eliminate the grounds for setting aside.'

arbitrator's request to correct an admitted mistake; and (4) material fresh evidence discovered after the award.[29] In due course an ill-defined fifth category of 'procedural mishaps' justifying remission emerged; but by and large, the approach adopted kept the power of remission in tolerable bounds.

In the last four years three judgments have been given which significantly expand the power of remission. In *Indian Oil*[30] a judge of the Commercial Court remitted an award to arbitrators to consider a point which at the hearing the applicant's legal representatives consciously and deliberately had decided not to advance. In *King* v. *Thomas McKenna*[31] the Court of Appeal examined the scope of the power to remit. That case also concerned an application for remission as a result of a mistake made by the applicant's lawyer. Lord Donaldson of Lymington gave the leading judgment. Lord Justices Ralph Gibson and Nicholls agreed. Lord Donaldson observed that the jurisdiction was unlimited. Turning to the way in which the jurisdiction is to be exercised, Lord Donaldson stated:[32]

> In my judgment the remission jurisdiction extends beyond the four traditional grounds to any cases where, notwithstanding that the arbitrators have acted with complete propriety, due to mishap or misunderstanding some aspect of the dispute which has been the subject of the reference has not been considered and adjudicated upon as fully as or in a manner which the parties were entitled to expect and it would be inequitable to allow any award to take effect without some further consideration by the arbitrator. In so expressing myself I am not seeking to define or limit the jurisdiction or the way in which it should be exercised in particular cases, subject to the vital qualification that it is designed to remedy deviations from the route which the reference should have taken towards its destination (the award) and not to remedy a situation in which, despite having followed an unimpeachable route, the arbitrators have made errors of fact or law and as a result have reached a destination which was not that which the court would have reached. This essential qualification is usually underlined by saying that the jurisdiction to remit is to be invoked, if at all, in relation to procedural mishaps or misunderstandings. This is, however, too narrow a view since the traditional grounds do not necessarily involve procedural errors. The qualification is however of fundamental importance. Parties to arbitration, like parties to litigation, are entitled to expect that the arbitration will be conducted without mishap or misunderstanding and that, subject to the wide discretion enjoyed by the arbitrator, the procedure adopted will be fair and appropriate.

These two cases concerned mistakes of a party's lawyers. Given the terms of Lord Donaldson's judgment, logically the next step was to allow remission in the event of a mistake of a party. That is what happened in *Breakbulk Marine* v. *Dateline*.[33] A judge of the Commercial Court decided that he had jurisdiction to remit an award in circumstances where the applicant had failed to find a material letter before the award, although such letter was in no sense fresh evidence.

---

[29] Mustill and Boyd, *op. cit.*, pp. 549 *et seq.*
[30] *Indian Oil Corporation* v. *Coastal (Bermuda) Ltd* [1990] 2 Lloyd's Rep 407.
[31] [1991] 2 QB 480.
[32] At p. 491 C–F. It is interesting to note that the jurisdiction issue had been argued in an appeal which was settled and withdrawn before the judgments were handed down. The same issue did not arise in the only extant appeal. It seems arguable that the observations on the jurisdiction are *obiter dicta*. This may seem technical but the *stare decisis* doctrine has its technical features.
[33] 19 March 1992 (unreported).

For my part I regard this development as a retrograde step. In the field of international commercial arbitration it will be regarded as an excessive judicial intrusion in the arbitral process.[34] I would respectfully suggest that in the light of the conflicting state of the authorities a re-examination of the scope of the power to remit is not precluded. In the meantime the DAC was faced with a difficult problem. On the one hand, there was something to be said for spelling out in the Bill the circumstances in which a court may exercise a power of remission. It is however, an exceptionally difficult exercise. And the DAC did not want to enshrine the effect of *King* v. *Thomas McKenna* in a statutory provision. On balance the best course would to be to retain the language of section 22(1) in the Bill in the hope that developing case law will confine the power to remit more narrowly.

(f) *Equity clauses*

Article 28(3) of the Model Law provides as follows:

> The arbitral tribunal shall decide *ex aequo et bono* or as *amiable compositeur* only if the parties have expressly authorised it to do so.

As a broad generalization that provision mirrors a type of arbitration which is quite common in civil law countries. States in the common law family of nations are usually less comfortable with notions of good faith, and that type of arbitration is less common.

It is necessary to consider whether English law at present recognizes such a form of arbitration. Equity clauses are common in reinsurance contracts made in England. On the other hand, such clauses have been given only a limited effect. If an equity clause is expressed to involve a power in arbitrators to disregard the rules of substantive law, the orthodox view is that English law does not at present recognize the concept of arbitrators acting in this way.[35] This is, however, a complex subject and it is not impossible that the courts may liberalize our arbitration law. The fact that distinguished commentators such as Sir Michael Kerr,[36] Mr Stewart Boyd QC[37] and Mr V. V. Veeder QC[38] have argued in favour of such a development guarantees that the prospect must be taken seriously. But in our case law the supporting planks for such a development are as yet insecure.

Protagonists of a *lex mercatoria* were encouraged by the important decision of the Court of Appeal in *Deutsche Schachtbau-und Tiefbohrgesellschaft m.b.H* v. *R'As al-Khaimah National Oil Co. ('DST* v. *Rakoil'.*)[39] The case concerned a Swiss

---

[34] V. V. Veeder, QC., 'Remedies Against Arbitral Awards: Setting Aside, Remission and Rehearing', *1993 Yearbook of the Arbitration Institute of the Stockholm Chamber of Commerce*, pp. 125 *et seq*.
[35] *Orion* v. *Belfort* [1962] 2 Lloyd's Rep 257; *Eagle Star Insurance Co.* v. *Yuval Insurance Co.* [1978] 1 Lloyd's Rep. 357; *Home Insurance Co.* v. *Administratia Asigurarilor de Stat* [1983] 2 Lloyd's Rep. 674; *Overseas Union Insurance Ltd.* v. *A.A. Mutual International Insurance Co.* [1988] 2 Lloyd's Rep. 63.
[36] '"Equity" Arbitration in England', 1993, 2 *American Review of International Arbitration*, p. 377.
[37] (1990) 6 *Arbitration International*, p. 122.
[38] British Insurance Arbitration Lecture 1992.
[39] [1990] 1 A.C. 295.

arbitration and a Swiss arbitration award. The arbitrators recorded that they were applying 'internationally accepted principles of law governing contractual relations'. The issue was whether an English court should enforce the award under the New York Convention of 1958. The Court of Appeal held that the award was enforceable. The critical point is that the court held that there was no head of public policy militating against the enforcement of the award. A contrary decision would, of course, have placed England beyond the pale among the signatories of the New York Convention. But the judgments do not tell us what the position would have been if the arbitration had taken place in England and if it had been an English award. In *Home and Overseas Insurance* v. *Mentor Insurance Co (UK) Ltd*[40] the validity of an equity clause was again considered by the Court of Appeal. Lord Justice Parker made clear that he regarded an arbitration clause allowing arbitrators to decide according to good conscience as invalid. Since Lord Justice Balcombe agreed with this judgment I regard Lord Justice Parker's view as the *ratio decidendi* of the case. In a lengthy judgment Lord Justice Lloyd commented on *DST* v. *Rakoil*. He said:[41]

> [Counsel for the Plaintiffs] argued that *DST* v. *Rakoil* was concerned only with the enforcement of a foreign award, and that it has no bearing on the present case, where the contract calls for arbitration in London. But why not? If the English courts will enforce a foreign award where the contract is governed by 'a system of law which is not that of England or any other state or is a serious modification of such a law', why whould it not enforce an English award in like circumstances? And if it will enforce an English award, why should it not grant a stay?
> [Counsel] argued that it would be impossible for the court to supervise an arbitration unless it is conducted in accordance with a fixed and recognisable system of law; he even went so far as to submit that the arbitration clause in the present case is not an 'arbitration agreement' at all within the meaning of the Arbitration Acts 1950–1979. It is sufficient to say that I disagree. I would only add (although it cannot effect the argument) that if [he] is right, no ICC arbitration could ever be held with confidence in this country for fear that the arbitrators might adopt the same governing law as they did in *DST* v. *Rakoil*.

I share Lord Justice Lloyd's instinctive reaction. But it seems to me that we are dealing with a complex and fundamental problem which will require further analysis. If a wide equity clause is invalid, it must be because it is subversive of a head of public policy governing arbitrations conducted in England and awards made in England. About that point *DST* v. *Rakoil* can in truth tell us very little. On the other hand, some seventy years after *Czarnikow* v. *Roth Schmidt & Co.*,[42] it may be arguable that there is no longer such a head of public policy. That issue may turn on an historical review of the swing of the pendulum from excessive judicial scrutiny to a better recognition of the imperative of party autonomy. It may be possible for a court to rule that an award made under an equity clause is nevertheless an arbitration award

---

[40] [1989] 1 Lloyd's Rep 473., [1990] 1 WLR 153; [1989] 3 All ER 74.
[41] [1987] 2 Lloyd's Rep. P. 489 col. 1.
[42] [1992] 2 K.B. 478.

governed by our arbitration statutes. Conceivably, a court might also rule that such an award is not subject to the limited appellate jurisdiction under section 1 of the Arbitration Act 1979. On the other hand, even if a court regarded such a development as beneficial, the court might take the view that it is a matter for reforming legislation. Uncharacteristically, I will not express any concluded view on the point. But I am firmly of the view that the issues have not yet been comprehensively debated in a English court and that *stare decisis* ought not to preclude a re-examination of this question.

Lastly, if the consultation process shows that there is a widespread desire on the part of commercial men to be able to arbitrate in England under fully effective equity clauses that might be a factor which could conceivably weigh with a court seized with the problem. After all, while our courts do not have the advantage of Brandeis briefs, judges do like to have a window to the real world. And, if such a development is beyond the capacity of the courts, a widespread desire for such a liberalization of our arbitration system may have to be considered by Parliament.

V. CONCLUSION

In conclusion I would only say that, while I have sketched some of the policy objectives of the DAC, it will be essential for the DAC to examine the whole Bill in the light of the responses to the consultative process.[43] There will be ample scope for further improvements of the Bill. But something broadly like the Bill represents the best attainable arbitration legislation in England. And it would represent an enormous improvement of our arbitration legislation.

Note

After this lecture was given, the Arbitration Act 1996 was drafted under the guidance of Lord Seville of Newdigate (then Lord Justice Saville) who took over from Lord Steyn in 1994 as Chairman of the Departmental Advisory Committee of the Department of Trade and Industry on Arbitration Law.

---

[43] Apart from departmental representatives from the Department of Trade and Industry, the present membership of the DAC is as follows: The Rt Hon Lord Justice Steyn; A.W.S. Bunch Esq; Stewart Boyd QC; Dr K.G. Chrystie; Clifford Clark Esq; Lord Dervaird; J. B. Garrett Esq; Professor Roy Goode QC; Martin Hunter Esq; Mrs P. Kirby-Johnson; R. A. MacCrindle QC; Arthur Marriott Esq; Oliver Parker Esq; Kenneth Rokison QC; David Sarre Esq; J.H.M. Sims Esq; Professor D. R. Thomas; Professor John Uff QC; V. V. Veeder QC; and its Secretary (Miss Maureen Dodsworth).

Part Seven

Westminster Abbey

[26]
Address at Memorial Service for The Rt Hon The Lord Williams of Mostyn Q.C.

Lawyers come and go. But Gareth Williams was no ordinary lawyer. He has left a huge imprint on the way we think, or ought to think, about a just society.

The very heart of the man lay in his Welsh roots and experiences on the Welsh circuit. His was a rare combination of towering intellect, gentle humanity and unfailing humour. These qualities made him one of the pre-eminent barristers of his day. He was a highly successful Chairman of the Bar before he was made a peer and subsequently attained high offices of state.

In a profession not noted for innovation his plainness of speech and his radicalism stood out. For him ethical considerations demanded of lawyers that they conduct themselves in a spirit of civility, generosity and humanity conducive to the welfare of the public whom they serve. For him the law was an honourable calling which involved more than the pursuit of personal gain.

Gareth Williams' philosophy is illustrated by his approach to criminal law. For him the purpose of the criminal law was decidedly not punishment for its own sake. Its sole aim is to permit everyone to go about their daily lives without fear of harm to person or property. In the language of John Stuart Mill he believed that the only purpose for which power can be rightfully exercised over any member of a civilized community is to prevent harm to others.

Gareth Williams was a profound lawyer steeped in constitutional history and constitutionalism. He believed that the people should play a full and effective role in a participatory democracy. He insisted that all public power must be limited to ensure that it is only exercised for the welfare of the people. His allegiance to the rule of law was unswerving. For him a cardinal principle of a civil society was that the doors of Her Majesty's courts must always be open to all, citizens and foreigners alike, who seek just redress of perceived wrongs.

Gareth Williams believed that the dominant theme of the common law was the spirit of liberty. But what does this mean? During the

Second World War, in Central Park, New York City, Justice Learned Hand gave an explanation which reflects strands of Gareth Williams' most profound beliefs. He said:

> "What then is the spirit of liberty? I cannot define it; I can only tell you my own faith. The spirit of liberty is the spirit which is not too sure that it is right; the spirit of liberty is the spirit which seeks to understand the minds of other men and women; the spirit of liberty is the spirit which weighs their interests alongside its own without bias; the spirit of liberty remembers that not even a sparrow falls to earth unheeded; the spirit of liberty is the spirit of Him who, near two thousand years ago, taught mankind that lesson it has never learned, but has never quite forgotten; that there may be a kingdom where the least shall be heard and considered side by side with the greatest."

In common with other liberal democracies our country faces enormous challenges in an era of change and upheaval. The untimely death of Gareth Williams has deprived the country of the guiding hand of a deeply thoughtful man of great wisdom, a man of steel with an educated heart.

Name Index

Ackner, Lord 231
Allanbridge, Lord 177
Angelos, Peter G. 271
Arbour, Madame Justice 200
Aristotle 258
Atkin, Lord 162, 196

Bagehot, Walter 109
Balcombe, Sir John 145, 301
Barak, Aharon 68, 209
Bates, Lord 31
Beaton, Stuart 144, 145
Bellamy, Sir Christopher 144, 145, 146
Bellknapp, Professor 204
Bentham, Jeremy 11, 44
Bingham, Lord 75, 149, 161, 164, 166, 184, 213, 214, 216, 274, 277, 278, 280
Blackburn, Lord 49
Blackstone, Lord 9
Blanchard, Claire 295
Boanerges, Lord 245
Bogdanor, Vernon xvii
Boyd, Stewart 300
Brandeis, Justice xx, 22, 23, 61, 115, 119, 269
Brennan, Justice 42
Bridge, Lord 35, 36, 51, 52, 76
Brightman, Lord 85
Brooke, Lord Justice 145
Browne-Wilkinson, Lord 21, 29, 30, 38, 40, 56, 135, 259
Buccleuch, Duke xxi
Bunch, Anthony 290
Bush, George W. 200
Buxton, Justice 293

Calabresi, Guido 58
Cardozo, Justice 65, 240, 267, 268, 269

Cave, Lord 246
Chang, Dr P.C. 154
Churchill, Sir Winston 106, 157, 178
Cole, Professor David 206
Collins, Justice 166
Collins, Lawrence 135
Cooke, Lord 129
Corbett, Chief Justice 187
Corbin, Lord 240
Cross, Sir Rupert 56, 62, 135
Cumaraswany, Paran 188
Curran, J. Joseph, Jr. 271

Dale, Sir William 290
Danelski, Professor 204
Davies, Owen 93
Denning, Lord xvi, 15, 30, 49, 149, 151, 198, 232, 256
Devlin, Lord 78
Dicey, A.V. xvi, xvii, 133
Dickens, Charles 112
Dickson, Brian 57
Dickson, Chief Justice 65
Diplock, Lord 100, 148, 276, 298
Dixon, Sir Owen 77
Donaldson, Lord 295, 299
Donne, John 209
Drewry, Professor 122
Dworkin, Professor Ronald 32, 68, 101, 207

Eckersley, Basil 289, 290
Eldon, Lord 26, 108, 216
Ewing, K.D. xv

Falconer, Lord 39
Feltham, J.D. 247
Fleming, John 270
Forsyth, Dr 121
Foster, John Galway 208
Frankfurter, Justice 28, 59

Gibson, Lord Justice 299
Goff, Lord 21, 89, 229, 255
Graef, Ralph 280
Griffiths Lord 90, 91

Hailsham, Lord xiii, 81, 122
Haldane, Viscount 13
Hamilton, Alexander 97
Hart, Herbert 27
Hayhoe, Lord 50
Hazlitt, Lord 25
Hepple, Professor Bob 159
Herbert, A.P. 81
Hill, Jonathan 277
Hitler, Adolf 167
Hobhouse, Lord Justice 145, 246, 249, 250
Hoffman, Lord 11, 45, 135, 138, 147, 172, 259
Holmes, Justice 4, 269
Holmes, Oliver Wendell 42, 231
Hope, Lord 75, 182, 184
Howard, Michael 116
Howell, John 146
Hunter, Martin 287
Hutton, Lord 76
Hyde, Edward 202

Irvine, Lord xx, 112

Johnson, Samuel 237
Jones, Glower W. 247
Jones, Lloyd 166

Kafka, Joseph 207
Keith, Lord 21
Kelly, Delphine 253
Kelly, John Maurice 253
Kennedy, Ian 279
Kennedy, Justice 208
Kentridge, Sir Sydney 277
Kerr, Lord Justice 198, 300
Khan, Sir Mohammad Zaffrulah 155
Kissinger, Henry 200
Klug, Francesca 173

Koh, Professor 208
Korematsu, Ahita 196, 197
Kraus, Lawrence B. 272

Laws, Lord Justice 262
Le Quesne, Sir Godfray 86, 90, 91
Learned Hand, Justice 61, 269, 307
Lester, Lord 37, 39
Lew, Dr Julian 296
Lewis, Anthony 207
Lincoln, Abraham 176
Lloyd, Lord Justice 301

MacCormick, Professor 12
Mackay, Lord 30, 112
MacKinnon, Lord 245
Major, John 122
Malik, Charles A. 154
Markesinis, Professor Basil 142, 253, 267, 277, 280
Marriott, Arthur 289, 290
Marshall, Dr Geoffrey 37
Marshall, John 102
McCluskey, Lord 55
McLachlin, Justice 67
Mill, John Stuart 4, 130, 306
Morris, Lord 87, 275, 276
Morritt, Lord Justice 277
Murr, Marc 272
Murray, Sir James 235
Mustill, Lord 21, 287, 289, 297

Nicholas, Professor Barry 247, 288
Nicholls, Lord 31, 299
Nolan, Lord 21, 99, 118, 132

Oliver, Professor 122
Oltmann, Karen 241, 249

Pannick, David 207, 277
Parker, Lord Justice 301
Pearce, Lord 276
Pearson, Lord 276
Phillips, Lord 205
Pinochet, General Agusto 109, 163, 164, 165, 166, 167, 168, 200

Polden, Dr Patrick 245
Pollock, Lord 16, 17, 48
Pollock, Sir Frederick 61
Powell, Professor Raphael 220
Priestley, J.B. 106

Randolph, Judge A.R. 204
Rehnquist, Chief Justice 208
Reid, Lord xiv, 15, 16, 18, 34, 41, 51, 61, 223, 232, 276, 279
Rodger, Lord 177
Roosevelt, Eleanor 154, 155
Roosevelt, Franklin Delano 153, 197
Roskill, Lord 149, 245, 250, 295
Roxburgh, Sir Ronald 276, 277

Salmon, Lord 256
Scalia, Justice 207, 208
Scarman, Lord 85
Schiemann, Lord Justice 146
Schuster, Sir Claud 246
Scrutton, Lord Justice 245, 249
Sen, Amartya 171
Simon, Lord 242
Simonds, Viscount 15, 232, 256
Sterndale, Lord 249
Steyn, Johan (Lord Steyn) 3-9, 11-26, 27-40, 41-56, 57-69, 71-83, 85-93, 97- 108, 109-23, 125-7, 129-42, 143-8, 151- 62, 163-70, 171-6, 177-84, 185-91, 195-209, 213-23, 225-34, 235-44, 245-51, 253-74, 275-84, 287-302, 305-7
Straw, Jack 116

Templeman, Lord 91, 149, 215
Thatcher, Lady Margaret 10
Thomas, Justice 207, 208
Thompson, Professor 130
Todd, Professor 266
Trollope, Anthony 245

Upjohn, Lord 276

Veeder, V.V. 300

Wade, Sir William 121
Wakeham, Lord 117
Waldron, Jeremy 32
Waller, Lord Justice 277
Ward, Judith 190
Warnock, Lord 177
Waterhouse, Eliza 42
Weir, Tony 264
Wetter, J. Gillis 24
Wheatley, Derek 249
Wilberforce, Lord 24, 28, 42, 54, 87, 168, 213, 240, 287
Williams, Gareth 305, 306, 307
Williston, Lord 240
Wittgenstein 42
Woodhouse, Professor 112
Woolf, Lord 105, 60